AF624077

Concept Publishing Co.
Rs 500/-

CONTEMPORARY URBAN ISSUES

PERSPECTIVES IN URBAN GEOGRAPHY
VOLUME EIGHT

Concept's International Series in Geography

No. 1 Perspectives in Agricultural Geography (In Five Volumes) Edited by NOOR MOHAMMAD

No. 2 Perspectives in Geomorphology (In Four Volumes) Edited by H.S. SHARMA

No. 3 Perspectives in Urban Geography Edited by C.S. YADAV

1. New Directions in Urban Geography
2. Comparative Urban Research
3. Comparative Urbanization: City Growth and Change
4.A Models in Urban Geography (Theoretical)
4.B Models in Urban Geography (Mathematical)
5. Urban Research Methods: Central Place, Hierarchical and City Size Models
6. Contemporary City Ecology
7. Slums, Urban Decline and Revitalization
8. Contemporary Urban Issues
9. Rural-Urban Fringe
10. Morphology of Towns
11. Cities and Housing
12. Perceptual and Cognitive Image of the City
13. Urban Economics
14. City Planning: Problems and Prospects
15. City Planning: Administration and Participation
16.A Urban Planning and Policies: Reorientation of Policy Norms
16.B Urban Planning and Policies: Cross-cultural Urban Policies

Concept's International Series in Geography No. 3

PERSPECTIVES IN URBAN GEOGRAPHY

VOLUME EIGHT

CONTEMPORARY URBAN ISSUES

Edited by
C. S. Yadav

CONCEPT PUBLISHING COMPANY, NEW DELHI–110015

First Published 1987
© The Editor

Published by

Naurang Rai
Concept Publishing Company
H-13, Bali Nagar
NEW DELHI 110015 (India)

Printed at

New Gian Offset Printers
495, DDA Complex, Shahzada Bagh
NEW DELHI-110035

Preface

NATURE OF URBAN GEOGRAPHY

THERE are several studies on urban geography which reveal that, as a major sub-discipline, it has a long tail but a short body. However, the spectrum is so vast and broad that researchers are able to make general statements in defence of its conception, philosophy, nature and orientation. Urban geography today encompasses and interfaces with various disciplines which are interested in urban studies. As an introduction to this series, our task here is to make an attempt to briefly review the development of geographical interest in various aspects of cities.

There are several reviews of the early development of urban geography which have been dealt with by Berry and Harton (1970)[1] and Carter (1974).[2] Berry and Harton in their book, **Geographical Perspective on Urban System**, have made an attempt to introduce readers to its present-day status. They have clearly resolved that "the formative years of the social science in the late nineteenth century and early twentieth century were also the years in which urban studies first developed,"[3] thus providing the context for geography's emerging interest in cities. However, the emergence of urban studies dates back to the writing of Greek scholars, but as a sub-discipline, it has reached its present-day status only in the past 30 years.

In their historical perspective the works on urban geography show that the pre-20th century studies primarily concerned themselves with themes of location, size and shape of the cities. The initial findings were strongly subjective, descriptive and dependent more on observation such as the works of Hassert (1907)[4] and Blanchard

(1911).[5] In the succeeding years the conceptual framework of site and situation was criticized by Aurousseau (1924)[6] and Crowe (1938)[7], their conception being that cities were not inanimate objects in landscape, but also organic elements which involved people and their movements. The morphologist, later in 1960, truly brought the indigenous line of evolution in the sphere of urban geography and studies on the build-up fabric of cities (Conzone, 1960).[8] Smails (1955)[9] constituted the prime base of urban geography, which remained articulated without any major conceptual change till early 1960s. The studies on the morphological aspects of the urban system were influenced by external forces, consequently the methodological frameworks got impetus within the discipline. At this juncture the evolution of concepts was not based on environment but took shelter under the umbrella of economics of location, and incorporated analysis of land values and rents, and the concept of nodality and accessibility. These concepts were derived from the economic theories of Cooley (1894)[10], Weber (1899),[11] and Hurd (1903).[12]

The Chicago School of Urban Ecology hastened the evolution of urban geography. In his monumental work Park (1925)[13] developed the idea of order and analysis of towns. Further, a powerful thrust and much of the rationale was provided to the studies of urban geography by the Central Place Theory of Christallar (1933).[14]

The impact of the statistical method was powerful and it brought rapid and enormous changes in the field of urban geography. It also brought new insights into the development and application of urban geography towards increased quantification. Brian J. Berry, a pioneer in the field, analysed the spatial order, size and location of towns and cities. There was widespread use of innovative techniques to explore the nature of urban problems, hypotheses were tested, new theories propounded and old theories remodelled. The statistical methods were put to a variety of uses. Smith (1965)[15] evaluated the classification of settlements; Berry and Garrison (1956)[16] examined the utility of the rank-size rule for urban populations. The models of Park and Burgess (1925),[17] Harris and Ullman (1945)[18] and Homar Hoyt (1939)[19] were tested and re-examined by various geographers.

A new impetus to urban geography came from social area analysis which was initially propounded by Shevky and Bell (1955)[20] and later on this provided a basis for factorial ecology. The collaboration of this stream in urban geography was offered by Berry (1971)[21], Herbert (1972)[22] and Johnston (1971).[23] As a consequence of these thrusts in geography after 1960, the techniques of investigation were sharpened and this has provided the basis for a scientific explanation of cities. Attempts were made to introduce new theories and frame laws to make the explanation of events more rational and logical. Sophisticated models were propounded as urban geography entered a new era of rationalizing the subject matter of urban studies on the basis of new philosophies, new concepts, new theories, new methodologies and applications.

However, the status of contemporary urban geography has been elevated only recently by the behavioural approach. The studies of perception and cognition which have a long tradition in physiology were first introduced into the field of geography by Lynch (1960)[24] Dowson and Stea (1973)[25], Gould and White (1974).[26] At present there is a sudden spurt in the studies on the subject with a new paradigm. But the full impact of behavi oural approaches upon urban geography has yet to be realized.

The aim of this series is to seek reorientation of the discipline strengthened by new philosophies, methodologies, subject matters or application. The series has been arranged in such a way that all contemporary viewpoints are covered comprehensively. Hopefully, this series will inspire researchers to appreciate the work already done by geographers in studying cities. Geography by nature seems to be a synthesizing field of inquiry. As such we have made an endeavour to combine some of the otherwise disparate facts garnered by other disciplines in such a manner that we can gain a better understanding of the urban system. The study of urban geography is essential if we are to analyse the human consequences of the settlements in which we live. It is useful to planners, decision makers in government and corporations and also to each one of us as citizens. Finally, it gives us a perspective on what may be happening to our cities and to the nature.

To achieve the above goal only those contributions with originality and contrasting viewpoints were selected for inclusion in this series. In doing so the editor does not wish to compete with the journals in the field in which innovative research and methodological aspects are presented. But he does wish to convey, and convey with conviction, that significant researches are being undertaken in the different branches of urban geography and in other allied disciplines. The present series is an attempt to provide a selective reappraisal and rigorous examination of the assumptions and the urge to disseminate new knowledge created by the mutual interaction. Emphasis is also placed on the conceptualization and theorization of the subject matter so that general laws may emerge. A conscious effort has been made to organize the series in such a way that it reflects the philosophical approach parallel to that of the behavioural school. Finally, a vigorous attempt has been made to demonstrate throughout the series how geographers are basically involved in solving the urban problems.

C. S. YADAV

REFERENCES

1. Berry and Harton, **Geographic Perspectives on Urban Systems: With Integrated Readings**, New Jersey, Prentice Hall, Inc, Englewood Cliffs, 1970.
2. Carter, **The Study of Urban Geography**, Edward Arnold, London, 1974.
3. Berry and Harton, 1970.
4. Hassert, K., **Die Stadte Geographisch Betrachect**, Leipzig, 1907.
5. Blanchard, R., **Grenoble: Etude de Geographic Urbanine**, Paris, 1911.
6. Aurousseau, M., "Recent Contributions to Geography: A Review," **Geographical Review**, 1924, 14, p.444.
7. Crowe, P.R., "On Progress in Geography," **Scottish Geographical Magazine**, 1938, 54, 1-19.
8. Conzone, M.R.G., "The Plan Analysis of an English City Centre," In Norkorg (Ed), **Proceedings of I.G.U. Symposium on Urban Geography**, C.W.K. Gleerup, Lund, 1962.
9. Smails, A.E., "The Urban Mess of England and Wales," **Transactions and Papers**, Institute of British Geographers, 1946, 11, 85, p.101.
10. Cooley, C.H., "The Theory of Transportation," **Publications of the American Economic Association**, 1894, 9, p.5-7.
11. Weber, A.F., **The Growth of Cities in the Nineteenth Century: A Study in Statistics**, New York, 1899.
12. Hurd, R., **Principles of City Land Values: New York Record and Guide**, 1903, p. 19-21.
13. Park, R.E., "Suggestions for the Investigation of Human Behaviour in an Urban Environment," in R.E.

Park, E.W. Burgess, R.D. Mackenzie (eds), **The City**, University of Chicago Press, 1925.

14. Christallar, W., **Central Place in Southern Germany**, Gustar Fischer, Teno, 1933.
15. Smith, R.M.T., "Method and Purpose in Functional Town Classification," **Annals of the Association of American Geographers**, 1965, 55, pp.539-548.
16. Garrison, W.L., "Applicability of Statistical Inference to Geographical Research," **Geographical Review**, 1956, 46, 427, 429.
17. Burgess, E.W., "The Growth of City," in R.E. Park, E.W. Burgess and R.D. Mackenzie (eds), **The City**, University of Chicago Press, 1925.
18. Ullman, E.L., "The Nature of Cities," **Annals, American Academy of Political and Social Science**, 1945, 242, 7-17.
19. Hoyt, H., **The Structure and Growth of Residential Neighbourhoods in American Cities**, Washington, Federal Housing Administration, 1939.
20. Shevky, E. and Bell, W., **Social Area Analysis**, Stamford University Press, Stamford, 1955.
21. Berry, B.J.L. (ed), "Comparative Factorial Ecology," **Economic Geographic (Supplement)**, 1971, 47.
22. Herbert, D.T., **Urban Geography: A Social Perspective**, David and Charles, Newton Abbot, 1972.
23. Johnston, **Urban Residential Pattern**, Bell, London, 1971.
24. Lynch, **Image of the City**, Massachusetts, Cambridge, 1960.
25. Dowson and Stea, "Image and Environment", Chicago and London, 1973.
26. Gould and White, R., **Mental Maps**, London, 1974.

Acknowledgement

We Thank Editors Gerd-Michael Hellstern, Frithjof Spreer Hellmut Wollmann, **Heft 2, Vol. II** and **Vol. III** for their permission to use material from "Applied Urban Research", Proceedings of the European Meeting on Applied Urban Research, Essen, 2-4, Oct. 1981.

Contents

SECTION THREE
CONFLICT AND CRIME IN CITIES

SECTION FOUR
POLLUTION AND HEALTH IN CITIES

SECTION FIVE
THE SOCIAL CONSEQUENCES OF POPULATION

List of Contributors

Daniel Stokols: University of California at Irvine, USA.

Christina R. Victor: Research Team for the Care of the Elderly Welsh National School of Medicine, St. David's Hospital, Cardiff.

Henry Sanoff: Professor of Architecture, School of Design, North Carolina State University Raleigh, North California-07650, USA.

Vincent P. Miller, Jr.: Indiana University of Pa., Indiana Pa. 15705, USA.

Bernard Kayser: Professor, Institute de Geographie, Universite de Toulouse-le-Miral.

William W. Goldsmith: Department of City and Regional Planning Cornel University, Ithaka, New York.

William R. Arnold: University of Kansas, USA.

Steve W. Rawlings: Bureau of the Census, USA.

Manfred Kochen: Mental Health Research Institute, The University of Michigan, Ann Arbor.

Vijay K. Mathur: Department of Economics, Cleveland State University, Cleveland, Ohio - 44155.

Sheldon H. Stein: Department of Economics, Cleveland State University, Cleveland, Ohio - 44155.

S.A.Q. Rizvi: Head, Department of Geography, A.K. College, Shikohabad (India).

John C. Chicken: Culham Laboratory

Terrel L. Rhodes: Department of Political Science, University of North Carolina at Charlotte, North Carolina-28223, USA.

Kathleen K. Loewy: Department of Political Science, University of North Carolina at Charlotte, North Carolina-28223, USA.

C. Thangavel: School of Planning, Centre for Environmental Planning and Technology, Ahmedabad (India).

P. Jayapal: School of Planning, Centre for Environmental Planning and Technology, Ahmedabad (India).

K.M. Kulkarni: Lecturer, Department of Geography Gujarat University, Ahmedabad (India).

A.H. Harris: Department of Political Economy, University of Aberdeen, Adward Wright Building, Dunbar Street, Old Aberdeen, AB9 2TY.

K.M. Dykes: C/o Editor Gerd-Michael Hellstern, "Applied Urban Research"

Ira M. Sheskin: Assistant Professor, Department of Geography, University of Miami, Coral Gables, Florida-33124.

Howard G. Eisenstadt: Schimpeler Corradino Associates, Coral Gables, Florida-33136.

A.T. Salau: Senior Lecturer, Department of Geography, Ahmadu Bello University, Zaria, Nigeria.

Hans Blumenfled: Faculty of Urban and Regional Planning, University of Toronto.

C.S. Yadav: Reader and Head, Department of Geography, Shaheed Bhagat Singh College, University of Delhi, New Delhi (India).

ONE

C. S. Yadav

Introduction

Our cities are organic entities and hubs of human activities. They are the centres of automated industries, employment—permanent and temporary—consumer markets, political decision making and learning and culture. The new technological innovations are radically changing the habits, way of life and manmade environment. Today millions of people are seeking progress and fortune in urban centres and more and more people are adopting the urban way of living. Every day massive streams of human beings are flowing into the cities which have resulted in the awesome prospect of an urban explosion. And looking objectively there seems to be no doubt that three dynamic forces are shaping the future of the world's cities: first, an unprecedented growth in world population; second, a massive, unabated migration from rural areas and concentration in cities; and third, too rapid economic development and technological innovations. If any one of these dynamic forces goes out of control, and there are already signs in this direction, it will have an impact on man's urban habitat. If uncontrolled it could prove disastrous. It is a well-known fact that today's great metropolitan cities are the centres of large populations and wealth. They undeniably are the abode of the richest, the healthiest, the best educated and employed people in the world. Our cities are truly the staging ground for the mobilization of manpower and the expansion of product capital (Blair, 1974)[1]. This new stage of metropolitan development and quickening tempo of change results in grave and fundamental structural defects at all levels of city community and has resulted in tremendous problems. It seems that deep fissures have appeared in the urban system which have greatly affected the orderly life of the people in the cities. The problems the cities face are not extraordinary or unpredictable or maladies, with no cures. Nevertheless, they are the stark reflections of the social cost of adaptation to city life, and urban culture produces its own band of illnesses forcing the cities into a sorry state. The conscious academicians and administrators in the 1960s interpreted the city problems as an "urban crisis". Here it will not be wrong to assert that a crisis is a turning point of some sort, undoubtedly it is an unstable condition which denotes imminent change for the better or worse. During the 1960s, various urban researchers were confronted with a series of issues and problems which have restructured the urban systems. Stress and strain, poverty, crime and delinquency, migration, deficiency of amenities and transportation, problems of minority groups, threats of environmental deterioration, implications of population growth are some of the problems associated with cities and urban living. These problems, their causes and resultant frustrations, did not suddenly emerge in the sixties, but had been developing over several decades and the scars of these problems persist even today.

The Human Stress and Strain in our Cities

Today's urban centres are in a state of imbalance caused by various noxious or potentially so environmental forces pressing upon the individuals. This notion of pressing is known as stress. Strain, on the other hand, denotes an individual's reaction to stress. However, noxious environmental forces put strain on the individual's personality and group behaviour. However, Langer (1963)[2] has provided a good operational definition of stress: "A stress may be any influence, whether it is arisen from the internal environment or the external environment, which interferes with the satisfaction of basic needs or which disturbs or threatens to disturb the stable equilibrium."

The environmental stress in our cities, whether generated by interpersonal relations or by uncontrollable fluctuations in the physical world is always present in the action space of individuals and its effects play some role in decision behaviour (Julian Wolpart, 1965)[3].

Thus the terms 'stress' and 'strain' create amusive conditions in the physical environment of urban settings. The oppressive agents of stress in the city are numerous, however, behavioural effects of stress on health and environment of the city are largely produced by such agents as noise, high density, air pollution, traffic congestion, crime and migration of rural folk to the cities.

The research programmes pertaining to urban stress, learned

helplessness and life changes denote that positive forces of stress or stressors are analogous to insufficient environmental amenities. The urban stress researchers have always devoted their attention to the implications of environmental controllability for human wellbeing. Most of the research findings on urban stress and strain, for example, Glass and Singer (1972),[4] Abramson et al (1978),[5] Wortman and Brehm (1975),[6] Dorhren Wend (1974),[7] Glass (1977),[8] have shown the existence of pervasive human conditions in urban centres; they have pointed towards an urge for environmental control which largely determines the quality and intensity of people's reaction to their acute problems. These studies suggest several unresolved issues in stress research.

Pollution

Much of the human stress and strain is caused by city pollution. Urban pollution in a layman's language is defined as a state of severe contamination of the natural and manmade habitat which threatens human health and causes societal sickness. It is facilitated by the overloading of the environment with pollutants which are largely caused by burgeoning populations, their extravagant profit-making, waste-producing and energy-using activities. The city air is laden with the malodour emanating from industrial and human waste and garbage and poisonous fluids and gases besides the noise, heat and energy, detergents, fertilizers and pesticides adding their own share to the pollution. This all is the direct result of the "throwaway economies". Thus ultimately they become a wrong thing in a wrong place at a wrong time (Blair, 1974).[9] This unbridled human interest causes vandalic atmosphere, the city environment is filled with smog, streets are littered with waste and garbage and thus allows a city to suffocate and die a slow, smelly death. It is a truism that the central parts of cities the world over are the scene of huge day-time populations, jammed streets, confused commuters and frustrated office workers, unorganized shoppers, hasty motorists, intense sales and media competition, traffic congestion with long halts. This all together generates huge wastes and pollutes the air immensely, which ultimately results in stress on human beings.

Persistent day-to-day air pollution is caused in our cities by its citizens who pollute their habitat and environment through their incorrect styles of living. In the process of maintaining a successful life, huge quantities of water, food and fuels are consumed and waste discharged in the form of sewage and refuge. People themselves contaminate their environment with their own waste products. Thomas Blair (1974)[10] rightly observes that today's urban pollution is accompanied by high technological innovations and industrial wastes. Air pollution was unimaginable 150 years ago, on the other hand, clean air and water have become scarce commodities today. It seems that the decades immediately ahead will witness more production of goods and services because the industrial and consumer demands will be felt in five strategic markets of change: shelter, energy and power, food, transportation and communication.

This will certainly require more metals, chemicals and resources, and hence pose a bigger threat to our cities and assault grievously man and his environment. Urban pollution in essence will threaten the citizens of the city in two ways: first, it will pollute his city and life-support systems and, second, it will subject him to stress and chronic disorders, which together recklessly rob the city environment of its purity. If, therefore, planners and administrators want to avoid disaster, the rate of pollution will have to be drastically reduced. In the past vigorous appeals were made to citizens, industrialists, and city administrators, efforts have also been made to devise an anti-pollution technology to protect the environment, stiffer taxation and stricter enforcement have been tried too, but all these have proved of limited help. What is, therefore, needed is some more sensitive and socially responsible initiative, with a set of new rules effective enough to combat the problem in an efficient way.

Crime and the Causes

The urban population is increasing at an alarming rate which has resulted in an unplanned growth of big world cities. The existing infrastructure of these cities cannot cope with the ever increasing needs of adequate water supply, transportation, communication, health and sanitation, housing and law and order. As a result the gap between the supply and demand is widening tremendously. In addition, television and mass media have developed high expectations among the poorest. Unfulfilment of these leads to discontent, stress, bitterness and frustration which ultimately lead to aggression and in turn to deviation from the set norms. This deviant behaviour depending on what has been infringed upon is known as misconduct, misbehaviour or crime. Prevention of crime, that is, violation of law which ensures the safety and security of public life, is given the first priority.

Our cities are generally centres of felonious crimes (punishable by death or imprisonment and trial by jury) and misdemeanour crimes (less dangerous to society and carrying lighter penalties). Nevertheless, "crime itself is the greatest problem in the debilitated central areas of our cities (B. Adams, 1971)".[11] On an examination of the vast literature on crime it becomes evident that most studies deal with crime control and law enforcement and the administration of justice, but there are very few studies dealing with the crucial catalytical agents which force a law-abiding citizen into a criminal act. Abrahamson (1960)[12] made an effort to analyse the factors that led a person to succumb more readily to crime. The behaviour of rule-breaking is adopted by man primarily due to cognitive deficiencies in which the criminal incorrectly perceives rewards of rule-breaking. Sometimes an emotional cause also plays an important role in the commission of a crime as the criminal may be quite insensitive to the feelings of his victim. The third, more dangerous type of deviant behaviour, results when the criminal lacks moral training in which case he is not aware that his action is a deviant.

The problem of controlling deviant behaviour in our cities is really a difficult task because the deviant gangs are formed by the ecological processes which result in conflict, disorganization, weak family ties and enemic neighbourhood ties (Warren and Warren, 1977).[13] Uncontrolled play groups which are outsiders to the adult community, under conditions of high density, limited resources, weak social controls, find sources of adventure, excitement and enjoyment in activities of their own innovation which intensifies conflict and community disorganization. This strengthens group organization through conflict with other groups and thus gangs of deviant behaviour are formed. Thus it is a truism that there are more problems underlying urban crime and delinquency which cannot be adequately analysed in one study.

Crime as a problem has been part of the world cities for quite some time. However, only recently have social scientists, in general, and sociologists and economists in particular rationally and logically begun to examine the hypothesis proposed by Bentham (1962)[14] that certainty of apprehension and punishment and severity of punishment deter criminal behaviour. After his statement there was a sudden spurt of methodological works by sociologists such as Gibbs (1968)[15] Gray and Martin (1969),[16] Title (1969),[17] Bailey et al (1974)[18] who have provided some support to the deterrent hypothesis.

The literature of these scholars points out that living in today's cities is in a constant state of anxiety bordering on panic. There seems a crisis of human identity in cities and the illness lies somewhere down in the urbanized society itself. It seems that crime is an integral and exploitative part of urban culture. Studies have shown that organized crime take out billions from the private and public purse. It is also observed that respectable businessmen and professionals reap huge benefits from white-collar crimes like tax evasion, falsified business expenses, embezzlement and fraud. Cities the world over are infested with gambling, prostituton, drugs and by violent crime, so it is the city culture which has produced its own brand of illness.

GEOGRAPHICAL ASPECTS OF POVERTY IN THE CITY

Much has been written about the definition of poverty in the metropolitan cities. Geographers and other social and behavioural scientists as well as urban planners, health practitioners, and legal authorities during the past few decades have focussed their attention on the subject of poverty in cities. The prevalence of and spatial patterns of poverty, especially within the cities, are in part a consequence of the lower productivity of some occupations, a result of the forces of supply and demand and the organizational strength, that is, if there are too many in some occupations and they are disorganized, their employer need not pay the competitive wages and may indulge in social discrimination against minorities Morrill (1973).[19] Apart from these main causes of urban poverty, poverty and unemployment are a result of the transfer of rural poverty to the city, that is, of rural migrants to the city who have been displaced from agriculture and forestry, who do not possess the requisite skills for the available jobs and who have swarmed into the city in greater numbers than the city could absorb. It is a well-known fact that within the city the socio-geographic process of spatial segregation of the poor and ghetoization of the minorities help maintain poverty.

The culture of poverty in cities is unique. Lewis (1967)[20] identified a very large number of traits which he associates with the culture of poverty. "The lack of effective participation and integration of the poor in the major institutions is one of the crucial characteristics". The poor city dwellers are not fully integrated into the main stream of city life. They display a cynical distrust of the government, planners and elite residents. It is also observed that "there is a minimum of organization beyond the level of the nuclear and extended family... the low level of organization gives the culture of poverty its marginal and anachronistic quality." Looking at the family life it was visualized that the family life of the poor in the city is disorganized. "There is an early initiation in sex, a preponderance of free unions and consensual marriages and mother centred families. At the level of the individual the major characteristics are a strong feeling of marginality, of helplessness, dependence and of inferiority... the poor cannot defer gratification... the belief in male superiority is widespread, psychological pathology is tolerated, little knowledge of other places and periods exists and people do not see their own problems as part of wider issues. They are not class conscious" (Lewis, 1967).

Considering all these view points, it would not be incorrect to conclude that urban society is a gigantic productive unit with a distributive system that allocates assets like income, property, education, prestige and power. Broad inequalities exist; severe poverty, inadequate incomes and insecurity are the enduring facts of life for millions of urban dwellers.

Health and Disease

The mass media has given different versions of the urban crisis. Nevertheless the themes which have stimulated the thinking of academicians are familiar. Voice is raised that today's cities are becoming uninhabitable because living is unhygienic, there are health hazards. Although urban areas have more medical facilities than the rural areas, such facilities are still inadequate. It is a truism that urban health problems bear more heavily on the poor than the affluent. The inevitable congestion, insanitation, air pollution, all contribute to the ill health of the city people. Many studies correlate the illnesses included in the following diagnostic groups with poverty, heart disease, arthritis and rheumatism, mental and nervous conditions, high blood pressure, visual impairments, orthopaedic impairments, mental disorders, cancer and infant mortality (Carey, 1973).[21] There are several studies on the medical geography of towns, but Wilner as cited by Schorr (1966)[22] provided a fivefold classification of complaints:

1. Acute respiratory infections (cold, bronchitis, grippe), related to multiple use of toilet and water facilities, inadequate heating and ventilation, inadequate and crowded sleeping arrangements.
2. Certain infectious diseases of childhood (measles, chickenpox and whooping cough) related to similar casual factors.
3. Minor digestive diseases and enteritis (typhoid, dysentery, diarrhoea) related to poor facilities for the cold storage of food and to inadequate washing and toilet facilities.
4. Injuries resulting from home accidents related to overcrowded or inadequate kitchen facilities, poor electrical connections and poorly lighted and rickety stairs.

5. Infectious and non-infectious diseases of the skin related to crowding and insufficient facilities for washing.

Schorr also made an attempt to discuss studies which show concomitant relationship of pneumonia, tuberculosis and lead poisoning to poor housing. He argues that stresses arising from crowding and the lack of personal satisfactions in a poverty-striken environment pose mental and physical health hazards Schorr (1966).[23]

In our cities, the health and disease problems are related to the poverty-striken areas of slum dwellings. Most of the academicians have concluded that "the aggregate impact of the physical and social environment of the poor, including their housing, nutrition, occupations and whole lifestyle, contributed to a burden of diseases and death that blights their lives much more than among the well-to-do".

In spite of the fact that access to medical care for the rich and poor alike is greater in the cities than in rural areas, the urban poor, receives it much less than the well-to-do, with the result that a given sickness is more likely to become worse, disabling and sometimes even fatal.

These problems of immediate attention arouse the concern of geographers interested in health. It is crucial for them to sort out the variations of these health-associated environmental, demographic, social and psychological elements of urban ecology. Therefore, they should make an attempt to identify the patterns of need for health services so that the problem of deploying medical technology to meet the need is brought under a sharp focus.

Demographic Problems

Every urban problem has a demographic aspect. Each urban problem is influenced by the rate of change in the population growth. The growth of population is assigned to two factors, natural increase and migration of rural people to the cities. The impact of increased rural-to-urban migration leads to problems like congestion, overcrowding, insanitation which in turn lead to problems of general health and living conditions. The inflow of greater streams of migrants have caused slumification in our cities, because there is no proportional increase in the living accommodation in the cities. In other words there is a lack of balance between the migration and the absorption rate. The indiscriminate influx of the people into the cities makes them houseless strangers or dishoused citizens.

Moreover, unregulated flows of the unemployed rural migrants, who do not possess skills essential for city employment, create chaotic conditions. This results in the baffling of the city environment which leads to more human misery and greater social unrest. The rural migrants when they land in an unfamiliar urban atmosphere find themselves in inhospitable circumstances. Lack of housing compels them to encroach on public or private land or make the already crowded shacks more crowded with the result that slum conditions and the concomitant problems only worsen.

Thus it is evident from the foregoing that cities are the focal point of a great variety of ills. Overflowing city dwellers everyday clog the highways, befoul air, contaminate water, overburden the sewerage system, make streets hazardous and public places unsafe and create congestion and insanitation. There is evidence that their sick, indigent, aged and deviants make demands, thus slums spread. Most of these problems which are identified with urban systems are not unique to this growing sector of society. It is patently impractical, undesirable and almost meaningless in a complex society undergoing rapid and widespread change to separate the city (McElrath, 1965)[24]. Cities are a part and parcel of greater societies where everyday activities are linked to greater politics, economics and extended networks of kin and friends. The problems which have been identified in cities as a matter of fact relate to wider social set-ups of which cities are a part.

ABOUT THIS VOLUME

This volume is designed primarily for those readers who are interested in contemporary urban affairs or urban problems. Its each essay formulates a point of view about a critical sector of urban issues. Each essay is cogent, readable and indicative of the standing literature on a given aspect of the contemporary urban conditions. A careful reader may find contradictions between the essays and the readings. This is because the urban condition is fraught with contradictions and is in all respects vastly more complex than the ideas and data we use to interpret it. But in combination, the readings provide a sample of the contemporary ways of thinking, scientifically about the urban condition.

The dominating interest which has affected the content and direction of every essay and the selection of most of the readings is my interest in the quest for practical solutions to urban problems. Hopefully this will serve as an antidote to a body of literature on urban geography which is unbearably long on description and problem identification and painfully short on the consideration of solutions.

The articles in this volume have been so selected as to serve several purposes. The volume itself has been designed to reflect some of the research and study which geographers and other social scientists have been engaged in and which bear social relevance to the contemporary issues and problems. It is intended to provoke a greater participation of geographers in the study and analysis of contemporary issues. Besides, the present volume will definitely assist in the teaching of relevant contemporary issues and problems pertaining to modern metropolises.

The volume has been divided into five distinct parts: i. Environmental Deterioration and Human Stress; ii. Poverty and the poor in Cities; iii. Conflict and Crimes in Cities iv. Pollution and Health in Cities; and v. The Social Consequences of the Pollution. The topics treated are rather general. However, it is done to provide a systematic analysis which is easier to comprehend. However, it is extremely difficult to separate the contemporary issues and problems of urban society into distinctly separate parts since they are intrinsically interrelated. How can one isolate poverty from slums? How can one isolate problems of environmental deterioration and stress and strains from problems of air pollution, crime and population pressure? While the five sections may be found overlapping, each one is, to some extent, sufficiently distinct so that they can, at least for organizational purposes, be treated under separate headings. The arrangement of each section primarily offers some continuity to the highly interrelated overall dimension of the issues and problems presented.

It is my contention and observation that some of the scholarly studies remain scattered in professional journals, discussion papers and other sources which vary in their accessibility to a greater number of readers. Therefore, it was necessary to bring relevant studies together which had an appeal for every present-day reader concerned.

The articles included in this volume comprehensively analyse the breadth of the problems at hand, and most where the case approach is adopted, offer depth both to the problem and the methodology employed. It is my sincere hope that this volume will prove itself worthy as a principal text in current or newly developing courses on contemporary urban problems. It is also my hope that this volume will be found useful and helpful by the students of courses in allied disciplines.

The first section of this volume is introduced by Daniel Stokols who in his article, "A Congruence Analysis of Human Stress", examines recent developments, unresolved issues and research priorities in the field of human stress. He provides a clear examination of the use of the term stress. Stress refers to a state of imbalance within an organism that (a) is elicited by an acutal or perceived disparity between environmental demands and the organism's capacity to cope with these demands and (b) is manifested through a variety of physiological, emotional and behavioural responses. This response syndrome occurs as a result of the organism's exposure to excessive environmental demands or stressors. In this discussion the author provides a glimpse of the diverse yet complementary conceptualization of human stress. Recent attempts to integrate and refine these perspectives have spanned several focussed areas of research. The first section of this paper examines recent developments in three of the most active areas of stress research: urban stress, learned helplessness and stressful life events. These areas are emphasized because together they reflect a wide range of conceptual and methodological perspectives on Stress. The second part of the paper identifies a major emphasis and unresolved issues in stress research. The third section introduces a theoretical framework for further research, linking the dimensions of environmental alience and control liability, the final section examines the relationship among components of the proposed model and highlights priorities for future research.

The research involvement by geographers in the field of urban stress studies is of comparatively recent origin. Nevertheless a contemporary urban problem, such as social deprivation, has an extensive history. Geographers have received stimulus to explicitly examine the problems of urban areas due to higher level government interest to resolve the contemporary social issues. As a response to this greater research interest in urban problems Christina R. Victor in her paper, on "Housing Stress and Social Stress: A Study of Nottingham C.B.", analyses the interrelationship aspects of urban stress, namely, housing disadvantage and social deprivation. The author first discusses the ecological tradition of studying urban social problems, examines the hypothesized relationships between housing problems and social problems, describes the methodological procedure and evaluates the results from the Nottingham case study. The urban stress in the study area, Nottingham C.B., is divided into its two constituent aspects—housing stress and social disadvantage. Using canonical correlation analysis the statistical and spatial relationships between these two dimensions are discussed. The resulting conclusions are then discussed in terms of the assumed relationships between these two aspects of urban deprivation.

Most of the researchers have indicated that injuries, illness, incapacity and death are not the only dangers or problems in housing and its environs. It is a well-recognized fact that threat of such physical harm from human violence and non-human dangers inhibits a state of emotional well-being. The most disadvantaged groups are usually sensitive about the security that housing should provide against the most blatant of threats. Henry Sanoff in his article "Stress and Density in the Residential Environment", clearly reveals that one's home is a symbolic extension of one's self. According to the author, deteriorating housing conditions cannot fully guarantee the security for one's family and the people who inhabit in such devastating conditions cannot control their own destiny and provide a stable family environment. The author clearly visualizes that the physical and social disorder of the congested housing presents a constant temptation to give up or to retaliate in kind. He feels that a relationship between mental health state and inadequate sanitation and the physical structure of the dwelling has not been completely established. The present paper is a step towards this neglected aspect of research.

Bernard Kayser in his article "Urban Poverty and Rural Poverty" points out that after the invention of the term Third World and the notion of under development the term poverty defines itself in many different ways, and after having convinced all the exploited people they were only underdeveloped, the poverty is entering now as an economic and political concept between the leading powers of the world. The author, reminds the readers that we cannot disagree with observants who raised the alarm everywhere in Third World the increasing of urban "proto-proletariat" coming from the rural zones in crisis and now perpetuated by the urban system itself, create bad environments and living conditions.

Widespread and oppressive poverty is an undeniable counterpart of booming, dynamic industry in the capitalist city. William W. Goldsmith in his article, "Poverty and Profit in Urban Growth and Decline", through the example of Manchester and Sao Paulo, tries to convince that accumulation of wealth at one pole is ... at the same time accumulation of misery, the torment of labour, slavery, ignorance, brutalization and degradation at the other pole. Academicians have recognized that Manchester was "the city of despair", "a great gloomy city", but this city of despair was also the greatest engine of production and accumulation the world had ever seen. In support the author visualizes that in both these cases, Manchester in the early 19th century, Sao Paulo in the late 20th century, as well as New York, Philadelphia. Chicago, Cleveland and many other cities of the USA, as we shall see, the forging of an impoverished proletariat, at work for low wages, on relief, or barely surviving on the edges of society, is the recognized counterpart of a spectacular achievement of industrial growth and capital accumulation. It is the intention of the author in this chapter to suggest that two popular observations about how urban development proceeds are seriously incomplete. Indeed, many times progress and poverty are reciprocal, rooted in the same basic social forces. The present paper begins with a discussion of how forces for development, in general, operate in market run societies. It then turns to show how the city is related to the economy. These two discussions will lead to arguments about the unity of profits and poverty and finally to a discussion of the geography of accumulation.

Most areal analysis of crime and juvenile delinquency has been referred to as ecological analysis. Most past studies have been designed to produce theoretical inferences about some non-geographical cause of crime or delinquency, most often poverty, social class or some feature of life associated with poverty or low social class standing. The evidence is overwhelming that indicators of low class standing of areas within cities are associated with high levels of both adult and juvenile official crimes. William R. Arnold and Steve W. Rawlings in their article, "Urban Areas and Self Reported Delinquency", report an areal analysis of self-reported offending by high school sophomores. The main thrust of this paper has been to demonstrate that when youthful offending, long thought to be concentrated in certain ecological zones, is measured by self-reports and disaggretgates by zones such as the socio-economic status areas, it is not meaningfully concentrated in lower status areas or populations. It seems safe to say that the concentration is certainly not as great as we have long thought. The implications of the findings for explaining juvenile misconduct are clear—low social class standing cannot be the cornerstone of future explanations of law violations. Similarly our social amelioration of juvenile delinquency should not focus on solving problems of poverty however valuable solving the problems may be for other reasons.

The earth's population is expected to increase by nearly two billion in the next two decades. That was the population of the earth at the turn of this century. Most of the young people will be in the large cities of the "South", countries in Africa, Asia and Latin America. They will definitely cause unplanned growth of cities like Bombay, Delhi, Calcutta, Mexico and Cairo. The infrastructures of these cities have for some time not been able to provide adequate water, transportation, communication, health and sanitation, police and other services to much of their population and the discrepancy between need and capacity is increasing consistently. Deficiencies in the home, school, and neighbourhood often do not raise the hope that should go with rising expectations. The obvious result is discontent, stress, bitterness and frustration. Frustration sometimes leads to aggression and if that deviates from social norms it is considered an offense. It is also termed as crime which is an act or failure to act that violates a law to protect the public. It is a public wrong. Manfred Kochen in his article, "Can Information Systems Help prevent Urban Crime?" examines the play groups of preschool children in the streets of disintegrated urban neighbourhoods as occasioning the formation of deviants and offenders. The process is modelled as the eventual conversion of, say, nine susceptible children in a group of 10 by one child; inviting them to join him in deviant acts, such as stealing fruits. The central idea is reversing this process, where the nine susceptibles simultaneously and independently convert the deviant by coherent peer pressure to joint them toward socially constructive goals. This is to be done by selecting or designing the group so that this inversion is possible and then providing them with an initial burst of external input in the form of know-how, motivation, aid and reinforcement. Thereafter the process is to become self-sustaining. It is modelled as a set of four non-linear differential equations of epidemiology and remembling those encountered in describing of other self organizing. Co-operative phenomena in science, spatial patterns of some infectious diseases.

Crime as a problem has been part of the American scene for quite some time. But only recently, social scientists have seriously and methodically begun to examine the hypothesis that certainty of apprehension and punishment and severity of punishment deter criminal behaviour. Past studies have supported the contention that certainty and severity are significant deterrents to various crimes. These studies have also established that for a majority of crimes certainty is a greater deterrent than severity. But no one has yet considered whether certainty poses a greater deterrent to crime when the punishment is more severe as opposed to the case when punishment is less severe. The answer to this question is provided by Vijay K. Mathur and Sheldon H. Stein in their article entitled "Certainty of Punishment and Mandatory Sentencing: Theory and Evidence". The primary purpose of this paper is twofold: to examine whether or not the theory proposed by Ehrlich can provide an answer to the questions posed above and, secondly, to provide empirical evidence to that effect. In Section I of the paper a brief version of Ehrlich's model and its comparative static implications are presented. Section II presents the supply of offence function to be estimated for various crimes, the variables included in the study and the postulated relationships between crime and its determinants. Section III discusses the methodology and empirical results. Finally Section IV sums up and draws conclusions.

Sanitation is not merely a physical and visual cleanliness, it also envisages control of environmental pollution, clear air, clean water and even unpolluted soil which must be provided to every citizen. It is, therefore, imperative to make a rational approach to and proper understanding of the existing environmental conditions which affect human health and activities. The planners and administrators should probe possibilities to improve the city environment and suggest measures for its betterment. Dr. S.Q.A. Rizvi in his article, "Changing Direction and Intensity of Air Pollution in an Urban Centre: A Case Study of Gorakhpur City", has tried to offer such measures so that the city environment of Gorakhpur City may be improved. The author in this paper provides a background for a thought-provoking problem known as "Pollution". He assesses the causes of environmental pollution which is a gift of modern scientific and mechanical development. He identifies air pollutions as solid, liquid and gaseous. Taking an example of Gorakhpur he outlines certain measures to deal with air pollution.

Throughout the world the use of nuclear power has grown considerably. At least eight per cent of the whole world's electricity is generated by nuclear power. In some countries the percentage has reached 20 and in Britain it is 14. As the nuclear power grew in Britain as also the external factors that had conditioned the environment the policy-making machine had to work in. During the early years there was growth of concern about the environment, then there was growth of terrorism from mid 1960s onwards and from mid 1970s onwards there was the growth of the movement for more open government. The origins of the anti-nuclear movement can perhaps be seen as developing as part of the environmentalist movement which in some way was a response to the public concern generated by Rachel Carson's book, **The Silent Spring** (1962) which dealt with the environmental problems related to the use of DDT. John C. Chicken in his article, "Community Organization's Influences on Local and Regional Decision Making", describes some of the findings from a study which the author made of various factors that have influenced the formulation of a nuclear power hazard control policy in Britain. The striking feature of this particular policy is that it shows how public interest in the policy has changed over the years and how the administrative procedures have been modified in response to the political pressures of the various interest groups. The public inquiry that was held to examine the proposal to extend the nuclear fuel processing plant at Windscale provides a useful case study of the way community organizations interact with the policy-making machine and the type of influence they have. The paper concludes with a description of a model of the way the interactions of various groups may change with time. The findings of the study are not peculiar to nuclear policy but are relevant to the impact all major technology developments have on policy.

Nuclear generation of power is a fact of life in many countries and will be in more by the end of the century. The initial promise has been modified by a more realistic assessment of relative costs and hazards posed by accidents and waste products. Recently the studies have identified that the worst situation will occur due to explosion of a nuclear weapon on or near a nuclear power plant which will affect a lethal zone of 500 square miles. In heavily populated areas, the potential danger of large-scale human contamination and injury is increased and, therefore, efforts that could prevent harm to the populace must have a very high priority. Dr. Terrel L. Pholcs and Dr. Kathlecrk Loewy in their paper, "Policy Issues: Emergency Response Planning for Nuclear Power Plants", evaluate the dangers of the location of nuclear power plants. According to them, nuclear power generation has been a major source of controversy in the United States and Western Europe as the supply of fossil fuels has dwindled and alternative energy source have become necessary. The construction of nuclear power plants near major metropolitan areas has made the re-examination of the national energy policies that rely heavily on nuclear power generation imperative.

This study compares the modern policies of the United States particularly as they relate to safety regulations for the general population that live in the surrounding areas with those of the nations of Western Europe which rely heavily on nuclear power, the United Kingdom, the Federal Republic of Germany and France. The focus of authors is on the decision-making processes detailed in the policy guidelines as well as the actual safeguards in the event of a nuclear emergency. The emphasis on nuclear power generation and the location of plants near heavily populated areas makes this issue specially important to Western Europe.

The authors find that emergency response plans have some shared aspects, but they also vary greatly in the detail with which they assign actions and responsibility to specific individuals or organizations. Overall, there is a lack of coordination, communications are weakly developed and exercises that fully test the plans are virtually non-existent. These conditions greatly jeopardize the effectiveness of these plans and the lives of people who depend on them for their safety.

Urbanization and industrialization have their far-reaching influence on the urban mosaic, both positive and negative. As a matter of fact while they bring various advantages to the society in the form of agglomeration economies, they also have far-reaching negative effects such as overcrowding, which probably gives rise to several social problems such as social disorders, social tensions, social ill health and social injustice. The studies on medical geography of urban areas have attributed the cause of social diseases of urban areas to overcrowding. In such areas communicable diseases may spread quickly. C. Thangaval, P. Jayapal and K.M. Kulkarni in their article, "Spatial Patterns of Some Infectious Diseases: A Case Study of Ahmedabad City", have said: The process of urbanization and industrialization have greatly led to the process of agglomeration of people and activities without taking adequate care of human values and health. The diversified economic activities over a wider area, operating on a large scale, have discarded the values of better living and have contributed a variety of unheard of diseases. Today, the urban living has become intolerable. The components of urban environment such as crowding, quality of drinking water, the conditions of sewerage lines and their performance in different seasons, routes and intensities of automobile traffic, the location of industries, the height of chimneys, the disposal of wastes, the urban facilities—their efficiencies, capacity and cost, etc.—have impoverished the urban dwelling. The quality of urban environment influences the physical and mental fitness of the urban dweller. An attempt has been made in this paper to assess the quality of urban environment in terms of few selected indicators and relate it to the incidence of some infectious diseases. The infectious diseases are "geographic" in nature as their spatial spread depends entirely on human interactions in space. It is not a great surprise that today the flights have widened the sphere of incidence of infectious diseases.

The use of aggregate data on populations to infer the health effects of a reduction in air pollution has been the subject of contention for some time. Many scientists have distrusted outrightly the result of statistical "natural experiments" on populations exposed to varying levels of environmental quality. They always preferred to rely on at best clinical tests or at least detailed individual case histories of exposure and health state. Most researchers would agree that before finally accepting any such evidence as casual we should be careful that any statistical association be.ween air pollution and health is supported by a consistent theoretical model specifying the disease mechanism. A.H. Harris in his article, "Economics and Epidemiology: A Critical Review of the State of the Art", postulates that individual and social behaviour influences the relationship between air pollution and health. Both the socio-economic environment facing individuals and their behavioural response to the environment may be important in the assessment of the damage to health associated with air pollution. The recent studies have advanced the statistical study of these phenomena to a considerable extent. The studies are examined with a view to assessing the confidence with which policy can be based on their result.

A movement for women's rights has surfaced every time a drastic change has shaken the established social order. The women's suffrage movement in the United States grew out of the drive to abolish slavery. The women's movement was begun largely, but not completely, by women who had been involved in the civil rights movement, in the anti-war movement, in student movements. The contemporary women's movement shares many of the concerns and motivations of the 19th century women's movement. They understood economic oppression, political and educational deprivation but did not understand sexual oppression in the concept of patriarchy. K.M. Dykes in her article, "The Women's Movement Relation to Social Movements in the United States", has reported on a specific aspect of the history of social formation and emancipation: the historical contributions of the American women's movement to a reorganization of the social sphere. She has pointed out that even as early as the turn of the century the women's movement had conceived programmes for a change of women's subordinate roles in a daily life dominated by the family. Suggestions for the development of women's cooperatives, communal kitchens and dining rooms— suggestions which had a lot to do with the social reform movements of the early socialists. The author finds it appropriate that these suggestions implied a recognition of the "one family home" as an obstacle to the development of the ideal self-administering community. Her report left open the question of how important the efforts towards reorganization of the much discussed "informal sector" are today; a question which remained unanswered in the discussion.

The elderly in the United States comprised about 11 per cent of the population in 1978. Florida, with its 1.6 million elderly residents, as the greatest proportion of elderly in the nation with 17.7 per cent of its total population. Dade county has one of the largest concentrations due in part to the large in-migration of the elderly from other States who seek the tropical climate and a somewhat lower cost of living than is found in the northern metropolitan areas. The past studies on the elderly have emphasized that due to decreasing physical and mental abilities of many elderly there is need for various para-transit programmes. Ira M. Sheskin in his article, "The Impact of Planned Dade County Rapid Transit upon the Accessibility of the Elderly", examines the effects of an expanding public transit system upon the accessibility of the elderly to various destinations including health centres, social service centres and the central business district. The author in his efforts first provides a brief description of Dade's elderly and planned rapid transit system, then he attempts the methodology which is used to analyse accessibility changes. Finally, selected results are shown. The author concludes that the elderly enjoy a somewhat greater level of accessibility than the general population and will experience decreased walk access times and total travel times.

Population movement within an urban system takes place on two levels. On a micro level, people move within a city in the process of carrying out their daily routines. On a macro level, urban residents also travel to locations outside their communities, in particular to other cities, for recreational, business or visitation purposes. All these movements are further categorized as Circulation and Migration. These movements are manifestations of part of the process taking place within an urban system. A.T. Salan in his article, "Population Movements within the Nigerian Sub-System", has dealt with the degree and nature of population movements within the Nigerian urban system. The present study is divided into two parts. The first part concentrates on the population movements between Nigerian cities (Inter-urban migration) while the second part focusses on circulation within the Nigerian cities (intra-urban movements). The author concludes that the continuing improvement in the standard of living of Nigerians cannot but lead to an increasing rate of mobility both between and within the cities. This shows an urgency that there is a need for effective spatial planning without which cities and highways could be plagued by mounting problems of traffic congestion. The study shows that population movement between and within cities occurs mainly in the efforts by the people to satisfy their needs. There is need to pay particular attention to the allocation and efficient arrangement of activities in space. The author evaluates that the lopsided concentration of activities in a few cities will ensure that most movements within the national urban system will be in their direction.

For several centuries a trend towards concentration of activity and population in relatively few urban centres has been observed. This trend has been generally accelerating and spreading from the developed to the developing countries. For at least a century this centripetal trend has been supplemented by a centrifugal trend from urban centres to their "Umland", the resulting new form of human settlement has been recognized as a "metropolitan area" which is potentially very large. Hans Blumenfeld in his article, "Where did all the Metropolitan Cities go?" clearly evaluates that in the United States there is an actual decrease in the population of some of the largest metropolitan areas in the country since 1970. The author finds that this surprising phonomenon give rise to various explanations, not necessarily mutually exclusive. A few researchers saw it merely as a repetition of the return of unemployed to their home communities, which had been observed during the depression. Some scholars interpret it as a "clean break", a return to life in the countryside and the small town. The author finds that the recent acceleration of the movement away from the metropolis and, in particular from its core, to more dispersed forms of settlement, both within and beyond the fringe, is due primarily to a basic shift in attitude, encouraged by prosperity, from seeking a place to make a living to choosing a place for living. This is reflected in the greatly increased emphasis on environment and on the quality of life. On the other hand, its relative disadvantages weighed far more heavily and were perceived as growing inexorably. They are numerous: congestion, pollution of air and water, noise, and insecurity of person and prosperity. The rural and small town environment is attractive—as it has always been—because it offers access to the world of nature, more space and privacy.

REFERENCES

1. Thomas Blair, **International Urban Crisis,** Mart Davis MacGibbon, London, 1974.
2. Langer, T.S. and Michael, S.T., **Life Stress and Mental Health,** Vol. II, Macmillan, New York, 1963.
3. Wolpart, J., Behavioural Aspects of the Decision to Migrate", Papers, Regional Science Association, XV, 1965.
4. Glass, D.C. and Singer, J.E., **Urban Stress: Experiment on Noise and Social Stressors,** Academic, New York, 1972.
5. Abramson, L.Y., Seligman, M.E.P. and Teasdale, J.D., "Learned Helplessness in Humans: Critique and Reformulation", **Journal of Abnormal Psychology,** 87, 1978, 49-74.
6. Wortman, C.B. and Brehm, J.W., "Responses to Uncontrollable Outcomes: An Integration of Reactance Theory and Learned Helplessness Model" in L. Berkowity (Ed.),

Advances in Experimental Social Psychology, Vol. 8, New York Academic, 1975, pp. 277-336.

7. Dorhren Wend, B.S. and Dorhren Wend, B.P., (Eds.), **Stressful Life-events, Their Nature and Effects**, Wiley, New York, 1974.
8. Glass, D.C., **Behaviour Patterns, Stress and Coronary Diseases**, Erlbanm, Hillsdale, N.J., 1977.
9. Blair, op. cit.
10. Blair, op. cit.
11. Adams, B. "Crime Prevention and Law Enforcement" in R.L. Chartrand (Ed.), **Hope for the Cities**, Spartan, New York, 1971, p. 56.
12. Abrahamson, **The Psychology of Crime**, Wiley, New York, 1960, p. 30.
13. Warren, R.B. and Warren, D.J. **The Neighbourhood Organizers' Handbook**, Notre Dame; U. Notre Dame, 1977.
14. Bentham, Jeremy, "Principles of Penal Law" in J. Browning (Ed), **The Works of Jeremy Bentham 1748-1832**, Y.N. Russel and Russell, 1962.
15. Gibbs, Jeck P., "Crime Punishment and Deterrence", **Social Science Quarterly**, 48, 1968, 515-530.
16. Gray, Lawis M. and David Martin J., "Punishment and Deterrence: Another Analysis of Gibbs Data", **Social Science Quarterly**, 49, 1969, 289-295.
17. Title, Charles, R. "Crime Rates and Legal Sanctions", **Social Problems**, 16, 1969, 409-423.
18. Bailay, William C., David Martin J. and Lawis M. Gray, "Crime and Deterrence. A Correlation Analysis, **Journal of Research in Crime and Delinquency** 11 July 1974, 124-143.
19. Morrill, R.L., "Geographical Aspects of Poverty in the United States" in Albanm M., **Geography and Contemporary Issues**, John Wiley and Sons, New York, 1973.
20. Lewis. O., **La Vida: A Puerto Rican Family in the Culture of Poverty**, Panther, San Juan and New York, 1967.
21. Carey, George W., "Urban Ecology, Geography and Health Problems" in Melvim Albanm, **Geography and Contemporary Issues Studies of Relevant Problems**, John Wiley and Sons, New York, 1973.
22. Schorr, A.L., Slums and Social Insecurity, Washington, D.C., Govt. Print. Office, 1966, p. 14.
23. Schorr, 1966, op. cit.
24. McElrath D.C., "Urban Differentiation: Problems and Prospects", **Law and Contemporary Problems**, 1965, Vol. 30, No. 1 Winter.

SECTION ONE
ENVIRONMENTAL DETERIORATION AND HUMAN STRESS

TWO

Daniel Stokols

A Congruence Analysis of Human Stress

RECENT DEVELOPMENTS IN STRESS RESEARCH

Impact of Urban Stressors on Health and Behaviour

The term urban stressor refers to a category of potentially aversive conditions of the physical environment that are prevalent in urban settings (although the occurrence of these stressors is not restricted to urban areas). Within the past few years, a substantial amount of research has been conducted on the health and behavioural effects of stressors such as noise (Cohen, Glass and Phillips, 1979; Glass and Singer, 1972), high density (Altman, 1975; Baum and Valins, 1977; Booth, 1976; Shokols, 1976), air pollution (Moos, 1976; Waldbott, 1973), traffic congestion (Novaco, Stokols, Campbell, and Stokols, 1978; Stokols, Novaco, Stokols and Campbell, 1978), and extreme temperature (Baron and Bell, 1976; Griffiths, 1975). Noise, for example, has been found to be associated with elevated blood pressure (Jonsson and Hansson, 1977; Cohen, Krantz, Evans and Stokols, Note 1), epinephrine secretion (Frankenhaeuser and Lundberg, 1977), skin conductance (Glass and Singer, 1972; Kryter, 1970), and impaired task performance (Glass and Singer, 1972; Weinstein, 1974).

The major thrust of recent research has been to identify cognitive and psychological factors that mediate the impact of physical environmental stressors on people. The research of Glass and Singer (1972) has been particularly important in identifying the role of predictability and perceived control as determinants of response to stressors. Specifically, their research indicates that although people are able to adapt physiologically and behaviourally to high-intensity noise in the short run, they frequently exhibit post noise aftereffects such as decreased tolerance for frustration and impaired task performance. Furthermore, when noise is predictable (periodic) or perceived as controllable, its negative aftereffects are reduced.

The differential effects of controllable and uncontrollable stressors have been documented in numerous laboratory and field investigations (Averill, 1973; Cohen, Glass and Phillips, 1979; Lefcourt, 1973). In lab settings, uncontrollable noise has been found to produce greater aggression among previously angered people (Donnerstein and Wilson, 1976), less helping behaviour (Sherrod and Downs, 1974), and lower tolerance for frustration (Glass and Singer, 1972) than controllable noise. Similarly, exposure to high-density noise results in fewer negative aftereffects when subjects believe that they are free (versus not free) to leave a crowded room if they so desire (Sherrod, 1974). Also, the detrimental impact of prolonged exposure to environmental stressors has been demonstrated in field investigations of the relationship between community noise (from airport and highway sources), decreased reading ability, and elevated blood pressure in children (Cohen, Glass and Singer, 1973; Cohen, Krantz, Evans and Stokols, Note 1), and in studies of urban commuting and physiological stress among adult workers (Novaco et al., 1979; Singer, Lundberg, and Frankenhaeuser, 1978; Stokols et al., 1978).

Several theories have been proposed to account for the relationship between perceived control and response to stressors (Averill, 1973; Cohen, 1978; Glass and Singer, 1972; Seligman, 1975). Cohen's (1978) theory of attentional overload assumes that individuals' capacity for attention is limited and that uncontrollable or unpredictable stimuli require more extensive monitoring (because of their novelty or complexity) than controllable events. The former stimuli are, therefore, more likely to deplete attentional resources and to result in impaired task performance and interpersonal relations. Consistent with this theory, Wohlwill and Heft (1978) found children from noisy homes to be less proficient on a selective attention task and less sensitive to auditory distraction than children from quieter homes. In two related studies, pedestrians in noisy areas were observed to be less helpful to strangers than those in quieter areas (Korte, Ypma and Toppen, 1975; Mathews & Canon, 1975). These findings, although subject to arousal-based (Easterbrook, 1959) as well as cognitive interpretations, are at least consistent with the notion that excessive environmental inputs result in decreased attentiveness to others' needs.

Learned Helplessness

Seligman's (1975) theory of learned helplessness provides an alternative explanation for the beneficial effects of perceived control. Helplessness involves a syndrome of cognitive, emotional, and motivational disturbances stemming from repeated exposure to uncontrollable events. Through exposure to such events, individuals come to believe that personal outcomes are independent of their behaviour, and consequently they reduce their attempt to influence the environment.

Seligman's formulation of learned helplessness has received substantial empirical support from studies with nonhuman and human subjects (cf. Hiroto and Seligman, 1975; Maier and Seligman, 1976). Among the findings from this research are that the exposure of animals to inescapable electric shock reduces on subséquent occasions their attempts to avoid escapable shock (e.g. by jumping over a barrier in a shuttle box, Seligman and Maier, 1976). Similarly, the debilitative effects of exposure to unavoidable aversive stimuli, such as loud intermittent noise (Glass and Singer, 1972; Hiroto, 1974; Krantz, Glass and Snyder, 1974; Sherrod and Downs, 1974) or a pattern of random reinforcement on difficult or insoluble tasks (Hiroto and Seligman, 1974; Roth and Bootzin, 1974), have been observed in several studies involving human subjects.

Recent research on human helplessness has identified several personal and situational variables that mediate the quality and intensity of people's reactions to uncontrollable events. The personality dimension of internal versus external (I-E) locus of control (Rotter, 1966), for example, has been found in laboratory experiments to mediate subjects' reactions to stressful situations, with externals exhibiting greater susceptibility to learned helplessness following exposure to uncontrollable aversive events (Cohen, Rothbart and Phillips, 1976; Hiroto, 1974). Moreover, the extent to which one attributes lack of control to either task difficulty or insufficient effort (Dweck and Reppucci, 1973; Klein, Fencil-Morse and Seligman, 1976; Wortman, Panciera, Shusterman and Hibscher, 1976), the amount of exposure to uncontrollable events (Krantz et al., 1974; Rodin, 1976; Roth amd Kubal, 1975), the aversiveness of these events (Benson and Kenelly, 1976), and the psychological importance of the situation (Roth and Kubal, 1975; Wortman and Brehm, 1975) have been identified as important mediators of helplessness effects.

Overall, the findings from research on human helplessness are considerably more complex than those of studies involving nonhumans. In certain experiments, for example, exposure of subjects to failure or random reinforcements on a series of tasks facilitated rather than impaired effort and performance on subsequent tasks (Roth and Bootzin, 1974; Roth & Kubal, 1975; Wortman et al., 1976). In an attempt to account for facilitation as well as helplessness effects of exposure to uncontrollable events, researchers have reformulated Seligman's (1975) original statements of helplessness theory (based primarily on animal studies), in terms of cognitive and social-psychological constructs. Wortman and Brehm (1975), in their review of the literature, point out that facilitation effects have been found in settings where subjects' initial expectations of being able to control the situation are high rather than low, and the amount of their exposure to uncontrollable events has been small rather than large (cf. Roth and Bootzin, 1974; Roth and Kubal, 1975). Moreover, they note that the intensity of both facilitation and helplessness effects appears to depend on the psychological importance of the situation to the target person. Thus, their reformulation of Seligman's theory predicts a pattern of psychological reactance (i.e., feelings of infringement following the preemption of one's control or freedom: (cf. Brehm, 1966) and enhanced efforts to reexert control over the situation under conditions of minimal exposure to uncontrollability, high expectancies for personal control, and a high degree of personal involvement in the situation; whereas the experience of learned helplessness is expected to occur in situations involving substantial exposure to uncontrollability, low expectancies for personal control, and a high level of personal involvement.

An alternative reformulation of Seligman's model in terms of attribution theory has been proposed by Abramson, Seligman, and Teasdale (1978). According to Abramson et al.'s restatement of helplessness theory, the kinds of causal attributions made by target individuals about the source or sources of uncontrollable events play a crucial role in mediating their response to such events. They note, for example, that the adverse impact of uncontrollable events is less pronounced when subjects attribute the source of their poor performance or lack of control to personally modifiable factors (e.g., insufficient effort: cf. Dweck, 1975; Miller and Seligman, 1976; Tennen and Eller, 1977) rather than to insurmountable or unchangeable conditions. Accordingly, Abramson et al. propose a classification of attributions relevant to learned helplessness, incorporating the dimensions of internal (personal) versus external (environmental), stable versus unstable, and global versus specific attributions about the source or sources of uncontrollability. These dimensions are assumed to mediate the chronicity, generality, and intensity of helplessness experiences.

An interesting implication of the Wortman and Brehm (1975) and Abramson et al. (1978) models is that helplessness, once experienced, might be reduced or even reversed by providing individuals with greater control over their environment, changing their expectations for personal control, or altering their attributions about the causes of prior failure and adversity. Consistent with this bypothesis, two recent studies found that control-enhancing interventions (e.g., increasing the predictability of visitors, Schultz, 1976; assigning personal responsibility for the caretaking of plants, Langer and Rodin, 1976) effectively reduced passivity and feelings of helplessness among institutionalized elderly people. Similarly, Dweck (1975) found that training children to atttribute their prior failure on problem-solving tasks to insufficient effort rather than task difficulty led to an enhancement of their performance on subsequent tasks.

Stressful Life Events

The relationship between exposure to stressful life events (i.e., circumstances requiring change in an individual's normal routine) and the subsequent onset of illness has emerged in recent years as a major focus of stress research (cf. Dohrenwend and Dohrenwend, 1974; Holmes and Rahe, 1967). The emergence of this area reflects a more general shift in the orientation of medical research from the traditional germ theory of disease toward a more holistic, social-epidemiologic perspective (cf. Cassel, 1964; Jenkins, 1971). The latter perspective places relatively greater emphasis on the contribution of social, psychological and behavioural factors to the etiology and distribution of disease in the community.

A systematic program of research on the health consequences of stressful life events was initiated by Holmes and Rahe (1967), who developed a standardized, paper-and-pencil inventory of life experiences, the Social Readjustment Rating Scale. This 43-item checklist incorporates a wide range of personal, family, and occupational situations that are weighted according to their relative impact on an individual's regular routine. The weights assigned to each item are based on the responses of an initial set of judges, who were asked to rate the selected events in terms of their relative intensity and the amount of readjustment required by each event.

The Social Readjustment Rating Scale has been utilized in several epidemiologic studies to evaluate the major hypotheses proposed by Holmes, Rahe, and their colleagues (cf. Dohrenwend and Dohrenwend, 1974; Rabkin and Struening, 1976). On the whole, these investigations offer strong support for the hypothesized relationships between the magnitude and number of stressful life events and the extent of both psychiatric and physical disability (Dohrenwend and Dohrenwend, 1974; Myers, Lindenthal and Pepper, 1971; Wyler, Masuda and Holmes, 1971).

Additional studies have identified personal and situational factors that mediate the relationship between life change and illness (cf. Dohrenwend & Dohrenwend, 1974). One such study found that, among Type A or "coronary-prone" individuals, the onset of myocardial infarction was more strongly predicted by prior exposure to uncontrollable rather than controllable life events (Glass, 1977). In other investigations, the relative desirability of life events has been identified as a significant predictor of well-being, with health impairments being linked primarily to undesirable rather than desirable life change (Sarason, Johnson and Siegel, Chap. 7 in this vol.; Theorell, 1976; Vinokur & Selzer, 1975).

The impact of societal conditions, such as economic change, on personal life events and health has also been examined in recent studies. Initial research by Brenner (1973) revealed a strong association between aggregate levels of unemployment and a variety of health disorders. Subsequent studies suggested that the relationship between community levels of unemployment and psychophysiological distress is mediated by depressed mood and increased exposure to life change at a personal level (Catalano & Dooley, 1977; Kasl, Gore and Cobb, 1975). Moreover, a recent study by Cohn (1978) found that the impact of job loss on emotional well-being is mediated by several contextual variables, including the availability of alternative roles and the degree to which unemployment is attributed to demographic conditions (external attribution) or to personal incompetence (internal attribution).

Cohn's (1978) research on job loss and self-dissatisfaction is noteworthy, as it provides a preliminary bridge between social-psychological models of learned helplessness (Abramson et al., 1978; Wortman & Brehm, 1975) and epidemiologic analyses of stressful life events. This preliminary integration of psychological and sociologic orientations signals several potentially important directions for future life-events research, including the delineation of cognitive, psychological, and social processes that mediate the relationship between life change and illness.

CURRENT EMPHASES AND UNRESOLVED ISSUES IN STRESS RESEARCH

Research developments pertaining to urban stress, learned

helplessness, and life change reflect certain emphases within the field as a whole. First, stress researchers have paid increasing attention to the implications of environmental controllability for human well-being. The dimensions of perceived and actual control over the environment are clearly central to recent formulations of urban stress (cf. Glass and Singer, 1972), learned helplessness (Abramson et al., 1978; Seligman, 1975; Wortman and Brehm, 1975), and stressful life events (Dohrenwend and Dohrenwend, 1974; Glass, 1977). Taken together, the findings from these areas suggest the existence of a pervasive human need for environmental controllability that plays a crucial role in determining the quality and intensity of people's reactions to their milieu.

A second trend in stress research is the increasing emphasis on cognitive and social-psychological variables that mediate people's response to environmental demands. In contrast with earlier analyses of physiological stress (Selye, 1956) and life change (Holmes and Rahe, 1967), which emphasized the direct linkages between environment and health, subsequent formulations have given far greater attention to the psychosocial processes that intervene among environmental conditions, human behaviour, and well-being (cf. Dohrenwend & Dohrenwend, 1974; Levi & Andersson, 1975). Moreover, the current emphasis on concepts such as perceived control, psychological reactance, and causal attribution in studies of urban stress (Glass and Singer, 1972 et al., 1978) and learned helplessness (Abramson et al., 1978; Wortman & Brehm, 1975) further reflect the trend toward explicit consideration of psychosocial mediating variables in stress research.

A third emphasis of the field is on the short-term consequences of acute environmental demands. Laboratory experiments on physical-environmental stressors and learned helplessness, for example, have been designed to examine subjects' reactions to salient aversive stimuli (e.g., bursts of loud noise, overcrowding) over relatively short periods. Also, naturalistic studies of urban stressors and epidemiologic surveys of life change and disease typically have focused on the behavioural and health impacts (e.g., performance deficits, onset of illness) of disruptive environmental conditions and life crises. This focus on the effects of acute environmental demands has led some researchers (e.g., Lazarus and Cohen, 1977; Lazarus and Launier, 1978) to call for a "transactional approach" to the study of stress, in which long-term processes of coping and adaptation (as well as the health-related outcomes of these processes) are analyzed and in which the potential benefits of exposure to enviromental demands (e.g., challenge and personal growth), as well as the more immediate costs of such demands, are considered.

The above-mentioned emphases of the field, on environmental controllability, psychosocial mediators of stress, and the short-term consequences of acute environmental demands, suggest several unresolved issues in stress research.

Questions of Environmental Controllability

Although numerous programs of research have emphasized the relationship between environmental controllability and personal well-being, the concept of control has remained relatively undifferenciated with regard to (a) the kinds of control available to people in specific settings (e.g., control over physical versus social dimensions of the environment), (b) the relative importance of different dimensions of control across settings and situations, and (c) the conditions under which perceived and actual control may be harmful as well as beneficial to well-being.

A significant gap in the research literature on stress is the lack of criteria for identifying relevant dimensions of control in particular situations. Control over the social environment, for example, may be of utmost importance in residential and work environments, yet less essential in more transitory situations. Similarly, reduced control over the physical environment brought about by conditions such as overcrowding and noise might be more salient in settings where people spend much of their time than in those where they do not. In general, it seems reasonable to expect that the adverse impact of a particular stressor will depend on the extent to which it interferes with personal control over psychologically important (rather than irrelevant) dimensions of the environment (cf. Stokols, 1976).

While emphasizing the benefits of personal control, reseachers have given less consideration to its potential costs (cf. Averill, 1973). The costs of control might arise where (a) the environment is too predictable, thereby leading to boredom and stagnation (Kaplan, 1975; White, 1959); (b) the initial perception of control is inappropriately high, resulting in frustration and disappointment from disconfirmed expectancies (Thibaut and Kelley, 1959); (c) too much energy is expended in gaining or maintaining control, resulting in premature depletion of adaptive resources (Selye, 1956; Lazarus, Cohen, Folkman, Kanner and Schaeffer, in press); and (d) the exertion of control over others promotes social conflict and personally aversive consequences (Thibaut & Kelley, 1959). At the same time, exposure to uncontrollable events might be beneficial in those situations in which efforts to cope with adversity result in feelings of competence and growth or lead to a constructive reassessment of personal goals and the choice of more functional behaviour patterns in the future (Wortman and Dintzer, 1978).

Questions of Mediational Mechanisms in Human Stress

Previous research has emphasized cognitive and social-psychological factors that mediate people's reactions to stressors, but little or no attention has been given in the literature to other categories of predisposing factors that may mediate susceptibility to stress, such as developmental and physiological variables. Moreover, most analyses of stress have emphasized single rather than multiple levels of mediation, and generally have neglected the complex interplay among different kinds of predisposing factors (e.g., cognitive, social, personality, developmental, and physiological variables).

The potential relevance of developmental factors in human stress has been noted by Greenberger and Steinberg (Note 2), who hypothesize that susceptibility to illness as a result of exposure to stressful life events may be greatest during critical periods of development, such as early childhood and adolescence. They also note that the impact of critical-period life events on health may be delayed and, perhaps, not manifested until adulthood.

Recent research on the coronary-prone behaviour pattern and stress underlines the importance of examining multiple levels of mediation associated with people's response to stressors. Studies by Friedman and Rosenman (1974), for example, suggest that coronary-prone, or Type A, behaviour is associated with certain pathogenic physiological processes (e.g., hormonal imbalance, atherosclerosis). These processes may account for the heightened susceptibility of Type A individuals to cardiovascular disease (Jenkins, 1971), especially following their exposure to uncontrollable life events (Glass, 1977). The health status of Type A's apparently is mediated by a variety of life circumstances, including occupational pressures (French and Caplan, 1970), social insecurity (Jenkins, Zyzanski, Ryan, Flessas and Tannenbaum, 1977), and routine exposure to traffic congestion (Novaco et al., 1979; Stokols et al., 1978).

In short, the effects of environmental demands on health and behaviour appear to be determined contextually by multiple features of the individual's life situation. The multivariate mediation of stress warrants explicit consideration in future theoretical and empircial research.

Questions of the Long-term Consequences of Chronic Exposure to Stressors

The emphasis of recent research on the short-term effects of exposure to acute stressors has resulted in the neglect of several important issues relating to long-term processes of coping and adaptation. Among these issues are (a) the adaptational costs of exposure to chronic versus acute stressors, (b) the carry-over effects of exposure to stressors across different situations (cf. Baum and Valins, 1977), and (c) the interactive effects of multiple stressors on health and behaviour (cf. Donnerstein and Wilson, 1976; Konecni, 1975; Evans, Stokols and Novaco, Note 3).

In an analysis of the costs associated with chronic exposure to stressors, Campbell (Note 4) distinguishes between ambient and acute stressors. The former stressors are less salient, of greater duration, and require fewer immediate behavioural adjustments than the latter. Ambient stressors are exemplified by chronic exposure to community noise, traffic congestion, and air pollution. Although people may become partially habituated to ambient stressors via perceptual and attitudinal processes, continual exposure to these stimuli may eventuate in physiological impairment (cf. Jansen, 1973). Priorities for future research are, thus, to examine processes of partial versus complete habituation to stressors, and the potential costs of chronic exposure to aversive stimuli (even when exposure to such stimuli is perceived as voluntary or personally controllable).

Although previous research on urban stress has examined the short-term after effects of exposure to noise and high density (cf. Cohen, Glass and Phillips, 1979; Glass and Singer, 1972; Sherrod, 1974), little attention has been given in prospective, naturalistic studies to the relationship between chronic exposure to stressors in one situation and subsequent sensitivity to stressors in other settings (cf. Baum & Valins, 1977; Cohen, Krantz, Evans and Stokols, Note 1). Specifically, under what conditions do innoculation or intensification effects occur as a result of exposure to stressors across different settings ?

An additional issue that, only recently, has been examined experimentally is the joint impact of multiple stressors on personal well-being (Donnerstein and Wilson, 1976; Konecni, 1975; Evans et al., Note 3). In many naturalistic settings, people are exposed to more than one source of stress (e.g., physical plus social stressors). Important questions for future research are, therefore, whether or not exposure to one stressor increases a person's susceptibility to other sources of stress in the same situation and whether the impact of multiple stressors is greater than that of isolated stressors.

A CONGRUENCE MODEL OF STRESS LINKING THE DIMENSIONS OF ENVIRONMENTAL CONTROLLABILITY AND SALIENCE

Most of the unresolved issues discussed above are directly or indirectly related to a major gap in stress research: that is, the failure of previous analyses, while focusing on the consequences of specific, uncontrollable stimuli or events, to consider the sociophysical context in which these events occur. This overemphasis on the impact of isolated, acute stressors has precluded an analysis of issues such as the ratio of uncontrollable to controllable events in a situation, the relative importance of those needs and goals with which a stressor (or set of stressors) interferes, and the extent to which the impact of stressors is ameliorated by the individual's exposure to concurrent, compensatory rewards. A systematic examination of these and related issues is crucial to the development of a more adequate conceptualization of stress than presently exists.

Central to a congruence model of human stress is the concept of environment-behaviour congruence, or the extent to which an environment accommodates the needs and goals of its users (cf. Barker, 1968; Michelson, 1976; Stokols, 1978; Wicker, 1972). The notion of congruence is germane to several of the contextual issues mentioned earlier, including the range of salient needs facilitated by an environment, as well as the proportion of significant needs that are constrained by uncontrollable features of the setting.

Although the importance of the congruence construct to the study of environment and behaviour has been suggested by several researchers, little attempt has been made to define the concept operationally or to specify its implications for research on human stress. In the formulation proposed here, environmental congruence is defined in terms of two measurable components: environmental controllability and environment salience. A major assumption underlying this analysis is that the joint utilization of the controllability and salience dimensions will yield a more adequate conceptualization of human stress than do existing models based on the controllability dimension alone.

The discussion of the proposed framework is organized in relation to three general concerns: the conceptualization of environmental congruence, controllability, and salience; the relationships among these components of the model; and the research priorities suggested by the model.

Conceptualization of Environmental Congruence, Controllability, and Salience

Environmental Congruence

The concept of environment-behaviour congruence has been variously labelled and defined in previous discussions (cf. Barker, 1968; French and Caplan, 1970; Kahana, 1975; Michelson, 1976; Mischel, 1973; Wicker, 1972), but generally, the term congruence has been used to refer to the degree of fit between individuals and their environment. Some writers, such as Michelson (1976), have distinguished between actual and perceived levels of congruence. Michelson defines **experiential congruence** in terms of how well the environment actually accommodates the characteristics and behaviour of people, and mental congruence as the extent to which people think that a given environment accommodates their desired activities (pp.30-31).

The present analysis builds upon Michelson's but places greater emphasis on perceived (mental) rather than experiential congruence. It is assumed that people's subjective appraisals of their environments provide a reasonably straightforward index of the quality of their experiences in those settings (cf. Lazarus, 1966; Thibaut & Kelley, 1959). At times, however, people may be quite unaware of the ways in which they are affected by environmental demands, as exemplified by situations involving stressors whose effects are subliminal (cf. Jansen, 1973; Campbell, Note 4) or where people simply have given little thought to the impact of the environment on their well-being (cf. Friedman and Rosenman, 1974). The circumstances under which perceived and experiential congruence diverge markedly, and their implications for the proposed model of stress, are examined more closely in a subsequent section of the chapter.

In the proposed formulation, congruence denotes a ratio between existing and ideal levels of need facilitation for a given situation. This need-facilitation index is determined through an interplay of personal attributes and environmental conditions. Personal variables that may influence the level of congruence in a setting include (a) psychologically important goals and plans, (b) expectancies regarding the fulfilment of goals and plans, which may be based on (c) prior experience with similar situations and the experiences of relevant others, (d) personal traits and behavioural styles, (e) developmental factors, and (f) physiological drives. Environmental determinants of congruence, construed most broadly, include what Chein (1954) referred to as environmental "supports" and "constraints," that is, those features of the environment that either facilitate or impair the fulfilment of personal needs and goals.

Throughout this discussion, personal determinants of congruence are represented by the term needs. Needs refer to emotional, physiological, and behavioural states of an individual that are actually advantageous, or are perceived as being necessary or advantageous, for personal well-being. Need fulfilment can be attained through active behavioural strategies (e.g., taking action to avert life-threatening events), or it can be experienced more passively as a result of existing environmental conditions (e.g., facilitation of personal comfort via optimal levels of ambient temperature and air quality). Needs, in this analysis, are not restricted to somatically determined drives but also subsume personally chosen goals and plans.

The term actual facilitation (AF) is used to refer to existing levels of perceived need fulfilment, whereas ideal facilitation (IF) refers to optimal or preferred levels of need fulfilment. Because need facilitation is so often functionally equivalent to individual's ability to control the environment or to regualte their exposure to it, we refer to the actual:ideal ratio of need facilitation as an index of environmental controllability.

As noted earlier, however, the degree of congruence or person-environment fit encompasses more than the relative controllability of the environment. That is, congruence is viewed as a joint function of the ratio between actual and ideal levels of need facilitation (controllability), and the motivational significance (salience) of those needs that are facilitated by the environment.

Environmental Controllability

The controllability of a setting concerns both the degree to which it can be modified or maintained in accordance with personal preference and well-being and the extent to which exposure to the environment can be personally regulated. The present analysis, by viewing environmental controllability as equivalent to an actual:ideal ratio of need facilitation, extends earlier discussions of personal control and stress in certain important respects. First, controllability here refers to a composite of several need dimensions, some of which may be facilitated and others constrained by the environment. The impact of an uncontrollable stimulus or event can therby be understood in the context of alternative dimensions of controllability (need facilitation) that are available to an individual in a given situation.

In addition to emphasizing the multidimensional nature of controllability, this formulation permits an analysis of different levels of controllability. Thus, we can consider not only the controllability of specific stimuli and events, but also the relative controllability of whole situations and settings, in terms of the range of environment conditions that are experienced as being personally controllable.

The proposed formulation of controllability must be stated in operational terms to be of use in future research. As a basis for arriving at a more detailed definition of controllability, let N represent those needs that are relevant to an individual in a particular situation. Further, let n_f denote each need within the set, N, that is perceived to be facilitated by environmental conditions, and let n_t denote each need among N that is perceived to be thwarted by the environment. Each need, n_f or n_t, is assumed to be weighted by an actual facilitation (AF) or thwarting (AT) score, respectively, and by an ideal facilitation (IF) score. The AF and AT scores reflect an individual's subjective rating of the degree to which a specific need is either supported or constrained by the environment, whereas the IF score reflects an individual's appraisal of the optimal or desired level of facilitation associated with that need. The level of environmental controllability, C, can be represented as an actual:ideal ratio of need facilitation, as follows:

$$C = \frac{{}_f(AF_{nf}) - {}_t(AT_{nt})}{{}_f(IF_{nf}) + {}_t(IF_{nt})} \qquad (1)$$

To illustrate the application of Eq. (1), suppose that an individual is asked to list those personal needs (N) that are relevant in the context of a work environment and to rate on 7-point scales the degree to which each need (n_f or n_t) is facilitated (AF) or thwarted (AT) by the environment. Let us assume that the individual lists privacy maintenance, opportunities for socializing, and lack of work interruptions as the major needs associated with this setting. Also suppose that the facilitation scores associated with these needs are 2, 5, and -4, respectively, where the latter number reflects thwarting score of +4. Assuming that the IF score for each of the three needs is +7, we can represent the perceived controllability of the individual's work environment as (7-4)/(14+7)= .14.

The degree to which a particular stressor reduces need facilitation can be gauged by comparing the levels of perceived controllability of the setting when the stressor is present versus absent. In the preceding example, let us suppose that a program of Muzak is installed in the work setting by the office manager and that this change in the environment reduces privacy from 2 to 1, increases socializing from 5 to 6, and increases the distraction associated with work interruption from 4 to 6. Also, assuming that the Muzak has been installed against the wishes of the worker, additional need dimensions relating to personal regulation of the work environment and respectful treatment by superiors may now be perceived as being constrained by the environment to the degree of 5 and 7, respectively. With the addition of Muzak, then, the controllability of the work setting shifts from .14 to (7 - 18)/(21 + 14), or -.31, reflecting a net loss of 45 points on a continuum ranging from complete uncontrollability (- 1.0) to complete controllability (+ 1.0).

The proposed index of controllability is essentially a static measure, summarizing actual and ideal levels of need facilitation for a given situation, at a particular point in time, rather than a process measure of adaptation and coping efforts. The impact of control-related processes, such as causal attribution, emotional experiences, and coping behaviour on environmental congruence is assumed to be summarized by the actual:ideal ratio levels of need facilitation at a given point in time. The static nature of this need-facilitation index, however, does not preclude its use as a repeated measure in conjunction with longitudinal assessments of coping processes and personal well-being (e.g., Lazarus and Cohen, Note 5). As discussed in more detail below, the occurrence and effectiveness of coping processes can be assessed in terms of the shift in levels of environmental controllability over successive measurement intervals.

Environmental Salience

Although the preceding discussion extends earlier analyses of stress by emphasizing the multiple dimensions and levels of controllability, it leaves unaddressed a fundamental theoretical issue, that is, which sources of uncontrollability will be most crucial in determining an individual's vulnerability to stress in a particular situation? Any attempt to address this issue must consider the concept of environmental salience, or the degree to which situations and settings are motivationally significant (Stokols, 1978; Wortman and Brehm, 1975) and perceptually prominent (Taylor and Fiske, 1978).

The concept of salience has been invoked in several areas of research, including studies of environmental perception (Brunswik, 1943; Kaplan, 1975; Lynch, 1960), causal attribution (Arkin and Duval, 1975; Heider, 1958; Jones and Nisbett, 1972; Taylor and Fiske, 1978; Neuman, Note 6), social exchange (Thibaut and Kelley, 1959), and information processing (Kahneman, 1973; Mandler, 1975). In the context of stress research, Lazarus (1966) and Wortman and Brehm (1975) have discussed the perceived importance of anticipated outcomes as a critical mediating variable in learned helplessness, and Stokols (1976) has examined the intensity of crowding experiences in relation to the psychological significance of the setting in which high density occurs (e.g., "primary" versus "secondary" environments). In previous discussions, however, the concept of salience has not been analyzed systematically in terms of its various components nor explicitly incorporated in most models of human stress.

The present analysis makes a distinction between **motivational** and **perceptual salience.** The former concerns the extent to which settings are associated with psychologically important needs (Stokols, 1976, 1978), whereas the latter category refers to the number and intensity of highly noticeable features of the sociophysical environment (cf. Lynch, 1960; Taylor and Fiske, 1978). Motivational salience depends largely on the idiosyncratic weightings of importance assigned by individuals to personal needs and goals, whereas perceptual salience is determined less by individual differences and more by objective features of the physical and social environment (e.g., brightness, contrast, novelty, movement). Also, as is true of environmental controllability, one can distinguish among different levels of salience, depending on whether one is referring to the salience of stimuli, situations, or settings.

To permit a more precise formulation of the components of salience and their relationship to environmental congruence, let MS denote the motivational salience (i.e., subjective importance rating) assigned by an individual to the need, n. Moreover, let PS denote the perceived prominence of an environmental element, **e**, which is perceptually salient but not immediately relevant to need facilitation. The ratio MS_n/MS_N represents the relative salience of the need, **n**, vis-a-vis the summated salience ratings of all situationally relevant needs, N. Similarly, the ratio PS_e/PS_E denotes the relative prominence of the element, e, vis-a-vis the summated salience ratings assigned to all perceptually prominent features of the environment, E.

It is assumed in this analysis that motivational salience affects over all levels of environmental congruence through its adjustment of actual and ideal levels of need facilitation. In operational terms, the facilitation (AF, IF) and thwarting (AT) scores associated with various needs are multiplied by the respective importance ratings (MS) of these needs, and the sum of these products is utilized to derive an adjusted index of environmental controllability, C':

$$C = \frac{{}_f(AF_{nf} \times MS_{nf}) - \quad {}_t(AT_{nt} \times MS_{nt})}{{}_f(IF_{nf} \times MS_{nf}) + \quad {}_t(IF_{nt} \times MS_{nt}} \qquad (2)$$

To illustrate the effects of motivational salience on need facilitation, we return to the earlier example of the work setting (prior to the installation of Muzak) where the actual facilitation (AF) scores associated with privacy, socializing, and freedom from interruptions were 2, 5, and - 4, and the ideal facilitation (IF) score for each need was 7. Previously, we assumed that the relative importance of these needs was equal. Now, however, let us assume that the importance ratings (MS) of these needs, on a 7-point scale, are 1, 6, and 3, respectively. The actual:ideal ratio of need facilitation is, thus, (2 + 30 - 12)/(7 + 42 + 21)= .29, compared to the previously unadjusted value of .14.

Equation (2) reflects the perceived impact of environmental conditions on need facilitation, or controllability. It neglects, however, the role of goal-irrelevant features of the environment that do not affect need-facilitation directly but do intensify the individual's sensitivity to existing levels of controllability. As a basis for delineating this perceptual intensification process, it is useful to consider a distinction, proposed by William James (1890), between voluntary and involuntary attention. Briefly, the former variety of attention requires effort whereas the latter does not. Voluntary attention occurs when one intentionally monitors those features of the environment that are relevant to task completion or goal satisfaction. Involuntary attention occurs spontaneously, in response to perceptually prominent stimuli (e.g., strikingly beautiful objects, sudden sounds).

The perceptual component of salience emphasizes involuntary rather than voluntary attentional processes. But in order to specify the contribution of perceptual salience to environmental congruence, it is necessary to differentiate between two kinds of involuntary attention: that which has a direct and perceived impact on the fulfilment of personal needs, and that which exerts a negligible or unrecognized effect on need facilitation. As an illustration of the former, exposure to novel or unexpected events sometimes offers a means of satisfying personal needs for diversity, challenge, or esthetic experience. At other times, complex or unfamiliar stimuli operate as a source of distraction, promoting cognitive overload (Cohen, 1978; Kahneman, 1973) and interfering with successful task completion. To the extent that perceptually salient stimuli enhance or reduce need-facilitation, they are viewed, respectively, in this analysis as environmental supports or contraints. Their contribution to congruence is, thus, represented in terms of the facilitation (AF) or thwarting (AT) scores associated with motivationally significant needs (see Eq.2), rather than in terms of perceptual salience (PS).

The term perceptual salience is reserved for those stimuli that are highly noticeable but are viewed by the individual as being unrelated to need fulfilment. According to the present analysis, such stimuli intensify our awareness of situations without directly modifying perceived levels of need facilitation. Specific illustrations of this intensification process are provided by experimental studies suggesting that salient features of the environment are evaluated more strongly and are construed as more causally signifcant than are less salient stimuli (cf. Arkin and Duval, 1975; Taylor and Fiske, 1978; Tesser and Conlee, 1975). In particular, stimulus complexity, novelty, and uniqueness have been identified as variables that heighten the evaluative and causal significance of the environment (e.g., Berlyne, 1960; Kaplan, Kaplan and Wendt, 1972; Taylor and Fiske, 1978).

The research on attention, evaluation and causal attribution suggests at least two mechanisms by which perceptual salience can affect environmental congruence. First, an individual's focus of attention on either personal or situational events may mediate the degree to which the environment is construed as controllable versus controlling (denoted by C' in Eq.2). Second, assuming that certain elements of a situation have been construed as uncontrollable, the individual's sensitivity to those events may be reduced to the extent that controllable or pleasant features of the setting are made more salient (e.g., via visual or acoustical interventions).

The relationship among environmental congruence (CG), controllability (C'), and perceptual salience (PS_E) is presumed to be multiplicative, as shown in the following equation:

$$CG = \frac{{}_f(AF_{nf} \times MS_{nf}) - {}_t(AT_{nt} \times MS_{nt})}{{}_f(IF_{nf} \times MS_{nf}) + {}_t(IF_{nt} \times MS_{nt})} \times c\ {}_p(PS_{ep}) \quad (3)$$

The term $E_p(PS_{ep})$, or more briefly, PS_E, denotes the summated subjective salience ratings associated with the set of environmental elements, E. The salience term is weighted by some constant, c, reflecting the fact that the exact relationship between perceptual salience and need-facilitation must be derived empirically for a specific situation or set of situations. For instance, the degree to which novel or unique elements of the environment affect congruence in a given situation could be determined by measuring the magnitude of change in subjects' congruence scores after different amounts of exposure to the setting.

In the above-mentioned example of the work setting, let us assume that the situation is novel for the worker (e.g., it is her or his first week on the job). Assuming further that the level of involuntary attention to various aspects of the environment is greater in novel than in familiar situations (cf. Berlyne, 1960; James, 1890), then it seems plausible to hypothesize that the worker's sensitivity to task-relevant constraints, such as interruptions by co-workers, will be higher during the 1st, compared to the 10th, week of work (even if the actual rate of interruptions remains constant over time). Thus, although the worker may not be consciously aware of the attentional demands of a novel situation, such demands may serve to heighten his or her sensitivity to goal-relevant supports or constraints in the setting. The magnitude of this increased sensitivity would depend on the pervasiveness and intensity of environmental conditions whose salience is amplified by the novelty of the setting.

At least three strategies can be utilized to assess perceptual salience: (a) structured questionnaire items pertaining to the perceived complexity and potency of visual, acoustical, aromatic, and tactile dimensions of the environment: (b) a combination of open-ended questionnaires in which respondents are asked to identify prominent features of the environment (that are also perceived to be unrelated to need facilitation) and a set of semantic differential scales on which the salience of these features are rated; and (c) nonverbal measures of reaction time designed to assess the salience and recognizability of environmental elements (cf. Hochberg and Gellman, 1977; Taylor and Fiske, 1978). The relative utility of these strategies must be determined empirically in future research.

RELATIONSHIPS AMONG KEY COMPONENTS OF THE MODEL

At least four major issues are raised by the preceding discussion of congruence, controllability, and salience: (a) the presumed separability of the controllability and salience dimensions; (b) the theoretical relationships among the terms congruence, environmental demand, and stress: (c) specific predictions derived from the proposed model of stress and empirical evidence pertinent to these hypotheses; and (d) the boundaries and scope of the proposed model.

Separability of the Controllability and Salience Dimensions

Throughout this discussion, environmental controllability and salience have been viewed as separate components of congruence (see Eq.3). This approach raises an important theoretical question: Are the dimensions of controllability and salience interdependent or orthogonal? On the one hand, the broadest conceptualization of controllability would subsume the salience dimension, inasmuch as the very existence of certain goals and needs within a situation is largely determined by (or confounded with) their psychological importance to the individual. On the other hand, controllability can be construed more narrowly as the degree to which personal goals and needs within a situation are facilitated by the environment, irrespective of their relative importance to the individual.

The controllability and salience dimensions are treated separately in this analysis for two reasons. First, the perceived importance of goals and needs often varies across individuals and settings. Only through separate measures of the environment's facilitation of personal needs (controllability) and the perceived importance of those needs (salience) can this interindividual and cross-situational variation be detected. Furthermore, certain components of salience, such as the perceptual clarity of the physical environment, may be negligibly related to personal goals or to individual differences in the perceived importance of these goals. Thus, the development of separate measures for salience and congruence seems heuristically and methodologically advantageous, despite the fact that at times these dimensions will be closely related rather than orthogonal to each other.

Theoretical Linkages among Environmental Congruence, Demand and Stress

The congruence ratio, depicted by Eq. (3), summarizes the degree to which an environment supports psychologically important goals and activities. The relevance of this formulation to the topic of stress becomes more apparent if we focus, instead, on the degree to which a setting constrains personal goals and activities. The level of environmental constraint in setting is represented in this discussion by the term environmental demand.

Specifically, environmental demand, D, is defined as the AT:IF ratio:

$$D = \frac{{}_t(AT_{nt} \times MS_{nt}) - {}_f(AF_{nf} \times MS_{nf})}{{}_t(IF_{nt} \times MS_{nt}) + {}_f(IF_{nf} \times MS_{nf})} \times c \quad {}_p(PS_{ep}) \qquad (4)$$

Furthermore, the demand of a particular stressor, D_s, is defined as the difference between the level of environmental demand when the stressor is present and when it is absent: $D_s = D_{(s\ pres.)} - D_{(s\ abs.)}$.

According to Eq. (4), the level of environmental demand is proportional to the number and preceived importance of personal needs that are thwarted by situational constraints. That is, environmental demand is heightened to the extent that controllability decreases and salience increases. This formulation is relevant to several unresolved issues in stress research. First, earlier analyses have defined stress as a state of imbalance in the organism arising from exposure to (or anticipation of) excessive enviromental demands. The psychological meaning and operational measurement of environmental demand, however, have been left rather vague in these discussions (cf. Dohrenwend and Dohrenwend, 1974). The proposed conceptualization extends earlier analyses by providing an operational definition of environmental demand in terms of the controllability and salience dimensions.

The definition of demand in terms of multiple dimensions of controllability and salience offers the basis for developing an ecological analysis of stress, namely, one that views stressors not as isolated stimuli but as situationally embedded events whose effects must be understood against the backdrop of salient personal needs and conditions of the environment. This ecological orientation would seem to be prerequisite for addressing more specific issues that have received little attention in the stress literature. For instance, the incorporation of need-facilitation (AF, IF) terms as well as need thwarting (AT) terms into the environmental demand equation permits an assessment of the conditions under which uncontrollable events result in positive as well as negative outcomes. The initial turmoil resulting from job loss, for example, might be offset later on by enhanced feelings of personal competence arising from the obtainment of an alternative job. Moreover, the cumulative costs of chronic exposure to stressful situations (e.g., the delays associated with traffic congestion) can be weighed against the perceived benefits of these conditions (e.g., the freedom, facilitated by long-distance commuting, to live in a desirable neighbourhood).

The assessment of environmental demand at successive points in time permits an analysis of an additional issue in stress research, namely, the relationship between unpredictability or suddenness of exposure to uncontrollable events and subsequent health impairment (Glass and Singer, 1972; Rabkin and Struening, 1976; Wortman and Dintzer, 1978). In the proposed framework, the impact of the rate of change in environmental demand (D/ t) on health and behaviour can be assessed, where the rate of change in demand is defined as:

$$\frac{D}{t} = \frac{(D_{t2} - D_{t1})}{(t_2 - t_1} \quad (5)$$

The present analysis suggests a number of hypotheses concerning the relationship between environmental conditions, stress and well-being. Before these are specified, however, it is necessary to clarify the theoretical status of the terms controllability, salience, congruence, demand, and stress. The terms, C', MS, PS, CG, and D, as defined in Eqs.(3-5) are intervening variables (cf. MacCorquodale and Meehl, 1948) that specify a set of functional relationships between condition of the environment, on the one hand, and physiological, emotional, and behavioural indexes of stress, on the other. The proposed terms intervene between environment and behaviour in the sense that they refer to an individual's subjective interpretation of the environment rather than to objective features of the environment. The degree of covariation between objective environmental conditions and perceived levels of demand can and should be empirically determined (e.g., through a systematic comparison of different individuals' responses to the same situations or settings), but the emphasis in this analysis is on the response side of the environment-behavior equation—on the linkages between the intervening variables, C', MS, PS, CG, and D, and the measurable manifestations of stress.

The term stress, as defined at the outset of this chapter, encompasses two closely related meanings: a hypothetical state of imbalance between environmental conditions and personal resources, and a measurable set of responses that are indicative of distrubance within the organism. In the present analysis, the variables C', MS, PS, CG, and D, are substituted for the more general, hypothetical meaning of stress as a state of imbalance. That is, the ratio variables of congruence and demand operationally define the degree of disparity between environmental conditions and desired levels of need facilitation. In the ramainder of this discussion, the term stress is, therefore, used exclusively to refer to the second meaning—a set of physiological, emotional, and behavioural indexes of disturbance.

Hypotheses Derived from the Proposed Model of Stress

A basic premise underlying this analysis is that people's responses to environmental demands are mediated by their subjective appraisals of those demands (cf. Lazarus, 1966). The term D has been proposed as an empirical index of subjectively appraised demands. The major hypotheses outlined below pertain to the degree of covariation between levels of environmental demand and indexes of emotional, behavioural, and somatic disturbance.

1. (a) As the magnitude of environmental demand, D, increases, the intensity of stress responses will also increase, as manifested by heightened levels of negative affect, performance deficits, physiological arousal, or somatic illness. (b) The particular combination of these responses will depend on the magnitude of demand, with higher levels of demand yielding more pervasive symptoms of emotional, behavioural, and somatic disturbance.

2. The intensity and pervasiveness of stress symptoms will increase to the extent that high levels of environmental demand are prolonged.

3. The intensity and pervasiveness of stress symptoms will increase as the rate of change in environmental demand, from low to high levels of demand, increases. Shifts from high to low levels of demand, on the other hand, will be associated with a decrease in the intensity and pervasiveness of stress symptoms.

These predictions regarding the magnitude, duration, and rate of change in environmental demand can be stated in terms of the dimensions of controllability and salience because environmental demand has been defined earlier as a joint function of C', MS, and PS. The more specific version of the first hypothesis, for example, states that, as controllability decreases, the intensity and pervasiveness of stress symptoms will increase. The main effects of controllability, however, will be mediated by motivational and perceptual salience, with higher levels of salience being associated with greater symptoms of stress in relatively uncontrollable environments (where—1 C' 0) and less stress in relatively controllable situations (where 0 C' 1). Similarly, the second hypothesis states that the disruptive impact of highly salient, uncontrollable events will increase to the extent that such conditions are prolonged. The third hypothesis predicts that abrupt (versus gradual) decrements in controllability and increments in salience will be associated with the most intense and pervasive stress symptoms.

Note that these hypotheses diverge from those based on earlier formulations of environmental demand in terms of life change units (cf. Holmes and Rahe, 1967; Wyler, Masuda and Holmes, 1971). Whereas the degree of demand associated with a particular life change is assumed in those analyses to be equivalent across individuals, uncontrollable elements of the environment are weighted in the present analysis by their salience to the individual and their impact on various facets of his or her life situation. Also, in contrast to earlier conceptualizations of nonspecific environmental demand (e.g., Holmes and Rahe, 1967; Selye, 1956), the present analysis suggests that the level of demand generated by unpleasant, negatively toned events will be greater than that associated with pleasant events (cf. Sarason et al., Chap.7 in this vol.; Vinokur and Selzer, 1975). For instance, although positive as well as negative events might tax physiological resources, only the latter would be expected to reduce cognitive and psysiological dimensions of congruence (thereby increasing environmental demand and subsequent symptoms of stress).

Although much of the recent literature on stress is directly relevant to the issue of environmental controllability and its implications for personal well-being[1] little systematic attention has been given to the role of motivational and perceptual salience in mediating the bahavioural and health consequences of uncontrollable events. Nonetheless, certain studies pertaining to urban stress and learned helplessness offer preliminary (allbeit indirect) evidence for the interactive effects of salience and controllability. First, a comparison of the findings from several crowding studies conducted in a diversity of settings suggests that high density exerts a more negative impact on health and behaviour when it occurs in psychologically important environments than in less salient settings (cf. Altman, 1975; Booth, 1976; Cohen, Glass and Phillips, 1979; Galle, Grove and McPherson, 1972; Stokols, 1976). As a case in point, a naturalistic study of the consequences of living in tripled-up dormitory rooms (originally designed for two rather than three students) found that those students who spent the greatest amount of time and felt most involved in their dorm rooms exhibited more negative reactions to their crowded living conditions (e.g., dissatisfaction with roommates, health problems) than those who spent less time and felt less involved in their dorm residence (Aiello, Epstein and Karlin, Note 7).

Second, experiments on learned helplessness further suggest that motivational salience mediates the intensity of stress reactions, with exposure to uncontrollable stimuli leading to more extreme symptoms of learned helplessness in situations that are of high rather than low importance to the individual (Roth and Kubal, 1975; Wortman and Brehm, 1975).

The contribution of perceptual salience to the environmental demand equation has not been assessed empirically, but indirect evidence for such a contribution is provided by recent research on attention, causal attribution, and emotion (cf. Taylor and Fiske, 1978). Specifically, this work indicates that perceptual salience heightens an individual's evaluation of positive as well as negative features of the environment (cf. Tesser and Conlee, 1975) and that the tendency to construe the environment as controllable versus uncontrollable depends in part on the focus of one's attention toward either situational or personal factors (cf. Arkin and Duval, 1975; Taylor and Fiske, 1978).

These hypotheses emphasize the impact of environmental demands on individuals, rather than the reciprocal influence of the person on the environment. The actual impact of environmental demands on well-being, however, will depend on an individual's ability to cope effectively with psychologically significant sources of uncontrollability. In the present framework, coping processes can be understood as efforts to enhance controllability or regulate the salience of personal needs and environmental conditions. These processes correspond roughly to Lazarus's (cf. Lazarus and Launier, 1978; Lazarus and Cohen, Note 5) categories of problem-focused and emotion-focused modes of coping.

Consistent with a transactional perspective (Lazarus and Cohen, 1977; Lazarus and Launier, 1978), the level of environmental demand may shift over time as an individual copes with salient sources of uncontrollability in the environment. The success of coping efforts can be gauged in terms of an individual's reduction of environmental demand (controlling for sources of reduced demand that are unrelated to the individual's efforts) and the subsequent enhancement of emotional and physical well-being.

In the present analysis, measures of emotional and physical well-being reflect personal needs that contribute to the environmental demand equation at Time 1 but also serve as indexes of stress and health outcomes at Time 2. These alternative uses of health-related measures at different points in time, rather than indicating a tautology between environmental demand and stress, reflect the cyclical nature of person-environment transactions. That is, an individual's experience and evaluation of the environment at Time 1 (demand) moderates the impact of the environment on that individual at Time 2 (stress), which in turn affects her or his evaluation of the environment at Time 3 (demand). Validation of the proposed model of stress thus requires an empirical analysis of the sequential shifts in environmental demand and personal well-being over two or more points in time.

Boundaries and Scope of the Proposed Model

In considering the utility of proposed model, it is essential to examine those factors that restict the model's range of applicability. One such factor is the model's reliance on subjective report measures for determining levels of environmental controllability, salience, and demand. Some theorists contend that people are inherently unable to access cognitive processes (cf. Watson, 1913), particularly those relating to the attribution of causality for behaviour to personal or situational sources (Nisbett and Wilson, 1977). Others take a more moderate position (cf. Smith and Miller, 1978), suggesting that people are often capable of accurately recounting their mental processes, provided that such processes are neither overlearned and routine nor excessively complex, and that respondents are given adequate time to analyze and report on their thoughts.

Consistent with the latter position, it is assumed in this analysis that people generally are able to identify and report accurately on their salient needs, their situational supports and constraints, but especially when they are prompted to consider such issues carefully[2]. The task of identifying salient goals and features of the environment would, after all, seem to be relatively straightforward and uncomplicated (e.g., in comparison with that of making subtle inferences about the causes of one's behaviour). As noted earlier, however, people are sometimes unaware of goal-relevant conditions of the environment or the ways in which they are affected by those conditions (e.g., the elevation of blood pressure as a subliminal but potentially dangerous effect of chronic exposure to aircraft noise). This divergence between perceived and experiential congruence (Michelson, 1976) is likely to be greatest in very complex settings where it is difficult to sort out salient environmental supports and constraints and in situations where people are either unable or unwilling to reflect on the quality of their relationship with the sociophysical milieu. Under such circumstances, then, the proposed model would be of limited utility for predicting the occurrence of stress reactions.

Another limitation of the model is that it does not generate predictions about the response profiles associated with particular environmental demands. Rather than specifying the qualitative pattern of responses, the present analysis makes the more general quantitative prediction that the level of environmental demand will be positively associated with the intensity and extent of stress symptoms. Investigation of the particular physiological, emotional, and behavioural responses elicited by different kinds of environmental demands remains as a relatively uncharted frontier of stress research (cf. Lundberg and Frankenhaeuser, 1978; Singer, Note 8).

Also it should be noted that the proposed model pertains exclusively to person-environment transactions rather than to those involving groups or organizations as the responding systems. Methods for representing salient group goals and measures of organization-environment congruence eventually may be devised but, for the time being, the scope of the model is restricted to the analysis of individuals rather than groups.

Finally, the proposed model is valid only to the extent that environmental supports and constraints are additively related to levels of environmental demand and stress, and the relationship between controllability and salience is multiplicative, as assumed by Eqs. (3) and (4). The adequacy of these assumptions and the circumstances under which they are not applicable must be delineated through empirical tests of the hypotheses outlined earlier.

PRIORITIES FOR FUTURE RESEARCH

The present analysis suggests several theoretical and methodological issues for future research. First, it is necessary to establish criteria for predicting the relative salience of personal needs and environmental events. A plausible hypothesis relating to this issue is that people orient to environments in terms of hierarchically ordered concerns (cf. Maslow, 1968). Among the major need categories associated with environments are those relating to (a) physical safety and emotional security, (b) environmental constraints and supports that are relevant to the fulfilment of important goals but pose no threat to personal security, and (c) environmental attributes not directly pertinent to immediate goals yet relevant to personal mood, comfort, and aesthetic experience. In general, these needs are arranged in a descending order of importance although their relative salience probably varies across different settings. The hierarchy-of-salience notion suggests that, when higher order concerns are neither threatened nor relevant in a given situation, environmental conditions associated with the next highest category of personal concerns become most salient and influential in determining the level of environmental demand in the setting.

Second, the specific mechanisms by which motivational and perceptual salience heighten environmental demand (and resultant stress) are yet to be delineated. Among the possible mechanisms by which increased salience might intensify stress are (a) via elevated arousal and hormonal response; (b) via the expenditure of attentional energy, resulting in fatigue; (c) via distraction and consequent behaviour disorganization resulting in ineffective coping efforts; and (d) via selectivity or biasing of attributional processes (Taylor and Fiske, 1978), resulting in personally threatenting interpretations of uncontrollable events.

Third, the contribution of various predisposing factors, such as developmental variables, to perceived levels of environmental demand remains to be assessed. An individual's stage in the life cycle, for example, might influence environmental demand by moderating the significance of certain personal needs (e.g, self-identity, intimacy, or generativity needs) or the perceptual salience of the environment (e.g., via physiological changes associated with aging).

Finally, to permit an empircal assessment of these issues and hypotheses, adquate measures of controllability and salience must be developed. As illustrated earlier, existing techniques for assessing attitudinal structure (e.g., Rosenberg, 1956) can be adapted for the measurement of personal needs and of the facilitation and importance scores associated with each. Moreover, the quantification of perceptual salience and its relationship to congruence will require both a classification of conditions that increase the prominence of environmental elements and the derivation of procedures for measuring the relative salience of those elements. The resolution of these measurement issues should permit a clear-cut assessment of the predicted linkages among environmental salience, controllability, and stress.

FOOTNOTES

1. The predicted main effects of environmental uncontrollability on personal well-being are generally supported by previous research on urban stress, learned helplessness, and stressful life events (cf. findings cited in the first section of this chapter).

2. The adequacy of this assumption ultimately must be tested by

developing procedures for cross-validating verbal reports of salient needs and environmental conditions. Among the strategies that could be employed for such purposes are the use of multiple response formats (e.g., forced-choice and open-ended questionnaires; systematic recording of behavioural patterns across different situations) for the assessment of personal goals and of situational supports and constraints; and the comparison of individuals' subjective reports with observers' (e.g., family and friends) projective estimates of their responses.

REFERENCES

Abramson, L. Y., Seligman, M.E.P., and Teasdale, J.D. Learned helplessness in humans: Critique and reformulation. **Journal of Abnormal Psychology**, 1978, 87, 49-74.

Altman, I. **The environment and social behaviour.** Monterey, Calif.: Brooks/Cole, 1975.

Appley, M.H., and Trumbull, R. (Eds.). **Psychological stress: Issues in research.** Englewood Cliffs, N.J.; 1967.

Arkin, R., and Duval, S. Focus of attention and causal attribution of actors and observers. **Journal of Experimental Social Psychology**, 1975, 11, 427-438.

Averill, J.R. Personal control over aversive stimuli and its relationship to stress. **Psychological Bulletin**, 1973, 80, 286-303.

Barker, R.G. **Ecological Psychology.** Stanford, Calif.: Stanford University Press, 1968.

Baron, R.A., and Bell, P.A. Aggression and heat: the influence of ambient temperature, negative affect, and a cooling drink on physical aggression. **Journal of Personality and Social Psychology**, 1976, 33, 245-255.

Baum, A., and Epstein, Y. (Eds.). **Human response to crowding.** Hillsdale, N.J.: Erlbaum, 1978.

Baum, A., and Valins, S. (Eds.) **The social psychology of crowding: Studies of the effects of residential group size.** Hillsdale, N.J.: Erlbaum, 1977.

Benson, J.S., and Kennelly, K.J. Learned helplessness: The result of uncontrollable reinforcements or uncontrollable aversive stimuli? **Journal of Personality and Social Psychology**, 1976, 34, 138-145.

Berlyne, D.E. **Conflict, arousal, and curiosity.** New York: McGraw-Hill, 1960.

Booth, A. **Urban crowding and its consequences.** New York: Praeger, 1976.

Brehm, J. **A theory of psychological reactance.** New York: Academic Press, 1966.

Brenner, M.H. **Mental illness and the economy.** Cambridge: Harvard University Press, 1973.

Brunswik, E. Organismic achievemnt and environmental probability. **Psychological Review,** 1943, 50, 255-272.

Cassel, J.C. Social science theory as a source of hypotheses in epidemiologic research. **American Journal of Public Health,** 1964, 54, 1,482-1,488.

Catalano, R., and Dooley, D. Economic predictors of depressed mood and stressful life events. **Journal of Health and Social Behavior,** 1977, 18, 292-307.

Chein, I. The environment as a determinant of behaviour. **Journal of Social Psychology,** 1954, 39, 115-127.

Cobb, S., and Rose, R.M. Hypertension, peptic ulcer, and diabetes in air traffic controllers. **Journal of the American Medical Association,** 1973, 224, 489-492.

Cohen, S. Environmental load and the allocation of attention. In A. Baum, J.E. Singer, and S. Valins, (Eds.), **Advances in environmental psychology** (Vol.1). Hillsdale, N.J.: Erlbaum, 1978.

Cohen, S., Glass, D.C., and Phillips, S. Environment and health. In H.E.Freeman, S.Levine, and L.G. Reeder, (Eds.), **Handbook of medical sociology.** Englewood Cliffs, N.J.: Prentice-Hall, in press.

Cohen, S., Glass, D.C., and Singer, J.E. Apartment noise, auditory discrimination , and reading ability in children. **Journal of Experimental Social Psychology,** 1973, 9, 407-422.

Cohen, S., Rothbart, M., and Phillips, S. Locus of control and the generality of learned helplessness in humans. **Journal of Personality and Social Psychology,** 1976, 34, 1,049-1,056.

Cohn, R.M. The effect of employment status change on self-attitudes. **Social Psychology,** 1978, 41, 81-93.

Dohrenwend, B.S., and Dohrenwend, B.P. (Eds.). **Stressful life events: Their nature and effects.** New York: Wiley, 1974.

Donnerstein, E., and Wilson, D.W. Effects of noise and perceived control on ongoing and subsequent aggressive behaviour. **Journal of Personality and Social Psychology,** 1976, 34, 774-781.

Dweck, C.S. The role of expectations and attributions in the alleviation of learned helplessness. **Journal of Personality and Social Psychology,** 1975, 31, 674-685.

Dweck, C.S., and Reppucci, N.D. Learned helplessness and reinforcement responsibility in children. **Journal of Personality and Social Psychology,** 1973, 25, 109-116.

Easterbrook, J.A. The effect of emotion on cue utilization and the organization of behavioor. **Psychological Review,** 1959, 66, 183-201.

Frankenhaeuser, M., and Lundberg, U. The influence of cognitive set on performance and arousal under different noise loads. **Motivation and Emotion,** 1977, 1, 139-149.

French, J.R.P., Jr. Person role fit. **Occupational Mental Health.** 1973, 3, 15-20.

French, J.R.P., Jr., and Caplan, R.D. Psychosocial factors in coronary heart diesease. **Industrial Medicine,** 1970, 39, 383-397.

Friedman, M., and Rosenman, R.H. **Type A behaviour and your heart.** New York: Knopf, 1974.

Galle, O.R., Gove, W.R., and McPherson, J.M. Population density and pathology: What are the relations for man? **Science,** 1972, 176, 23-30.

Glass, D.C. **Behaviour patterns, stress, and coronary disease.** Hillsdale, N.J.: Erlbaum, 1977.

Glass, D.C., and Singer, J.E. Urban stress: **Experiments on noise and social stressors.** New York: Academic, 1972.

Griffiths, I.D. The thermal environment. In D. Canter and P. Stringer, **Environmental interaction.** New York: International Universities, 1975.

Heider, F. **The psychology of interpersonal relations.** New York: Willey, 1958.

Hiroto, D.S. Locus of control and learned helplessness. **Journal of Experimental Psychological,** 1974, 102, 187-193.

Hiroto, D.S., and Seligman, M.E.P. Generality of learned helplessness in man. **Journal of Personality and Social Psychology,** 1975, 31, 311-327.

Hochberg, J., and Gellman, L. The effect of landmark features on mental rotation times. **Memory and Cognition,** 1977, 5, 23-36.

Holmes, T.H. and Rahe, R.H. The Social Readjustment Rating Scale. **Journal of Psychosomatic Research,** 1967, 11, 213-218.

James, W. **The principles of psychology.** New York: Holt, 1890.

Jansen, G. Non-auditory effects of noise: Physiological and psychological reactions in man. In W.D. Ward (Ed.), **Proceedings of the International Congress on Noise as a Public Health Problem.** Washington: U.S. Government Printing Office, 1973.

Jenkins, C.D. Psychologic and social precursors of coronary disease. **New England Journal of Medicine,** 1971, 284, 244-255; 307-317.

Jenkins, C.D., Zyzanski, S.J., Ryan, T.J., Flessas, A., and Tannenbaum, S.I. Social insecurity and coronary-prone Type A responses as identifiers of severe atherosclerosis. **Journal of Consulting and Clinical Psychology,** 1977, 45, 1,060-1,067.

Jones, E.E., and Nisbett, R.E. The actor and the observer: Divergent perceptions of the causes of behaviour. In E.E. Jones, D.E. Kanouse, H.H. Kelley, R.E. Nisbett, S. Valins, and B. Weiner (Eds.), **Attribution: Perceiving the causes of behaviour.** Morristown, N.J.: Silver Burdett, General Learning, 1972.

Jonsson, A., and Hansson, L. Prolonged exposure to a stressful stimulus (noise) as a cause of raised blood pressure in man. **Lancet,** 1977, 1, 86-87.

Kahana, E. A congruence model of person-environment interaction. In P.G. Windley, T.O. Byerts, and F.G. Ernest (Eds.), **Theory development in environment and aging.** Washington: Gerontology Society, 1975, pp. 127-141.

Kahneman, D. **Attention and effort.** Englewood Cliffs, N.J.: Prentice-Hall, 1973.

Kaplan, S. An informal model for the prediction of preference. In E.H. Zube, R.O. Brush, and J.G. Fabos (Eds.), **Landscape assessment: Values, perceptions, and resources.** Stroudsburg, Pa.: Dowden, Hutchinson and Ross, 1975, pp.91-101.

Kaplan, S., Kaplan, R., and Wendt, J.S. Rated preference and complexity for natural and urban visual material. **Perception and Psychophysics,** 1972, 12,354-356.

Kasl, S.V., Gore, S., and Cobb, S. The experience of losing a job; Reported changes in health symptoms and illness behaviour. Psychosomatic Medicine, 1975,37, 106-122.

Klein, D.C., Fencil-Morse, E., and Seligman, M.E.P. Learned helplessness, depression, and the attribution of failure. **Journal of Personality and Social Psychology,** 1976, 33, 508-516.

Konecni, V.J. The mediation of aggressive behaviour: Arousal level versus anger and cognitive labeling. **Journal of Personality and Social Psychology,** 1975, 32, 706-712.

Korte, C., Ypma, I., and Toppen, A. Helpfulness in Dutch society as a function of urbanization and environmental input level. **Journal of Personality and Social Psychology,** 1975, 32, 996-1,003.

Krantz, D.S., Glass, D.C., and Snyder, M.L. Helplessness, stress level and the coronary-prone behaviour pattern. **Journal of Experimental Social Psychology,** 1974, 10, 284-300.

Kryter, K.D. **The effects of noise on man.** New York: Academic, 1970.

Langer, E.J., and Rodin, J. The effects of choice and enhanced personal responsibility for the aged: A field experiment in an institutional setting. **Journal of Personality and Social Psychology,** 1976, 34, 191-198.

Lazarus, R.S. **Psychological stress and the coping process.** New York: McGraw-Hill. 1966.

Lazarus, R.S., and Cohen, J.B. Environmental stress: In I. Altman and J.F. Wohlwill (Eds.), **Human behaviour and environment: Advances in theory and research** (Vol.2). New York: Plenum, 1977.

Lazarus, R.S., Cohen, J.B., Folkman, S., Kanner, A., and Schaeffer, C. In H. Selye(Ed.), **Guide to stress research.** New York: Van Nostrand, in press.

Lazarus, R.S., and Launier, R. Stress-related **transactions** between person and envrionment. In L.A. Pervin and M. Lewis (Eds.), **Internal and external determinants of behaviour.** New York: Plenum, 1978, 287-327.

Lefcourt, H.M. The function of the illusions of control and freedom. **American Psychologist,** 1973, 28, 417-425.

Levi, L., and Andersson, L. **Psychosocial stress: Population, environment and quality of life.** Jamaica, N.Y.:SP Medical and Scientific, 1975.

Levine, S., and Scotch, N. (Eds.). **Social stress.** Chicago: Aldine, 1970.

Lundberg, U., and Frankenhaeuser, M. Psychophysiological reactions to noise as modified by personal control over noise intensity. **Biological Psychology,** 1978, 6, 51-59.

Lynch, K. **The image of the city.** Cambridge: M.I.T. Press, 1960.

MacCorquodale, K., and Meehl, P.E. On a distinction between hypothetical constructs and intervening variables. **Psychological Review,** 1948, 55, 95-107.

Maier, S.F., and Seligman, M.E.P. Learned helplessness: Theory and evidence. **Journal of Experimental Psychology: General,** 1976, 195, 3-46.

Mandler, G. Mind and emotion. New York: Wiley, 1975.

Maslow, A.H. **Toward a psychology of being.** New York: Van Nostrand, 1968.

Masuda, M., and Holmes, T.H. Life events: Perceptions and frequencies. **Psychosomatic Medicine,** 1978, 40, 236-261.

Mathews, K.E., and Canon, L.K. Environmental noise level as a determinant of helping behaviour. **Journal of Personality and Social Psychology,** 1975, 32, 517-577.

McGrath, J.E. (Ed.). **Social and psychological factors in stress.** New York: Holt, 1970.

McGrath, J.E. Stress and behaviour in organizations. In M.D. Dunnette (Ed.), **Handbook of industrial and organizational psychology.** Skokie, Ill.: Rand McNally, 1976, pp.1,351-1,395.

Meier, R.L. Communication stress: Threats and remedies. **Organizational Dynamics,** 1973, 1, 69-80.

Michelson, W. **Man and his urban environment: A sociological approach** (2nd ed.). Reading, Mass.: Addson-Wesley, 1976.

Miller, W.R., and Seligman, M.E.P. Learned helplessness, depression, and the perception of reinforcement. **Behaviour Research and Therapy,** 1976, 14, 7-17.

Mischel, W. Toward a cognitive social learning reconceptualization of personality. **Psychological Review,** 1973, 80, 252-283.

Moos, R.H. **The human context: Environmental determinants of behaviour.** New York: Wiley, 1976.

Myers, J.K., Lindenthal, J.J., and Pepper, M.P. Life events and psychiatric impairment. **Journal of Nervous and Mental Disease,** 1971, 152, 149-157.

Nisbett, R.E., and Wilson, T.D. Telling more than we can know:

Verbal reports on mental processes. **Psychological Review**, 1977, 84, 231-259.

Novaco, R.W., Stokols, D., Campbell, J., and Stokols, J. Transportation, stress and community psychology. **American Journal of Community Psychology**, 1979, 7, 361-380.

Proshansky, H.M., Ittleson, W.H., and Rivlin, L.G. (Eds.). **Environmental psychology: People and their physical settings** (2nd ed.). New York: Holt, 1976.

Rabkin, J.G., and Struening, E.L. Life events, stress and illness. **Science**, 1976, **194**, 1,013-1,020.

Rodin, J. Density, perceived choice, and response to controllable and uncontrollable outcomes. **Journal of Experimental Social Psychology**, 1976, **12**, 564-574.

Rosenberg, M.J. Cognitive structure and attitudinal affect. **Journal of Abnormal and Social Psychology**, 1956, **53**, 367-372.

Roth, S., and Bootzin, R.R. Effects of experimentally induced expectancies of external control: An investigation of learned helplessness. **Journal of personality and Social Psychology**, 1974, 29, 253-264.

Roth, S., and Kubal, L. Effects of noncontingent reinforcement on tasks of differing importance: Facilitation and learned helplessness. **Journal of Personality and Social Psychology**, 1975, 32, 680-691.

Rotter, J.B. Generalized expectancies for internal versus external control of reinforcement. **Psychological Monographs**, 1966, **80**, (1, Whole No. 609).

Schultz, R. Effects of control and predictability on the physical and psychological well-being of the institutionalized aged. **Journal of Personality and Social Psychology**, 1976, **33**, 563-573.

Seligman, M.E.P. **Helplessness: On depression, development, and death.** San Francisco, W.H. Freeman, 1975.

Seligman, M.E.P., and Maier, S.F. Failure to escape traumatic shock. **Journal of Experimental Psychology**, 1976, **74**, 1-9.

Selye, H. **The stress of life.** New York: McGraw-Hill, 1956.

Selye, H. **Stress in health and disease.** Woburn, Mass.: Butterworth, 1976.

Sherrod, D.R. Crowding, perceived control, and behavioural aftereffects. **Journal of Applied Social Psychology**, 1974, 4 171-186.

Sherrod, D.R., and Downs, R. Environmental determinants of altruism: The effect of stimulus overload and perceived control on helping. **Journal of Experimental social Psychology**, 1974, **10**, 468-479.

Singer, J.E., Lundberg, U., and Frankenhaeuser, M. Stress on the train: A study of urban commuting. In A. Baum, J.E. Singer, and S. Valins (Eds.), **Advances in environmental psychology** (Vol.1). Hillsdale, N.J.: Erlbaum,1978.

Smith, E.R., and Miller, F.D. Limits on perception of cognitive processes: A reply to Nisbett and Wilson. **Psychological Review,** 1978, 85, 355-362.

Stokols, D. The experience of crowding in primary and secondary environments. **Environment and Behaviour,** 1976, 8, 49-86.

Stokols, D. Environmental psychology. **Annual Review of Psychology.** 1978, 29, 253-295.

Stokols, D., Novaco, R.W., Stokols, J., and Campbell, J. Traffic congestion, Type-A behaviour and stress. **Journal of Applied Psychology,** 1978, 73, 467-480.

Taylor, S.E., and Fiske, S.T. Salience, attention and attribution: Top of the head phenomena. In L. Berkowitz (Ed.), **Advances in experimental social psychology** (Vol.11). New York: Academic, 1978.

Tennen, H., and Eller, S.J. Attributional components of learned helplessness and facilitation. **Journal of Personality and Social Psychology,** 1977, 35, 265-271.

Tesser, A., and Conlee, M.C. Some effects of time and thought on attitude polarization. **Journal of Personality and Social Psychology,** 1975, 31, 262-270.

Theorell, T. Selected illnesses and somatic factors in relation to two psychosocial stress indices-A prospective study on middle-aged construction building workers. **Journal of Psychosomatic Research,** 1976, 20, 7-20.

Thibaut, J.W., and Kelley, H.H. **The social psychology of groups.** New York: Wiley, 1959.

Vinokur, A., and Selzer, M.L. Desirable versus undesirable life events: Their relationship to stress and mental distress. **Journal of Personality and Social Psychology,** 1975, 32, 329-337.

Waldbott, G.L. **Health effects of environmental pollutants.** St. Louis: Mosby, 1973.

Watson, J.B. Psychology as the behaviourist views it. **Psychological Review,** 1913, **20,** 159-177.

Weinstein, N.D. Effect of noise on intellectual performance. **Journal of Applied Psychology,** 1974, **59,** 548-554.

White, R.W. Motivation reconsidered: The concept of competence. **Psychological Review,** 1959, 66, 297-233.

Wicker, A.W. Processes which mediate behaviour-environment congruence. **Behavioural Science.** 1972, **17,** 265-277.

Wohlwill, J.F., and Heft, H. Environments fit for the developing child. In H. McGurk (Ed.), **Ecological factors in human development.** Amsterdam: North Holland, 1978.

Wortman, C.B., and Brehm, J.W. Responses to uncontrollable outcomes: An integration of reactance theory and the learned helplessness model. In L. BerKowitz (Ed.), **Advances in experimental social psychology,** (Vol.8). New York:

Academic, 1975, pp.277-336.

Wortman, C.B., and Dintzer, L. Is an attributional analysis of the learned helplessness phenomenon viable? A critique of the Abramson-Seligman-Teasdale reforumulation. **Journal of Abnormal Psychology,** 1978, 87, 75-90.

Wortman, C.B., Panciera, L., Shusterman, L., and Hibscher, J. Attributions of causality and reactions to uncontrollable outcomes. **Journal of Experimental Social Psychology,** 1976, 12, 301-316.

Wyler, A., Masuda, M., and Holmes, T.H. Magnitude of life events and seriousness of illness. **Psychosomatic Medicine,** 1971, 33, 115-122.

REFERENCE NOTES

1. Cohen, S., Krantz, D.S., Evans, G.W., and Stokols, D. **Community noise and children: Cognitive, motivational and physiological effects.** Paper presented at the Third International Congress of Noise as a Public Health Problem, Freiberg, Germany, September, 1978.
2. Greenberger, E., and Steinberg, L.D. **Implications of stress for health disorders in childhood and adolescence.** Unpublished manuscript, University of California at Irvine, 1978.
3. Evans, G.W., Stokols, D., and Novaco, R.W. **Perceived control and multiple environmental stressors.** Unpublished manuscript, University of California at Irvine, 1978.
4. Campbell, J. **Ambient and acute stressors.** Unpublished manuscript, University of California at Irvine, 1978.
5. Lazarus, R.S., and Cohen, J.B. **Ways of coping, uplifts, and hassles scales.** Unpublished manuscript, 1978. (Available from the Stress and Coping Project, University of California, Berkeley, CA 94720.)
6. Neuman, K. **Sensitivity to novel environments and causal attribution.** Unpublished manuscript, University of California at Irvine, 1978.
7. Aiello, J., Epstein, Y., and Karlin, R. **Field experimental research on human crowding.** Paper presented at the Eastern Psychological Association Convention, New York, 1975.
8. Singer, J.E. **The psychological-physiological frontier of stress research.** Paper presented at the NATO Advanced Study Institue on Environmental Stress, Life Crises, and Social Adaptation, Cambridge, England, August 1978.

THREE

Christina R. Victor

Housing Stress and Social Stress
A Study of Nottingham C.B.

A research involvement by geographers in the field of urban stress studies is of comparatively recent origin. However, concern with the patterns of social deprivation has an extensive history, dating back to the social commentators of the nineteenth century (Booth, 1906). The relatively recent nature of the explicitly geographical contribution to the study of urban social problems can be explained by reference to several inter-related trends. A major influence was the realisation that the quantitative and spatial analysis approaches to urban studies were becoming increasingly sterile. The partial nature of the knowledge of urban social structure generated by multivariate studies of small area census statistics also prompted a search for a more wide ranging perspective towards urban studies. In addition there has been the growth of the 'radical critique' which has sought to concern geographers with socially relevant issues. A final stimulus for geographers to examine the problems of urban areas has been the higher level of government, media and grassroots concern with contemporary social issues.

As a response to this greater research interest in urban problems this paper is concerend with the inter-relationship aspects of urban stress—namely housing disadvantage and social deprivation. The paper first discusses the ecological tradition of studying urban social problems, examines the hypothesised relationships between housing problems and social problems, describes the methodological procedure and evaluates the results from the Nottingham case study.

Geography and the Study of Social Problems

It has been recognized for some time that various indices of abnormal behaviour, such as, delinquency (Shaw, 1925) and crime (Boggs, 1966) display marked areal patterns when analysed at an ecological scale. The urban ecologists in particular identified the distributional qualities of pathological behaviour and have described the regular decrease in incidence rates with increasing distance from the city centre (Shaw and Mckay, 1942; Faris and Dunham, 1939). Empirical studies in Britain have produced findings which deviated from the regualr American model and were explained by the distorting influence of the publicly owned housing stock upon the internal social organization of the city proposed in American studies (Timms, 1965).

This univariate perspective towards the study of urban social problems has recently been overshadowed by studies which sought to investigate the distribution of sets of problems. Although such studies have become fashionable in the post 1960 period, some do predate this era (Castle and Gittus, 1957).

Two distinct types of multiple-problem (or deprivation) studies have been produced. These approaches may be classified according to the data source employed and identify studies where the problem indices are derived from census statistics (Glasgow Corporation,1972) and those where alternative sources provide the information base (Amos, 1969).

An integral feature of census based problem studies has been the inclusion of both direct and indirect indicators which Craig and Driver (1972) term sufficient and aggravating problem measures. Victor (1980) has demonstrated that such works have been based upon the measurements of indirect problem indicators such as social class, ethnic status and demographic structure. The only direct form of social problem measured has related to dwelling conditions as defined in terms of variables measuring amenity provision, overcrowding and the multiple occupation of dwellings.

Implicit in such investigations are two basic assumptions. One is that certain social groups, for example, ethnic-minorities, are 'at risk' groups for the incidence of social disadvantage. The validity of this assumption has been discussed elsewhere (Victor, 1980). Secondly, it is assumed that the incidence of one problem carries with it a predisposition towards others. Therefore housing problems are employed to predict the distribution of other, less easily measured, forms of social disadvantage. It is this underlying assumption which is explicitly tested in this paper.

Although the explicit spatial and statistical relationships existing between housing problems and social problems have not received specific attention, a number of workers have described the concentration of specific forms of social deviance in sub-standard residential environments. The urban ecologists in Chicago described the high prevalence rates of vice (Reckless, 1926), juvenile delinquency (Shaw et al., 1929) and mental illness (Dunham, 1937) in the lowest quality residential districts. In Britain the works of social commentators writing last century described similar relationships (Mayhew, 1862; Engels 1969). However, these investigations failed to include a broad range of problem indices and concentrated upon behavioural abnormalities. As such the justification for the assumption that housing stress may be employed as a surrogate malaise index is limited.

RESEARCH STRATEGY

The concept of urban stress was operationalised in terms of five specific dimensions and twenty-six individual variables (Table 3.1). Four of these problems dimensions - the ill-health, housing, income and family stress groups - were derived from the deprivation categories defined by the Shelter Neighbourhood Achon Project (S.N.A.P., 1973). In addition some measure of criminal behaviour was included.

With the exception of the housing quality measures and the single parent families, these variables were derived from Local Authority agency records for the year 1972-1973. As such the information on which the indices were based relates to the known incidence of cases and not to the total population which may be eligible for, or affected by, the defined measure.

The topics listed in Table 3.1 are largely self-explanatory. However, a few general comments are offered concerning the measurement of these malaise syndromes. Housing stress was operationalised in terms of four specific aspects—amenity provision, overcrowding, dwelling, multiple occupation and the physical fabric of individual dwellings. This latter measure was not, unlike the rest, derived from the returns of the 1971 census. The ill health topic included the measurement of physical illness, mental illness and mental retardation. Included within the poverty category were two direct measures of low income (families with free school meals/school clothing grants) and two indirect (long term unemployment and council house eviction notices). Family stress measured both 'at risk' children and specific family problem groups (i.e., single parent families and multiple problem families). Three measures of adult criminal behaviour were included, namely disorderly behaviour (crime I), larceny (crime II) and offences involving violence (crime III).

A more detailed explanation of these variables is available elsewhere (Victor, 1980).

TABLE 3.1
Indices of Urban Stress

Housing

Households over-crowded (over 1.5 persons per room) (c)
Households sharing a dwelling (c)
Households with non-exclusive use of a hot water tap (c)
Households with non-exclusive use of a fixed bath or shower (c)
Households with non-exclusive use of an inside W.C. (c)
Dwellings disinfected from vermin, etc

Health

Mentally ill adults on social workers' case lists
Mentally handicapped adults on social workers' case lists
School children attending E.S.N. schools
Infant mortality (deaths to infants aged 0-12 months)
Cases of notifiable infectious diseases

Low Income

Families with school children receiving free school meals
Families with children receiving school clothing grants
Adults unemployed for one year or over
Local Authority tenants served with notices to quit

Family Problems

Children being statutorily supervised
Children being voluntarily supervised
Children received into the care of the Local Authority
Families discussed at social workers' conferences ('problem families')
Children disinfested from lice, etc.
Children persistently absent from school
Single-parent families (c)
Illegitimate births

Crime

Adults convicted of breach of the peace and relatd offences - Crime I
Adults convicted of theft, burglary and related offences - Crime II
Adults convicted of offences against the person - Crime III

Note: All variables marked (c) were derived from the census returns.

The incidence rates for each index were calculated for each of the 99 planning zones into which Nottingham C.B. was sub-divided. These areas are amalgams of the 596 districts into which the study area was divided for the 1971 enumeration. The data set was then divided into its constituent aspects— housing stress and social stress (i.e., the crime, income, health and family problem measures).

A two stage analytical procedure was employed to identify the precise statistical and spatial relationships exhibited by these two aspects of deprivation. Canonical correlation based upon factor scores was considered to be the most appropriate multivariate statistical technique for the identification of linkages between data sets (King, 1964; Clarke, 1975).

Whilst the uses of this technique in a geographical context are limited, some debate has emerged concerning the 'correct' input to such an analysis. Corsi and Harvey (1975) employed primary variables in their study of crime and social structure in Cleveland. In contrast, both Gittus and Stephens (1974) and Herbert (1977) used factor scores in their respective studies of crime and the urban environment. Briggs and Leonard (1977), in a recent paper, have argued that the former rather than the latter was the most appropriate statistical procedure.

It was found that using primary variables in such a complex satistical procedure resulted in highly specific canonical variates which failed to clarify the general associations existing between the two data sub sets under review. Therefore for this investigation factor structures were considered to form the most appropriate input for the canonical correlation. Hence the two data sets were first summarised by a principal axes factoring routine. An oblique rotation procedure with a delta value set at zero was used to simplify the factor structure.

The empirical results are therefore described in two sections. The first presents the results of the factor analysis whilst the second described the canonical correlation analysis. Subsequently the results of the canonical correlation are discussed with reference to the assumed relationship which is supposed to exist between housing and related social problems.

EMPIRICAL RESULTS

The two complex statistical analyses which formed the basis of the canonical correlation model are each briefly described.

The Structure of Housing Stress

Table 3.2 illustrates that all the estimated common variance in the seven variable data set was described by two factors with eigenvalues greater than unity. Rotation of the retained factor axes produced two loading matrixes, the factor structure and factor pattern matrices respectively. Following the advice of Harman (1967) and the precedent of Giggs (1973) the pattern matrix was used to interpret the nature of the factors (Table 3.3). The description of the character of each factor was based upon the identification of significant loadings (i.e., the variables with a loading of ±0.29).

TABLE 3.2

Housing Deprivation: Factor Analysis Summary

Factor	Eigenvalue	Variance (%)	Cumulative Variance (%)
1	3.55	59.3	59.3
2	1.65	27.6	87.0

TABLE 3.3

Housing Deprivation: Factor Pattern Loadings Matrix

Variable		Factor 1	Factor 2
1.	Share/Lack Fixed Bath	-0.89	0.29
2.	Share/Lack Inside W.C.	-0.95	0.08
3.	Share/Lack Hot Water	-0.97	0.26
4.	Overcrowding	-0.55	0.59
5.	Multi-occupation	-0.04	0.77

Employing this procedure the first factor was characterised by diagnostic loadings with each of the three amenity provision variables in addition to the statutory measure of overcrowding. Thus the first measure of housing stress in Nottingham identified the problem of amenity provision levels. In contrast the second dimension was typified by diagnostic loadings with the overcrowding and multiple occupation of dwellings indices. Hence this second dimension identified housing problems concerned with dwelling occupancy characteristics. These two aspects of housing stress were statistically independent (Table 3.4).

The Structure of Social Stress

Application of the same analytical procedure to the 21 social disadvantage variables produced seven factors with eigenvalues of one or over (Table 3.5). Table 3.6 lists the pattern matrix resultant from this analysis and from which the factors were interpreted as representing:

TABLE 3.4
Housing Deprivation:
Inter-factor Correlation Matrix

Factor	1	2
1	-	-
2	-0.25	-

(I) mental health-poverty; this negatively orientated factor was characterised by diagnostic loadings with two measures of mental illness (E.S.N. children and mentally ill adults) and two indices of economic deprivation (free school meals and unemployment).

(II) ill health; diagnostic negative loadings with three physical health indices; unemployment and crime I typified this factor.

(III) poverty; two measures of financial inadequacy were combined with the single parent families and crime II variables in describing factor II.

(IV) at risk children; variables measuring voluntary and statutory supervision orders combine with the school absence, E.S.N. children and children deloused at school indices to identify a composite measure of disadvantaged children.

(V) mental handicap; for this factor mental handicap is linked with the incidence of serious crime (III) and the free school meals index.

(VI) family stress; this factor is described by three separate indices of family stress.

(VII) crime; the final retained factor, which was negative in orientation, was described by the three measures of adult criminal residence.

Social disadvantage in this case study was summarised in terms of seven dimensions which measured poverty (factors I and III), ill health (factors IV and VI) and crime (factor VII). With the exception of the relationship between factors I and VII these dimensions remained statistically independent of each other (Table 3.7).

TABLE 3.5
Social Disadvantage: Factor Analysis Summary

Factor	Eigenvalue	Variance (%)	Cumulative Variance (%)
1	4.86	29.9	29.9
2	2.91	16.1	46.0
3	1.51	8.0	54.0
4	1.23	6.7	60.7
5	1.17	6.2	66.9
6	1.04	5.5	72.4
7	1.00	5.3	77.7

THE CANONICAL ANALYSIS

Table 3.8 summarised the canonical correlation procedure. Of the two variables produced only the leading structure was significant at the 99.9% confidence level. Interpretation of this variate was based upon those variables with a loading of ± 0.3 - a procedure recommended by Cooley and Lohnes (1974).

Each of the two district aspects of urban stress illustrated a relationship with the canonical variate (table 3.9). In terms of housing stress, it was the leading amenity provision index which was diagnostic of the variate structure. The dwelling occupancy aspect of housing stress displayed no significant association with the variate. Three dimensions of social stress were descriptive of the variate. Two were indices of financial inadequacy and mental health problems (factors I and III). Whilst the third was the adult crime measure (factor VII). These results would therefore seem to suggest that whilst low quality housing is linked with financial stress, mental illness and criminal residence, it seemed not to be associated with deprivation in a family context.

Figure 3.1 illustrates the spatial representation of this first canonical variate. In producing maps of canonical variables some difficulties are encountered. The major problem being that for each area two scores are produced by the analysis—one for each aspect of the variate. The methodology adopted to produce this map was based upon that employed by Corsi and Harvey (1975) and adopted by Herbert (1977). Hence in this example it is the simple direction of the canonical score (i.e. positive or negative) which constitutes the mapping criteria. At present it remains impossible to incorporate any concept of magnitude into this classificatory prodedure.

TABLE 3.6

Social Disadvantage: Factor Pattern Matrix

Variable	Factor 1	2	3	4	5	6	7
1. School Absence	0.03	-0.09	0.01	**-0.31**	-0.12	0.02	0.11
2. E.S.N. Children	**-0.59**	0.11	-0.04	**-0.37**	0.22	-0.08	0.03
3. Clothing Grants	-0.03	-0.28	**0.92**	-0.16	**0.39**	-0.08	0.03
4. Local Authority Notices to Quit	-0.10	0.007	0.10	0.07	0.04	0.28	0.27
5. Unemployment	**-0.91**	**-0.29**	0.13	-0.15	0.07	-0.02	0.05
6. Problem Families	0.007	0.06	0.04	0.005	-0.04	**0.79**	0.15
7. Care Orders	-0.02	0.01	-0.25	0.19	-0.12	**0.67**	0.01
8. Voluntary Supervision	-0.03	-0.05	0.13	**-0.45**	-0.14	0.22	0.25
9. Statutory Supervision	0.08	-0.07	0.04	**-0.61**	0.05	-0.04	0.03
10. Mental Handicap	-0.23	0.06	-0.16	0.16	**0.31**	0.19	0.02
11. Mental Illness	**-0.92**	-0.09	0.12	-0.01	0.17	-0.04	0.03
12. Crime I	0.06	**-0.29**	0.25	0.10	0.28	0.26	**-0.57**
13. Crime II	-0.04	-0.10	**0.29**	0.05	**0.29**	0.07	**-0.61**
14. Crime III	-0.12	-0.24	-0.17	-0.04	0.23	0.24	**-0.30**
15. Children Deloused	-0.23	-0.03	-0.15	**-0.59**	0.03	-0.15	0.07
16. Single-Parent Families	0.07	-0.03	0.39	**-0.11**	-0.11	0.10	0.09
17. Infectious Diseases	0.03	**-0.46**	0.04	0.002	-0.06	-0.12	-0.02
18. Infant Mortality	0.04	**-0.51**	0.02	0.08	0.06	0.23	0.19
19. Illegitimate Births	-0.28	**-0.37**	0.01	0.06	0.14	**0.42**	-0.14
20. Free School Meals	**-0.41**	0.07	**0.44**	-0.23	0.28	0.19	-0.02

TABLE 3.7

Social Disadvantage: Inter-factor Correlations

FACTOR	1	2	3	4	5	6	7
1	-						
2	0.19	-					
3	-0.25	-0.09	-				
4	0.28	0.02	-0.36	-			
5	-0.06	-0.01	0.01	-0.09	-		
6	-0.05	-0.01	0.18	-0.18	-0.09	-	
7	0.51	0.22	-0.29	0.23	-0.12	-0.04	-

A fourfold mapping typology was employed in this canonical investigation. Type A areas represent those zones which were typified by both aspects of the canonical structure and are clearly concentrated in the inner residential districts of the County Borough. The type B districts, however, indicate that a sub-standard housing environment is not universally linked with a defective social environment. In contrast, zones categorized as type C areas are linked only with the social disadvantage aspect of the variate and identify the Local Authority estates. However, as Figure 3.1 clearly shows, the majority of residential zones illustrated no specific relationship with urban stress in either of its manifestations.

DISCUSSION

These results, therefore, offer some guidance as to the nature and composition of deprivation in urban areas. Only one aspect of housing stress - low levels of amenity provision - was associated with the incidence of social disadvantage. Dwelling occupancy problems illustrated no statistical relationship with social stress. It is also obvious from the above analysis that only specific aspects of social disadvnatage - namely economic inadequacy, mental illness and crime - were related to housing stress. Problems more characteristic of a family situation were not associated with housing problems. Hence whilst amenity provision indices may be of some value in predicting deviant behaviour, they are of little value as a general indirect indicator of social disadvantage.

This conclusion that there is only a very limited degree of inter-relationship between housing problems and social problems has implications for British urban planning practice. Michelson (1970) notes that the assumed causal link between these two types of problem has been central to much of British planning practice. The assumed relationship also suggested that social problems could be eradicated. The solution was obvious if ex-

TABLE 3.8

Social and Housing Deprivation: Canonical Analysis Summary

Canonical Variate	Eigenvalue	Canonical Correlation	Wilk's Lamba	Chi Square	Df	Significance
1	0.474	0.689	0.395	86.3	28	0.000
2	0.148	0.385	0.752	25.4	18	0.110

TABLE 3.9

Canonical Variate: Diagnostic Loadings

Factor	Social Stress	Loading	Factor	Housing Stress	Loading
1	Mental health-poverty	-0.89	1	Amenity provision	-0.64
2	Ill-health	0.29	2	Dwelling occupancy	0.28
3	Poverty	-0.52			
4	Children 'at risk'	0.02			
5	Mental handicap	-0.29			
6	Family stress	0.14			
7	Crime	-0.72			

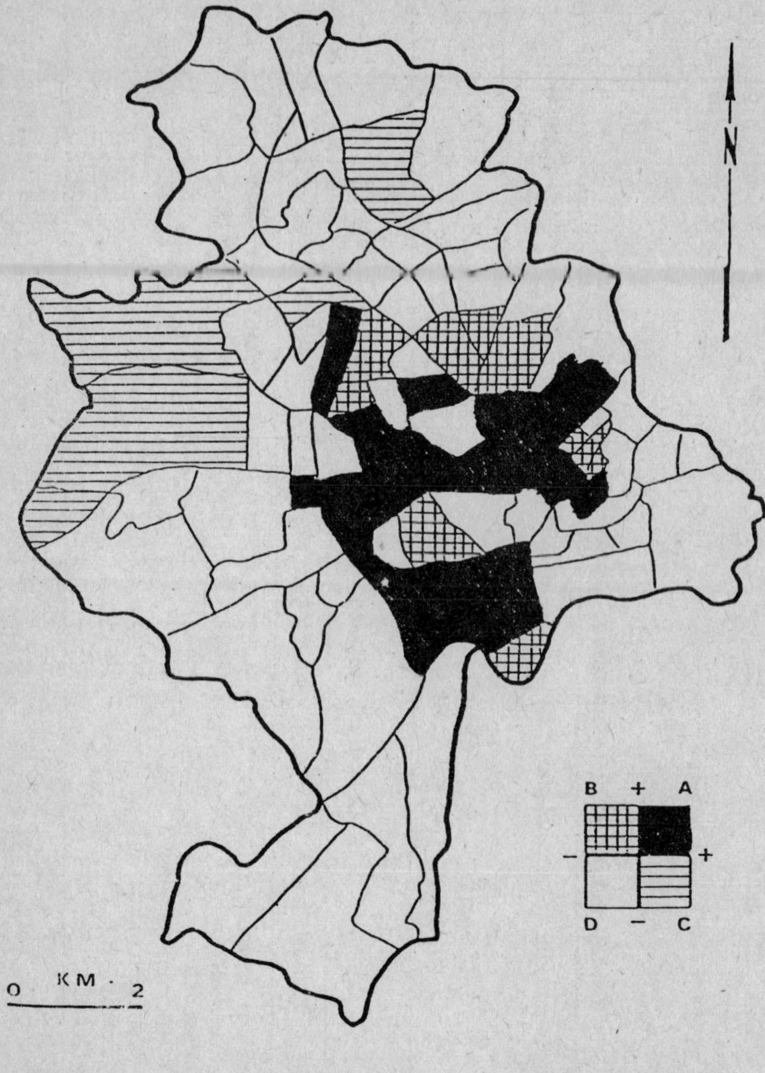

Figure 3.1 Housing stress and social disadvantage: Canonical variate one.

tensive - improve the quality of the residential environment and the associated problems would be removed. Rose (1972) and Williams (1967) have both suggested that this assumed causal relationship has been central to much of British social policy, especially the large scale slum clearance schemes initiated in the post war period. In addition, housing stress variables have been employed as surrogate deprivation indices in many of the recent urban policy initiatives (e.g. the urban Aid projects etc.). The results from this investigation in Nottingham clearly suggest that such a practice is erroneous.

REFERENCES

Amos, C.W., Social Malaise in Liverpool. Planning Department, Liverpool Corporation 1969.

Boggs, S.L., Urban crime patterns, **American Sociological Review**, 30, pp. 1966. 899-908.

Briggs, R. and Leonard, W.A., Empirical implications of advances in canonical theory, **Canadian Geographer**, 21, 1977, pp. 133-147.

Castle, I.M. and Gittus, E., The distribution of social defects in Liverpool, **Sociological Review**, 5, 1957, pp. 43-64.

Clarke, D., Understanding canonical correlation analysis, Concepts and Techniques in Modern Geography, 3, Quantitative Methods Study Group, Institute of British Geographers, 1975.

Cooley, W.W. and Lohnes, R.P., **Multivariate data analysis**, John Wiley, London, 1971.

Corsi, T.M. and Harvey, M.E., The socio-economic determinants of crime in the city of Cleveland, **Tijdschrift voor Economische en Sociale Geographe**, 66, 1975, 323-336.

Craig, J.A. and Driver, A., The identification and comparison of small areas of adverse social conditions. **Applied Statistics**, 21, 1972, 23-35.

Dunham, M.W., The ecology of functional psychosis in Chicago, **American Sociological Review**, 2, 1937, 467-479.

Engles, F., **The condition of the working class in England**, Panther, London, 1969.

Faris, R.E. and Dunham, M.W. **Mental disorder in urban areas**, Uniiversity of Chicago Press, Chicago.

Giggs J.A., The distribution of Schizophrenics in Nottingham, **Transactions Institute of British Geographers**, 59, 1973, pp. 55-76.

Gittus, E. and Stephens, C.J., Some problems in the use of canonical analysis; unpublished discussion paper, University of Newcastle upon Tyne, 1973.

Glasgow Corporation, Social deprivation in Glasgow, Planning Department, 1972.

Harman, H.H., **Modern factor Analysis**, University of Chicago

Press, Chicago, 1967.

Herbert, D.T., 1977. An areal and ecological analysis of delinquency residence: Cardiff 1966 and 1971, **Tijdschrift voor Economische en Sociale Geografie,** 68, 83-99.

King, L.J., **Statistical analysis in geography,** Prentice Hall, New York, 1969

Mayhew, H., **London Labour and London Poor.** Pilot Press, London, 1862

Michelson, W., **Man and his urban environment,** Addison Wesley, Reading, Mass, 1970.

Reckless, W.C., The distribution of commercialized vice in the city, Publications of the **American Sociological Society,** 20, 1926, pp. 164-176.

Rose, M.E., **The Relief of Poverty,** Macmillan, London, 1972.

Shaw, C.R., **Delinquency areas: a study of the geographical distribution of juvenile delinquents.** University of Chicago Press, Chicago, 1925.

Shaw, C.R., Mckay, H.D., Zorbaugh, F.M. and Cottrell, L., **Delinquency areas,** University of Chicago Press, Chicago, 1929.

Shaw, C.R. and Mackay, H.D., **Juvenile delinquency and urban areas,** University of Chicago Press, Chicago, 1942.

Shelter Neighbourhood Action Project, Another chance for cities, S.N.A.P., Liverpool, 1973.

Timms, D.W.G., The spatial distribution of social deviants in Luton, England, Australian and New Zealand, **Journal of Sociology,** 1, 1965, pp. 38-52.

Victor, C.R., A geography of Greater Nottingham, unpublished M.Phil. thesis, University of Nottingham, 1980.

Williams, G., **The Coming of the Welfare** State; George Allen and Unwin, London, 1967.

FOUR

Henry Sanoff

Stress and Density in the Residential Environment

Injury, illness, incapacity and death are not the only dangers or problems in housing its environs. The mere threat of such physical harm from human violence and non-human dangers, inhibits a state of emotional well-being. Many urban poverty groups are particularly sensitive about the security that housing should provide against the most blatant of threats[1]. The National Advisory Council on Civil Disorder points out that 47 per cent of the housing units occupied by non-whites were substandard and 24 percent were overcrowded in the 1967 civil disorder areas.

One's home is a symbolic extension of one's self[2]. Rats, overcrowding, the stench of inadequate plumbing and the inability to keep one's family from freezing in winter conveys to the slum dweller, in devastatingly graphic terms, their inability to control their own destiny and provide a stable family environment. The physical and social disorder of their world presents a constant temptation to give up or retaliate in kind[3]. The continuing disparity betwen the slum dweller's housing expectations and their lack of fulfilment has been stressed as a common source of recent ghetto rioting. The long term consequences for health and well-being of adaptation to these psychological and physiological problems associated with the residential environment are unknown.

Wilner,[4] in a longitudinal study of 5000 persons, found that rehoused slum families, in contrast to control families remaining in the slum, responded to greater space and improved dwelling conditions. The findings show that larger proportions of rehoused families liked their apartments, commented favourably on the safety of their children's places, felt then, were getting their money's worth for the amount of the rental, indicated an increased liklihood for personal privacy and reported less friction and dissension directly related to space. Other factors were:

(1) Better personal relations and lessened friction between family members (particularly in the mother's reaction to and discipline of children). The data showed an increase in mutually shared activities, both routine and leisure-time pursuits.

(2) Markedly increase assistance to neighbours with household chores, children, and in time of illness. Closer and more amicable relations with neighbours occurred among test families as a consequence of differences in their physical environments. Some of the factors in the housing project that were considered conducive to the formation of these relationships by the test group were: a dwelling architecture providing many opportunities for daily contact, a dwelling unit possessing some aesthetic qualities and sufficient room space, and the existence of facilities used in common under non-competitive circumstances.

(3) More pride and care in maintaining their immediate neighbourhoods. The rehoused families reported more activities devoted to keeping up the neighbourhood and gave far more favourable views regarding its adequacy as a place to live and raise children.

(4) An increased sense of improvement in their position in life, even without increases in income. The findings show that test respondents more than controls were likely to indicate felt improvement in their position in life and to report themselves rising in the world. Findings for a series of ten psychosocial scales consisting of variables pertaining to the self, revealed optimism and satisfaction with personal state of affairs as a result of moving from a generally depressed and deprived environment to good housing.

Psychiatrists believe that these factors indicate a more stable emotional state and better mental health. Rainwater[5] found that rehoused slum families evidenced a "dramatic drop in anxiety, about non-human threats within the dwelling" and viewed the improved house as a haven from human threats, but not a complete solution to human threats.

THE PHYSICAL ENVIRONMENT AND MENTAL HEALTH STATUS

A relationship between mental health state and inadequate

sanitation and physical structure of the dwelling has not been completely developed. While both of these housing qualities may be interpreted as stressful,[6] crowding has a stronger influence on mental health state. Crowding (living conditions which require people to interact with and relate to others in ways that are not desirable to them) can contribute very substantially to accelerated intellectual and physical deterioration of older people, to increased aggression, to withdrawal and sexual abnormalities among yound adolescents, and the general mental health of adults. The disparity between the number of people in a dwelling, and the capacity of the dwelling to contain them and allow them to perform important human activities can be reflected through a variety of physiological and psychological processes and many disturbances of human health.

It is recognized that adequate physical layout of the dwelling cannot cure mental ills already in existence (such as schizophrenia), but that it may prevent their further development, in the sense that physical layout does act as a reinforcing agent to personality trends already structured. Neither can adequate physical layout of the dwelling produce (in the sense of originating them) new and desirable personality traits. But an adequately planned and structured physical layout can be an end or objective. As such, it should be flexible, to permit the flow of the process of adjustment and readjustment rather than regarded as an end in itself.

There are two factors of physical layout which may be considered in relation to crowding : (1) privacy in the dwelling as related to mental health, and (2) circulation in the dwelling as related to the mental hygiene of its occupants. Overcrowding affects privacy and often results in family members spending more time outside the home[7]. When recreation is not available, families have been observed to show aggravation of any predisposition to neurotic behaviour[8]. When overcrowding forces children to find activity space outside the dwelling, children's study habits suffer and parental supervision and control is reduced[9]. Weakened supervision and exposure of children to the life of the street may, in turn, contribute to the development of many of the social problems of youth, assumed to be characteristic of high density impoverished communities around the world[10].

When discussing privacy, we assume that freedom to be by one's self is a value; and that hindrances to its realization lead to frustrations, irritation and resentments. Thus privacy becomes a value. Privacy is needed for thinking, reflection, reading, study, and for aesthetic enjoyment and contemplation.

Intrusions on the fulfilment of personal desires need to be shut off in order to avoid the internal tensions that are built up from frustrations, resentments, and irritations of continual multiple contacts with others. If we now turn to the physical factor of circulation within the dwelling, we infer that this factor although related to the factor of privacy, in some obvious respects, also plays a part in the mental health of occupants.

Ease and freedom of circulation within the dwelling relieves cramped muscular conditions and attendant irritations. It facilitates the normal performance of family functions, an easy flow of sequences of overt behaviour without interruptions to freedom of movement, or unwanted and unexpected intrusions on a train of thought.

Historically, government housing planners have viewed "housing" in terms of quantity of units. Emphasis has always been placed upon producing "units" to meet existing "needs"[11]. Often housing needs are not "units" but clear water supply, addtional bedrooms, or bathroom installations. Too often the only possible result of government housing efforts are new three-bedroom, single-family units or new two-bedroom apartments. Families are expected to conform their housing needs to the product which the government produces, rather than the government dealing with the people to determine what improvements are needed.

To adequately assess local housing needs, government housing efforts must move closer to the people with housing problems. The quality of improvements must be given the same consideration as quantity. Programs must be designed to deliver the type of housing service that conforms to the individual life style of the family.

POPULATION DENSITY AND CROWDING

Overcrowding in the dwelling unit has been reported to contribute to the spread of infectious diseases and affect the response of individuals, as well as society, to many of life's stresses[12].

Secondary attack rates of tuberculosis have been found to be over 200 per cent higher for people on relief living in overcrowding dwellings than for all economic status groups living in less crowded structures - one person or less per room[13]. Studies have shown, that overcrowding, is associated with the frequency of disabling illness lasting a week or longer[14], the number of respiratory infections in infants, infectious childhood diseases[15], skin diseases, and the number of home accidents[16]. Overcrowding interacts with home heating and ventilation to produce increases in morbidity and mortality in the young and the aged[17].

Overcrowding also conditions personal and group behaviour and mental health. Doubled-up families in multi-storey buildings tend to develop higher levels and emotional illness and hostility[18]. In the 167 metropolitan areas in which rioting occurred during 1967, 24 per cent of all dwellings occupied by non-whites were overcrowded, against only 8.8 per cent of the white occupied units[19]. Obviously, overcrowding is not the single element that produces a "culture of poverty"; more likely, crowding heightens the effects of other deprivations, each reinforcing the other, to shape the personality of those residing in poor housing. Cassel[20] argues that there is a considerable amount of confusion concerning the health consequences of crowding and the narrowness of migration theory. To support that conclusion, a brief review of morbidity rates would be appropriate. Death rates for all causes in the United States were indeed higher in urban areas than in rural prior to 1950. By 1960, however, the ratio had become reversed, rural rates being higher than urban and since 1960, the ratio of rural to urban deaths has been steadily increasing. Thus, paradoxically, even though cities have been increasing in size since 1940, death rates have fallen more rapidly in these crowded circumstances than in the more sparsely populated rural areas. Part of this phenomenon may be due to the improved medical care and sanitation in the cities, leaving an older, more susceptible population behind in the rural areas. While the rural excess in both incidence and mortality rates from typhoid fever, for example, may well be due to differences in sanitation, and the more effective immunization programs in cities account for the lower urban rates of diphtheria and pertussis, the rural excess in the incidence of scarlet fever can hardly be due to either of these processes, as there are no adequate means to prevent the occurrence of streptococcal infections. Similarly, as far as the migration hypothesis is concerned, this could not explain the excess mortality rates in children, both black and white, male and female.

Even from the fragmentary illustrative cases, population density and/or crowding does not inevitably lead to poorer health status. Crowding under certain circumstances may be associated with certain factors which themselves can influence health, such as poor housing, but the relation of crowding to disease states may be a reflection of other factors than crowding, per se.

An important factor influencing health consequences is the human environment associated with housing. Holmes[21] in his studies on tuberculosis in Seattle, has shown that the disease occurs most frequently in "marginal" people; that is, those individuals deprived of meaningful social contact. He found higher rates of tuberculosis in those ethnic groups who were distinct minorities in the neighbourhoods in which they lived, in people living alone in one room, in those who had multiple occupational and residential moves, and who were more often single or divorced, than was true of the general population.

Cassel argues for the importance of the social environment under conditions of increasing population density and urbanization. The rapid urbanization of rural areas in the U.S., particularly when it is associated with deterioration in housing, is usually accompanied with increased death and disease which we are now witnessing.

The situation or environment as a determinant of crowding is a factor described by Schmitt[22] where he distinguishes between inside and outside density. Inside density refers to the number of people per unit of living space within a residence, whereas outside density refers to the number of people per unit of space as a larger environmental unit within which the inside density unit is embedded, for example, street, neighbourhood, census tract, etc.

Altman[23] describes another aspect of the environment that is the richness of environmental resources. Two homes with equivalent space and density can differ enormously on how space is laid out, the interior decor, and the quality of facilities, in general. An environment that is poor in resources might be more susceptible to the effects of crowding.

There are also interpersonal determinants of crowding. Much has been written about personal space, privacy, and territoriality. Central to these concepts is the idea that people establish boundaries around themselves to maintain their psychological integrity, protect their environment and pace and manage interactions with others. Control of interpersonal interaction is accomplished in a variety of ways, including manipulation of the physical environment, verbal and non-verbal communication, etc. Regarding the use of the environment, we open and close doors, arrange furniture in certain ways, establish seating patterns around tables, etc.

Where the cost of controlling interaction is high, where contact with other people is continuous, where environmental resources are limited, there can be a social and psychological breakdown.

The implications are that the popular conception of the negative effects of crowding seem largely an issue of too many people in too little space and consequently massive low-cost housing programs are generated that are designed to provide more space per person or per family. Altman suggests that if environmental richness is also a factor then more attention be directed towards interior spatial planning and design.

Previous research on crowding has generally lacked a theoretical perspective[24]. Moreover, there has been a tendency to view crowding in terms of spatial considerations alone and a failure to distinguish between physical condition (density) and the psychological experience (crowding). Personal and social variables do have a direct bearing on an individual's perception of spatial restriction as well as on his attempts to cope with this constraint.

REFERENCES

1. Rainwater, L. "Cricible of Identity: The Negro Lower Class Family", in Daedalus, 95:172, 1, Winter, 1966.
2. Schorr, A. **Slums and Social Insecurity**, Washington, D.C.: Government Printing Office, 1963.
3. Rainwater, L., op. cit.
4. Wilner, D., Walkley, R., Pinkerton, T., and Tayback, M. **The Housing Environment and Family Life**, Baltimore: The John Hopkins Press, 1962.
5. Rainwater, L., op. cit.
6. Schorr, A., op. cit.
7. Mitchell
8. Strotzka, Wiener-Klinische. **Wochenschrift 573**, June 2, 1961, pp.389-92.
9. Lewis, O. **Children of Sanchez**, New York: Random House, 1961.
10. Mitchell
11. Chapin, F.S. "The Relationship of Housing to Mental Health", Geneva, Switzerland: World Health Organization, Expert Committee on the Public Health Aspects of Housing, Working Paper No. 3A, 1961.
12. Dubos, R. **Man Adapting**, New Haven: Yale University Press, 1965.
13. Britten, R.H., Brown, J.E, and Altman, I. "Certain Characteristics of Urban Housing and their Relation to

Illness and Accidents: Summary of Findings of the National Health Survey", **Milbank Memorial Fund Quarterly**, Vol.18, 1940.

14. Ibid.
15. Wilner, D, op. cit.
16. Spence, J., Walton, W.S., Miller, F.J.W., and Court, S.D.M. **A Thousand Families in Newcastle-upon-Tyne**, London, Toronto, New York: Oxford University Press, 1954.
17. Gilbertson, W.E. "New Challenge in Environmental Health Control", **Transaction and Studies of the College of Physicians of Philadelphia**, Vol.31, April, 1964, pp.294-98.
18. Mitchell
19. Kerner Commission, Report of the National Commission on Civil Disorder, 1968.
20. Cassel, J. "Health Consequences of Population Density and Crowding", in R. Gutman, **People and Buildings**, N.Y. Basic Books, 1972.
21. Holmes, T.H. "Multidiscipline Studies of Tuberculosis", in P.J. Spaner, ed., **Personality Stress and Tuberculosis**, N.Y. International University Press, 1956.
22. Schmitt, R.C. "Density, Health, and Social Organization", **Journal of the American Institute of Planners**, 1966, p.32.
23. Altman, F. "Crowding and Human Behavior", in **Environment and the Social Sciences**, by D. Carson and J. Wohlwell, eds., Washington, D.C.: American Psychological Association.
24. Stokols, "A Socio-Psychological Model of Human Crowding Phenomena", **Journal of the American Institute of Planners**, March, 1972, p.72.

FIVE

Vincent P. Miller, Jr.

The Political Geography of Upper Class urban Stability

Conceptualization and Refelections on a case study

William Stringfellow notes in **My People are the Enemy** that the poor are intercessory for the rich[1]. What Stringfellow means is that the poor soften the role of and provide for the rich. That is indeed an unusual view of poverty, at least from a middle class perspective. But after reading various works of this author one becomes intrigued with the thesis. Throughout these works a picture of the politics of poverty is formed—a picture that one has become accustomed to: the ward boss, the shylock, etc., as well as the politics of "law and order" (for the poor).[2] In this last respect a dialogue between Richard Peet and Keith Harries clearly points to what Stringfellow is saying.[3] Peet asserts (regarding crime, its cures and prevention) that the priorities of society are wrong, whereas Harries demures, essentially insisting that society has perhaps gone wrong, but that liberal academic managerial techniques can be used as a corrective element. The difference of course is between liberal and radical mentalities. Stringfellow's chronicle of the politics of poverty, as gleaned throughout the corpus of his work, is now well recognized and understood by both liberals and radicals alike.

Of what malaise do we speak? Are political payoffs, exhorbitant prices, poor schools, the illness or symptoms of the illness? The liberal and radical mindsets would disagree here. Of course crime contributes to urban destitution, but is crime and other forms of deviant behaviour a major or minor actor on the stage of our cities? What have been the priorities of our society, and have they led to the microareal differences we call the ghetto and the suburb? That is a large question that cannot be easily answered. Previous research by this author has yielded some discomforting conclusions, but let us go on to better frame the viewpoint explored here.

Let me become autobiographical at this point. When I was very young, perhaps three or four years of age, my parents moved from one borough to the next borough in the Pittsburgh SMSA in order to take advantage of the obviously superior schools in the new residential area. Although the move was only about one mile, the two political units represented different educational worlds. While growing up I often wondered about the essential differences between these adjacent boroughs. Why was one "good" and the other "bad"? Why did the Westinghouses and the Rockwells live in Edgewood, not Swissvale? Why did such a high percentage of the graduates of Edgewood High School go on to college, but not so in Swissvale? Why did in fact Edgewood "maintain" itself as a community while Swissvale was unable to do so?

Did Edgewood in fact maintain itself? The question is loaded, scientifically speaking. Here we see a controversy, not dissimilar from the Peet-Harries controversy. Bertalanffy would apparently deplore such vitalistic terminolgy. For example he says that human invention is roughly equivalent to the number of permutations and combinations of available elements (not the product of e.g. intuitive leaps).[4] This logic delivers us to the conclusion that living organisms (and human societies) are essentially open systems that interact with their environment.[5] From this perspective, the affluence of Edgewood is a product of the prosperity of the residents, a product of a type of environmental interaction. One could thus assert; "What Edgewood did other communities could do." Yet Boulding states that images, what could better be termed here spatial character, akin to the German concept of raumgefuhl,[6] cannot be represented by a set of variables. Boulding seems to say that systems have a dynamic all their own.[7] In Bertalanffy's terms Edgewood, **per se**, could not maintain itself, it is maintained by its residents. Boulding would say Edgewood and Swissvale had opposite inertial forces that propelled them in different directions. If Boulding doubts Bertalanffy's "liberal" conceptualization of causality, so does Driesch with his vitalism, Kafka with his castle, Stringfellow with his piety of poverty, and Mackinder with his going concern, to give but a few examples.

The contrived controversy between Bertalanffy and Boulding serve to raise some basic questions about the topic at hand, community stability. Our purpose is not to focus on vitalism and similar arguments beyond the kith and kin of science, but to reflect on systemic momentum in the urban setting. What evidence can be offered that in fact the political units of our cities have momentum all their own? What is the molar behaviour of these political entities, whether they be wards or boroughs?

Ecological psychologists have had a lot to say about molar behaviour, concepts of potential usefulness here.[8] Molar behaviour is the behaviour of the mass, a notion closely allied to the hypotheses of Stringfellow and Riesman. David Riesman conceives of molar behaviour in terms of "other directedness", where the clues of acceptable behaviour are taken from others.[9] The process would appear to be recursive, I observe you and you observe me and so we bahave like one another. Stringfellow notes an overarching moral dimension to such behaviour in his conceptualization of the piety of poverty.[10] The imminence of death in the poor areas of the city gives a certain definitive meaning to life which also has its recursive aspects. The more one sees of death the more one taunts death and so the more one risks death. In Stringfellow's terms such a relationship becomes a moral imperative, there is a type of secular religious morality (piety) that arises in the environment of constant danger.

Ecological psychologists tend to affirm the notion noting that particular behaviour settings elicit highly predictable responses. Behaviour settings entail microspatial areas ranging from the scale of a store front church to perhaps that of a city block. Can it be said that behaviour setting theory aids in the resolution of the twin controversies, the liberal-radical debate and the debate over the causes of molar behaviour, cited here? With respect to criminality the work of Pyle **et al.**,[11], Roth and Sidhu[12] and Brunn[13] offer possibilies for the construction of behaviour theory in larger territorial units, say the size of Zorbough's "natural area" of the city,[14] the equivalent of a ward or the politically autonomous suburbs. At this point all sides in the debate can said to have weighty evidence in their favour, and so the debate is likely to be unresolved. Understanding the ecological causes of behaviour is an essential step in searching out the merits of the liberal or radical explanations of alienating behaviour. One could dream of a spatial theory of behaviour so powerful that the manipulative management techniques of liberal theory would be eclipsed by the only obvious alternative of restoring equality to the society. But the millennium has not arrived.

Another approach is available. This is to adopt the methodology suggested by Swartz in his collection of essays on local-level politics.[15] Local-level political analysis assumes that more or less self-determined isolated groups exist in political systems. Local-level analysis focuses on events rather than functions and structures. Swartz claims that such analysis is more defensible than that of the structuralists and functionalists in that it allows us to see what really occurs. Structuralist analysis is really the analysis of authority whereas local-level analysis concentrates on the "residuum" that may occur when authority is pitted against local-level goalful political activity. Swartz's emphasis on the goalfulness of political activity allows the analyst to understand the distance or the closeness between particular local-level groups and state-idea.[16] Local-level political activity would form the basis of Hartshorne's centrifugal and centripetal forces. Increasing "distance" between local-level political activity and the state-idea would be indicative of centrifugal forces; the opposite would hold true for centripetal forces. Where there is nearly universal agreement on the part of individuals with the state-idea an organic state system would be present, to use the terms of Eugene Lauer.[17] Here the "residual" between political goals and accomplishment would be minimal and so political activity as such would be non-existant and unnecessary. Peoplekind would live for the law; but the law does not exist for the people, a type of beggar's democracy, is to be seen.[18] This is the so far vainglorious hope of much materialistic theory. Solve the production problem says Keynes and "...then foul will be fair" and peace and prosperity will reign.[19]

Nevertheless, we are far removed from the problems of a close identity between people and the state-idea in many areas of our cities. Laws in our system are not the end-all but merely a means to an end. Laws, the visible and conspicuous reminder of the state-idea, exist for people in our non-organic state structure. That is, there is something higher than the law; law exists not for itself but for something higher, presumably civil order and civil betterment. This should be an obvious fact, a truism, in any democracy. If laws impede civil order or the betterment of the social condition then those laws become ends, rather than means to an end, and therefore dangerous to the state-idea.[20] The whole point is that local-level political analysis could contend that structuralists and functionalists may well mistake trees for the forest in misunderstanding the relationship between people and the law.

The local-level analytical approach then brings us to the "advocacy" position that has gained attention recently, as with Kasperson and Breitbart's paper on advocacy planning.[21] Advocacy planning denies important aspects of structuralist and functionalist political analysis. Anarchist architecture, as explained by Goodman, plays a role here. Goodman contests the validity of "look at" architectural design and for that matter "look at" urban design if it fails in satisfying human needs.[22] Here it would seem that human needs are always local-level in nature, even coming down to the microlevel of the ecological psychologists conceputalization of behaviour space.[23]

The originators of local-level political analysis are in fact anthropologists rather than political scientists. Their perspective is genetic, evolutionist in a uniformitarianist sense. The concept of political field is important to the analysis. Such a field is made up of actors directly involved in the political phenomena being studied. The field involves both social and territorial components. It is important, says Swartz, to assume that no particular state of change is any more normal than any other,[24] The political field in turn is surrounded by a social and cultural arena immediately adjacent to the field. The arena and the field play a vital role in influencing, limiting, and facilitating the processes of change. Political principles governing the arena radiate into the field motivating individuals, inducing or reducing tensions in a way to bring about the (temporary) distribution of power. Geographers will recognize that there is a similarity between Swartz **et al.**, arena and field and the component parts of S.B. Jone's field theory,[25] although the terminolgy is not strictly comparable. Jone's synthesis of some concepts of political geography makes considerable note of Gottmann's notion of **circulation**,[26] termed "movement" by Jones. Every political decision, states Jones, involves movement. As will be shown this certainly seems to be true in the case study examined here. Swartz's arena is determined by the social and cultural milieu of the group studied. In the case of the American city one important component is seen the idea of movement in the literal sense, very akin to the "transience" of Alvin Toffler.[27]

By way of all of the foregoing it follows that from the geographer's purview local-level political analysis (local-level political geography) can potentially give a picture of the distribution of power. In so doing local-level political geography can map the spatial distribution of the power and then help us to understand its genesis and evolution. If, as Stringfellow suggests is the case in Harlem, ongoing political momentum brings about a disparity between goals and achievements, we can then attempt to focus on those processes—structures and functions—causing the centrifugal motion. Here then the immediate task is to recognize the "islands in the stream", that is the politically and economically stable segments of geographical space. Once done the genesis and evolution of the politics of stability and instability should be researched. This becomes a search for the decisions that have led to stability. What is the political nature of said decisions? What trade-offs were involved? Have adjacent areas been adversely affected by these trade-offs? In this respect does Stringfellow's thesis of the intercessory role of the poor for the rich have merit as a basic critique of our system? Putting it another way, is poverty a **de facto** product of growth or a **de jure** consequence of absolutizing the law? If the law has been absolutized it fails in its task as an instrument of social and economic justice; we have made it a god. Can the natural areas of our city maintain themselves or are they, in the case of poor areas, overwhelmed by their unfortunate images and the prestigiousness of neighbouring communities (with apologies to Bertalanaffy and Boulding). Local-area political geography makes it possible to give answers to such questions.

A CASE STUDY

By way of growing up in one of Pittsburgh's East Boroughs (Edgewood) this author has been intrigued with the overall picture of the evolution of community development. The fact that some areas are more subject to deleterious change than others is obvious from even a cursory reading of the urban landscape. Some communities apparently can withstand the ravages of time, that is blight, the twin phenomena of economic decline and spiralling property taxes, as well as changes in the nature and the quality of services available. One might say that the preservation of a neighbourhood's identity may be a very undemocratic thing, as if an area has erected some kind of cultural boundary to fend off alien influences.

Differences in land use as an urban spatial phenomena have been well investigated by planners and economists. Some theories of community stability invite controversy. Thus Jane Jacobs' theory of the successful neighbourhood has had considerable verbal challenge since its introduction in 1961.[28] Jacobs' model says that a successful neighbourhood is characterized by diversity. In a 1973 publication Weicher concludes that the Jacobs' formula for neighbourhood success was counter indicated.[29] Jacobs says that crime will fall as diversity increases which Weicher concludes is untrue (signs of the coefficient are wrong). Generally speaking Jacobs likes land use diversity and the policy makers, the planners and the politicians, dislike it. Diversity or the lack of it could be said to be part of the "prestige" (negative or positive) factor of communities. Weicher calculates partials in order to understand the point of diminishing returns with respect to the negative relationships between neighbourhood success and Jacobs' criteria of success. He does not take an essential next step, however, and elaborate on the requisite variety that may become the basis neighbourhood success for all people.[30]

Tepper's conclusion in a study of mobility within the City of Pittsburgh is that stability can never be understood through using just economic criteria.[31] Tepper found that low economic groups (income less than $5000 per year) tended to have considerable intra-area mobility whereas higher income groups enjoy greater inter-area mobility. Do areas of diversity and homogeneity "maintain" themselves through such processes? We do not know the role of prestige in such mobility, nor do we understand the role of other non-economic factors. The intra-urban political geography of poverty and of wealth needs to be investigated before we can understand the relationship between "prestige" and the legal factors that maintain or destroy prestige.

What is the requisite variety of land use types that will afford the best juxtaposition of the rich and the poor? What are the politics of such change? What are the politics of the intercessory role of the poor for the rich? These are large questions, I will attempt a tentative answer for the latter question through all to brief reference to a case study of my home local area and arena.

The Arena

The arena or surrounding area of the focus of this study is the East Boroughs of the City of Pittsburgh. This is comprised of 58 census tract districts on the eastern edge of the Pittsburgh SMSA. These census tracts include the Boroughs of Penn Hills, Wilkensburg, Edgewood (the focal point of the study), Swissvale, Rankin, Braddock, North Braddock, Braddock Hills, Forest Hills, Turtle Creek, Chalfant, East Pittsburgh, and certain districts within the City of Pittsburgh proper, notably the declining area of Brushton and the stable area of Regent Square. For the purpose of this analysis census tracts are defined as local areas. A number of local areas with like socio-economic characteristics will be identified as communities. The analysis of this arena of 58 local areas is an attempt to define the types of communities to be found, following an earlier study of the author.[32] The earlier study of focussed particularly on the economic aspects of segregation in the area and has yielded information that takes us beyond aspects of such **de facto** segregation.

The statistical approach is simple. The 58 neighbourhoods

are analyzed with respect to eighteen socio-economic criteria using factor analysis. The statistical approach allows the socio-economic variables to be grouped (as it turned out) into four factors. These socio-economic variables are then subjected to a different statistical technique, cannonical analysis. Here the eighteen variables were analyzed with respect to five additional variables. These five new variables, called the "predictors" in the jargon of cannonical statistical techniques, are used heuristically to link the larger array of socio-economic characteristics to aspects of change as represented by the five predictors of the cannonical analysis. The variables (criteria, C) are:

C-1:	total population,	C-10:	number employed,
C-2:	white population,	C-11:	number unemployed,
C-3:	black population,	C-12:	number employed as professional workers,
C-4:	number of children,	C-13:	number employed as managers,
C-5:	mean school age completed,	C-14:	number employed as sales workers,
C-6:	mean income,	C-15:	number employed as service workers,
C-7:	families at poverty level	C-16:	number employed as clerical workers,
C-8:	mean value of house,	C-17:	number employed as craftsman,
C-9:	gross rent paid,	C-18:	number employed as labourers (ex. farm).

The factor analysis of the eighteen socio-economic variables is shown in table one. The four factors (A through D) of Table 5.1 accounts for 87.662 per cent of the variance of the study area. Analysis of Eigen values indicates that very little additional information would be gained by attempting additional factor interpretation.

An analysis of Table 5.1 indicates that Blacks C-1 load heavily on factor B, children (C-4) on factor D, whites (C-2) less heavily on factor A. The pattern follows in seemingly logical fashion through the eighteen variables: professional workers (C-12), managers (C-13) load high on A, weakly or negatively on the other three factors. Service workers (C-15) and labourers (C-18) load more heavily on B, minimally on A and even less on C and D. The loadings of the professions coupled with those of C-5, 6, 7 indicates something of a dichotomy between factors A and B. Thus C-5 and C-6 load heavily on A whereas C-7 on factor B. Factor A seems to be saying something about well educated, affluent individuals, many who are white rather than black (compare C-2 white population, with C-3, black population). Factor B in turn says something about blacks (C-3) and the poor (C-7), and those who are labourers. Factors C and D seem to relate to blacks (But only weakly so) and to children respectively; factor D especially seems to be of little interest to the purposes of this essay. Factor C could indicate something about the very poor black population, but further analysis is necessary and is beyond the scope of this paper.

TABLE 5.1

Rotated factor matrix showing 18 variables (C.1—C.18) and their loadings on four factors (A.D). Rotation is the varimax procedure

	A	B	C	D
C-1	.641	-.719	.095	-.181
C-2	.843	.307	.116	-.308
C-3	-.084	-.971	-.004	.081
C-4	-.385	.172	-.775	-.044
C-5	.798	-.062	.027	.345
C-6	-.023	.104	.023	-.793
C-7	-.039	-.861	-.203	-.012
C-8	.902	-.054	.029	.250
C-9	.918	-.100	.073	.112
C-10	.791	-.499	.316	-.067
C-11	-.001	-.065	-.841	-.146
C-12	.963	-.023	.123	-.056
C-13	.942	-.002	.165	-.116
C-14	.884	-.032	.030	-.258
C-15	.144	-.935	.192	.005
C-16	.823	-.505	.039	-.011
C-17	.755	-.257	.264	-.353
C-18	.185	-.720	.125	-.359

Source: Author's Computations

Some general conclusions emerge. Blacks and whites, rich and poor, managers and professionals as opposed to service workers and labourers are located differently with respect to the 58 local areas analyzed. These conclusions are not very sensational. Such **de facto** segregation is common place in the city, as are ghettos and well-to-do suburbs, i.e., declining and stable communities.

The cannonical analysis adds an important dimension to our understanting of the social and economic geography of Pittsburgh's East Boroughs.[33] The predictors (P) used in the cannonical analysis consist of five variables indicative of change. The group of five are associated with residential tenure characteristics, and are responses to the census takers question:

"When did you move into your house?"

P-1: 1968-March 1970
P-2: 1965-1970
P-3: 1960-1964
P-4: 1950-1959
P-5: 1949 or before

TABLE 5.2
Cannonical correlation matrix showing the relationship between 18 criteria and 5 predicator variables.

See text for the identification of the criteria and predicators. Significant correlations (defined as .700 or above) are in bold type

	P-1	P-2	P-3	P-4	P-5
C-1	.747	.923	.937	.939	.694
C-2	.578	.821	.834	.883	.714
C-3	.294	.110	.112	-.002	-.145
C-4	-.038	.003	.002	-.006	-.017
C-5	.318	.462	.441	.420	.337
C-6	-.027	.049	.105	.068	-.024
C-7	.455	.323	.339	.225	.090
C-8	.387	.591	.591	.591	.382
C-9	.450	.619	.558	.606	.285
C-10	.712	.901	.911	.948	.713
C-11	.197	.211	.158	.119	.061
C-12	.685	.852	.796	.848	.597
C-13	.588	.817	.766	.831	.569
C-14	.661	.838	.845	.880	.621
C-15	.696	.647	.695	.678	.462
C-16	.790	.904	.848	.878	.733
C-17	.597	.787	.854	.895	.726
C-18	.507	.581	.682	.587	.517

Source: Author's Computations

Table 5.2 shows the Cannonical Correlation Matrix. Some of the characteristics of stability and change that emerge from Table 5.2 follow: Blacks (C-3) change their residence more than whites (C-2). Additionally there is a complex relationship between five of the seven vocations and a residential tenure of more than three but less than twenty years (P-2, 3, 4). In contrast there seems to be a correlation between a residential tenure of more than twenty years (P-5) and clerical workers and craftsmen, although both vocations score more highly on other predictors.

Even though cannonical correlations are notoriously difficult to interpret, Table 5.2 suggests a dualism with respect to the arena of the East Boroughs. Those neighbourhoods that show tendencies toward brief residential tenure (two years or less, P-1) and long tenure (twenty years or more, P-5) can be linked to clerical workers (C-16), blacks (C-3), and the unemployed (C-11). Blacks show their greatest correlation with young neighbourhoods, although the relationship is not strong. Clerical workers are associated most strongly with "moderately" young (P-2) neighbourhoods but have significant correlations with all neighbourhoods. The unemployed (C-11) are most significantly associated with P-2.

Table 5.3 facilitates additional analysis of Table 5.2. Table 5.3 gives a profile of the "tenure-types" represented by P-1 through P-5. (C-1, population, is ignored in Table 5.2, only correlations of .500 and above are listed). Table 5.3 would appear to tell an interesting story (given the difficulty in interpreting cannonical correlations). In looking at the rank-order of tenure-types from column to column, P-3 and P-4 show considerable similarity. The variables of the two columns are identical but some of the rank-orderings are different. Number of employed is ranked first in both P-3 and P-4. Whites change places with clerical workers. Craftsmen, professionals, managers, education, labourers, value of house, and rent have identical rankings in P-3 and P-4. A number of these categories, (managers, education, value of house, rent), drop from the list in P-5. Whites, education, value of house are added to the list in P-3. Columns P-3 and P-4 would appear to give picture of affluent stability found in the arena of the East Boroughs.

To generalize, category P-1 forms a picture of "transcience", to use Toffler's terms.[34] This group is highly mobile, some of whom are educated young professionals and managers. The P-2 tenure-types, in the main, are lower economic strata persons who rent homes. The P-3 and P-4 categories are more dominately home owners who are better educated, of a higher economic strata. P-5 tenure characteristics, those who have lived in their house the longest, appears to be similar to P-1 or P-2 tenure profiles, except that C-10, the number of people employed, ranks lower, probably because of the lower economic position of the group or else the number of retirees found. Table 5.3 affords a picture of the stability patterns of the more affluent of the study area. They tend to have lived in their homes from 1950 to 1964 as of the 1970 census. To further generalize, the more affluent are neither excessively long nor excessively short stayers in a neighbourhood, with a tenure range of from six to twenty years.

TABLE 5.3

Tenure Profiles, Categories P-1 through P-5

P-1	P-2
C-16 Clerical	C-16 Clerical
C-10 No. employed	C-10 No. Employed
(C-15 Education)	C-12 Professionals
C-12 Professionals	(C-14 Sales Workers)
C-14 Sales Workers	C-13 Managers
C-17 Craftsmen	C-17 Craftsmen
C-13 Managers	C-9 Rent
(C-2 Whites)	C-18 Laborers
C-18 Laborers	
(C-7 Poverty)	

P-3	P-4
C-10 No. Employed	C-10 No. Employed
*C-2 Whites	C-16 Clerical
C-17 Craftsmen	C-17 Craftsmen
C-16 Clerical	C-2 Whites
C-12 Professionals	C-12 Professionals
C-13 Managers	(C-13 Managers)
*C-15 Education	(C-15 Education)
C-18 Laborers	C-18 Laborers
C-8 Value of House	(C-8 Value of House)
C-9 Rent	(C-9 Rent)

P-5
C-16 Clerical
C-17 Craftsmen
C-2 Whites
C-10 No. employed
*C-14 Sales Workers
C-12 Professionals
C-18 Laborers

Underlined variables are those newly added, not appearing in previous category.

Variables marked with asterisk (*) are those that reappear in list, having once appeared and then dropped.

Variables in parenthesis are dropped in the next succeeding category.

Population (C-1) is omitted.

Only correlations over .500 are included in the table.

Source: Table 5.2

What is the geographic distribution of affluent-stability (P-3 and P-4) within the arena of the East Boroughs? The statistics given so far are mute on the geography of affluent stability. If the mix of categories P-1 through P-5 was geographically homogeneous in the East Boroughs then we could expect to find no islands in the stream of decline. The raw economic data, newpspaper reports, library research, field work and experience indicate such is not the case. For example, a recent newspaper article indicates that Wilkensburg, one of the communities of the "arena" of study, has a declining housing stock.[35] Housing stock decline results when housing and zoning code violations go uncorrected and the properties fall into disrepair. Often the property is placed on the demolition list to force the owners to comply with the codes. Such tactics often do not work, partly bacause absentee landlords milk the property for the rent and then essentially abandon it through sheriff's sale and demolition. Another problem encountered by many cities is the rate of property assessment. For example, New York City's 130 year old Community Service Society states that the real estate property tax has evolved in a way that discriminates against multi-family units.[36] Single family homes are favoured because of the higher rate of assessment against multi-family units. This practice forms the recursive link of the cycle of poverty: housing code abuse...disproportionally high assessment against multi-family units...further code abuse...thus decline of the housing stock. The extent to which this pattern is found in the East Boroughs of the Pittsburgh SMSA is unclear at this stage of the research. Whatever the case, the city fathers of Wilkensburg seem to think that the answer to their housing crises is stricter code enforcement.[37] One could doubt the efficacy of the approach given a true evolution of so-called "racist" tax assessment policies. Such pragmatic enforcement of codes will not undo long standing policies that have plunged entire communities into decay.

The Community Service Society's emphasis on the evolution of tax assessment disparties would seem to be of potential interest to geographers. In general, what has been the nature of the evolution of stable communities? In this respect a great deal of knowledge is lacking for the East Boroughs but some general details are known. Many of the communities, Boroughs and Townships, of the area are factory towns. Rankin and Braddock for example were and are dormitory communities housing workers of the steel complexes found along the Monogehela River. Wilmerding was a "company town" for the large Westinghouse complex found in the Turtle Creek valley.[38] Even as late as 1926 the Westinghouse corporate interests owned "more than half" of the houses of Wilmerding.[39] Even the evolution of at least one of the upper middle class communities was hypothetically influenced by corporate policy, the case in point is the Borough of Edgewood.

In thinking of company towns, isolated mining communities usually come to mind. In general the play of forces is familiar: the company owns everything, the land, the workers houses, the mine, the store, the social services, the church, etc. Such total control is rarely associated with suburdan communities growing on the edge of large metropolitan areas. However, a cursory reading of the history of the East Boroughs indicates that indeed corporate control of the area's communities was strong. In the case of Wilmerding, the Borough was "...a brake town (Westinghouse's air brake) as Crewe was a London and Northwestern town, or Essen a Krupp town.[40] To what extent did the corporations affect town politics? Since history has not been written in such a way as to tell us, one must guess, interpolate from the references that do exist. In Wilmerding Westinghouse interests "refrained" from influencing town policies at all, or so says a biographer of George Westinghouse. Indeed troublesome men were elected to office and "radical socialistic" tendencies have sometimes prevailed, but the Westinghouse Company went "serenely" on.[41] The implications of this paraphrase of Prout's biography of Westinghouse (apparently written on commission from Westinghouse corporate interests) is that politics had little if any effect on corporate policy.[42] What effect did corporate policy have on local-level politics? Only grassroots research into the relationships between corporate policy and local-level politics can provide us with answers, indeed a worthwhile but onerous and difficult task. Official biographies doubtfully tell the complete story.

Edgewood: The Evolution of Local-Level Politics

More information is to be had for the case of the upper middle class community of Edgewood. Note some of the facts of the history of Edgewood: In 1857 Edgewood was a cluster of seven or eight homes with a population of 60 ... after 1857 more and more houses were built owing to the increasing importance of Westinghouse interests...in 1886 George Westinghouse bought the Allegheny Car and Transportation Company...in 1889 Edgewood became incorporated after a court fight over the location of the boundary line with neighbouring Swissvale...1894 H. H. Westinghouse (George's brother) elected to council, served until 1900 when he was elected burgess, served until 1902. The aforementioned court fight focused on the placement of the boundary between Swissvale and Edgewood, i.e., whether Westinghouse's Union Switch and Signal would be part of

Swissvale or Edgewood.[43] When Edgewood succeeded from Swissvale, the Westinghouse plant also succeeded, broadening the tax base of the new Borough but considerably shrinking the tax base of Swissvale.

Down through its history Edgewood has been solidly Republican in its political character, with Westinghouse interests represented from almost the beginning. The Borough was not only the home of George and Herman Westinghouse but also that of a string of Westinghouse corporate officials. In speaking of the politics of Edgewood one analyst notes that the incumbents usually succeed themselves unless they wish to retire. The election contests are usually keenest in the primaries. The incumbents appear on a slate together, and any man who wishes to break into council has a difficult time. New people are elected only when an incumbent desires not to run.[44]

According to one local historian, the suburban character of Edgewood has been maintained since the beginning. Councilmen have guarded the community from the intrusion of commercial contacts.[45] Two streets and only two streets where zoned "commercial" out of the entire community. The zoning laws were and are still rigidly enforced, an approach helpful in inhibiting the deterioration of the housing stock.

As noted with the neighbouring community of Wilkensburg, code enforcement alone will doubtfully insure community stability. Indeed the rigidly enforced zoning laws of Edgewood have not single-handedly maintained the "suburban character" of the Borough. Another aspect of local-level politics has become crucial: the politics of continuing school segregation. The full scenario will not be repeated here; it is enough to say that the Edgewood School District, one of the smallest and yet most prestigious in the state, has continued to resist jointure through a series of court manoeuvres. Various proposals have been put forth to join the Edgewood Schools with those of Swissvale and North Braddock. At this writing the forces of integration have been forestalled. This analyst suspects that the quality of the Edgewood schools has long been the necessary condition of the community's stability. Zoning and housing code enforcement merely a kind of tandom factor, a sufficient condition of stability.

Should the Edgewood Public Schools be obliged to integrate by force of law the community would undoubtedly suffer from disastrous instability. Returning to the factor analysis cited in an earlier section of this essay, the upper middle class residential stay (the time that upper middle class families remain in a community) is from six to twenty years. Experience indicates that this indeed is the pattern of Edgewood. People buy (rather than rent) the out-sized homes of the community in order to provide their children with a quality and sheltered education. Once the children are out of the nest the larger homes become cumbersome and expensive and so are sold to younger upper middle class executive types seeking sheltered, quality, education. In this way the Borough maintains itself through periodic renewal.[46]

Edgewood, like Wilmerding and undoubtedly many of the other boroughs of the arena studied, is in a sense a "company town". The general algorithm is this: the dependent variable is community stability, i.e., young higher middle class families periodically replacing older higher middle class families; the independent variables are: **longstanding** (prudential rather than pragmatic) zoning and housing code enforcement, self-generating polity leading to extreme political homogeneity, a stable tax base with stability augmented by the presence of the Union Switch and Signal Corporation, careful regulation of behaviour space through "exclusiônary" zoning (commercial areas and certain business types, as well as multi-family units in many areas of the Borough being excluded), and last but not least the politics of the survival of the small but high quality Edgewood Public Schools. All of this is indeed micro-spatial polities or local-level political geography.

At this point in the research it is difficult to spell out the political role of corporatism in the case of Edgewood. Undoubtedly the presence of a large manufacturing plant cushioned the tax burden of the Borough's residents and perhaps (probably?) that of the manufacturing plant as well. This last statement must remain hypothetical as corroborating data has not been found.[47] Saying all of this in another way, the prestige of Edgewood as an upper middle class residential area has been carefully managed down through the years. The chief surrogate of prestige in the case of Edgewood is its quality school system, further justifying Kains' contention that education is indeed a useful surrogate of prestige.[48]

CONCLUSIONS

This essay interweaves threads of analysis from several different analytical perspectives, that of political geography, ecological psychology, and political anthropology. Singularly the concepts of these disciplines fail to provide an integrated picture of community stability, together they afford an avenue of potential usefulness for understaning the antonymous forces of change in the urban landscape. The "algorithm" presented in the summary of the case study is seen as a hypothesis that in combination with a similarly constructed perspective for unstable neighbourhoods would become a theory of urban change, not dissimilar to the "cumulative causation" theories of say Myrdal and Prefisch.

Confirmation of Stringfellow's hypothesis of the poor being intercessory for the rich must wait upon the creation of a micro-level theory of cumulative causation. However, strong hints that indeed more wealthy communities prosper at the expense of poorer communities have been shown. The factors are subtle in that they are buried in the historical record. Of considerable interest is the role of law, that is zoning and housing codes. When are such codes to be blamed for **de facto** segregation?, **de jure** segregation? Is it the fault of such ordinances that certain economic classes are unable to migrate into certain neighbourhoods? Can communities be blamed for desiring stability? But, what is the price of such stability for larger urban arenas,...SMSAs? No doubt the price to the poor is very high. Our cities have a dilemma, and willy-nilly pragmatic prescriptions for that dilemma (such as rigid code enforcement) may well help to kill the patient. Where do we go? We might try calculating the requisite variety needed to promote community stability and they try rewriting our laws in such a way as to promote the correct requisite variety for stability. This in tandom with the correction of (other) civil and economic injustice should help.

To what extent is human society, as exemplified by the case study, an open system. The question here is not "Are they open systems?" but, "To what extent are they open systems?" How well does materialistic scientific philosophy serve in the analysis of change? Is change merely the product of environmental interaction, or does "on-goingness", the Gestalt, help in understanding the direction and momentum of change. This discussion was introduced early in the paper by way of the contrived disagreement between Bertalanffy and Boulding and the introduction of the concept of **Raumgefuhl.** Of course the controversy becomes a matter of philosophy, indeed even metaphysics, and certainly will not be laid to rest here. However, evidence has been presented that Edgewood as a system has had "going concern" type of momentum (the term is that of Mackinder), a system that increasingly has been able to become oblivious to its outside environment. An important component of such movement towards a closed system is seen to be prestige. While we have surrogates for prestige, such as Tepper's use of social rank dimension criteria[49] or Kain's use of median education, the non-economic component is not easily modelled with accuracy. If economic variables fail in our analysis then we must consider the noneconomic; a dimension all too frequently ignored in a world obsessed with economic thinking.

Postscript

Recently, within the last year, the Edgewood School District has been forced to amalgamate with other surrounding districts including the poorer boroughs of Swissvales and Braddock as well as the richer area of Churchill. This event is seen as changing the entire nature of the local level politics of the area and as well affecting the nature of transience in the entire area, but particularly that of Edgewood. Appeals are still pending and it will likely be some years before the final impact of the court's decision will be felt in the area. The decision came too late to have any probable affect on the 1980 population census, but its full manifestation will no doubt be felt by the time the 1990 census is taken. Thus one will have to wait until that time to ascertain the correctness of the ideas put forth in this paper.

FOOTNOTES

1. See Willian Stringfellow, **My People is the Enemy**, Garden City: Anchor Books, 1964. The thesis of the poor being intercessory for the rich is given in Chapter One, "Initiation".
2. William Stringfellow, a lawyer and advocate for the poor, has written a number of other works setting forth his perspectives on the origins of poverty, such as **A Private and Punblic Faith,** and **Free in Obedience.**
3. Richard Peet, "The Geography of Crime: a Political Critique," and Keith D. Harries, "Rejoinder to Richard Peet: 'The Geography of Crime: a Political Critique" **The Professional Geographer** XXVII-3, pp. 277-282.
4. Ludwig von Bertalanffy, **General Systems Theory**, New York: George Braziller, 1968, p.16.
5. **Ibid,** p.32.
6. Raumgefuhl or "spatial-feeling" is a concept little known in anglo-Saxon geography. The concept, among others, is explored in an early essay by the author, see Vincent P. Miller, "Observations on the Goals and Methods of Regional Courses," **The Journal of Geography** 59 (1960) pp. 371-377.
7. K.E. Boulding, "National Images and International Systems," reprinted in Kasperson and Minghi, eds. **The Structure of Political Geography,** Chicago: Aldine Publishing Co., 1969, beginning on p. 347. The research of the author's colleague

Leonard Tepper suggests that "image" can be translated into "prestige" at the local-level of politics. "Prestige" as defined by Tepper is a social rank dimension having a close association with high income and education levels as well as white collar and professional occupations. See Leonard P. Tepper, "Residential Mobility of Selected School Families in Pittsburgh, Pennsylvania, 1960-1966, unpub. Ph.D. dissertation, Department of Geography, University of Pittsburgh, 1971, pp. 95-96. John F. Kain uses of median education as an indication of prestige. See John F. Kain, **Essays on Urban Spatial Structure,** Cambridge: Ballinger Publishing Co., 1975, p. 268.

8. For example see Roger Barker, **Ecological Psychology,** Stanford: Stanford University Press, 1968. Chapter 6, "A Theory of Behavior Settings," develops a rationale for the relationship between the environment and behaviour. Bertalanffy **(op.cit.)** explores the controversy between molar (or Gestalt) and molecular psychology in his chapter "General System Theory in Psychology and Psychiatry."
9. David Riesman, **et al, The Lonely Crowd,** Garden City: Anchor Books 1953.
10. Stringfellow, **op. cit.** pp.28-33.
11. Gerald Pyle, **et al, The Spatial Dynamics of Crime,** Chicago: The University of Chicago, Dept. of Geography, Research paper no. 159, 1974.
12. Irvin J. Roth and Sherry Sidhu, "The Fear Factor in Public Transportation Usage." **The Pennsylvania Geographer,** XIII-3 (November 1975), pp. 19-22.
13. Stanley D. Brunn, "Jury Selection, Justice, and Geography," **The Pennsylvania Geographer,** XIII-3 (November 1975), pp.23-30.
14. Harvey W. Zorbaugh, "The Natural Areas of the City", reprinted in George A. Theodorson, **Studies in Human Ecology,** Evanston: Row, Peterson and Co., 1961, pp. 45-49.
15. Marc J. Swartz ed., **Local-Level Politics,** Chicago: Aldine Publishing Co., 1968.
16. The concept of state-idea is that of Hartshorne. See Richard Hartshorne, "The Functional Approach in Political Geography," reprinted in Kasperson and Minghi, eds., **op.cit.**
17. Eugene Lauer is a professor of philosophy at Duquesne University. This "organic" concept is important to this essay, thus organic political systems would be the source of morals, hence amoral, in the Hegelian sense. Our political system is **not** so constituted; the law is not an end unto itself but a means to an end. If the law should ever become an end unto itself, say for example, the enemy of the poor rather than the advocate of the poor, then, so reasons Lauer, the disadvantaged have a right to practice civil

disobedience.

18. Karl Wittfogel comments on the beggar's democracy in his **Oriental Despotism,** New Haven: Yale University Press, 1963, see Chapter 4 "Despotic Power-Total and Not Benevolent," particularly pp. 108-125.
19. E.F. Schumacher explores these notions and in so doing suggests avenues for change. To what extent is the "technological optimism" of the Design School of Thought linked to the "managerial optimism" of Keynes? So far as this author knows the subject has not been explored. See Schumacher"s **Small is Beautiful,** New York: Perennial Library, 1973, Chapter 2 "The Role of Production" pp. 40-52.
20. See footnote 17.
21. R. E. Kasperson and M. Breitbart, **Participation, Decentralization, and Advocacy Planning,** Association of American Geographers, Resource Paper no. 25, 1974.
22. Robert Goodman, **After the Planners** New York: Simon and Schuster, 1972. Goodman is an architect who has much to say about "design mentality", critisizing the city beautiful that is not for people.
23. Barker, **op.cit.** This point is discussed on page 6.
24. Swartz, **op.cit.** Swartz says that if the actors at some particular time are more or less at peace with one another the truce cannot be assumed to be normal or optimal or exceptional...only temporary. In this respect the originators of local-level politics see it as being value free, a controversial point indeed.
25. S. B. Jones, "A Unified Field Theory of Political Geography," reprinted in Kasperson and Minghi, **op.cit.**
26. According to R.K. Wolfe **circulation** spans the rigid boundary seperating communication and transportation. See R. K. Wolfe, **Transportation and Politics,** Searchlight Book no. 18, Princeton: Van Nostrand Co., 1963, p.7
27. Alvin Toffler, **Future Shock,** New York: Bantam Books, 1971. Toffler's "transience index" is described on p. 456.
28. Jane Jacobs, **The Death and Life of Great American Cities,** New York: Random House, 1961, see part two "The Conditions for City Diversity," pp. 143-222.
29. John C. Weicher, "A Test of Jane Jacobs' Theory of the Successful Neighborhoods," **Journal of Regional Science** 31-1 (April 1973) pp.29-40.
30. Requisite variety may be defined as the correct mix, the degree of heterogeneity, permissible for systemic stability. To this author's knowledge the concept has never been applied in the social sciences. The development of the philosophy of requisite variety would enable the abandonment of the "progress mentality", hence a more lively debate in

the social sciences between the two schools of thought. Shiw Singh makes an interesting start in this direction in his "The Stability Theory of Rural Central Place Development," reprinted in Singh **et al** eds, **Readings in Rural Settlement Geography,** Varanasi: National Geographical Society of India, 1975, pp. 416-423.

31. Tepper, **op.cit.**
32. Vincent P. Miller, Jr. "De Facto Segregation and Residential Stability in Pittsburgh's East Boroughs," **The Pennsylvania** Geographer, XI-4 (December 1973), pp. 19-25.
33. The conceptual basis for this approach is to be found in H. L. Gauthier, "Transportation and the Growth of the Sao Paulo Economy," **Journal of Regional Science,** 8-1 (1968), pp. 78-94.
34. Toffler, **op.cit.**
35. "Wilkensburg Fights to save its Houses," Pittsburgh **Press,** February 12, 1978, section G, p.2.
36. Peter Kihss, "City Property Tax Called 'Racist' by Community Service Society," **New York Times,** March 5, 1978, section A, p.50.
37. See footnote 35. The law in the form of code enforcement actually becomes a dilemma for the advocates of the poor. To not enforce housing codes is to tolerate substandard housing environments, to enforce codes would cause the houses to be priced beyond the ability of the poor to pay. In a general sense Stringfellow treats the problem in his section "The Law as the Enemy of the Outcast", **op.cit.** pp. 57-64..
38. Wilmerding has been labelled a company town by Westinghouse biographer Henry G. Prout in his **A Life of George Westinghouse** New York: Charles G. Scribner Sons, 1926, p.295.
39. Ibid.
40. Ibid.
41. Ibid.
42. This impression is also given in **George Westinghouse Commemoration,** New York: The American Society of Mechanical Engineers, 1937, p.49.
43. References as to the issues in the court fight are vague. Whatever the case boundary determination awarded most of the property to Edgewood although Swissvale desired the boudary to run through a hollow called Nine Mile Run, which would have placed the entire property within the confines of Swissvale. This was indicated in a conversation with Milford Holliday, archivist, Borough of Edgewood, March 12, 1978.
44. Clark Benjamin Kistler, "The Government of Edgewood," unpub. M.A. thesis, University of Pittsburgh, 1930, p.12.

45. **Borough of Edgewood, Allegheny County, Pennsylvania, A History**, "Edgewood," (by Mrs. T.S. Grubbs), Pittsburgh: Reed and Witting, 1934, pp.5-6.
46. Groups throughout the Pittsburgh SMSA seem to have an intuitive sense of local-level politics and their value to community stability. For exxample bussing is seen to be disruptive to local area and community stability. Edgewood has an advantage over lower-middle class communities with respect to stability in that many Edgewoodites own their own homes and so have greater political clout which is particularly manifest in the politics of school integration and segregation. The Edgewood schools have not merged with those of neighboring communities at this writing.
47. Tax data are available. For example Kistler (op.cit. p.31) notes that in 1929 the Union Switch and Signal Corporation paid a tax of $ 20,000 to the Borough out of a total tax revenue of $ 98,371.24. Without expertise on the fairness of this ratio, no opinion can be offered on whether the "Switch" was paying its share of the tax burden. The issue of industrial tax burdens in "company" towns is a potentially fruitful path for further analysis for those interested in the topic of economic justice
48. Kain, op.cit., p. 268.
49. Tepper, op.cit., p. 95.

SECTION TWO
POVERTY AND POOR IN CITIES

SIX

Bernard Kayser

Urban Poverty, Rural Poverty
Sharing of Crumbs

After the invention of the term "Third World", and the notion of underdevelopment, defines itself in many differet ways, and after having convinced all the exploited people they were only underdeveloped, the poverty is entering now as an economic and a political concept (or as a slogan) between the leading powers of the world...Milton Santos has ironically well described this story:

"Poverty, a qualitative phenomenon until now, was changed gradually in a quantitative question reduced in numerical data. Those indicators were used in accordance to demonstrate the difference between poor and rich countries and for making the proof of a necessaray imitation of rich countries by the poor ones.

"This has conducted a need for everything coming from rich countries, from money to foods; in this way was constructed the aid ideology..." [1]

Now it's useful to investigate the poverty concept, in analysing statistical informations and in measuring their differential evolutions: that's the way for having a clear view of today's real problems, because we can't, in fact, make correctly our own mind from only the study of enterprises and governments strategies. It's obvious because these informations are not sufficient in the understanding of reality.

The way how to evaluate the level and the living conditions of the urban and rural inhabitants, of underdeveloped countries, in quality and quantity, gives us a precise direction: it's a way to understand, in a prospective manner, the real problems and challenges of today's humanity.

Professor, Institut de Geographie, Universite de Toulouse-Le-Mirail

A Differential Pauperization

In lack of other sources, let's refer to the World Bank's published calculations[2]. Absolute poverty concerned in 1975, about 770 million people, 37% of the third world population. This sort of poverty is corresponding to a 50$ income per year for each inhabitant, a revenue which put people in position to survive, within malnutrition, analphabetism and misery, with less than 30 cents per day (based on United States consumption level[3] Also, a further analysis of these informations positively reveals that the pauper's proportion is clearly higher in rural zones:

Rate of "absolute poverty" in rural population 43%
Rate of "absolute poverty" in urban population 30%

But,—and this is not only a statistical observation but also a factual well-known phenomenon—it's rather essential to notify that urban pauperization level is growing up. The rate was 18% in 1969, first reference year known. Chiefly, we must recognize that in some countries, like those entering in a "middle income level" (as Nigeria, Morocco, Malaysia and Brasil) absolute misery rate, of both towns and rural zones, became sensibly the same.

TABLE 6.1
Rate (%) of Absolute Poverty in Middle Income Level Countries in 1975
(Reference : World Bank data)

	Towns	Countryside
Mediterranean Zone	27	25
Africa	27	29
Asia	17	25
Latin America	18	18
Total	21	24

For instance, it seems to be proved that, as data concords, the large inegality of revenues is relatively less higher in rural zones than in urban zones (where, obviously, are concentrated the most important finances) and in consequence, statistically, this fact appears for the whole population.

TABLE 6.2
Part (%) of Revenues owned by 40% of the Poorest Peoples

	In rural zones	In the whole country
Bangladesh (1963)	18,5	18,0
India (1963-1965)	20,0	16,0
Malaysia (1970)	12,4	11,6
Pakistan (1963)	18,0	17,5
Philippines (1971)	13,3	11,6
Sri Lanka (1973)	17,0	15,1

It's useful to note that everywhere the 40% most poorer peoples share only 20% of the global national revenue, and often less.

Concerning the evolution and tendency over which it's difficult to obtain sure information, we can see, for example, the status quo or aggravation of numerous individual situations, both in the town and in the countryside. It's well known for India. In the whole land the monthly consumption per person appears, in steady roupies, as following:

TABLE 6.3
India—Direct estimation of the Monthly Consumption per Person (in 1960 roupies)

	rural zones	urban zones
1960	21,5	29,5
1965	16,7	22,3
1970	19,4	29,3

Contrary to Malaysia,[5] the difference between urban and rural revenues—which is a ratio of one to two—is continuing to be accentuated. The middle familial revenue increased by 7% in the country, between 1957 and 1970, while the urban revenue shot up in a proportion of 24%. But it's less for Sri Lanka where in ten years (1963-1973) the rural revenue increased about 13% when, in the same time, the urban revenue retreated by 20%, the difference between these revenues continued, anyway, to be important (223 to 317 roupies in 1973).

What's the meaning of these insufficient and unequal data other than to expose clearly the complex problem of differential pauperization? Because the basic conditions are different, because the evolution stages are not the same, because from one country to another the investment rate brings a different result, none of statistical studies can conduct to global conclusions over the question of expansion or retraction of misery.

This phenomenon is extremely binded to circumstances (climatic phases, prices of raw materials, political events etc.) that we can well judge it only with a long term observation.

Then, it's more convenient to develop a logical reflection, inspired from observations and informations rather qualitatives than statisticals.

The Evidence of Urban Pauperization

After having believed, with the ideologists of the fifties, to a city as the centre pole of development, today we must submit ourselves to this fact; over a third world urban population of 380 million people the extreme poverty, which means an only fight for survival, concern at least 115 million people. A little more than half the country people, the so-called "drifters from the land", to whom urban integration was a bit successful over the past twentyfive years, are surely in a better living condition, but for the rest we can ask ourself what's the point of being rejected by the countryside if it's not the only possibility, real or ideal, to proclaim, to the whole society's face, the right to exist?

Today's urban growth doesn't slow down. It generally reaches and exceeds 5% per year because of the drifting from the land and the rise or birth rate, half and half. Such a development, in which the part of young adults is considerable, is confronted to a national and urban economic growth of about the same scale: 3% for the most poorest countries between 1970 and 1976 and 6% for the middle income lands. This confrontation leaves sometimes only crumbs to share, because of profusion of intermediaries, all the way to the most deprived neighbourhoods.

The crumbs are one thing and the development is another. The dominating capitalistic system doesn't multiply productive employments, it's just the opposite. In Philippines, the worker's part in industry passed from 13 to 10% between 1957 and 1972. In Indonesia, the textile industry modernization (with a 20% growth per year) between 1966 and 1971 has ended to the redundancy of half the workers. A company can create, for 100,000 dollars a plastic shoe shop in which 40 workers are employed which at the same time created unemployment for more than 5,000 persons imvolved in a traditional shoes and sandals making.

It's not surprising that even the smallest part of growth profit leaved to dominated classes is first serving, in the lower circuit of the economy described by M. Santos[6], those who are part of the proliferating redistribution activities. Everybody who can't survive otherwise has cropped up the redistribution circuit. In the time of the triumphant town planning process these ones were considered as spongers, a derogatory term today difinitively forsake for good reasons. The recent Mr Pain's works[7] about Kinshasa demonstrate the existence, in this large town, of about one microcommercial centre for 6 to 8 families and a single cellar for 15 to 18 persons... without counting all those little occasional merchandise stocks that are possessed by housewives, nobody knowing exactly how in 1975, in reference to a very serious inquiry, the "complementary revenues" were constituing half the income of Kinshasa's families... that's the reason why the families' expenses were growing up more than salaries (+ 150% against + 60% for the salaries, in current money).

It's not surprising, in that condition, to learn that the major part of urban population is devoting a great part of income in daily feeding, in accordance with some familial budget and consumption inquiries. The assessment for Kinshasa[8], for example, gives more than a 67% average rate for daily feeding (15% for housing, 7% for clothing). This proportion reaches 80% in the most poorer districts elsewhere, such as in the Indian cities (where the population is underfed). What's remaining for services consumption, the very reason of urban living? It's true that doctors are more numerous in town than in the countryside (1 for 1,500 persons in urban zones against 1 for 10,000 in rural zones in the Philippines, 1 for 3,700 against 1 for 24,200 in Pakistan, 1 for 880 against 1 for 50,000 in Kenya), but access to medical cares is equally available in town for everyone ? Concerning schooling, a report of the World Bank reveals a schooling rate of 36% for the poorest town districts and 90% for the rest of the surrounding neighbourhoods.

In fact, the rapid development of the Third World's urban population doesn't fit neither to an equal global revenue growth nor an expansion of employments in up to date economic sectors. The city dwellers are, every day, much numerous to share a gross national product growing less rapidly than the population (especially in Southern Asia and in Africa). At the same time the sharing is more and more unequal. The investments give a favourable mood for large fortune setting up (with a large exit of money from the national circuit). The process is then perfectly suitable for a rapid growing of masses underproletarization.

At last, beyond current observations, the fast growing up of urban poverty is appearing as a logical obviousness. The new philosophy of the World Bank, an organization in charge of preventing social disruptions all over the world, indicate, with a proclamation style, "that it's absolutely necessary to revalue the town's function in development process". "Anywhere in the world it doesn't exist a good remedy to urban pauperism without considering the city as an open organism favourable to the integration of needy inhabitants and newcomers by the multiplication of productive employments. Any realistic strategy must have a goal of creating, for the poors, new well-paid employments in traditional sectors"[9].

The differential evolution of rural zones

Today's rural population growth, for the entire Third World and since a few years, is near a 2% annual rate (in the last twenty years, 1.3% in Latin America for 2, 2% in India). For all the great geographical units, except Africa, foodstuffs production can sustain the population explosion, any sign of production per inhabitant growing or, worse, stabilizing.

TABLE 6.4
Foodstuffs Production FAO Indicators Per Inhabitant (1951–1965 = 100)

	1971	1974	1975	1976
Latin America	103	103	102	107
Asia (except China)	103	99	106	105
Near-East	103	105	109	109
Africa	99	93	93	94
China	110	111	112	112
Total	105	103	105	107

There are considerable differences between a land and another, as we see in the annual growing rates of rural production (not only foods), for some great States.

Nevertheless, the second report on Asian agriculture, published in 1977 by the Asian Development Bank[10], notes, after analysing the last decade, that, in spite of the "green revolution", the foodstuff production per inhabitant is lowering and the rural poverty is seriously extending in the same way, as numerous studies demonstrate especially for the rural Bihar, the number of persons "living in abject poverty" is passed, between 1960 and 1970, from 17 to 30 millions, from 41 to 49% of the population. For the rural Punjab as well, and during the same period, despite growing up of the middle standard of living these proportions had passed from 18 to 23%, it's the same case for Java where, in 1970, the farmer's standard of living was clearly lower than at the end of the fifties[11].

TABLE 6.5
Average Agricultural-Annual Growth Rate

	Period 1960 1970	Period 1970 1976		Period 1960 1970	Period 1970 1976
Egypt	2,9	3,0	India	1,9	1,4
Ivory Coast	4,2	3,5	Pakistan	4,9	1,6
Zaire	3,9	1,9	Indonesia	2,7	4,0
Ghana	3,7	1,3	Mexico	3,9	1,4
Nigeria	-0,5	-0,2	Colombia	3,5	4,5
Turquey	2,8	4,9	Brasil	1,9	5,5

But, except for lands and regions particularly exploited or deprived, current observation and thought process confirm unexpected growing rates understandable but often lesser than the real ones.[12] In fact it's difficult to analyse how the progress and the individual or occasional high-value can be immediately accounted.

The farmer is producing more because of the demand reinforced espansion: family is growing up, urban population needs are extending, with government instigation cultivations for exportation are growing. In the other hand production increase is happening because of new selected seeds, fertilizers, labour (from the family), collective hydraulics as a result of State intervention... in total, productivity, in most cases, is not decreasing.

How to conciliate these observations, apparently conflicted, with the rural pauperization problem we saw before?

The Egyptian case is interesting for that.[13] Familial revenue analyses from 1958-1959, 1964-1965 and 1974-1975 inquiries show that after a notable reduction of poor peasants we see a spectacular increase, in the last decade, of these ones. A population of 22% is under the "poverty line" for 1958 and 17% for 1964. This rate was growing to 28% for 1974, touching 6 million people (for a global number of 21 million peasants). Many causes can explain this evolution in accordance with S. Radwan. It's, after all, an effect of a lack in the agrarian reform redistribution system. Of course during the fifties the number of farmers without fields was lowering and revenues growing up a bit. But at the end of the sixties this tendency was completely reversed. Consumption expenses rate between social stratum are more unequal than twenty-five years ago. A little progress is known for the land owners, even the little ones, but the countrysiders without land are increasing in a way that these people, with their families, are counting now for half the rural total population. Also salaries, a major revenue source, are stagnating since the Second World War and deteriorating since the very last years.

However with good qualitative observations[14] we may think that the Egyptian situation is not so bad as what we see in statistics and calculations. Besides, Egyptian economists held up in a 1977 Le Monde newspaper, was asserting that 40% of the whole country agricultural production was not accounted in the official statistics. It's because of the fellahs who developed, in the same time that they were improving their self-subsistence system, a considerable and spectacular commercial microproduction sold directly in urban markets (or serving at the help of family members living in towns). Who can account the production of thousands of gardens and little orchards spontaneously appearing in response to the demand? This phenomenon is yet taking a great part in the consumption level of Cairo : 22% of the total Egyptian population and 45% of the whole country's foodstuffs production, as the Egyptian supply Minister said. The city-countryside confict is clearly appearing.

What Assessment, What Principle?

We can't disagree with observants who raised the alarm. Everywhere in the Third World the increasing of urban "proto-proletariat" coming from the rural zones in crisis and now perpetuated by the urban system itself, create bad envrironments and living conditions. The betterment time required is difficult to predict? In the other hand how can't we see that, in a large number of countries, a certain growth of differential agricultural revenues (what about the drift from the land...) was creating a pauperization slowering and, sometimes, a relative improvement of individual situations?

Can we conclude that cities are passing in a negative tendency in reverse of countryside? This thinking is too global and too restrictive because the elementary ratio is not sufficient for a correct situation analysis. The humanity doesn't live, and lesser will accept to live "of only bread". In evidence the differential services availability disadvantage the rural people.

In reality we can't make a serious assessment neither an affirmation over which the Third World cities must have the greatest part. But it's essential to put attention on cities problems in a necessary integrate development philosophy. Successive styles launched by ideologists and relieved by international organizations gave a split up struggle for the underdevelopment problem, or worse a certain multinational action favouritism; growth centres, modern industrialization, great industrial manpower operations in traditional sectors...just when it was necessary to consider all the whole social and economic system those actions stood always sector-based. Global national policies, and even better, additive local integrated policies are required.[15]

FOOTNOTES

1. Milton Santos, Planning underdevelopment, Antipode, December 1977.
2. Banque Mondiale, Rapport sur le development dans le monde, aout 1978.
3. R. MacNamara, speech pronounced at the Governor's Council, Nairobi, 1973.
4. World Bank, India, Occasional paper, Washington, 1978, no 279. Note; Estimation for 1978-1979 seems to indicate that there is a notable amelioration of the consumption level.
5. International Labour Office, Poverty and landlessness in rural Asia, Geneve, 1977.
6. M. Santos, les villes du tiers monde, Paris, Ed. Genin, 1971.
7. M. Pain et al., Atlas de Kinshasa et travaux connexes.
8. M. Houyoux, Les budgets menagers à Kinshasa, 1973.
9. R. MacNamara, Speech pronounced at the Governor's Council, Washington, 1975.
10. Asian Development Bank, Second Asian Agricultural Survey, Manila, 1977.
11. CF. P. 696, No 5.
12. B. Kayser, La survie imprevue du tiers monde, revue Tiers Monde, no 47.
13. S. Radwan, Agrarian reform and rural poverty, Egypt 1925-1975 Geneve, International Labour Office, 1977.
14. Conversation with H. Attia, Tunisian Geographer and Sociologist, 1978.
15. Mac Gee, the persistence of the proto-proletariat, Australian National University, Research school of Pacific Studies, Mimeo, 1974.

REFERENCES

Bailey, William C., J. David Martin, and Louis N. Gary, "Crime and Deterrence: A Correlation Analysis," **Journal of Research in Crime and Delinquency** 11 (July 1974), 124-143.

Bailey, William C., and Ronald W. Smith, "Punishment: Its Severity and Certainty," **Journal of Criminal Law, Criminology, and Police Science** 63 (Dec. 1972), 530-539.

Becker, Gary, "Crime and Punishment: An Economic Approach," **Journal of Political Economy** 76 (Mar/apr 1968), 169-217.

Bentham, Jeremy, "Principles of Penal Law," in J. Browning (ed.), **The Works of Jeremy Bentham 1748-1832** (N.Y.: Russell & Russell, 1962).

Ehrlich, Isaac, "Participation in Illegitimate Activities: A Theoretical and Empirical Investigation, **Journal of Political Economy** 81 (May/June 1973), 521-565

Gibbs, Jack P., "Crime, Punishment and Deterrence," **Social Science Quarterly** 48 (March 1968), 515-530)

Gray, Louis N., and J. David Martin, "Punishment and Deterrance: Another Analysis of Gibb's Data," **Social Science Quarterly** 49 (September 1969), 289-295.

Mathur, Vijay K., "Economics of Crime: An Investigation of the Deterrent Hypothesis for Urban Areas", **The Review of Economics and Statistics** 60 (August 1978), 459-466.

Tittle, Charles R., "Crime Rates and Legal Sanctions," **Social Problems** 16 (Spring 1969), 409-423.

U.S. Department of Commerce, Bureau of Census, **Census of Population 1960, Characteristics of Population** (Washington, D.C.: Government Printing Office).

U.S. Department of Commerce, **City Government Finances**, 1960-61 (Washington, D.C.: Government Printing Office).

U.S. Department of Justice, Bureau of Prisons, **Characteristics of State Prisoners, 1960 National Prisoner Statistics** (Washington, D.C.: Government Printing Office).

U.S. Department of Justice, Federal Bureau of Investigation, **Uniform Crime Reports**, 1960 (Washington, D.C.: Government Printing Office).

SEVEN

William W. Goldsmith

Poverty and Profit in Urban Growth and Decline

> . . .Accumulation of wealth at one pole is. . .at the same time accumulation of misery, the torment of labour, slavery, ignorance, brutalization and moral degradation at the other pole. . .[1]

Widespread and miserable poverty is an undeniable counterpart of booming, dynamic industry in the capitalist city. Two well known, perhaps unsurpassed, examples of territories for viewing both the terror and the power of industrialization are Manchester, England, and Sao Paulo, Brazil. Manchester was the prototypical city of the industrial revolution, and Sao Paulo is the most thriving industrial centre in the "developing" world today.

As Raymond Williams has reminded us, the 19th century English city was the city of despair, Dickens' city, "murky, swarming, rotting," "a great gloomy city, webbed and meshed, as it were, by the spinnings of a huge poisonous spider"[2], in which a worker's life expectancy was 17 years—less than half that of the upper middle classes[3].

Prominent visitors to Manchestar all noted two things:

> . . .The first was the sheer squalor of conditions. . .a squalor which was difficult to relate to either their experience of their reading. The second was the emergence of a new class, the industrial prolateriat, which was substantially excluded from English society[4].

But this city of despair was also the greatest engine of production and accumulation the world had ever seen. Manufacturing of textiles was the prime industry. In 1806 power-looms were fitted to a Manchester factory, the first successful installation in England; by 1850, there were nearly a quarter-million looms in England. Application of steam, improvement and speeding up of machinery, and other innovations reduced the price of cotton yarn more than 30 per cent in the 1820s. Similar innovations led to a 20 per cent price reduction in piece goods between 1830 and 1850.[5] Growth rates in the city itself were overwhelming: in 1790 there were 1240 spinners, weavers, and printers employed in Manchester factories; this grew to be 48,300 in 1801. Total employment grew nearly five-fold from 1790 to 1821. Between 1774 and 1831 the number of houses increased by 615 per cent, the density by 790 per cent, the total population by 780 per cent, to a quarter of a million persons.[6]

In some places things are the same today. In the Sao Paulo Metropolitan Region the infant mortality rate fell by 30 per cent between 1940 and 1950. By 1960 it had fallen 32 per cent more. "By contrast, in the 13 years up to 1975 it rose by 45%."[7] Cardinal Arns, the Archbishop of Sao Paulo, wrote in June 1976 of "the widespread violence" that is "used against the people":

> cutting short lives through malnutrition and appalling health and sanitary conditions, through excessive work hours, fatigue and impoverishment, through lack of jobs and through wages which do not cover even basic necessities, through lack of housing and grossly inadequate public transport, through fear and the stifling of the rights of association, information and trade union activities.[8]

Yet this, too, is despair accompanied by extraordinary rates of accumulation. In 1969 the State of Sao Paulo, with about 19 per cent of the country's population, accounted for 35.6 per cent of Brazil's domestic output, about 44 per cent of capital accumulation, and half of the national property rental income. In the previous 40 years, the city grew from three-quarters of a million to six million persons. By 1975, when its population was about 11 million, it housed 26 of the country's 50 biggest companies.[9]

In both these cases, Manchester in the early 19th century, Sao Paulo in the late 20th, as well as New York, Philadelphia, Chicago, Cleveland, and many other cities of the U.S. in the late 19th and early 20th centuries as we shall see, the forging of an impoverished proletariat, at work for low wages, on relief, or barely surviving on the edges of society, is the recognized counterpart of a spectacular achievement of industrial growth and capital accumulation.* Indeed, until the early 20th century, and in some places still, the only defense uttered by most apologists of urban industrial development was that its poverty would one day be absorbed by the munificence of its production.[11]

In spite of considerable rhetoric to the contrary, recent evidence suggests that this distressing complementarity persists, though in new guises. The popular association of post-war urban economic growth with almost uniformly improved conditions for all city dwellers is misleading: a sizeable and substantially impoverished group remains within most cities, alongside rapid growth. Neither do the daily reports of unemployment, reduced services, and impoverished residents in urban industrial cities, such as New York, Detroit, Newark, Gary, Cleveland, and Akron, tell the whole story of urban decline: much business is still profitable, and accumulation still takes place. To be sure, neither of these situations, post-war urban growth or post 1974 decline, is the same as the 19th century prototype or the current situation in the Third World, but there are enough parallels to warrant careful investigation.

It is my intention in this chapter to suggest that the two popular observations about how urban devleopment proceeds—either progress with relative plentitude, or decline with misery—are seriously incomplete. Indeed, many times progress and poverty are reciporcal, rooted in the same basic social forces. The chapter begins with a discussion of how forces for development, in general, operate in market-run societies. It then turns to show how the city is related to the economy. These two discussions will lead to arguments about the unity of profits and poverty, and finally to a discussion of the geography of accumulation.

---

* Many migrants from Irish or Lancaster farms to Manchester did marginally improve their conditions, as Vigier points out. The same is true for migrants from the U.S. South to northern cities, or from the Northeast of Brazil to Sao Paulo. It is worth remembering, though, that many of these migrants are expelled from the land, that many others would have fallen below subsistence by staying behind. A paltry "improvement" this is for migrants. See Saint and Goldsmith for elaboration. Note that, perhaps because migrants to the city (from Lancashire and Ireland) formed a cohesive working class while landowners and industrialists were divided, Manchester's working class was "highly radicalized." "Major working class riots swept through the streets of the city every few years. . . At times, the city was completely taken over by the rioters."[10]

I. Forces for Development in Market Society

Urban problems are often not understood because they are examined in the wrong context, or in no useful context at all. In the United States—and many other places—most such problems arise from, and are best studied with reference to, the private market economy. Second, profits are important for expansion of the private economy. Third, technological innovation arises from concentrated ownership and control of production. Fourth, profits and rents come from work done for the benefit of others, hence inequality arises. Fifth, the inequality tends toward resistance.

The first consideration, the persistent and tight connection between politics and the economy, shows up most clearly in times of recession. The differences between the great crash and the contemporary crisis in the United States are particularly instructive. The principal difference is this: today the state is giant, the private economy is inextricably entangled with it, and therefore the 1929 resolution to the crisis—the crash—is no longer feasible. Even were it so, still the form of struggle that led to regained stability could not be repeated. Then there were massive union organizing efforts in basic industry, big increases in public invtervention in industry and trade, and the construction of a floor, however inadequate, beneath which labour could not fall.[12] And there was World War II, followed by gigantic U.S. investment in a destroyed Europe. Furthermore, much industrial activity has come to be critically dependent on government. (For one small, but typical example, nearly 20 percent of U.S. exports of manufactured products are financed by the government's Export/Import Bank.)[13] The unwillingness of the government to deal forcefully with stagflation derives from these changed conditions.

The results of this unwillingness are striking. In the seven recessions from 1920 to 1949, wholesale prices declined 9.4 per cent in an average year, retail prices fell 2.4 per cent, and the manufacturing wage rate dropped 1.8 per cent.[14] These changes restructured the economy so that profitability would each time rise to attract investors to expand production. Conservative, liberal, and Marxist economists all agree that these business cycles, without govenrment intervention, disciplined workers and inefficient industries and, in most cases, put the economy back on a growth path. In the six recessions from 1953 until 1980, however, wholesale prices increased 5.3 per cent in an average year, retail prices increased 5.6 per cent, and the manufacturing wage rate increased 5.1 per cent.[15] The dip in the business cycle did not, after the 1940s, restructure the economy with deflated prices. Conservative economists have told us why: the liberal government, in order to avoid rapidly falling incomes and rising unemployment, intervenes to prevent depression.

Economists as radically different in their politics as the arch-conservative Nobel prize winner Friedrich von Hayek,[16] the widely read liberal historian Robert Heilbroner, and the Marxist editors of **Monthly Review** Paul Sweezy and Harry Magdoff all agree that there are three alternatives: continued and increasing inflation, a deep depression, or a planned economy.[17] One thing is sure. The choice lies not simply with actors in the private economy. What the government does, or does not do, is crucial. It makes little sense to discuss them as though they were independent.

In complex urban societies the state is also responsible for numerous expenditures on what is called collective consumption, such as transportation, schooling, public health facilities, and other such services that provision the propulation. Some of these activities are undertaken by the state because they would not be profitable for private firms. In all cases, however, these activities lower the pressure on wages, which again ties the state to the private economy. By the reckoning of many astute viewers, this relationship is a crucial element of Third World urbanization.[18]

The growth of a capitalist economy depends on private investment. Investment is undertaken only in search of profit, indeed, only when profit is expected. A constant profit rate, which insures a return on investment, can be maintained only when the volume of investment, hence the level of overall economic activity, is increasing. ". . .however much they disagree on other matters, all economists who have studied capitalism—from Smith through Marx, Marshall, and Keynes—agree on the necessity of expansion."[19] The recognition that capitalism must be expansionary to survive, and that investment decisions are made by private owners of funds and facilities, leads governments to try to create conditions that make investment profitable.

After a crash, it is possible for such expansionary policy to reflate the economy, stimulate investment, and promote employment simultaneously. In a period of stagflation, however, the government is pressed between the demands of workers and citizens for wage guarantees, employment, public services, and for health and safety regulations, and the demands of businessman for reductions in all these, so as to re-establish profitability and growth. In a period when a large segment of the population is "marginal" to production, because of innovation and the shift of production abroad, and when inflation feeds the instability, the pressures on the government become critical. In a stagnant and inflationary period, there are not enough funds to satisfy demands for wages and for profits, for production and for services.[20]

Technological change, which comes about largely as a result of the competitive need to reduce costs of production, is a mixed blessing. It does reduce costs and therefore has the potential to make living easier for all, but it also tends to further concentrate both control over enterprise and participation in production.[21] These latter tendencies are not inherent characteristics of technological progress; they are results of the fact that selection of invention and innovation take place under the control of the owners of enterprise. To give but one example: cash registers are designed for ever less comptent and trained persons to operate, with coded merchandise and electronic wands, or with buttons marked with the item purchased (as in fast food chains) and less programmed to change prices without the cashier even needing to know. Such innovation, because it allows employment of persons (with fewer skills) at lower wages, cuts costs.* (This has important implications for the shift from manufacturing to service employment in U.S. cities.)

---

* If legislation or union organization effectively prohibited such low wage employment (as they prohibit child labour, the ten-hour day, and work under a variety of dangerous conditions) then the innovation would not be made, and the cash register designers would be instructed to look for other ways of cutting costs. More radical departures in technology, such as the celebrated silicon electronic chip, or robot control of machine production, also are developed under conditions that guarantee they will be appropriate for centralized control. The current emphasis, by government and industry alike, on nuclear rather than solar power, is another example. These innovations, as mentioned, also concentrate participation, that is, tey lead to unemployment. This, of course, is an impact that can be treated separately from the technique, if the latter could be separated from control. Cost cutting and unemployment could be spread around; nothing but social arrangements prohibits this. If there is 20 per cent employment, than all could work 8 hours less each week, with no one unemployed. Such social innovation, however, is made less likely by the technology that concentration produces.[22]

The core of the private market system, the driving force at the centre, is the search for profit that is derived from employing people who produce more than they are paid. It is here that profitability, technological change, and the pressure from workers for higher wages come into clearest conflict. Workers try to take home more of the value of what they produce, which is determined by their wages (fought for in direct negotiation, strikes, etc., and in general rises in the standard of living) and by the social wage (government services, social security, health benefits, etc.). The more workers are successful, the less businessmen have left over after buying materials, amortizing their plant and equipment, and paying for services. Here, in the distribution of control over production and its proceeds, originates the inequality that appears later in the distribution of rewards, in income, and in goods and services.

These inequalities are augmented by those of race and sex, and they are exacerbated by problems of violent crime, environmental degradation, neighbourhood decay, and decline of social services. From such a situation there naturally arises resistance, which in the absence of overt repression is likely to lead to organization and social and political struggle.* The purpose of the remainder of this paper is to see how the process of urbanization arranges and mediates the geography of this profitability and inequality.

II. The City and the Economy

The geographical imprint of these social and economic forces is not constant. It tends sometimes toward uneveness, sometimes toward territorial equality. Much discussion of urban and regional economics understandably focuses on these large territorial questions. Thus Manchester was a booming city, Cleveland is now in decline; Sao Paulo is thriving, as are U.S. southwestern cities, but the northeast megalopolis is in trouble.[23] What follows, in contrast, focuses on some of the details of growth and decline. In particular, a close examination shows that there is much poverty with growth, much wealth in decline. In both cases there exists an urban underclass, whose condition is an outcome of market and political processes.

----

* As Wolfe writes (p.25): "Hence it should come as no surprise that the major theorist of the new capitalism, Jeremy Bentham, was also the major theorist of police reform."

For present purposes, let us divide history into four rather vague periods and take examples from the development of cities in the northeastern and midwestern areas of the United States. The first period is from the beginnings of rapid urban growth, in the early to mid-19th century, until World War I. The second period goes until about the Second World War. The third runs from then through about 1970; the last period, until the present. We shall see how both expansion and decline are accompanied by a process of distribution that is uneven, creating both wealth and poverty, often in the same urban area. In each period the connection between business expansion (at local, national, and international levels) and distribution (with local consequences) is crucial.[24]

A. The Engines of Industry

The period of rapid urban growth coincided with the maturing of American industrial capitalism. Take Cleveland as the first example.[25] From 1830 until 1870 the city grew at least 70 per cent each decade. From 1870 until 1920, while the country's urban population shifted from one-quarter to over one-half the total, Cuyahoga County, which encompassed the Cleveland urban area, grew by nearly 50 per cent each decade. In 1870, following the opening of the Ohio and Soo Canals and the rise of Civil War demand for iron, steel and chemicals, there were 180,000 people. In 1910, with over half-a-million people, Cleveland was the sixth largest city in the U.S. By 1920, after an intense period of industrial development that included the founding of Standard Oil, growth and consolidation of iron and steel works, various enterprises of heavy manufacturing, food processing and textiles, ship building and auto manufacturing (Peerless and White Motors), the metropolitan population was just over a million. Expansion continued throughout the 1920s, as American business merged, consolidated, and centralized control. (The most prominent merger in Cleveland was Republic Steel.) Many forutnes were made in this period. In Cleveland those of Mark Hanna, the National City Bank, Standard Oil of Ohio, and Cyrus Eaton are well known examples.

At the beginning of this period (which in part preceded the growth of Cleveland), accumulation took place through the destruction and replacement of small producers by industry. Here the connection between accumulation and distribution is clear. Impoverishment of the labour force and the rapid expansion of class inequality were counterparts of the more centralized control over capital. This transformation from self-employment of farmers and urban artisans to an urban proletariat has been clearly depicted in the history of

Philadelphia. From the turn of the century until 1860, there were decades of resistance, but by the end artisans and migrants had been roughly demoted, not "picked up" by concentrating capital, and owners had become an opulent elite.[26]

Later, when industry was being further concentrated both for technical and political reasons, the drive for profits centred on vast programs of plant expansion in heavy industry, on the assembly of large labour forces and the concentration of markets, and on the many efficiencies that urbanization made available. The stratification and exploitation continued but on a much larger scale. Breaking the power of factory workers now became a most important prerequisite for growth and profits. As Catherine Stone has shown, in the early steel industry "the men ran the mill and the foreman had little authority." The crucial battle to change this took place when in 1892 Andrew Carnegie transferred control of his Homestead mill to Henry Frick, who made use of barbed wire fences, the sheriff and the State Militia, 300 armed Pinkertons, and a barracks for strikebreakers to kill dozens of men and break the union. Union memebership was 25,000 that year; by 1910 there was no steel union.[27] Worker organization was repressed by industrialists promoting conflict between immigrants and natives, between blacks and whites, by urban political machinery whose function was "much like that a banage has for running score,"[28] by suburbanizing production to protect plants from urban mods,* and as in the Homestead case at times by raw, armed violence.

In Gary, Indiana, where in 1909 U.S. Steel finished the largest and most modern plant in the world, high profits and rapid growth took a heavy toll from eastern and southern European immigrants:

----

* Pullman and U.S. Steel both utilized suburban operations to minimize worker organization. Pullman, incorrectly, thought his company town would work this way. "With such surrounding and such human regard for the needs of the body as well as the soul...the disturbing conditions of strikes and other troubles that periodically convulse the world of labour would not need to be feared here."[29] Around the suburban Gary steel works the Grand Calumet Canal was rechannelled to resemble "a veritable moat in times of stress... Perhaps no great industrial plant...occupies a position so impregnable to mob attack and so calculated to withstand a prolonged industrial siege."[30] See also Gordon's analysis of industrial suburbanization to escape labour demands.[31]

> . . . Poverty was only the beginning of their misfortune. Their working conditions in the mills were grim. Although the average American manufacturing work week was sixty hours, the 'new migrant' steel workers put in six twelve-hour days each week. (On the other hand, even in prosperous years, the average labourer could anticipate about two months of unemployment) The work was so physically taxing that 'old age at forty' was the popular expression of the day. And it was frightfully dangerous; each year a quarter of the unskilled workers were injured or killed on the job.[32]

The massive concentration gave rise to very large holdings of profits and political power. The concentration of industry also led to concentration of workers in crowded cities; their miserable conditions followed. Lincoln Steffens described St. Louis at the time of the 1904 World's Fair:

> The visitor is told of the wealth of the residents, of the financial strength of the banks, and of the growing importance of industries, yet he sees poorly-paved, refuse-burdened streets and dusty or mud-covered alleys; he passes a ramshackle fire-trap, crowded with the sick, and learns that is the City Hospital. . . . Finally, he turns a tap in the hotel, to see liquid mud flow into wash basin or bath tub.[33]

For many residents of Gary, low wages for the "new migrant" steel workers meant that for a man with a family:

> . . . his wife and children were obliged to enter the labour market to work to supplement his income. Alternatively, if he saved up enough to purchase a house, his 'wife (was) a drudge and slave(d) incessantly for her household,' which was filled with paying boarders.
>
> The infant mortality rates among the children of the unskilled workers were over double of those of the skilled workers. Even at the end of World War I—after real wages had increased one-third from their pre-war level—two-thirds of the children of Gary's foreign born workers had no milk, fruit, or eggs in their daily diet. Over half of them had no vegetables. . . and one-third lacked any meat.[34]

Things were probably worse for the half of the immigrants, doubtless the least able to succeed, who returned to Europe.

It is at the end of this period when the American economy reached maturity. There was a transition from rapidly growing competitive capitalism, in which busts were overridden by booms, to monopoly capitalism, in which overproduction, stagnation, and related problems began to seem endemic, except insofar as they were avoided by war mobilization.[35]

B. From Boom through Depression

In the second period, sometime before 1920—in response to new attempts at unionization, to rapid increases in industrial productivity and the increasing division of labour, to widespread hostility to the monopolies, and the need for purchasing power to allow continued industrial expansion—there emerged an economic dualism, in which the competitive sector began to stagnate and a dynamic monopoly sector, with wages increasing along with productivity, began to cooperate with the growing state.[36]

By the 1920s this dualism began to be expressed in several ways in big industrial cities. First, the very prosperity of the rapidly growing cities was a reflection of the concentration in them large, monopoly, industrial establishments. It also reflected the separation and concentration of head office activity from plants themselves, an important component of the mergers.[37] An extended hierarchy of economic activity began to appear, so that even as big cities began to exhibit less and less of their regional "character,"[38] they became uniformly more distinct from small cities and the hinterland.

Second, the configuration of the cities allowed the appearance of general prosperity in the midst of continued inequality and poverty. With a segment of the industrial workforce beginning to be well paid, the poor could begin to be isolated in neighbourhoods and, as we have subsequently seen, blamed for their own poverty.* There was plenty of poverty and even unempoloyment in the 1920s—estimates range from an average of 5 to 13 per cent[40] but the buoyancy of the top segement of the dual economy kept them partly hidden. Accumulation in this period was then logically accompanied by the growth of a reasonably well off and residentially separated industrial workforce, who shared in the prosperity of increasing productivity, and who, in contrast to their European counterparts, who had gone through the destruction of the war, could support a liberal image of unending urban progress.[41]

----

* Engels, in a brilliant presursor of urban ecological studies, noted how the spatial arrangement of Manchester allowed the bourgeoisie to avoid seeing the residences of the working classes.[39]

When the Great Depression came, industrial cities were hard hit, and the miserable part of the economy, previously manifested in a substantial inequality, became pervasive. Still, the hardest hit segments of the population were the bottom of the industrial workforce, who were laid off with no cushion, and, in the case of black workers, concentrated in the most difficult and dangerous jobs. Immigrant workers from Mexico were deported from industrial cities, the legal proceedings being arranged by the steel companies.[42] (Fifty years later we observe similar responses to recession in European countries with international migrant workers.) The political response to the depression, manifested in more state participation and power in the economy as well as in the establishment of safeguards for labour against future calamities, provided the rules for future growth.

Throughout this extended period, which may be stretched to run from some time before World War I through most of World War II, urban inequality was politically managed—contained, in a strong geographical sense—by the cities themselves, within their jusisdictional boundaries. In prosperous times, especially, poverty was masked in neighbourhoods segregated by class, and when it escaped into public view it was filtered through visions of unending progress and mobility. City governments were able to provide services to the majority, and the commercial, industrial, and cultural hegemony of the city was never in doubt.

C. The False victory of Liberalism

As war production expanded slowly in 1941 and more rapidly in the following years, then investment, production, and employment in U.S. industrial cities grew rapidly. Between 1939 and 1946, for example, the value of manufactured goods in Cleveland (Cuyahoga County) multiplied nearly 2.7 times; the industrial payroll grew 2.8 times.[43] This growth continued, throughout the decade of the 1950s, with real force, in some places through the 1960s and until the 1974 recession. Incomes for Americans rose rapidly in these years, as they accompanied rapid increases in productivity and investment. This was the period of flushed success of the American dream, of suburban expansion, of more housing, more space, more highways and cars, more of everything for metropolitan populations. Median family income (including inflation) increased from $1200 in 1939, to $3200 in 1950, to $5200 in 1960, to $8900 in 1970. Growth of industrial production from 1947 until 1970 averaged 4.5 per cent per year. Gross national product, in constant dollars, doubled from 1947 to 1965. Corporate profits after taxes trebled from 1950 to 1974.[44]

In these 30-odd years, urban industrial growth in the United States seemed for many to be strongly associated with the abatement of poverty and with the disappearance of an impoverished class working at low wages or on relief. Perhaps the most succinct statement of this stance on cities is Banfield's in 1968:

> The plain fact is that the overwhelming majority of city dwellers live more comfortably and conveniently than ever before. They have more and better housing, more and better schools, more and better transportation, and so on. By any conceivable measure of material welfare the present generation of urban Americans is, on the whole, better off than any other large group of people has ever been anywhere. What is more, there is every reason to expect that the general level of comfort and convenience will continue to rise at an even more rapid rate through the foreseeable future.[45]

This growth, however, had its counterpoint. The ideologues of the period, who convinced themselves that all was working smoothly on the urban scene, ignored the immense inequality, by this time mostly racial, of the urban areas. The U.S. Civil Rights Commission held hearings in Cleveland in 1966, for example, and theirs not a typical findings revealed a pattern of police brutality, segregated and inadequate schooling and housing for blacks, and discrimination in employment and labour unions. The drop-out rate for black high school students (14%) was twice that for whites. Median family income for blacks was only $4,768; for whites it was 54% higher. There were only 17 black apprentices among more than 1000 in Cleveland's 22 building trade unions, only 13 blacks among more than 2000 police officers. Blacks comprised 38% of the population, 29% of the municipal employees (in low paying jobs) and only 17% of the employed labour force.[46] The riots that came to Cleveland (soon after the hearings) also came to several hundred other American cities.[47] Investigations that followed the riots left no doubt of the poverty in which rapid postwar urban growth had either pushed or left many people.

It is quite possible that one of the strongest reasons for the myopic estimates of uniform progress pronounced by these who saw an "end of ideology" is precisely the fact that much of the poverty associated with this period of accumulation was the poverty of black people. Just as the worst off members of the working class were hidden in the 19th century by strict class separation, and then in the early 20th century by neighbourhood arrangements, by income and class isolation, so in this later period blacks were hidden by their "invisibility."

This invisibility was helped along by two national trends, both of which were strongly influential in the industrial cities. The first was the shift from manufacturing to service employment, the second was shift of jobs and then residences from city to suburb. This dual transformation had dramatic results. Even as the general economy continued to grow rapidly, the shift out of manufacturing into the lower paying service sector resulted in lower incomes and lower rates of growth of employment than adequate for the urban populations. This relegated ever larger numbers of people into poverty. Furthermore, the suburbanization of business along with the better off of the population—both thereby being removed from the central city's taxing (and schooling) jurisdiction—led poor and otherwise needy people to be left behind with insufficient power to finance their affairs. As a planner for the city of Cleveland noted:

> The process of suburbanization is selective in that those employed in higher paying, more prestigious occupations are more likely to have the resources to move from the central city to the surrounding suburbs.[48]

This segregation by income and race has even psychological manifestations, with serious political consequences. As Sennett suggests, a set of adolescent attitudes, based on vicarious rather than real experience with social differences and conflict, is developed in the minds of suburbanites. These people, who then govern the most influential economic and political isntitutions, are unable to resolve the most crucial problems.[49] In this way a colonial attitude is superimposed on the problem of invisibility.

D. Stagflation

If in the post-war boom most attention was turned to the benefits of urban and economic growth, then, after the first phase of ghetto riots had passed and a brief feeling of official smugness had been worried off, by the mid-1970s most attention on northern industrial cities was turned to their decline. Suddenly it was all Cowboys versus Yankees, sunbelt growth versus frostbelt decline. The liberal view of post-war progress and general prosperity had been clouded in the 1960s by evidence of racism, inequality, and severe urban dependency. But in the 1970s the cloud seemed to rain poverty on the majorities of big city people in the northeast.

Although the roots of these tendencies can be found long before, by the mid-1970s the statistics do indicate dramatic urban difficulties in the north, not only for black but also for white urban populations. The true picture is of course more complex. Northeastern cities have suffered most. But compared to previous periods of rapid growth, the entire north is stagnant. Though not by any means the worst case, the figures for Cleveland, once again, are instructive. Cleveland lost 14 per cent of its population and 17 per cent of its jobs in the 1960s. Between 1970 and 1976 the 4-county Cleveland metropolitan region had net annual loss of 2,200 jobs. From 1969 to 1976 the metropolitan area lost 21 per cent of its manufacturing employment, some 65,000 jobs. Manufacturing production jobs have gone down even more rapidly, by 25 per cent. In the city of Cleveland, since 1947, more than half of all production jobs have been lost.[50]

The impact on the people of Cleveland has been tremendous. Already by 1969, the median urban family income in the U.S. ($10,196) was 12 per cent above Cleveland's ($9,107). Nearly a quarter of the families in Cleveland earned less than $5,000 that year. From 1950 to 1960 the number of welfare recipients increased by 18 per cent; the following decade they increased by 59 per cent. In 1977, 33 per cent of all children in Cleveland received welfare payments (ADC).[51]

Unemployment in Cleveland (which probably is grossly understated compared to national figures because it counts neither discouraged workers nor those who have migrated from the city after losing or not finding jobs) was until 1977 consistently higher than unemployment in the metropolitan area, the state, or the nation, often being between nine and twelve per cent. Since 1978 rates for the state of Ohio have been the same as Cleveland's about 8 per cent in late 1980.[52]

Health conditions in Cleveland today are very poor. The premature birth rate (which is associated with serious illness, such as retardation, blindness, and cerebral palsy) in 1975 was 43 per cent higher in Cleveland than in the state of Ohio. In 1977, the state of Ohio reported that 14 per cent of the state's children were not in compliance with its immunization program for communicable diseases. In Cleveland things are more than twice as bad: nearly one-third of Cleveland's children were not in compliance.[53]

Other conditions are equally poor. It was estimated in 1976 that 40 per cent of all 7th grade students in Cleveland will never finish high school! (The rate is probably about 15 per cent for the state of Ohio.) Of those who remain, Cleveland's 10th graders in 1975 scored far below the national norms for reading scores.

11th GRADE 1979 READING SCORES

	United States	Cleveland
Top U.S. Third	23%	6%
Middle U.S. Third	54%	45%
Lowest U.S. Third	23%	49.1%

In Cleveland 35 per cent of the housing units were substandard in 1976. More than half of all Cleveland's households were eligible in 1970 for housing assistance, but only 14 per cent of those eligible were getting it.

In this period as earlier, the most dismal aspect of Cleveland's contemporary crisis is racial. Theoretically the rise, stagnation, and decline of the city could have happened without racism, but it is impossible to know in America if this would have been the case. There is a sizeable group of successful black businessmen and professionals,* but for the most part the black population of Cleveland is the poorest segment. It is also the least employed and in the worst jobs. Its children have the worst time in school. Its health rate is lowest. And it is segregated into the most crowded and poorest housing in the city. This is the segment of the population in Cleveland (as Puerto Ricans, other Hispanics, and other minorities in other cities) that bears the largest portion of the costs of uneven growth and decline.

---

* There is in many cities a notable group of black professionals and businessmen and women. In Cleveland, e.g., 247 black men and 76 black women earned $25,000 or more in 1969. (The figures for Hispanic men and women were 149 and 9, respectively.) There were in addition 139 blacks and 287 Hispanics who earned over $15,000. For black families, the figures were 965 ($25,000) and 8674 ($15,000), out of 77,808 families, a total of 12%, compared to a national figure of 17% for black families and 40% for white families in 1969. For comparison, there were over 138,000 non-black families who earned over $15,000 in Cleveland that year, about 31%.

All of these difficulties, of course, have "neighbourhood" effects, not least of all on the administration of public offices in the city. Response in Cleveland has meant the virtually forced fund raising sales of the city's zoo (1970, for $1 million), the sewer treatment plant (1973, $3 million), and the transit system (1975, $9 million) to metropolitan authorities; has led to struggles regarding sale of the electric generation and distribution system (MUNY) to a private utility; and (on December 15, 1978) resulted in the first major U.S. city bond default since Detroit in 1933. The city's remaining capital plant is still dismally in need of repair and renovation. Sound estimates call for $250 to $500 million for the water system, another $150 million for 30% of the city's several hundred bridges rated unsatisfactory or intolerable, and $340 million for the sewer system simply to avoid flooding. Experts attribute the problem to lack of maintenance plus aging and obsolescence. They also conclude the problems are shared by many other cities in the north.[54] These problems also arise with private industry. For example, multi-storey heavy industrial plants are inefficient to use but too costly to tear down, and they blight neighbourhoods, prevent alternative development, and lose tax revenue.

The widely accepted opinion that there has been aggravated decline in the northern industrial areas is, then, basically sound. But, following the analysis of the other periods, we should ask if the critically high unemployment, dependency, and neighbourhood difficulty in northern cities (particularly of black, central city residents) has been matched by a severe retardation in accumulation. What has happened to business?

In this period of generlized decline there have been, to be sure, massive shutdowns and layoffs in steel, rubber, automobile, and other industrial plants. There have been plant closing, much more extensive generalized disinvestment, and markedly slowed population growth, or decline. But what has been the impact on profits? In the midst of a period of crisis, and before the changes are played out, it is of course difficult to know, and it is also difficult to isolate the industrial cities from the rest of the economy. Nevertheless, it is clear that the crisis of the cities is not equally a crisis of their corporations. Take, once again, Cleveland as an example. Although the population of the Cleveland metropolitan area declined by 4.3 per cent from 1970 to 1975, all metropolitan areas combined in the state of Ohio only declined by one per cent in the entire decade, to 1980, and the state's non-metropolitan population grew by 9.2 per cent. Non-agricultural employment in the state grew 14 per cent from 1960 to 1978.[55] The economy is not entirely stagnant. Cleveland, itself, after New York, Chicago, and probably Los

Angeles, is by volume of sales the third or fourth largest U.S. centre of major corporate headquarters. Forty-one of its corporations are among the Fortune Top 1000. Their worldwide sales were $5 billion in 1962. By 1972 sales had grown over 12 per cent a year, to $15.6 billion. They grew an additional 14 per cent per year to a 1975 total of $23 billion. (Even when deflated by the Consumer Price Index, the annual increment is 7 3/4 per cent over 13 years.)[56]

Indeed, there is a segment of the business community that envisions Cleveland as a centre of multinational banking, finance, and services.[57] Even in the manufacturing sector alone, where the employment decline has been greatest, there have been dramatic increases in value-added. "Sales and receipts of the establishments engaged in (manufacturing, trade, and selected services) have grown at a considerably greater rate than employment." "In short," states a report by the Cleveland City Planning Commission, "businesses and industries in the Cleveland area are healthy and growing in terms of sales and production. It is their capacity to employ the available labour force at adequate wages that is questionable."[58] Even in the city of Cleveland, at least until 1967, while employment in manufacturing was falling, value-added increased by 20 per cent from 1954, and capital investments by 93 per cent.[59]

The Geography of Poverty and Profit

First, a quick review. The complexity of urban development in the United States over te past 150 years can be understood in terms of epochs in which investment and low wages stand in varying relations to one another. In the earliest period of rapid urbanization the situation can be compared to Manchester's industrial revolution, to Sao Paulo's progress with poverty: profits were made directly from the labour of a brusquely crushed class of migrants, independent farmers and artisans, who became workers in small factories. Somewhat later, large industries came to dominate northern cities, and profits were won also through more efficient arrangment of large-scale production which went hand in hand with destruction of organization and control by workers. These are the familiar pictures, in which Dicken's England is reproduced, though in the U.S. less severely and for a smaller portion of the population, mostly for the European immigrants, freed slaves, and their children. In those times, poverty and profit were linked directly in particular U.S. cities.

Later when a well-off industrial workforce was created in the monopolies, poorly paid workers in competitive business were segregated and isolated. Vast fortunes were made in industry, still in part based directly on an impoverished workforce, but the accompanying poverty was closeted in neighbourhoods. The separation of corporate finance and planning from management, from production, began to take place, so that profits in production were also likely to be somewhat more concentrated, low wages in some places, profits in others.

From the Second World War until 1960 or later, with enormous accumulation of capital in the American economy, many viewers saw no accompanying poverty, until it was pointed out in The Other America, until the Civil Rights Commissions began their hearings. The complex geography of the global division of labour makes the connection between accumulation and urban poverty more difficult to specify.

In sharp contrast, in the most recent period, northern industrial cities have declined, and but for transfer payments, the poverty of their residents would grow much more severe, through unemployment, lower real wages, and cuts in services. Although it is frequently assumed that this decline can be generalized, and that business is losing as well, the situation is complex. For much business, there are losses, but as we have seen for Cleveland, many large corporations, even in the northeastern cities, continue to be profitable and even to invest locally. To oversimplify the case, there is profit in decline.

These cases of urban growth and accompanying poverty, and urban distress and accompanying profits, are overly abstract notions, which require elaboration. The more recent periods are, of cours, vastly different from the industrial revolution. The current recessions are different from the 1930s. One principal transformation with strong effects on the nature of urban growth and the position of the underclass is the globalization of the economy. In some respects, it makes no sense to speak of "urban economies" even 150 years ago as though they operated in isolation. It makes no sense whatsoever in today's cities. The profits of Cleveland corporations during the city's recent loss of population and manufacturing employment, for example, are in large part derived from operations those corporations control outside Cleveland, outside Ohio, and outside the United States. Furthermore, the corporations "belong" significantly less to Cleveland: for example, the per centage of large manufacturing plants controlled by interests outside Cleveland grew from 27 per cent in 1968 to 40 per cent in 1972.[60]

By most accounts a worldwide capitalist economy has existed from the 16th century. Since then, at least, productive wealth has always been accumulated in cities, from mercantile activity, from war and plunder, from investment elsewhere, and from local production of goods and services. In recent periods in the U.S. we have been made particularly sensitive—and properly so—to relations that appear almost mercantile, as capitalist profits are transferred from one city or region of the country or world to another. There is no doubt of the power of large corporations to suck dry the surplus product of a region in order to invest it elsewhere, leaving the first stranded and without command over its destiny. These are matters of the first political importance. But there is danger that in our attempts to deal with these problems we will lose sight of the fact that an underclass would be created, has been created, in cities not being exploited by other places. Thus we are inclined not to identify problems of the underclass in booming cities, such as Houston or Dallas, and we are similarly inclined to think underclass problems in declining cities such as Cleveland would disappear if interregional capital loss were stemmed. Nothing could be further from the truth, theoretically and practically.

The history of urban accumulation and poverty, when examined in light of our understanding of how market forces work, suggests why this is so. In a nutshell, the argument is that the normal operation of capitalist production and exchange leads to inequality: there is private ownership of profits that result from workers producing more than they are paid.* First consider the role of the state. In the early period, typified by the destruction of artisans in Philadelphia, the government was seen precisely as providing the condition for unfettered labour markets. (Alan Wolfe calls it the Accumulative State.) Remember, Adam Smith's **Wealth of Nations**, published only a few years earlier (1776) was a defense of this position, which openly argued for the need of inequality (and severe poverty and loss of skills by workers) to allow accumulation. The state helped make this legitimate, through legislation and in other ways, for example, in the general abdication of power to private corporations. It also enforced inequality ultimately with centralized control of violence, used, for example, when the police and national guard were employed as strike breakers, as at Andrew Carnegie's Homestead Steel plant. Still later the state expanded its strictly urban functions: for example, the provision of utilities, public services, even streets so business-

---

* If there is interregional division of labour, then certain segments of the exchange system can be without any underclass (Scarsdale and Scandinavia are examples) because wealth there can be based on accumulation and poverty elsewhere.

men could get to work from suburbs without seeing the slums, then land use regulation to protect both industry and the middle class from competition by the poor. Throughout this entire period the state regulated immigration, going so far as to expel foreign steel workers in the Depression. By the 1950s, the state and the economy had become so thoroughly entwined that, you will recall, it was President Eisenhower who warned of the "military-industrial complex." The most urban of these entanglements was activity magnifying the race, class, and fiscal separation of cities and suburbs: principally the FHA suburban home mortgage guarantees and the Interstate Highway Act. In the period of stagflation, the state has acted in numerous ways to make foreign investment feasible, which contributes to the decline of U.S. cities, and, most recently, it has acted to reduce business taxes by assaulitng hard-won protection and provision of public services: less stringent pollution requirements, higher transit rider fees, etc. All these activities help provide conditions whereby profits can be made and kept concentrated.

Profitable investment appears as a mainstay of the dynamics of urbanization in each of the periods we have looked at. Urban growth is, in this market economy, basically a function of private investment, which is in turn a function of the expectation of profits. When the Philadelphia capitalists struggled against artisans, they saw potential profits in the reorganization and exploitation involved in their urban investments. When Carnegie and Frick reorganized steel production, they were quite explicit about the way new investment could make more profits by manipulating the urban labour force, including moving it to the suburbs. When the corporations separated head offices from production plants, to f'nd cheap labour and avoid unions, they also arranged the geography of their investment to insure profits. When Cleveland multinationals now gradually disinvest there, they do so to take advantage of profitable opportunities in other cities and places. All these decisions, narrowly rational, are enforced by competition.

Technological innovation further contributes to the urban changes. Manchester capitalists depended on the introduction (not the invention) of the machine loom and the steam engine to make concentrated (urban) use of the helpless labour expelled from the rural areas. Rapid industrialization in the northern U.S. cities depended heavily on the railroads, on machine making, and on the assembly line, which further encouraged agglomeration of population, as well as an agricultural technology to push farmers from the land, while concentrating control. The automobile (and truck) made industrial suburbanization (which preceded suburbanization of population) possible; and cheap transportation, dependable communication and machine-aided administration facilitated separation of office and factory, and later, the building of the global economy. Technological innovation also plays an ironic role in interurban conflict: older cities were built with transport arrangements and factories that do not remain competitive (or functional, as with Cleveland's sewer system), and maintenance or replacement with alternative systems is prohibitively expensive in comparison with new plant or infrastructure.

All of this is conditioned by the competitive struggle for more efficient use of labour, as a "factor of production," either by making it more productive, by cutting its wages, or by replacing it with machines. All the way through the urban history from the early 19th century until today, the need to reduce costs in face of competition makes poverty the natural counterpoint of profit.

There is one additional element to the story. The poverty engenders resistance. And, potentially at least, the resistance leads to enhanced consciousness and political organization. In order to emphasize the bare economic outlines of uneven urban development, I have left resistance and politics out of this account. As a consequence, to the extent my arguments are of use, it will be because they make it impossible to avoid acknowledging that capitalist growth generates poverty. But here, in conclusion, mention must be made of the other part of the story, for resistance and politics precisely will be more and more the mainsprings for change.

Resistance to exploitation has been an influential element over the entire urban history we have dealth with. In Manchester there were constant rebellions; at times the city was lost to the working class mobs. In Sao Paulo there is brutal repression by well-equipped policemen and soldiers. In Chicago, Gary, Cleveland, and other U.S. cities there were struggles at factory gates and in city streets. In Harlem, Bedford-Stuyvesant, Hough and hundreds of other ghettos there have been riots. The debates over the causes of rebellions and their immediate consequences—whether they arise in times of acute stress or are stimulated by rapid change, and whether they are the negotiations they provoke lead to material improvement or cooptation—are not pertinent here. What is important is that this more or less continuous series of rebellions provides strong evidence of resistance, which is an essential ingredient for political organization. Another element is the existence of related social movements, such as the Welfare Rights Movement of the 1960s and 1970s.

Whether such a radical politics will grow is an open question. U.S. cities have seen populist and socialist parties in the past, in the 1890s and 1910s, for example, and there are now scattered cases of socialist or populist municipal governments throughout the country. One possibility, perhaps optimistic, is that there is a very long struggle ahead, in which locally based democratic action—to control city hall, to take over shut down plants, to provide social services—will ascend to influence national politics so that the roots of poverty in the free-market economy will be attacked.

FOOTNOTES

1. Marx, p. 799.
2. The words are by G. Gissing, **Introduction to Oliver Twist** (1900), quoted by Williams, p. 224.
3. Marx, p. 785.
4. Allison, p. 205.
5. On price reductions, Smelser, pp. 147-156; other statistics, Vigier, pp. 129, 139, Tables 5 and 7.
6. **Sao Paulo**, p. 46, emphasis added. This little book is, to my mind, the best case study relating capital accumulation and urban poverty, and I have learned much from its methodology. It is worth noting that the authorities in Sau Paulo have made public their great displeasure with the book.
7. Ibid., p. 14.
8. Ibid., pp. 18-19.
9. Shirley, pp. 164-165.
10. This approach is consistent with much work in international development economics. The old theory stated, with little equivocation, that severe inequality—therefore poverty—was an essential ingredient of capitalist growth. Liberal theorizing simply drops the analytical connection between production and distribution, in an attempt to force basic equality into being, without accompanying structural changes. New conservatives, on the other hand, see the old connections and insist once again that inequality be made to play its part in operating accumulation. What they miss is the extent to which politics will resist such repression. The only alternative is structural change. See Goldsmith, 1978.
11. See, e.g., Heilbroner.
12. **New York Times**, Business Section, Friday, Feb.13, 1981.
13. **Morgan Guarantee Survey**, quoted in Sweezy and Magdoff.
14. Ibid.
15. **Business Week** (Dec.15, 1980).

16. See Sweezy and Magdoff.
17. Campanario.
18. Dowd, p. 79.
19. For one such argument, see O'Connor.
20. Gordon, "Capitalist Efficiency."
21. Braverman.
22. See, e.g., Bluestone and Harrison, Brous, Markusen, Goldsmith (1978) which relate these regional shifts to economics and politics.
23. Castells.
24. For the information on Cleveland throughout, I am indebted to two research assistants, Cynthia Coleman and Jeffrey Coleman.
25. Warner, Chs. 1-4.
26. Stone, pp. 65-66.
27. Dowd, p. 169.
28. Beaker, **Marshall Field**, quoted in Greer, p. 64.
29. Taylor, **Satellite Cities**, p. 180, quoted in Greer, too.
30. Gordon, "Class Struggle."
31. Greer, p. 76.
32. Steffens, P. 31, quoted in Dowd, p. 168.
33. Greer, pp. 76-77.
34. Dowd, pp. 86, 91ff.
35. Ibid.
36. Hymer, and Goldsmith, 1977.
37. Markusen.
38. See part 3, "The Great Towns."
39. Dowd, pp. 88, 91. National unemployment estimates were 12 per cent in 1980, 1914, and 1915.
40. On the destruction of liberalism in Great Britain and Europe see Carr, Ch. 2. Also see Goldsmith and Roth.
41. Greer, p. 90.
42. Bonner, p. 21.
43. U.S. Census data.
44. Banfield, p. 4.
45. Coleman.
46. Mueller, p. 1 ff.
47. Bonner, p. 33.
48. Semaj has reported on related problems.
49. Knight, "Economic Transition. . ."
50. These statistics have been collected from numerous sources and compiled in **The Cleveland Profile**.
51. U.S. Department of Labour.
52. **Cleveland Profile**. Statistics for health, reading scores, and housing.
53. Humphrey, Wilson and Peterson.
54. U.S. Census reports.
55. Knight, **Cleveland**.

56. Ibid.
57. Bonner, pp. 73-75.
58. Ibid.
59. Donahey.

REFERENCES

Allison, Lincoln. "Association Football and the Urban Ethos," in Wirth and Jones, pp. 203-228.

Ammans, Linda. "Unequal Justice: Cleveland's Other Default," **Encore** 8 (Feb., 1979).

Banfield, Edward C. **The Unheavenly City** (Boston: Little, Brown, 1968).

Bluestone, Barry and Bennett Harrison. **Capital and Communities** (Washington: The Progressive Alliance, 1980).

Bonner, Ernest. **Employment and Income** (Cleveland City Planning Commission,).

Braverman, Harry. **Labor and Monopoly Capital** (New York: Monthly Review Press, 1974)

Brous, Ira. "Economic Decline of the Northeast: Capital Flight and Counter-planning," **Working Papers in Planning** WP #38 (Department of City and Regional Planning, Cornell University: Ithaca, NY, 1980).

Campanario, Milton. "Land Rent and the Reproduction of Labor Force: Some Evidence from Sao Paulo," unpublished Ph.D. thesis, Cornell University, 1981.

Carr, E.H. **What Is History** (New York: Vintage Books, 1961).

Castells, Manuel. "Multi-National Capitalism, National States and Local Communities," 1980.

Clavel, Pierre, John Forester, and William W. Goldsmith, eds. **Urban and Regional Planning in an Age of Austerity** (New York: Pergamon Press, 1980).

Cleveland Profile, Published by the Greater Cleveland Inter church Council (1978).

Cohen, Robert "Cleveland's Future as an International City: The Globalization of U.S. Business," unpublished manuscript, c. 1980.

Coleman, Cynthia. "Corporate Control versus Populism: A Comparative Study of Five Cleveland Mayors," manuscript, 1979.

Donahey, Kierain. "Corporate State and Capital Flight in Cleveland," unpublished manuscript, Cornell University, 1981.

Dowd, Douglas E. **The Twisted Dream: Capitalist Development in the United States Since 1776** (Cambridge, Mass.: Winthrop, 1974).

Engels, Frederick. **The Condition of the Working-Class in England** (Moscow: Progress, 1973).

Goldsmith, William W. "The War on Development," **Monthly Review** (March 1977).

__________ "Marxism and Regional Policy, An Introduction," **Review of Radical Political Economy**, Vol.10 (Fall, 1978), pp. 13-17.

Goldsmith, William W. and Deborah Roth. "The Myths of Planning," Department of City and Regional Planning Working Paper #15, Cornell University, January 1979.

Gordon, David M. "Class Struggle and the Stages of American Urban Development," in Perry and Watkins.

__________, "Capitalist Efficiency and Socialist Efficiency," **Monthly Review** (July-Aug., 1976).

Greer, Edward. **Big Steel: Black Politics and Corporate Power in Gary, Indiana** (New York: Monthly Review Press, 1979).

Heilbroner, Robert. "Inflationary Capitalism," **The New Yorker**, Oct. 8, 1979, pp. 121-127.

Humphrey, Nancy, George Peterson and Peter Wilson. "The Future of Cleveland's Capital Plant," (Washington, D.C.: The Urban Institute, 1979

Hymer, Stephen. "The Multinational Corporation and the Law of Uneven Development, in J.N. Bhagwati, ed., **Economics and the World Order from the 1970s to the 1990s** (New York: Macmillan, 1972).

Knight, Richard V. "Economic Transition and Opportunity: Corporate Headquarters and the Future of Cleveland" (Greater Cleveland Growth Association, n.d.).

__________, "The Cleveland Economy in Transition" (Cleveland: State University, 1977).

Markusen Ann. "Regionalism and the Capitalist State," in Clavel, et al. (1980).

__________, "Regions and Regionalism: A Marxist View," Working Paper 326, June 1980.

Marshall, Dan and OPIC, eds. **The Battle of Cleveland: Public Interest Challenges Corporate Power** (Washington, D.C.: Conference on Alternative State and Local Policies, 1979).

Marx, Karl. **Capital**, Vol.I (New York: Vintage, 1977).

Mueller, Carol E. "Riot Negotiations: Conditions of Successful Bargaining in the Urban Riots of 1967 and 1968," unpublished Ph.D. thesis, Cornell University, 1971.

New York Times, February 11, 1981, p. D9.

O'Connor, James. **The Fiscal Crisis of the State** (New York: St. Martin's, 1973).

Perry, David C. and Alfred J. Watkins. **The Rise of the Sunbelt Cities** (Los Angeles: Sage, 1977).

Saint, William S. and William W. Goldsmith. "Cropping Systems, Structural Change and Rural-Urban Migration in Brazil," **Working Papers in Planning**, WP #20 (Department of City and Regional Planning, Cornell University, Ithaca, NY, 1979).

Sao Paulo 1975: Crescimento e Pobreza (Sao Paulo: Edicoes Loyala, 1976) translated as **Sao Paulo: Growth and Poverty**

by Candido Carmago, et al. (London: Bowerdean, 1978).

Semaj, Leachmi. "The Development of Racial Evaluation and Preference: A Cognitive Approach," **Journal of Black Psychology**, 1979, in Press.

Shirley, Robert W. "Legal Institutions and Early Industrial Growth," in Wirth and Jones.

Smelser, Niel J. **Social Change in the Industrial Revolution** (Chicago: University of Chicago, 1959).

Steffens, Lincoln. **The Shame of the Cities** (New York: McClure, 1904).

Stone, Katherine. "The Origins of Job Structures in the Steel Industry," **Review of Radical Political Economics** IV. (Summer, 1974), pp. 61-97.

Sweezy, Paul and Harry Magdoff. **Monthly Review**, Vol. 32, No. 2 (Jan. 1981).

U.S. Department of Commerce, **Statistical Abstract of the U.S.** (1979).

________ **Historical Statistics of the U.S.**, Bicentennial Edition, (1976).

________ **The National Income and Product Accounts of the U.S.**

Vigier, Francois. **Change and Apathy: Liverpool and Manchester during the Industrial Revolution** (Cambridge, Mass.: MIT,1970).

Warner, Sam Bass. **The Private City: Philadelphia** (Philadelphia, Pa: University of Pennsylvania Press, 1968).

Wirth, John D. and Robert L. Jones, eds. **Manchester and Sao Paulo: Problems of Rapid Urban Growth** (Palo Alto: Stanford, 1978).

SECTION THREE
CONFLICT AND CRIME IN CITIES

EIGHT

William R. Arnold and Steve W. Rawlings

Urban Areas and Self-Reported Delinquency

The purpose of this paper is to report an areal analysis of self-reported offending by high school sophomores. The data were gathered in a middle-sized city (250,000 population, called here Lake City) in the U.S.A.

REVIEW OF PERTINENT LITERATURE

Most areal analysis of crime and juvenile delinquency has been referred to as ecological analysis. The term was obviously borrowed from biology and environmental studies and, for sociologists, refers simply to counts of populations (offenses or offenders) in different portions of a geographical area. Most past studies have been designed to produce theoretical inferences about some non-geographical cause of crime or delinquency, most often poverty, social class, or some feature of life associated with poverty or low social class standing.

The evidence is overwhelming that indicators of lower class standing (such as median income or proportions of the population below some identified poverty level) of areas within cities (enumeration districts of virtually any type) are associated with high levels of both adult and juvenile official crime. This has been demonstrated beginning in the nineteenth century and extending to cities in the United States (Shaw and McKay, 1969;

----

* The research on which this paper is based was funded by a Faculty Research Grant from the University of Texas at Austin and National Association of Mental Health grant MH 1103301.

Chilton, 1964; Voss and Peterson, 1971: part II: Wolfgang, Figlio, and Sellin, 1972: Table 8.4), England (Morris, 1958; Edwards, 1973), Mexico (Hayner, 1946), Guatemala (Caplow, 1949), Argentina (Defleur, 1970), and a variety of African and Asian countries (Clinard and Abbott, 1973).

Surprisingly, however, studies of individuals who have had official contact with the police or court reveal that the negative association between social class standing and illegal behaviour is quite weak, generally on the order of -.04 to -.20 (Hindelang, Hirschi, and Weis review twelve studies, 1981: 186-197). The difference in the per cents of all boys in the various classes who have official contact is generally not more than five to ten per cent. As Robinson (1950) and Hannan (1971) have pointed out, "... ecological correlations generally overestimate individual-level correlations by a substantial margin" (Hindelang, Hirschi, and Weis, 1981:184).

The clearest evidence, however, that delinquency is uniformly distributed across the social classes in the United States was based on self-reports. Eliciting self-reports has most commonly taken the form of interviews with or questionnaires distributed to youngsters in schools and hangouts. These have been demonstrated to be quite valid and reliable indicators of juveniles' illegal acts (Hindelang, Hirschi, and Weis, 1981: Chs. 4 and 5; Arnold and Brungardt, 1983: Appendix). Almost universally (see Bytheway, 1975 for a re-analysis of earlier studies questioning the gerneral conclusion), these self-report studies have reported minimal associations between various measures of social class and the incidence of delinquency (for lists of these studies, see Elliott and Ageton, 1980:95; Hindelang, Hirschi, and Weis, 1981:188-197; and Arnold and Brungardt, 1983:Ch. 6). It has been widely noted, however (most recently by Elliott and Ageton, 1980: 96-97 and Hindelang, Hirschi, and Weis, 1979:997-998, 1009), that the questions on self-report instruments typically over-represent less serious offenses. This has occurred, in part, because many of the earlier self-report studies undertook to develop unilinear scales of illegal acts (Short and Nye, 1957-1958; Scott, 1959; Arnold, 1965). Among the criteria for Guttman scaling is the stipulation that no item should be included on which fewer than ten per cent of the respondents differ from the other respondents. Since fewer than ten per cent of most juvenile populations have committed serious acts such as armed robbery, forcible rape, or homicide, such items were not included. Further, many of the earlier self-report questions were either asked or coded so that all frequencies of committing illegal acts over some minimum (sometimes as low as one or two or, in our

Lake City study, eleven) were lumped together, thus overlooking the possibility that one social class might include a disproportionate number of persons who had committed exceptionally high numbers of offenses (Elliott and Ageton, 1980:97).

Both Hindelang, Hirschi, and Weis' Seattle study and Elliott and Ageton's National Survey of Youth eliminated both these problems of self-report research by asking for and reporting total admissions of all the acts normally reported by police departments in the United States. Neither reports the results in an altogether satisfactory manner, unfortunately. Hindelang, Hirschi, and Weis found quite low associations between social class measures and both official delinquency (1981:194) and self-reported delinquency (1981:196), but they completed the social class analysis only for white males. They found, further, that the white males' responses were equally valid at the various social class levels and for different types of offenses. Elliott and Ageton, on the other hand, found significant concentrations in the lower class of total self-reported delinquency (a ratio of about 6:5) and predatory crimes against persons (a ratio of about 3:2). Predatory crimes against property were also concentrated in the lower class, but the difference was not statistically significant (Elliott and Ageton, 1980:102). Elliott and Ageton do not present an analysis of social class variation within races. After discussing race and offending, we will return to the apparent disagreement between these two research reports.

The official data for the distribution of crime among the races at the individual level reveals, as does the ecological unit level of analysis, concentrations of law violation by racial minorities, especially Blacks, in the United States. In sharp contrast, many self-report studies have revealed almost equal probabilities of offending by Whites and Blacks, the only interracial comparison which has been made often enough and on large enough populations to hold our attention here (see Hindelang, Hirschi, and Weis, 1979:999-1002; 1981:158-159 for reviews of both the official and unofficial, self-report data). Since the Seattle study and the 1977 National Youth Survey are among the few self-report, studies to overcome the above-noted shortcomings of earlier self-reports, we will again pay special attention to their findings. With adjustments for population size, officially known violent offenses are committed from three to over nine times more frequently by Blacks than by Whites. Less serious offenses are committed only a little more frequently by Blacks than by Whites according to police records (Hindelang, Hirschi, and Weis, 1979:1001). Elliott and Ageton's self-report data indicate the average Black respondent admitted about one and one half times as many offenses as did White respondents and that the higher level of offending by Blacks was especially notable among the more serious offenses. Further, Blacks were more likely than Whites to have committed large numbers of offenses (Elliott and Ageton, 1980:102-106). In the Seattle study, Hindelang, Hirschi, and Weis, using questions very similar to Elliott and Ageton's, found no meaningful differnces in the offending of Blacks and Whites except for the weapons offenses and personal violence offenses (Hindelang, Hirschi, and Weis, 1981:166-169). Overall, Blacks committed only 1.1 times as many offenses as Whites. However, Blacks were particularly likely to fail to report offenses which checks of police records had revealed the youths had been apprehended for. These were, of course, relatively serious offenses. When the self-reports are adjusted for offenses known not to have been reported, the Blacks committed about one and one half times as many offenses overall and about three times as many violent offenses as the Whites (Hindelang, Hirschi, and Weis, 1981:171-180 with certain of the above conclusions drawn by the present authors). Elliott and Ageton made no validity check with police data, but all their data were acquired by interview, and there is evidence that Blacks are more likely to report offenses in interviews than on questionnaires (Handelang, Hirschi, and Weis, 1981:123). It appears that our best self-report efforts at this point in time indicate that the overall Black-White offense ratio is 1.5:1 and the ratio for more violent offenses is about 3:1.

Let us return, for a moment, to the discrepancy in the findings of these two focal studies regarding the social class distribution of offending. Elliott and Ageton combined the races to conclude that offending was concentrated in the lower social classes, while Hindelang, Hirschi, and Weis found no variation in offending by different social classes of Whites. Since Blacks are disproportionately lower class in the United States, it is obvious that at least part of the concentration in the lower classes Elliott and Ageton found is a function of the concentration of offending by Blacks. They report a high level of statistical interaction between social class and race measures (1980:106), high enough to allow us to suggest that had they analyzed their data differently they, too, would have found little association between delinquency and social class for Whites.

The more important question these studies leave unanswered, however, is what explains the difference between the self-reported race ratios for offending and much higher ratios in official data. Certainly a part of this difference is accounted for by the fact that the most frequent and most serious offenders are arrested (Elliott and Ageton, 1980:107), but this fact does not seem to account for the magnitude of the difference. Both the studies on which we have been focusing imply that the difference lies in the self-report instruments. Hindelang, Hirschi, and Weis state explicitly, partly because victimization studies support official data on the racial composition of offenders with victims, that official records are "...a true account of an event having taken place in the past. Whatever the justice or validity of these events, they did occur and can, therefore, be taken as irrefutable data" (1981:179-180). Evidence from observational studies of police operations allows us to call into serious question the facticity of police records. Rather, what are reported as facts in offense reports are constructions of scenes and conclusions about the offenses reported (Daudistell, Sanders, and Luckenbill, 1978:98-106 and the many supporting studies done by these authors). The character and demeanor of the reporting party, the suspect, and the locality all are major influences on whether or not a crime is perceived as "real" and therefore recorded. When handling juveniles, of course, it is perfectly appropriate to consider the child's overall situation--demeanor, family ability to exercise control over the child in the future, the known (officially, of course) delinquency rate in the child's neighbourhood, and whether or not the child is performing acceptably at school. Each of these considerations is institutionally racist, i.e., without using race as a criterion in decisions, these considerations will work to make Black children's crime seem more "real" and more serious than White children's crime. We agree with Liska and Tausig (1979) that although the racial discrimination at each step of the juvenile justice system is relatively small, the discrimination at all the steps add up to a significant difference in the way juveniles of different races are handled (see also, Arnold, 1971). We conclude, in other words, that Blacks are more frequently and more seriously delinquent than Whites (for varied historical and social reasons) but that some of the diferences between self-reported and official ratios by race is accounted for by the defining processes of the juvenile process system.

All the foregoing leads to a little answered question. If the social class and race distributions of juvenile law violation at the individual level are as uniform (or relatively uniform, in the case of race) as they appear to be, would not the geographical distibution of offending also appear relatively uniform if the data were disaggregated by geographical area? Answering this question seems like a logical step in the resolution of conflicting conclusions of past studies, especially the conflict between those taking ecological areas as the unit of analysis and those taking the individual as the unit of analysis. It is not surprising that relatively few self-report studies have resulted in ecological analysis of the data, for most of the studies have been in smaller communities in which analysis by census enumeration districts is impossible (census data are not so analyzed for cities of less than 50,000 population), done in only one or two schools in a metropolitan area, or done by national survey yielding too few cases in any given city to provide data for an ecological analysis. Clark and Winniger did compare self-report offenses for schools in two "status areas" in the Chicago metropolitan area. Less misconduct was reported in the higher than in the lower status are (1962:833). Mc. Donald drew her respondents from four different schools in different parts of the London, England metropolitan area and presents the data separately for each of the schools. Although she concludes that the youths in the lower class areas are more delinquent, our reading of her tables suggests that only serious theft is consistently more common in the inner-city than in the middle class and suburban schools. The concentration of the different types of petty theft were variable among the schools; the property damage, violence, and general misconduct were as common in outlying schools as in those in the city core (1969:126-131, 233). It is obvious that the data for the Seattle study referred to extensively above were disaggregated by census tract (Hindelang, Hirschi, and Weis, 1981:194), but the only findings presented are distributions by social class when the socio-economic status of census tracts is used as the criterion for placing youths in social classes. The logic of disaggregating self-report data by parts of a metropolitan area and the paucity of past research in which such an analysis was reported allow us to hypothesize:

Hypothesis 1: Self-report offending will be uniformly distributed across areas differing in social status characteristics, such as median income.

Hypothesis 2: Self-report offending will be uniformly distributed across areas differing in concentrations of racial minorities.

Two other pertinent matters may be addressed here. First, since the ecological studies of offending placed the concentration of offending in lower class areas, delinquency appeared to be associated with other pathologies, such as broken homes. Although there is evidence that even official delinquency is weakly associated with broken homes when other conditions are held constant (Rosen and Nielson, 1978:407-410), there is evidence that broken homes are used as a criterion for a declaration of delinquency but are not a cause of delinquency

(Short and Nye, 1957-1958:208-209; Richards, 1979:491; and Hennessey, Richards, and Berk, 1978:516-517). It follows from our discussion above about the ecological disaggregation of self-reported delinquency that the association of delinquency and broken homes should disappear in self-report data. Accordingly, we also hypothesize that:

Hypothesis 3: Self-report offending will not be associated with broken homes.

Second, since officially-known offending is concentrated in parts of a city characterized by indicators of lower socio-economic status, such as lower median income, if hypotheses 1 and 2 above are correct, it must follow the neighbourhoods differentially absorb (Gold, 1970:Ch. 6 implies, at least, that there would be variation by neighbourhood) their delinquency and/or official agencies enforce the law differentially by neighbourhoods. Absorption occurs when parents, neighbours, and others never report offenses to the police even though they may handle them some other way, such as punishing the children themselves or using private counsellors. Officials, of course, patrol some areas more heavily than other areas and select some offenders into official channels and filter others back to the community without giving the youths official records (Williams and Gold, 1972:221). Although the data at hand do not allow us to distinguish between offenses absorbed by the community and offenses filtered out by the police, they do allow us to observe the operation of the two processes together. We hypothesize that:

Hypothesis 4: Juvenile justice system operations produce official delinquent population characterized by lower class and minority racial group membership and residence in broken homes.

It is reasonable to suppose that this "production" is a result of the historic philosophy that those who "need" the supervision of the state are those who should get more extensive handling, those from the lower class, minority races, and broken homes presumably having the greatest needs for supervision.

METHODOLOGY

For collecting self-reports—The methodology used to gather self-reports of delinquent behaviour in Lake City has been described previously (Arnold, 1965). The high school sophomores in a city of 250,000 population were asked to report on a variety of their misbehaviours during the ten year period since they had entered school. About 8% of the questionnaires were discarded on the same general grounds Short had used earlier (Nye and Short, 1957:327). It is not surprising that our proportion of unusable forms was higher than Nye and Short's, because we had to rely on college students to administer some of our instruments. A total of 2639 responses were considered "usable", but it will be noted that omissions of responses to questions placing persons in the various categories of analysis produced somewhat varying N's for the different tables. In part to eliminate a large proportion of the self-reported offenses that were so minor as to be unlikely to appear in official reports and in part to select acts clearly identified in the offense categories used by the police, solving at least some problems noted in self-report research (Elliott and Ageton, 1980:96-97), analysis is here limited to auto theft, felony and misdemeanor theft, assaults, vandalism, fighting and disturbing the peace, drinking, and petty theft. This necessarily makes our self-reports and official records comparable, but our response categories do limit the number of acts we can relate to the official reports.

<u>For acquiring police data</u>—The intended method of data collection from Lake City police agencies was to check their records for high school sophomores during the 1963-1964 school year and to develop cumulative totals of offenses for this cohort of the population by checking the records for offenses by high school freshmen during the 1962-1963 year, offenses by eighth graders during the 1961-1962 year, etc., to the time that the cohort started to school. The information from the police would, then, cover the same period as did the self-reports. Several problems arose, however, in following this relatively simple procedure. (a) Local police agencies did not keep class in school on their records of offenses by juveniles. The cohort was re-defined as those who were sixteen at the time of an apprehension in 1964, 15 at the time of an apprehension in 1963, etc. This adjustment means that the police cohort is slightly older, on the average, than the school class and would have, accordingly, a slightly higher total arrest rate than would the sophomore class. (b) Police data processing is by location of offense rather than location of residence. This need not be thought of as a serious blemish on the analysis, however, for, "... the places at which crimes are committed are close to the residences of the criminals" (Sutherland and Cressey, 1978:188). (c) The boundaries of the Lake City school district go somewhat beyond the boundaries of municipal Lake City at which, of course, the jurisdiction (and records) of Lake City police stop. The district does not, however, cover all of Lake Country, so the data for the age cohort in the country outside the city had

to be selected from sheriff's records by the address of the offender. (d) The police chief refused to grant direct access to police records but provided from their data processing cards the needed data only for 1963 and 1964, earlier records not having been put on such cards. The sheriff of Lake County permitted access to his records for the full ten year period. This permitted the estimation of the ten year total for the city police data from the ratio of police to sheriff data for 1963-64. The estimate for each type of offense then, could be computed by the formula for this cohort:

$$\frac{\text{1963-64 police figure}}{\text{1963-64 sheriff figure}} = \frac{\text{unknown 10 year police figure}}{\text{10 year sheriff figure}}$$

and adding together the police total thus derived and the sheriff total. This figure is an estimate of offenses reported to law enforcement officers and known to have been committed by juveniles of the cohort.

The appropriateness of this estimate from a ratio depends, of ocurse, on the constancy of the proportion of youths subject to the two different law enforcement jurisdictions. Although the population of the area has grown dramatically, the city boundaries have been expanded accordingly so that the proportion of the county population subject to the sheriff's jurisdiction had remained fairly constant—17.7% in 1950, 12% in 1960, and 14.7% in 1970. The city has two small suburbs, neither of which accounts for as much as 1% of the county population. It appears that this ratio estimate of law enforcement contact with our cohort is reasonably accurate.

The population of the city and county, however, was about 84% greater in 1970 than it was in 1950. This means that a sizeable portion of the youths who answered our questions committed at least part of the law violations they reported in communities other than the one studied. Since most of these violations probably took place in the last three or four years before our questionnaires were responded to, however, the comparability of the various records is considerable if not precise. Even if one were to argue that the "true" official records of the youths studied would reflect 84% more offenses than do Lake City records, the differences between self-report and official records would still be striking.

For acquiring juvenile court data—The chief probation officer of the Lake County juvenile court made his records available to us. Neither grade in school nor age at time of referral was typically recorded on the records of the court, so the cohort was defined by bithdate, using the inclusive dates of birth of those who entered first grade ten years prior to the year in which the survey was completed. Records are kept in this court by family units. Each folder was examined briefly to determine whether or not it contained a member of the relevant cohort. The decision whether to handle a case formally and the decision for disposition at a formal hearing were recorded for seperate analysis of each of these two decisions. Each offense by a member of the cohort was taken as a unit for analysis just as it was in self-reported and police records. Thus, although the court's informal or formal disposition of a case often disposed of several offenses, the data were treated as if each offense had been given the disposition actually accorded the case as a whole.

For putting data into areas of differing socio-economic status—The self-report data were gathered from high school sophomores by school districts. Police offense data were reported to us by the census tracts where the offenses occurred. Juvenile court data contained addresses of those referred to the court. Because we feared that asking for addresses on the questionnaires would make respondents feel they were not really anonymous, we know only the school from which the respondents come. Court cases, of course, could be put into census tracts by address of residences. Happily for us, school district boundaries often corresponded to census tract boundaries. This occurred as often as it did because census tracts were originally designed to contain relatively homogeneous populations, and school district boundaries in Lake City correspond so closely to the boundaries of residences of the racial minorities that the federal courts have, on several occasions, ordered the school district to provide for increased racial integration. Further, certain geographical features, especially a long, thin lake which goes down one side of Lake City and cuts off the southern portion of the city from the rest of the city is both a census tract and school district boundary. Where the two types of boundaries did not correspond, income data and all police cases were put into the school district containing most of the area of the census tract. The median of the medians of family income in the census tracts in each school district is taken to be the median income in each school district. This obviously allows school districts to be ranked by median income.

FINDINGS

To test the first hypothesis, a decision had to be made

about how frerquency data for offenses would be computed, for the response categories in the questions were ranges: None, 1 or 2, 3 or 4, 5 to 10, and over 10. Since we anticipated that the offenses reported would be far more numerous than official offenses, in order to blunt criticism that our figures were exaggerated, we counted the lower edge of each response category. The results of the analysis appear in Table 8.1

TABLE 8.1
Mean number of offenses admitted by youth in each school District

	Median Income of School District (1960 Census)	Mean Number of Offenses Admitted
1.	56433	21.35
2.	5505	17.74
3.	5300	20.74
4.	5256	20.41
5.	2995	19.63
6.	2785	14.63
All Schools		18.86

While the mean number of offenses committed in the various school districts is not uniform, there is clearly no monotonic trend toward higher offense rates in the lower status areas. We can accept the hypothesis that geographically disaggregated self-report data indicate general uniformity in offending in the various social classes, given the limitations noted above about the form of questionnaire used and the variation in validity by race of respondent.

The racial composition of the student bodies in the various schools is pertinent here. All the students in school 6 in Table 8.1 are Black. In school 5 the population is quite mixed, approximately 40% Latin-American, 20% White (Anglo), and 20% Black. About 60% of the students in school 3 are Whites. The majority of the remainder is Latin-American, and a few Blacks attend school 3. School 1 is about 70% White with most of the remainder Black, but some Latin-American also attend this school. The remaining two schools are almost entirely White, with each having a few Latin-American and a few Black youngsters. These figures suggest that the second hypothesis will also be supported, but we can test the hypothesis directly by comparing the mean numbers of offenses admitted by youths of the different race/ethnic groups: for Latin-Americans, 20.05; for Blacks, 14.59; and for Whites, 18.67. Again, these are hardly the same, but they do tell us that the majority Whites are about as law-violating as the minority races. These figures must, of course be considered relative to the conclusions cited about the concentration of violent crime among Blacks (we asked about no seriously violent offenses) and the fact that Seattle Blacks' self-report responses were less valid than were White responses. It seems reasonable, however, to accept our hypothesis about uniform distribution of offending among the races, given these limitations.

Our deduction from the uniformity of delinquency across social classes and races that delinquency would also not be associated with broken homes is not supported by the data. Unfortunately, the present analysis does not bear directly on marital status of parents. Rather, it focuses on the persons with whom youngsters were living at the time of their responses. Those living with both natural parent and a step-parent (usually the result of a divorce) to a mean of 24.20 offenses; and those living in other households to a mean of 19.42 offenses. Partly because the lack of uniformity in these figures is in the direction official data would lead us to expect, we must reject the hypothesis of no association between broken homes and self-reported offending.

Our fourth hypothesis suggesting that the juvenile justice system produces our impression that delinquent youth are from the lower class, minority races, and broken homes is supported by the data in Tables 8.2, 8.3, and 8.4. The most obvious apparent exception to this generalization is in the second row of Table 8.2 in which it appears that the youth from a relatively high status school are the most likely to appear in police records. This exception to the general trend in Table 8.2, however, is likely a result of the police data's being based on location of offense. The district in which school 2 is located includes the central business district of the city and most of the heavily used portions of the lakefront. We suggest that the officially-noted offending in these areas is, in large part, by youths from other parts of the city and that if police data had been available by the location of youths' residences, the experiences of youths attending school 2 would have conformed with our hypothesis (Fabrikant, 1979 and others support such an interpretation, calling youthful offending in business areas near their homes "spillover").

It should be noted that interpretation of Table 8.3 calls for knowing the proportion of the Lake City youth population falling in the three major race/ethnic groups. About 70% are White; 20% are Latin-American; and 11% are Black. For unknown reasons, only 16% of our respondents indicated they were

TABLE 8.2

Comparison Of Volume Of Seven Offenses By Juveniles In School Districts Of Decreasing Median Income

School	Number Self-Reported	Number in Police Reports	% of S/R in police Reports	Number Referred to Court	% of S/R Referred to Court	Number in Formal Hearings	% of S/R in Formal Hearings	Number Resulting in Declaration of Delin.	% of S/R Resulting in Declaration of Delin.	Number Being Referred to Youth Council.	% of S/R Being Referred to Youth Council.
1 (N=496)	10,609 (21.87%)	84 (8.88%)	.79%[1]	46 (9.35%)	.43%	5 (4.72%)	.05%	4 (3.92%)	.04%	1 (1.56%)	.015
2 (N=663)	11,763 (24.25%)	520 (54.97%)	4.42%	185 (37.60%)	1.57%	42 (39.62%)	.36%	41 (40.20%)	.35%	33 (51.56%)	.285
3 (N=247)	5,124 (10.56%)	25 (2.64%)	.49%	20 (4.07%)	.39%	1 (.94%)	.02%	0 (---)	--	0 (---)	---
4 (N=531)	10,847 (22.37%)	83 (8.77%)	.76%	52 (10.57%)	.48%	11 (10.38%)	.10%	7 (6.86%)	.06%	3 (4.69%)	.039
5 (N=327)	6,280 (12.95%)	148 (15.64%)	2.36%	123 (25.00%)	1.96%	30 (28.30%)	.48%	30 (29.41%)	.48%	22 (34.38%)	.355
6 (N=265)	3,876 (7,97%)	89 (9.41%)	2.30%	81 (16.46%)	2.09%	22 (20.75%)	.57%	21 (20.59%)	.54%	7 (10.94%)	.185
Totals	48,501 (100%)	946 (100%)		492 (100%)		106 (100%)		102 (100%)		64 (100%)	

[1] All decimals throughout the table are to be read as hundreths of a per cent.

TABLE 8.3
Comparison of Volume of Seven Offenses By Juveniles of Differing Race and Ethnicity

Race/ Ethnicity	Number Self-Reported	Number in Police Reports	% of S/R in Police Reports	Number Referred to Court	% of S/R Referred to Court	Number in Formal Hearings	% of S/R in Formal Hearings	Number Resulting in Declar-ation of Delin.	% of S/R Resulting in Declar-ation of Delin.	Number Being Referred to Youth Council.	% of S/R Being Referred to Youth Council.
Latin-American (N=392)	7,859[1] (17.56%)	435.16[2] (46%)	5.54%[3]	165 (32.42%)	2.10%	40 (38.10%)	.51%	40 (40.00%)	.51%	30 (46.15%)	.38%
Negro (N=365)	5,323 (11.89%)	236.5 (30%)	4.44%	142 (27.90%)	2.67%	40 (38.10%)	.75%	40 (40.00%)	.75%	27 (41.54%)	.51%
Anglo (N=1690)	31,569 (70.54%)	283.5 (25%)	.90%	202 (39.69%)	.64%	25 (23.81%)	.08%	20 (20.00%)	.06%	8 (12.31%)	.03%

1. Per cents in all columns total 100% except for errors due to rounding.

2. Figures are based on per cents of youths reported in police annual reports arrested for robbery, aggravated assault, burglary, theft, auto theft, other assaults, liquor law violations, drunkenness, and DWI. An average per cent was computed for several relevant years, and these per cents were divided into the 946 offenses officially known to have been committed by the cohort under study.

3. All decimals are to be read as hundredths of a per cent.

Latin-Americans, while nearly 15% of our respondents indicated they were Black. We noted above that Latin-American youths do admit to more offenses per person than either Whites or Blacks, but their 17.56% of the self-reported offenses hardly suggests that 46% of the offenses in police files would be by Latin-Americans. Similarly, the percent of the offenses self-reported by Blacks does not prepare us for the percent of official offenses commited by Blacks or, even less, for the percent of the offenses resulting in persons being sent to the Youth Council. Most youths sent to the Youth Council are incarcerated in state training schools.

Although we rejected above the hypothesis that the broken home is not related to self-reported offending, the data in Table 8.4 indicate that coming from a broken home has a far greater effect on becoming an official delinquent than the 3 to 2 ratio of admitted offenses would lead us to expect. While police data did not indicate the marital status of the parents of those apprehended, the court data indicate that those from broken families are referred to the court in numbers several times greater than their proportion in the population. It is even more astounding to observe that fully 95% of the offenses resulting in youths' being sent to the Youth Council were by youths from homes with one natural parent and one stepparent.

IMPLICATIONS

The conclusion that socio-economic status of area of residence is not associated meaningfully with admitted offending while becoming an official delinquent is implies that living in a low status area is grounds for discriminatory action by juvenile justice system officials. This implication must be held tentatively, however, for several reasons: (1) The questions to which answers are reported here did not include those violent offenses for which youths are most likely to be dealt with harshly and extensively. (2) The data about offending cannot take into account such variables in official handling as attitude, demeanor and prior record of offenders. An earlier analysis of the operations of the juvenile court in Lake City, however, indicated that even when all tangible, legitimate variables in cases were taken into consideration, there was still some discrimination in favour of white youths (Arnold, 1971). (3) Certain characteristics of youths, such as official delinquency rate in the area of youths' residences and the marital status of parents (as an indicator of future family capacity to control youths' behaviour) are legitimate considerations in deciding which youths need the care of the state.

TABLE 8.4

Comparison of Volume of Seven Offenses by Juveniles from Differing Types of Homes

Living With[2]	Number Self-Reported	Number in Police Reports	% of S/R in Police Reports	Number Referred to Court	% of S/R Referred to Court	Number in Formal Hearings	% of S/R in Formal Hearings	Number Resulting in Declaration of Delinquent	% of S/R Resulting in Declaration of Delinquent	Number Being Referred to Youth Council.	% of S/R Being Referred to Youth Council.
Both Natural Parents (N=1990)	35,810 (74%)	No Data		210 (54.98%)	.59%[1]	2 (1.90%)	.01%	2 (2.00%)	.01%	1 (1.54%)	.005%
Parent[2] and one step-parent (N=230)	4,677 (9.7%)	Available from		179 (46.02%)	3.83%	95 (90.48%)	2.03%	94 (94.00%)	2.01%	62 (95.38%)	1.33%
Other Family Situations (N=381)	7,401 (19.42%)	Police Records		53 (13.62%)	.72%	8 (7.62%)	.11%	4 (4.00%)	.05%	2 (3.08%)	.03%

1. All decimals are to be read as hundredths of a per cent.

2. The question on the self-reported questionnaire on which this analysis is based asked the respondent whom he was living with. The court records reflect marital condition of the home, but this is, of course, normally the home in which the child is living.

In any case, the main thrust of this paper has been to demonstrate that when youthful offending, long thought to be concentrated in certain ecological zones, is measured by self-reports and disaggregated by zones such as the socio-economic status areas, it is not meaningfully concentrated in lower status areas or populations. It seems safe to say that the concentration is certainly not as great as we have long thought. The implications of this finding for explaining juvenile misconduct are clear--low social class standing cannot be the cornerstone of future explanations of law violation. Similarly, our social amelioration of juvenile delinquency should not focus on solving problems of poverty, however valuable solving these problems may be for other reasons.

REFERENCES

Arnold, William R. (1965): "Continuities in Research: Scaling Delinquent Behavior." **Social Problems** xIII, 1 (Summer): 59-66.

------(1971): "Race and Ethnicity Relative to Other Factors in Juvenile Court Dispositions." **American Journal of Sociology** LXXVII, 2 (Sept.): 211-227.

Arnold, William R. and Terrence M. Brungardt (1983): **Juvenile Misconduct and Delinquency.** Boston: Houghton-Mifflin

Bytheway, Bill (1976): "The Statistical Association between Social class and Self-Reported Delinquency." **International Journal of Criminology and Penology** III, 3 (Aug.): 243-251.

Caplow, Theodore (1949): "The Social Ecology of Guatemala City." **Social Forces** XXVIII, 2 (Dec.): 113-133.

Chilton, Roland J. (1964): "Continuity in Delinquency Area Research: A Comparison of Studies for Baltimore, Detroit, and Indianapolis." **American Sociological Review** XXIX, 1 (Feb.):71-83.

Clark, John P. and Eugene P. Wenninger (1962): "Socio-Economic Class and Area as Correlates of Illegal Behavior among Juveniles." **American Sociological Review** XXVII, 6 (Dec.): 826-834.

Clinard, Marshall B. and Daniel J. Abbott (1973): **Crime in Developing Countries.** New York: Wiley.

Daudistel, Howard C., William B. Sanders, and David F. Luckenbill (1979): **Criminal Justice: Situations and Decisions.** New York: Holt, Rinehart, and Winston.

DeFleur, Lois (1970): **Delinquency in Argentina: A Study of Cordova's Youth.** Pullman: Washington State University Press.

Edwards, Anne (1973): "Sex and Area Variations in Delinquency Rates in an English City." **British Journal of Criminology** XIII, 2 (April): 121-137.

Elliott, Delbert S. and Suzanne S. Ageton (1980): "Reconciling

Race and Class Differences in Self-Reported and Official Estimates of Delinquency." **Americai. Sociological review** XLV, 1 (Feb.): 95-110.

Fabrikant, Richard (1979):"The Distribution of Criminal Offenses in an Urban Environment: A Spatial Analysis of Criminal Spillovers and of Juvenile Offenders." **American Journal of Economics and Sociology** XXXVIII, 1 (Jan.): 31-47.

Gold, Martin (1970): **Delinquent Behavior in an American City.** Belmont, CA: Brooks/Cole.

Hannan, M. (1971): **Aggregation and Disaggregation in Sociology.** Lexington, MA: Lexington Books.

Hayner, Norman S. (1946):"Ciminogenic Zones in Mexico City." **American Sociological Review** XI, 4 (Aug.): 428-438.

Hennesy, Michael, Pamela J. Richards, and Richard A. Berk (1978): "Broken Homes and Middle Class Delinquency: A Reassessment." **Criminology** XV, 4 (Feb.): 505-527.

Hindelang, Michael J., Travis Hirschi, and Joseph G. Weis (1979): "Correlates of Delinquency: The Illusion of Discrepancy between Self-Report and Official Measures." **American Sociological Review** XLIV, 6 (Dec.): 995-1014.

------ (1981): **Measuring Delinquency.** Beverly Hills: Sage.

Liska, Allen E. and Mark Tausig (1979):"Theoretical Interpretations of Social Class and Racial Differentials in Legal Decision-Making for Juveniles." **The Sociological Quarterly** XX, 2 (Spring): 197-207.

McDonald, Lynn (1969): **Social Class and Delinquency.** London: Faber and Faber. See below, at end of references for Morris.

Morris, Terrence (1958): **The Criminal Area.** London: Ekgan Paul.

Nye, F. Ivan and James F. Short, Jr. (1957):"Scaling Delinquent Behavior." **American Sociological Review** XXII, 3 (June): 326-331.

Richards, Pamela (1979):"Middle-Class Vandalism and Age-Status Conflict." **Social Problems** XXVI, 4 (April): 482-497.

Robinson, W.S. (1950):"Ecological Correlations and Behavior of Individuals." **American Sociological Review** XV, 3 (June): 351-357.

Rosen, Lawrence and Kathleen Neilson (1978):"The Broken Home and Delinquency," in Savitz, Leonard D. and Norman Johnston, eds. **Crime in Society.** New York: Wiley, pp. 406-415.

Scott, John F. (1959)"Two Dimensions of Delinquent Behavior." **American Sociological Review** XXIV, 2 (April): 240-243.

Shaw, Clifford R. and Henry D. Mckay (1969): **Juvenile Delinquency and Urban Areas,** rev. ed. Chicago: Chicago.

Short, James F., Jr. and F. Ivan Nye (1957-1958):"Reported Behavior as a Criterion of Deviant Behavior." **Social**

Problems V, 3 (Winter): 207-213.

Sutherland, Edwin H. and Donald R. Cressey (1978): **Criminology,** 10th ed. Philadelphia: Lippincott.

Voss, Harwin L. and D. Peterson, eds. (1971): **Ecology, Crime, and Delinquency.** New York: Appleton, Century, and Crofts.

Williams, Jay R. and Martin Gold (1972):"From Delinquent Behavior to Official Delinquency." **Social Problems** XX, 2 (Fall):209-229.

Wolfgang, Marvin E., Robert M. Figlio, and Thorsten Sellin (1972): **Delinquency in a Birth Cohort.** Chicago: Chicago.

NINE

Manfred Kochen

Can Information Systems Help Prevent Urban Crime?

SELF-IMAGE REVERSAL IN THE SHAPING OF A DELINGUENT

The earth's population is expected to increase by nearly two billion persons in the next two decades (Brandt, 1979; O.E.C.D., 1979). That was the population of the earth at the turn of this century. Most of these young persons will be in the large cities of the "South", countries in Africa, Asia, and Latin America. They will add to the unplanned growth of cities like Bombay, Calcutta, Mexico, and Cairo. The infrastructures of those cities have for some time not been able to provide adequate water, transportation, health, communication, sanitation, police and other services to much of their present population, and the discrepancy between need and capacity is increasing. At the same time, children exposed to television or other mass media, which reach even the poorest, develop high expectations at an early age. Deficiencies in the home, school and neighbourhood often do not raise the hope that should go with rising expectations. The result is discontent, stress, bitterness, and frustration. Frustration sometimes leads to aggression, and if that deviates from social norms, it is considered offensive. We will henceforth refer to offensive, deviant or sociopathological behaviour.

Crime is an act or failure to act that violates a law to protect the public. It is a public wrong, a transgression against the public order, as opposed to a private wrong against an individual that is not punishable by the state. In the U.S., apart from treason, crimes are felonies (punishable by death or imprisonment and trial by jury) and misdemeanors (regarded as less dangerous to society and carrying lighter penalties). Crimes require both a criminal act and criminal intent. A criminal is an adult who commits the crime, either by himself, by an inanimate agency, or by an innocent human agent, or who aids in the commission of a crime. A corresponding non-adult is called a delinquent (Marshall & Clark, 1962).

"Crime itself is the greatest problem in the debilitated central areas of our cities" (B. Adams, 1971). Because we cannot yet identify the crucial catalytic agent which transforms a law-abiding citizen into a criminal, most efforts at crime control appeal to law enforcement and the administration of justice. But the search for such a "catalytic agent", perhaps for a combination of several, should not be abandoned. To be sure, that "a multiplicity of causative factors go into the making of criminal behaviour" has been called the first law of criminology (Abrahamson, 1960). In addition to constitutional (e.g. genetic) factors that may predispose a person to succumb more readily than others to certain conditions (i.e. the lack of opportunity for wider forms of responsibility), events or catalytic agents, and in addition to these conditions and agents, defects in at least three faculties play a role in rule-breaking. The first is a cognitive deficit. The deviant may reason incorrectly that the expected rewards or rule-breaking exceed the expected costs or else he may not reason consistently at all. The second is an emotional deficit. The deviant may be insensitive to the feelings of victims that breaking a rule, such as theft, causes. The third is a moral deficit. They do not regard their acts as deviant; they may be unaware of the rules they break or choose to ignore them as not applying to them or to exist as an obstacle to overcome.

A decisive turning point in the transition toward deviance may be a reversal of self-image. The deviant feels free to break a rule when he ceases to regard the rule as would an insider to the group that formed the rule. Instead, he regards it as the uninformed or unjustified convention of outsiders. He has switched from being an insider of the rule-forming group to being an insider of the rule-breaking group, and regards his former colleagues as outsiders (Becker, 1963). The catalytic agency that effects such a reversal may act over several occasions.

This does not imply that the new group to which the deviant then belongs is without rules. There are large illegal organizations of deviants who belong to small, highly structured reference groups within it. These have their own goals, codes of conduct, and a high level of mutual obligation and support. Its members thus preserve their psychic integrity, stability and mental health. Sociopathology does not imply individual psychopathology, though schizoid traits are obviously present when a person behaves normally when alone but as a barbarian when in the company of others like him (e.g. the storm trooper squads in Nazi Germany or sadistic gangs, as in the movie "Clockwork Orange").

CRIME AND URBAN SYSTEMS

An obvious way to reduce the incidence of crime is to reduce the number of occasions that bring about such self-image reversals, i.e., that arouse or reinforce sociopathy in persons at risk—i.e., those who are constitutionally susceptible to deviation from normalcy. Assuming that there is an opportunity to reduce the number of such occasions, the problem is to anticipate sufficiently soon and accurately when and where such occasions are likely to occur. If encounters with influential peers who are socially deviant—e.g., engage in theft-arouses or reinforces imitative behaviour in susceptible youngsters, and the occurrence of such encounters can be controlled, then there is a need for the information to exercise that control. An example is information about which street play groups have a mix of "infectives"—i.e., influential deviants—and "susceptibles", plus when and where they meet.

The issue of control is, of course, critical. According to Thrasher's conceptualization, which still appears to be the best available (Bordua, 1961), gangs are formed by the ecological processes shaping a city that result in conflict, disorganization, weak family ties, and anomic neighbourhoods (Warren & Warren, 1977). Uncontrolled play groups form spontaneously to meet the needs of children, such as the need for recognition and new experiences. Under conditions of high population density, limited resources, weak social controls, such play groups find sources of adventure, excitement, and enjoyment in activities of their own invention, governed by rules of their own making rather than those of the adult community to which they are outsiders. Competition for space, prestige etc., intensifies conflict. Conflict with "established" communities further weakens family ties and neighbourhood organization and turns a "play group" into a gang. Prior to being a gang, the group engages heavily in petty larceny, stealing from stores, parents, empty houses, etc., though more out of a sense of adventure and play than economic need, according to Thrasher. He viewed the lure of fun, profit, glory and freedom, all in one package, irresistible in contrast with that of "being a good child". More modern analysts, however, dropped Thrasher's assumption that deviance and delinquency was fun—that young gangsters thrilled at eluding the police chase, shooting dice, skipping school—but believe that they are driven instead away from conformity into rebellion by economic and psychic necessity. In any case, by the time most of a group's members become insiders in the group that might exert social controls on them, it is too late to control the occurrence of encounters between "infectives" and "susceptibles".

Cities, by their nature, breed information systems as well as conditions for crime. A city is an information engine. It has been viewed as a "device to enlarge the range and reduce the cost of individual and social choices" (Deutsch, 1960). For those who know a city's potential wealth of information sources and the networks by which to access and update them, there are limitless options. These are the information-rich. For some of them, the amount of information becomes an embarrassment of riches. The number of options available to them exceeds their ability to choose wisely. Nonetheless, it is possible to devise an information system that helps its users to avoid encounters with criminals, to avoid high-crime areas, etc. It does not require an information system for residents of a neighbourhood to realize that they are no longer safe in their homes or going to and from home. The feeling of being unsafe is one of the major reasons that people move in a city. But deciding where to move with regard to being safe in the new neighbourhood in the future can be enlightened by information, provided reliable information exists.

Most of a city's inhabitants are not information-rich, however. If criminals are deprived of opportunities to choose their victims among the information-rich, they will victimize the information-poor. The needs that caused sociopaths to act criminally do not disappear. Their expression merely surfaces at another site.

The information-rich tend also to be politically and economically more influential. If they are victims of crime also, then attempts to reduce crime are more likely than if criminals are deprived of opportunities to victimize them. That this is already happening in the U.S. was evidenced by a telephone survey of 1047 adults that found four out of ten were so fearful of being victims of crime that they feel unsafe, with 52% owning guns for protection (Raab, 1980). It is therefore more effective to allocate resources given to develop crime-control information systems almost entirely toward reducing the number of sociopathogenic situations, assuming that such investments produce effective yields.

It is, of course, most desirable to change the social, economic and political conditions, or the constitutional factors afflicting the susceptible population that are at the root of crime. We cannot, however, expect to do this with an information system as a primary means, which is the focus of attention in this paper. It is also too vast and unrealistic an undertaking to merit diversion of attention from more modest and feasible steps. Yet, these underlying conditions and trends in them must be understood. As stated in Section I, we should expect uncontrolled growth of cities that are already too large to adequately support their present populations by an unprecedented number of children. Couple this with advances in technology that make it more economical to produce goods and even some services by machine than by human labour—and we can expect massive structural unemployment in North and South alike. Unless there are carefully planned and radical changes this grim scenario seems assured. Assuming that wars will be disapproved as a means of settling the resulting conflicts and tensions, and that attempts will be made to control organized terrorism, that leaves the breakdown of individual psyches, or of social institutions on a large scale, as one of the remaining outlets. Individuals' breakdown can take the form of mental illness. Because the facilities to cope with widespread mental illness are inadequate, as they have already been for some time, this imposes a great social burden on other social institutions inadequate to cope with them, such as the criminal justice system. Finally, breakdown can take the form of sociopathology, such as organized crime and gangs or sociopathology combined with individual psychopathology, such as crimes of passion, insanity, etc. It is sociopathology that is largely free of psychopathology that we address next. We are concerned with the sub-cultural delinquent as opposed to the neurotic, psychopathic, organic or psychotic delinquent, whose aggressive antisocial behaviour is largely the result of imitative social learning (Bandura & Walters, 1959).

FORMATION OF SOCIOPATHOLOGICAL PEER GROUPS: PROBLEM ANALYSIS

Because there are more problems underlying urban crime and delinquency than can be adequately analyzed in one study, we restrict our attention to one. It concerns the identification of frequent situations in which pre-school children who are susceptible to socio-pathology are started on a deviant track due to the influence of peers and in which there is a possibility of reversing the direction and quality of the negative influences. We are not examining the role of the criminal justice systems, law enforcement, the role of crime in financing legitimate aims (Jacobs, 1969), the suggestion to incarcerate career criminals for longer periods of time (Peterson et al., 1981) and the numerous other important approaches to coping with crime, such as individual rehabilitation, general deterrence and social retribution. Rehabilitation efforts are weakening because of a low success rate and deterrence alone will not work either (Sedgwick, 1980). There appears to be a reversal toward retribution in the form of demands for captial punishment and longer imprisonment administered more swiftly, surely and harshly (Stinchcombe, 1980). We selected our approach because early intervention aimed at prevention seemed promising for its importance if successful, and because it is relatively unexplored (National Advis. Comm. on Criminal Justice, Standards and Goals, 1976; Johnson et. al., 1979), and closest to our expertise in the design of information systems. To indicate the importance of early intervention, note that drug use has been found among ever younger schoolchildren, and junior high schools in the U.S. are afflicted with crime—e.g. 9.5% of urban students reported robberies and 8.2% reported being assaulted (Toby, 1980).

To clarify the problem, we introduce a simple mathematical model that uses an analogy to infection in epidemic processes. Let A denote a person capable of negatively influencing certain others, such as B, in an appropriate situation. For example, A might be a 6-year-old stealing fruit from a street market and enticing a small group of peers who meet regularly on the street to join him. B might be a 5-year-old from that group living under unbearable home conditions and feeling trapped. The first problem is to identify that B is susceptible to "infection" by A—to becoming thoroughly converted to a life punctuated by the thrills of such misdemeanors and the enjoyment of the spoils as a result of A's negative influence—and that A is an "infective." The second problem is to identify, accurately, and in advance, when and where this peer group meets. Solving even these two difficult problems is not sufficient. Attempts to prevent A from influencing B would be cleverly circumvented. It is too feeble a step to try to prevent this. Instead, a forceful and bold attempt at reversing the influencee seems worth exploring. That is the central point of this paper. What, if instead of A influencing B negatively, B and his/her peers could influence A positively, toward socially constructive goals?

Under what conditions is that possible? Clearly, all concerned, but especially A, must find greater personal rewards in the reversed than in the usual situation. If the peer group consisted of A and 9 B's, what would it take for the 9 B's to suggest to A, simultaneously and independently, that they plant a garden instead of swiping apples, as proposed by A? Even if the hopelessness, frustration, entrapment and desperation is not altogether alleviated by one reversal, sufficiently repeated, consistent reversals may have an effect, somewhat as appropriate behaviour modification techniques occasionally do more than symptom relief or substitution. At least it might limit the violence of the usual behaviour or the crimes these eventually turn into if reversal fails. B by him-or himself is not likely to have the persuasiveness of convert A. But sufficiently coherent peer pressure applied all at once and spontaneously may do it. The problem is then to mobilize potential peer pressure and bring it to bear on converting A. Once A is a member of the positively oriented peer group, his talents add significantly to peer pressure, the effeccts of which are then extended to convert others like A.

Assuming that this can be done, how will it bear upon the problem? An epidemiological approach appears to be appropriate (Eisner, 1969). To start our analysis, let p denote the probability that A exerts negative influence on B as usual. If I(t) is the number of infective persons like A in a certain urban region at time t, then, according to the equations of epidemiology (Daley & Kendall, 1965),

$$dI/dt = pIS + a - cI$$
$$ds/dt = -pIS + b$$

where S is the number of susceptible persons like B in the same region at the same time. It is assumed that I increases not only due to the conversion of "susceptibles" to "infectives" but that "infectives" are generated at a constant rate a as well. (In a more realistic model a fluctuates randomly). Their number is, however, diminished because a fraction constant c of the I "infectives" ceases to be active each time period—due to age, death, arrest, disability, or rehabilitation or conversion. The number of "susceptibles" also increases at a constant rate b (also a random variable or a stochastic process in a more realistic model) due to an excess of birth over death rates and the continuing conditions of social entrapment, even while that number is diminished due to conversion into "infectives".

There is, of course, a third group in the population under consideration that is neither "infective" like A nor "susceptible" like B, but non-deviant, in established groups that perform normally. Call them C's. It is generally the largest proportion of the population, with the B's second and the A's in a minority. If A's are removed by causes other than death, they become B's or C's, and B's who do not indefinitely remain susceptible become A's or C's. Ideally, most A's would convert to C's, possibly by passing through a stage of being B's again and most B's would convert to C's.

In the metastable group of youngsters we are discussing, it is plausible to assume that there are only A's and B's, and it the earliest stage just one or two A's with the rest all B's. Without intervention, over a few years all these B's become A's, gangs are formed and may turn into organized crime cells or count as their alumni career deviants or career criminals. Many of these deviants will be offenders, but a few may also convert later to become great artists or leaders in other fields.

Suppose now that r is the probability or **B and peers** converting A from "socially deviant" to a "socially desirable" state. Then

$$dI/dt = pIS - rIG + a - cI$$

where G is the number of peer groups capable of reversal. If z is the size of each such peer group, G = S/z. The value of r depends on the amount and quality of peer pressure which depends, in turn, on size z: assume that $r = z / (1 + z)$. It follows that z increases with success: $z = r/(1 - r)$.

But what can make a peer group cooperate spontaneously and simultaneously to reverse the influence of A on B and substitute for it a conversion of A to socially useful purposes? Perhaps an appropriately constituted peer group can become self-organizing as information, know-how, motivation and aid is supplied from the outside. This external input must bring about like-mindedness within the peer group about what is socially desirable, commitment and will for converting A, as well as coordination and mutal support to do so. Let i(t) denote the intensity of this external input, measured by the number of person-hours of effort of a quality exceeding some threshold expended during a time period (t, t + T). It is simplest to assume r to be related to i by:

$$r = i/(1 + i)$$

We then have

$$pIS - rIG = IS(p + r - 1) = IS(p + i/(1+i) - 1) \text{ and}$$

$$dS/dt = -c'I - IS[p - 1/(1+i)] + b. \qquad (1)$$

Where c', by analogy to c, is the remission rate at which susceptibles cease to be susceptible, and

$$dI/dt = -cI + IS[p - 1/(1+i)] + a \qquad (2)$$

Assume further that

$$di/dt = -ei + Sx \qquad (3)$$

where e is the rate at which advisors, motivators, and aides cease to be active due to fatigue, disillusionment, etc., and x is a potential for reversal of "infectives" like A. We may interpret x as the excess of B's who are ready to suggest a socially constructive (e.g. plant a garden) alternative to A's socially disruptive suggestion (e.g. swipe apples) over the number of B's who are ready to try A's proposal.

Finally, assume that

$$dx/dt = k - k' x + giS$$

where k is a constant rate at which the potential is replenished by seeking out or planting persons like A who are converted; k' is the decay rate of this potential; and g is the coupling constant that expresses the effect of information and the number of susceptibles on the reversal potential x.

We would like for now to increase S at the expense of I.

(1) to (4) are nonlinear differential equations that resemble those encountered in other self-organizing cooperative phenomena, e.g., Laser Theory (Haken, 1978). If the method of analysis can be transferred, then there are interesting results. A sufficiently large reversal potential x may lead to a metastable soulation far from equilibrium. As i is increased, S may attain a new stable equilibrium, maintaining a high value of x and that gives rise to sustained values of S, indicating the possibility that the kind of peer groups we considered organize and maintain themselves so as to effect a conversion of infectives to susceptibles. These are conjectures rather than results of analyzing equations (1) - (4), based on their approximate resemblance to equations that have been analyzed. But the analysis remains to be done.

EFFECTING REVERSAL: WHAT CAN BE DONE?

Is there an opportunity to prevent delinquency where the need to do so is also greatest? In the decades ahead, we are about to witness the unplanned, uncontrolled growth of cities such as Mexico, Bombay, Cairo and others to unprecedented sizes. The number of persons at risk of social deviancy—susceptible to sociopathology—will increase enormously and rapidly. Hence there is a significant need to prevent, if possible, such susceptibles from realizing the potential for sociopathological behaviour. Because much of this potential is not yet fully actualized, there is still the possibility of prevention by early intervention. If it is possible to form and/or identify appropriately constituted peer groups in such cities, and to introduce into them external inputs, both of the kind discussed in the last section, then there is an oportunity to reduce the incidence of future crime.

The first step is to identify social groups in early formative stages that have only one or two youngsters of type A (infectives), and not too many of type B (susceptibles), and which have a potential within the group of converting A's to B's and B's to C's. Alcoholics Anonymous and Synanon have formed such groups with considerable success. Probably, it is necessary that none of the A's in the group have charismatic or strongly dominant personalities, and that not too many of the B's have excessively weak or dependent personalities. Generally, youngsters belong to more than one play group but those who belong to just one are probably more prone to be B's than those who belong to several, who are probably C's.

Teams of sociologically trained persons could, initially on a volunteer basis, survey the street scenes and established playgrounds (if any) of cities to inventory and classify existing groups. They must have at least the political support and cooperation of civic authorities, such as welfare, police and crime prevention agencies. Volunteerism as a form of public participation in criminal justice has been suggested but not, to my knowledge, tried in a significant way (U.S. Dept. HEW, 1971; Cook and Scidi, 1980). They may be motivated and possibly underwritten by reinforcement from scholarly and scientific societies and support agencies in the form of invitations to present published results, prize competitions, and grants. Once such a team has identified an appropriate group, it can enlist the assistance of that group in its work. Computerized data base management systems could be used effectively by this person; these are now available from local community learning centres for less than $ 3000 and the associated microcomputer can serve many other functions as well. Computers have been used in this general area but primarily to support established authorities (National Council of Juvenile Court Judges, 1974).

The second step is to develop or mobilize what will be external inputs of know-how, motivation and aid to the selected groups. An external stimulus intended to raise the hope and enthusiasm of such a group is no substitute for indigenous, spontaneously generated goals and enthusiasm within the group. But it is to serve as the spark that sets off the latter. Examples of such externally injected aspirations include: construction of community facilites, such as a swimming pool, a potable water plant, a garden, a fishery, a forest, a bicycle factory, or forming a marketing organization, a research team as mentioned above, a sanitation squad or a police-like task force. Know-how to be supplied must be in a form that eventually makes the group self-sufficient and self-motivating. It includes both technological and managerial/organizational aspects. Motivation must eventually come from immediate rewards of the activity itself, even though reinforcement from an advisor may be essential at the outset. Aid from external advisors is to be rendered only initially, and so that the group does not become dependent upon them. As soon as possible, the advisors are to leave the group, for it to sustain itself in that activity.

As the group transforms the increasing external inputs into self-sustaining inernal energy so as to require only minimal external inputs, it is also charged with converting A's to B's and B's to C's by the spontaneous formation of coherent peer pressure and attracting the A's into slots for which they are needed. Imagine that A commits petty larceny and has tried to get his peers to join him. Suppose that the group is about to discover planting a garden as a substitute. When A tries to mobilize a few B's to join him in a larceny foray, word of this immediately spreads to the rest. They suggest, instead, that A lead them or apply his skills to help them build a garden. Is it believable that A could trade the immediate adventure, challenge and potential profit of a larceny for the uncertain postponed and assumed reward of a garden? Is it believable that influential external information sources, like the "role model" of adult criminals in the crime-susceptible urban environment, can be overridden? Such criminals are often the only role models visible in the environment to which high-status attributes such as money, material possessions, freedom, and power have accrued. These roles are much more common and for cultural and other reasons probably communicated more effectively than the role of gardener or farmer, for example. Only if the latter could be regarded as equally adventurous, challenging, important and rewarding would this happen or else if the group learns to replace these values by those of postponed gratification, etc. It is the group's task to reduce the positive values A sees in larceny and increase the positive values A will see in the tasks it asks him to trade larceny for. It is, of course the role of the family and other institutions involved in the socialization of children to inculcate and nurture such values. The problem we are discussing exists because these institutions have failed or because these values have become eroded in the culture. Nor can the external advisors be parental surrogates, for that makes them suspect. They must be accepted as insiders to some extent, at least for a time. That is critical when a play group has already turned into a gang, and it takes a long period of arduous training to supply workers who can infiltrate a gang to earn its memebrs' confidence and on their own terms redirect their energies.

This has been a more successful technique than working with pre-delinquents, who are not yet in trouble with the law using indigenous leadership to help high delinquency neighbourhoods work out their own problems. Use of humanitarian, common-sense counselling as well as conventional professional casework has proved to be of questionable value with pre-delinquents (Johnston, et al, 1962). Yet, what I propose here does not seem to have been tried.

The next step is to pump such external inputs into selected groups. Doing the latter requires persons outside the group with the requisite skills, personalities, and dedication who will be accepted as advisors by the group. The previously mentioned corps of sociologically trained investigators who inventory and classify the groups could also do so for potential advisors. Some of these could come from their own ranks. The task of assigning advisors to groups and bringing them together requires a full-time management team. Such teams are readily formed in large cities, where the necessary concentration of talents can be mobilized by experiment and capable organizers, who must also procure the required funding and check goodness of fit.

Is all this feasible? There are many reasons to believe that it is not, that the barriers are not likely to be overcome. One reason is that the privileged are likely to agitate for the expenditure of resources to protect them from crime; it will then surface among the less privilged who lack the clout to commit resources toward crime prevention and control in their environments. This requires an act of political will by politicians who do not depend on the support of the privileged; possibly such a politician could come to rely on the kinds of group we discussed who adopted by and for themselves a goal of raising turnout of voters who support this politician. Another reason is the difficulty of mobilizing the needed know-how, motivation and aid. A third reason is the lack of complete understanding about group dynamics and how the hoped-for consequences follow from the proposed measures despite the rather voluminous literature (Giallombardo, 1966; Conger & Miller, 1966; Hirschi & Selvin, 1967; Phillipson, 1971). Much of what we assumed in this paper may be wrong. But we will not know unless it is tried.

The research done so far on which to base a judgment of feasibility or which to use in designing a workable intervention strategy is inconclusive. There is, for example, a six-stage mode of moral development, but it is not supported by available data.

Enterprises of this kind are vulnerable to being 'twisted by knaves to make traps for fools," to quote Rudyard Kipling. Citizen groups can easily be corrupted and become fraudulent. The reason that gangs form is that we permit and even facilitate their formation. That is easier than the high-risk, hard work of social control.

Feasibility depends very much on the existing culture. Large administrative budgets are unlikely to exist where they are needed most. A large-scale attempt to provide jobs for the very poor in New York City using behaviour modification approaches lapsed into its prior state after the external input was withdrawn, indicating no or only a transient effect. The most promosing avenues are perhaps to build upon existing structures such as the stronger ties of kinship and religion.

There are grounds for believing the proposal to be feasible. There is at least one successful precedent for similar enterprises despite a great dearth of good scientific work. A carefully controlled study showed the feasibility of preventing 5th and 6th graders from becoming cigarette smokers, reducing the number of potential smokers by 50% in four years (Dielman, 1982). While it is agreed that preventive efforts should be directed primarily at juveniles, all forms of treatment and prevention for all age groups have been tried with varying degrees of impact (UN, 1965). Too much of the literature deals with medical models that stress one or another form of therapy (Slavson, 1965) as opposed to prevention. One early follow-up study of non-delinquents in high-delinquency regions (Scarpitti, et al, 1960) showed that "once a favourable self-image has been internalized by pre-adolescents with respect to friends, parents, schools and the law, there is every reason to believe that it is as difficult to alter as a delinquent self-image". There is something inherently attractive about the idea that, much as a crime breeds more crime according to a law of cumulative disadvantage—losers act so as to become bigger losers, in a spiralling social trap—socially constructive effort can be infectious and follow the law of cumulative advantage. It is quite plausible that pump-priming with increasing external input gives rise to coherent internally generated energy that sustains itself, and which inverts the interaction between infectives and susceptibles.

CONCLUSIONS

If a system of the kind we proposed is set up as an experimental vehicle, results of social importance are very likely to result. Because these systems are aimed at reform, a strictly controlled experimental design is not feasible. Results that are valid in the tradition of rigorous experimental science cannot be expected. Instead, quasi-experimental designs are suggested (Campbell, 1969). To be sure, reforms and their undoing seem to repeat in cycles (Bell, 1953), but that is better than constantly or geometrically increasing crime, and it is possible that these oscillations could decay. The expected cost of such a design is negligible in comparison to the expected value of results, even if they disprove feasibility and possibly lead to a more feasible alternative. We therefore recommend urgently that such an experiment be undertaken immediately.

Paradigms for highly-leveraged behaviour modification of crime-encouraging environments are badly needed; it would be desirable to have them in place before undertaking the propsed quasi-experiment. Ideally, a classification of the various compartments in the urban-social environment, such as street play groups with emphasis on which are still controllable, on their development, on the interactions among them and on relations between them and possible early interventions, should logically precede the design of quasi-experiments. We may not, however, have the time to wait for such methodological perfection if we are to win the race against the demographic explosion of disillusioned young that is in progress now.

REFERENCES

Abrahamson, D. **The Psychology of Crime**, New York: Wiley, 1960, p. 30.

Adams, B. "Crime Prevention and Law Enforcemennt," **in Hope for the Cities** (R.L. Chartrand, ed.), New York: Spartan, 1971, p. 58.

Bandura, A. and Walters, R.H. **Adolescent Aggression**, New York: Ronald, 1959.

Becker, H.S. **Outsiders**, New York: **Free** Press, 1963.

Bell, D. "Crime as an American **Way** of Life," **The Antioch Review 13**, June 1953, 131-154.

Bordua, D.J. "Delinquent Subcultures: Sociological Interpretation of Gang Delinquency," **The Annals of the Amer. Acad. of Polit. and Social Sci. 338** Nov. 1961, 120-136.

Brandt, W. North-South: A program for Survival, Cambridge: MIT Press, 1980.

Campbell, D.T. "Reforms as Experiments", **The Amer. Psychologist 24**, 4, April 1969, 409-429.

Conger, J.J. and Miller, W.C. **Personality, Social Class and Delinquency**, New York: Wiley, 1966.

Cook, T. and Scidi, Jr., F. **in Crime and Criminal Justice** (John A. Gardiner and Michael A. Mulkey, eds.), Lexington Books 1975.

Daley, D.J. and Kendall, D.G. "Stochastic Rumours", J. **Inst. Maths. Applics.** 1 1965, 42-55.

Dielman, T.E. **et al.** Resisting Pressures to Smoke: Short Term Results of an Elementary School Based Smoking Prevention Project. Tech. Memo 82.1, University of Michigan, 1982. (Submitted for publication)

Deutsch, K.W. "On Social Communication and the Metropolis", in **The Future Metropolis** (L.Rodwin, ed.), New York: Braziller, 1971, p. 129.

Eisner, V. **The Delinquency Label**: The Epidemiology of Juvenile Delinquency, New York: Random House, 1969.

Friedman, Lawrence and Macaulay, Stewart. **Law and the Behavioural Sciences.** Indianapolis: Bobbs-Merrill Company, Second Edition, 1977.

Giallombardo, K. **Juvenile Delinquency: A book of Readings,** New York: Wiley, 1966.

Haken, H. **Synergetics,** Berlin: Springer, 1978, pp. 225-230.

Hirschi, T. and Selvin, H.C. **Delinquency Research,** New York: Free Press, 1967.

Jacobs, J. **The economy of Cities,** New York: Random House, p. 222.

Johnson, G. et al. **Delinquency Prevention: Theories and Strategies,** U.S. Department of Justice. 1979.

Johnston, N., Savits, L. and Wolfgang, M.E. **The Sociology of Correction,** New York: Wiley, 1962, pp. 311-12.

Marshall, W.L. and Clark, W.L. "The Legal Definition of Crime and Criminals", **in The Sociology of Crime and Delinquency** (M.E. Wolfgang et al, eds.), New York: Wiley, 1962, pp. 14-19.

National Council of Juvenile Court Judges, **Computer Applications in the Juvenile Justice System,** Reno: University of Nevada, 1974.

National Advisory Comm. on Criminal Justice Standards and Goals, **Juvenile Justice and Delinquency Prevention,** Washington DC: U.S. Government Printing Office, 1976.

Organization for Economic Cooperation and Development. **Facing the Future,** Paris: OECD, 1979.

Peterson, M.A., Braiker, H.B., and Polich, S.M. **Who Commits Crimes,** Cambridge: Oelgeschlager, Gunn & Hain, 1981.

Phillipson, M. **Sociological Aspects of Crime and Delinquency,** London: Routledge & Kegan Paul, 1971.

Raab, S. "Report (by H.E. Figgie, Jr.) Finds Fear of Crime Changing Life Nationwide", **The New York Times,** September 17, 1980, B5.

Scarpitti, F.R. et al. "The 'Good' Boy in a High Delinquency

Area: Four Years Later", **Am. Soc. Rev.,** August 1960, **25,** 555-558.

Sedgwick, J.L. **Deterring Criminals: Policy Making in the American Tradition,** Washington DC: American Enterprise Inst., June 1980.

Slavson, S.R.**Reclaiming the Delinquent,** New York: Free Press, 1965.

Toby, J. "Crime in American Public Schools", **The Public Interest 58,** Winter 1980, 18-42.

Thrasher, F.M. **The Gang,** Chicago: U. Chicago, 1927.

United Nations, **The Young Adult Offender**: A Review of Current Practices and Programmes in Prevention and Treatment, New York: United Nations, 1965.

U.S. Department HEW, **Volunteers in Court,** Washington DC: U.S. Government Printing Office, 1971.

Warren, R.B. and Warren, D.J. **The Neighborhood Organizer's Handbook,** Notre Dame: U. Notre Dame, 1977.

Wright, K.N. (ed.) **Crime and Criminal Justice in a Declining Economy,** Cambridge: Oelgeschlager, Gunn & Hain, 1981.

TEN

Vijay K. Mathur and Sheldon H. Stein

Certainty of Punishment and Mandatory Sentencing

Theory and Evidence

Crime as a problem has been part of the American scene for quite some time. But only recently have social scientists in general, but sociologists and economists in particular, seriously and methodically begun to examine the hypothesis proposed by Bentham[4] that certainty of apprehension and punishment and severity of punishment deter criminal behaviour. Empirical works of sociologists like Gibbs[6], Gray and Matin[7], Tittle[9], Bailey et al.,[1] provide some support to the deterrent hypothesis. However, their statistical analysis is not sophisticated enough to isolate the deterrent effect of certainty and severity of punishment.

Starting with the seminal theoretical paper by Becker[3], a number of economists have attempted to verify the hypothesis by using more sophisticated statistical techniques. For example, Ehrlich[5] has not only extended Becker's model but also has clearly shown in his cross-section study of states for the year 1960 that certainty and severity are significant deterrents to various crimes. Mathur's[8] empirical work for a cross-section of cities of 100,000 population or more came to the same conclusion for both 1960 and 1970. In general, both these studies as well as others, e.g., see Gibbs[6], Bailey et al.,[1], also establish that for a majority of crimes certainty is a greater deterrent than severity. But no one has yet considered whether certainty poses a greater deterrent to crime when the punishment is more severe as opposed to the case when punishment is less severe. The answer to this question assumes a greater importance now because a growing number of states are leaning towards some kind of mandatory sentencing law which is intended to make punishment more severe. The primary purpose of this paper is twofold: to examine whether or not the theory proposed by Ehrlich can provide an answer to the questions posed above and, secondly, to provide empirical evidence to that effect. In section I, a brief version of Ehrlich's model and its comparative static implications are presented. Section II presents the supply of offense function to be estimated for various crimes, the variables included in the study and the postulated relationships between crime and its determinants. Section III discusses the methodology and empirical results. Finally, section IV sums up and draws conclusions.

MODEL OF CRIMINAL BEHAVIOUR

Here we present a simplified version of Ehrlich's model and some theoretical results which follow from the model:

Assumptions

1. A utility maximizing individual can participate both in illegitimate activity, $\underline{i}$, and a legitimate activity, $\underline{l}$, Entry into and exit from these activities is costless.

2. Income in both activities is an increasing function of time devoted to these activities.

3. Safe activity $\underline{l}$ brings a net return $\underline{w_l} \cdot \underline{t_l}$ with certainty where $\underline{w_l}$ is a constant wage rate and $\underline{t_l}$ denotes time spent in activity $\underline{l}$. Activity $\underline{i}$ is risky and the net incomes are conditional upon two states of the world; $\underline{c}$ is a state of being caught and punished with probability $\underline{p_i}$ (later on termed as certainty of apprehension and punishment or certainty for short) and $\underline{n}$ is a state of not being caught and punished with a probability $(1 - \underline{p_i})$. In state $\underline{n}$ the offender receives the return from illegitimate activity $\underline{w_i t_i}$ (net of any cost associated with the inputs used in i) but in state $\underline{c}$ his net return from $\underline{i}$ is reduced by the amount $\underline{s_i}$ $(\underline{t_i}) = \underline{s_i} \cdot t_i$, the discounted value of the penalty for his entire activity $\underline{i}$ where $\underline{s_i}$ represents the average penalty (later on termed as severity of punishment) assumed to be independent of $\underline{t_i}$.

4. $\underline{P_i}$ is assumed to be independent of $\underline{t_i}$ and $\underline{t_l}$ in order to keep the economic model simple.

5. Time allocated to the consumption activity is assumed to be fixed. Hence, total net time $(\underline{t_o})$ available can be allocated to only activities $\underline{i}$ and $\underline{l}$. Dropping this assumption will not change the main thrust of the analysis.

More formally the individual is interested in maximizing the following expected utility function subject to constraints.

$$EU = p_i\ U(I_c) = (1-p_i)\ U(I_n), \text{ Where} \quad (1)$$

$$I_c = w_o + w_i \cdot t_i + w_1 \cdot t_1 - s_i \cdot t_i, \quad (2)$$

$$I_n = w_o + w_i \cdot t_i + w_1 \cdot t_1. \quad (3)$$

w_o represents the market value of the individual's assets. In addition to constraints (2) and (3), the individual faces the time constraint: $t_o = t_i + t_1$ where t_i o, t_1 o. To keep the analysis simple, we ignore the possibility of a corner solution. Interested readers should consult Ehrlich's paper for these possibilites. The problem of allocation of time boils down to the maximization of expected utility (equation 1) subject to income constraints (2) and (3) and a time constraint.

Properties of the Expected Utility Function

Before obtaining the conditions for maximization and comparative static results let us point out some of the properties of the expected utility function. Rewriting equation (1) we have,

$$EU = p_i\ U(I_n - S_i) + (1 - p_i)\ U(I_n) \quad (4)$$

If $S_i = 0$ is follows that $EU = U(I_n)$ for all values of P_i. Therefore in the absence of any penalty, i.e., severity of punishment, certainty of punishment (p_i) does not matter. Similarly, if $p_i = 0$, $EU = U(I_n)$ for all values of S_i which shows that if certainty is zero severity of punishment does not matter even if the individual is boiled in oil. This may be why some sociologists refer to certainty and severity as "additive factors" (see Bailey and Smith[2]) although not as precisely and clearly as the present analysis has demonstrated. This analysis suggests that we need both certainty and severity to deter crimes. But to answer the question posed in this paper, i.e., does a high level of severity increase the effectiveness of certainty in deterring crimes, we need to analyze the complete model of criminal behaviour.

Utility Maximizing Conditions

To maximize the equation (1) subject to constraints (2), (3) and $t_o = t_i = t_1$ we form the following Lagrange function after substituting equations (2) and (3) into (1):

$$L = P_i\ U(W_o + w_i \cdot t_i + w_1 \cdot t_1 - s_i \cdot t_i) + (1 - p_i)$$
$$U(W_o) w_i \cdot t_i + w_1 \cdot t_1) + \quad (t_o - t_i - t_1), \quad (5)$$

Where y 0 is the Lagrange multiplier. The first order conditions are

$$\frac{L}{t_i} = p_i U_c (w_i - s_i) + (1 - p_i) U_n w_i - \quad = 0, \qquad (6)$$

$$\frac{L}{t_l} = (p_i U_c + [1-p_i] U_n) w_l - ?y = 0, \qquad (7)$$

$$\frac{L}{Y} = t_o - t_i - t_l = 0, \qquad (8)$$

where U_c 0 and U_n 0 represent partial derivatives. These conditions are necessary and sufficient for a global maximum if the indifference curves are strictly convex to the origin and the opportunity boundry is strictly concave. The second order condition for a constrained local maximum requires that bordered Hessian determinant

$$H = -(p_i U_{cc} (w_i - s_i - w_l)^2 + (1-p_i) U_{nn} (w_i - w_l)^2) \quad 0, \qquad (9)$$

where U_{cc} and U_{nn} are second partials. For a detailed discussion of the conditions under which individuals with different attitudes towards risk participate in activities i or l or both, see Ehrlich[5], (pp. 527-528.)

Comparative Static Results

1. Effect of Severity and Certainty of Punishment

Assuming $dw_i = dw_l = dt_o = dp_i = 0$ it can be shown tnat in the neighbourhood of the optimum,

$$\frac{t_i}{si} = - P_i (U_c + U_{cc} t_i w_i - s_i - w_l)/H \qquad (10)$$

For an interior solution we require that s_i $w_i - w_l$, i.e., average penalty must exceed the differential wage from illegitimate activity. Therefore, assuming U_{cc} 0 it follows that t_i/ s_i 0. The result would be ambiguous when U_{cc} 0, i.e., in the case of a risk preferer. Similarly, assuming $dw_i = dw_l = dt_o = ds_i = 0$ we obtain in the neighbourhood of the optimum,

$$\frac{t_i}{p_i} = U_c (w_i - s_i. - w_l) - U_n (w_i - w_l)/H. \qquad (11)$$

Since $w_i - w_l$ 0, it follows that t_i/ p_i 0.

Cross Effect of Certainty and Severity of Punishment

We can now investigate the effect of certainty (p_i) in the presence of increased severity (s_i) of punishment. To do that we wish to look into the sign of the cross partial of (11) with respect to s_i. But in order to take its cross partial one has to know the sign of the third order partial of U. There is a simpler way to handle this problem without speculating about the sign of third partial. We know from Young's theorem that for continuous functions

$$\frac{{}^2t_i}{p_i\ s_i} = \frac{{}^2t_i}{s_i\ p_i} \qquad (12)$$

Therefore we can investigate the sign of the left hand side of the equation (12) by examining the sign of the right hand side of the equation (12). To that end we take the cross partial of the equation (10) with respect to p_i after substituting equation (9) for H into equation (10). We obtain in the neighborhood of the optimum,

$$\frac{{}^2t_i}{s_i\ p_i} = (U_c+U_{cc}\ t_i(w_i-s_i-w_1))\ (U_{nn}\ (W_i-w_1)^2)/(K_1+K_2)^2p_i^2 \qquad (13)$$

where

$$K_1 = U_{cc}\ (w_i - s_i - w_1)^2 - U_{nn}\ (w_i - w_1)^2,$$

$$K_2 = U_{nn}\ (w_i - w_1)^2\ /\ p_i$$

Assuming U_{cc} 0, U_{nn} 0 and $w_i - s_i - w_1$ 0 it follows that ${}^2t^1/\ s_iep_i$ 0.[1] Hence from (12) we have $e^2\ t_i/ep_ies_i$ 0. Ambiguous results will follow if U_{cc} 0.

This is a very significant result which our economic theory permits us to obtain. It shows that the effect of certainty of punishment (p_i) on crimes is augmented when severity of punishment increases. In other words we should expect, given the assumptions, that certainty will be a greater deterrent to crimes in the presence of high severity as opposed to low severity of punishment. Earlier studies by Ehrlich and Mathur demonstrated that severity, even though a significant deterrent to crimes, is of lesser importance for a majority of the crimes than the certainty. However, the present theoretical result clearly demonstrates the importance of severity in making certainty a more effective deterrent to crimes and vice versa. Therefore the main hypothesis to be tested in this paper is that the deterrent effect of certainty is enhanced by higher levels of severity of punishment.

SUPPLY OF OFFENSE FUNCTION

The following aggregate crime function for the ith crime (c_i) which can be obtained from individual crime functions (see Ehrlich[5], pp. 533-538, for details) has been estimated to test the above hypothesis obtained from the theoretical model.

$$C_i = A\ P_i^{\ 1i} S_i^{\ 2i} I^{\ 3i} U^{\ 4i} NW^{\ 5i} G^{\ 6i} \exp(\ ). \qquad (14)$$

The subscribed variables are crime specific while the rest are city specific and u is the error term.

Variables Included in the Econometric Model

The following is a description of the endogenous and exogenous variables used in the present empirical work for the cities of the United States of America[2].

1. Endogenous Variables

C_i: reported crime rate per 100,000 population.

P_i: certainty of apprehension and punishment obtained by dividing the number of admissions to prisons for an offense by the number of reported crimes[3]. It ranges from 0 and 1 where 0 indicates that no one was convicted and imprisoned.

2. Exogenous Variables

S_i: severity of punishment. It is defined as the median number of months served in prison by released felons.

I: median income.

G: gini coefficients to measure income inequality in a city. It ranges from 0 (perfect equality) to 1 (perfect inequality).

U: per cent unemployed.

NW: per cent nonwhites.

SCH: median years of shcool completed by persons 25

years of age and over.

W: per cent white collar inhabitants.

N: population in thousands.

R: per capita general revenue of the city government.

For clarification purposes it might be worth mentioning that the complete econometric model for each type of reported crime consists of three equations. In addition to the crime equation (14) there is an equation for certainty (P_i) describing the production function of the criminal justice system and an equation for police expenditure (E) denoting the demand for police. It is assumed that P_i is a function of C_i, S_i, E, N, NW, W and SCH and E is a function of C_i where i = 1,...,7, and R. Therefore the complete model consists of three endogenous and ten exogenous variables. Since our interest in this paper is to estimate the crime equation we have not presented the complete model here.

It should be noted that since certainty (P_i) and severity (S_i) data are not available for cities, state data is used as proxies. One may also observe that police expenditure is not included in the crime equation (14) but rather is included in the equation for P_i. It is our contention that police effort as measured by police expenditure does not influence crime directly. It affects certainty of apprehension and punishment which in turn affects crimes.

Brief Description of Postulated Relationships in the Crime Equation

Our economic model shows that under certain assumptions we expect P_i and S_i to have a negative impact on crimes as they tend to increase **ceteris Paribus** the marginal cost of punishment. In the absence of data on individual criminal's gains and losses we use measurable proxies. Average income and the opportunity cost associated with criminal activity can be approximated by median income (I) and the unemployment rate (U). We expect U to enter positively but the effect of I is not clear as it also represents the amount of transferable wealth in the community thereby increasing the potential payoffs to crimes. The gini coefficient (G), a measure of income inequality, is included to measure potential gains from criminal activity and is expected to enter positively. We expect nonwhites (NW) to be more attracted to illegal activities not only because of less discrimination in such activities but due to their low level of income and high unemployment rates.

The Effect of Severity on the Elasticity of Certainty

We demonstrated in (13) that it is reasonable to expect that

$$\frac{t_i}{S_i \; P_i} \qquad 0$$

In the empirical work reported here, we compare the certainty elasticity of crime ($E_{ti}P_i$) obtained in high severity cities with that obtained in low severity cities. We expect to find that the certainty elasticity of crime is larger in high severity cities than in low severity cities. To see this, let,

$$E_{t_iP_i} = \frac{t_i \cdot P_i}{P_i \; t_i} \qquad (16)$$

be the certainty elasticity of crime. Differentiating $E_{ti}P_i$ with respect to severity, we obtain (remembering that P_i and S_i are parameters from the criminal's point of view),

$$\frac{E_{t_iP_i}}{S_i} = \frac{P_i \; {}^2t_i}{t_i \; P_i \; S_i} - \frac{P_i \; t_i \; t_i}{t^2{}_i \; P_i \; S_i} \qquad (17)$$

Since (${}^2t_i/ \; {}_i \; S_i$) < O from (13), ($t_i/ \; P_{i-}$) and ($t_i/ \; S_i$) are negative given the assumption of the model, it follows that ($E_{ti}P_i/ \; S_i$) O. This result implies that in high severity cities we expect a higher absolute value, and in low severity cities we expect a low absolute value, of the certainty elasticity of crime.

METHODOLOGY AND EMPIRICAL RESULTS

Methodology

In order to linearize equation (14), all the variables have been converted into natural logs, a specification commonly used by other criminologists, e.g., see Ehrlich[5], (pp. 537). The total sample consists of 112 cities of the United States of 100,000 population or more. Initially we started with all cities in this population group but, due to the missing data problem, especially in the case of certainty and severity of punishment, we finally ended up with the above sample. The crimes included in this study are murder, assault, rape, robbery, burglary, grand larceny and auto-theft. To test our main hypothesis, we sub-divided the whole sample of 112 cities into two groups for each crime.

1. Cities which have higher than average severity of punishment for a particular crime. We call them high severity cities.

2. Cities which have lower than average severity of punishment for a particular crime which we label as low severity cities.

The average severity used for a given crime represents the average for the whole sample. This classification scheme is used because severity is assumed to be an exogenous varibale in the econometric model. The equations for each crime in each group were estimated for the year 1960 for a cross-section of cities. Due to the presence of simultaneity in the econometric model, we use the two stage least squares method to estimate each crime equation. We made an effort to conduct the analysis for the year 1970 as well but due to the unavialability of certainty and severity data for a number of states the total sample of cities was not large enough to get a meaningful and significant sample in each group[4].

Empirical Results

The results for the high severity subsample and low severity subsample are reported in Table 10.1 and 10.2 respectively. Our results are in general supportive of our main hypothesis, in spite of the imperfect nature of the data, particularly for certainty and severity of punishment. Comparing the results of Table 10.1 (high severity) and 10.2 (low severity) we find that the certainty coefficient is significant and negative for all crimes in the high severity city subsample but is positive, though insignificant, for most crimes in the low severity city subsample. This finding implies that certainty is a greater deterrent to crime in the presence of high severity of punishment, but is either less of a deterrent or not an effective deterrent at all when severity is low, a result consistent with our theoretical result obtained in equations (13) or (16). In Table 10.1, the elasticity of certainty ranges from −0.085 for robbery to −2.11 for murder and, with the exception of robbery and auto-theft, the results support our hypothesis. In order for the hypothesis to hold, we should expect the coefficients of LP_i to be smaller (i.e., a larger absolute value) for high severity cities than for low severity cities for each crime. Such is the case for murder, assault, rape, burglary and grand larceny if we compare the results of Table 10.1 and 10.2. Saverity of punishment (LS_i) enters negatively in five crime equations in Table 10.1 (high severity subsample) and is significant for three crimes. It enters negatively in three equations for low severity cities (Table 10.2), and is significant for two crimes.[5]

As far as socioeconomic variables are concerned, all enter positively in a majority of the crime equations with the exception of the results for LINC in Table 10.1 and 10.2, thus lending some credibility to our **a priori** expectations. Most importantly, the nonwhite variable is very significant and positive in a majority of the equations in both high as well as low severity cities.

SUMMARY AND CONCLUSION

It has been well established in the criminological literature that certainty of punishment is an effective deterrent to various crimes. With regard to severity of punishment, some sociologists like Tittle, Bailey, **et al.**, may doubt the deterrent effect of severity along; but economists like Ehrlich and Mathur, who utilize more sophisticated statistical techniques, have shown severity also to be a significant deterrent to a majority of crimes. In this paper, we carried the debate on deterrence a step further. The theoretical model shows that under certain assumptions about the criminal's utility function, the effectiveness of certainty is enhanced when the severity of punishment increases. This result should not be confused with what sociologists call the 'additive effect' of certainty and severity. The 'additive effect' only means that "when punishments are severe and administered with certainty, maximum deterrence results" (see Bailey and Smith[2], pp. 531). Our concern is with the partial effect of certainty when severity increases. The economic model shows that under certain assumptions this partial effect of certainty increases when punishment is more severe as compared to when punishment is less severe. Therefore, we should expect the partial regression coefficients of certainty in the estimated equations for the high severity case to be smaller (i.e., absolute value larger) than those of the low severity case.

To test this hypothesis, we divided the whole sample into two groups: (1) cities having higher than average, and (2) cities having lower than average severity of punishment for a particular crime where average severity pertains to the whole sample. The empirical analysis for the year 1960 confirms our hypothesis for a majority of the reported crimes in this study.

In the states of Illinois, Maine, California and Indiana, a mandatory senteceing law or a system of predetermined sentenc-

TABLE 10.1
Two Stage Least Squares Estimates of Crime Equations for high Severity Cities

	LMUR	LASST	LRAPE	LROB	LBUR	LLAR	LAUTO
Constant	-13.64 (-1.20) ***	-1.27 (0.11)	-7.89 (-0.86) ****	-5.85 (-0.579)	12.26 (1.45) **	6.45 (0.28)	0.636 (0.10)
LINC	1.04 (0.91) ****	0.261 (0.171)	1.26 (1.11) ***	0.989 (.85) ****	-0.253 (-0.32)	0.935 (0.416)	0.424 (0.711)
LNW	0.958 (5.91) *	0.713 (5.49) *	0.479 (3.44) *	0.581 (4.89) *	0.20 (2.82) *	-0.137 (-1.20) ***	0.161 (1.77) *
LU	0.114 (0.27)	-0.652 (-1.43) **	-0.131 (-0.257) ****	1.12 (1.90) *	-0.065 (-0.16)	0.041 (0.07)	0.443 (1.54) **
LGINI	1.16 (1.10) ***	0.621 (0.84)	1.50 (2.13) *	-0.65 (-0.94) ****	-0.758 (1.94) *	0.583 (1.01) ****	-0.279 (-0.54) **
LP	-2.11 (-1.90) *	-0.226 (-0.97) ****	-0.748 (-1.31) **	-0.085 (-0.16)	-0.313 (-0.89) ****	-0.413 (-1.05) ***	-0.197 (-0.95) ****
LS	0.689 (1.59) *	0.681 (0.59)	-0.474 (-0.79)	-0.68 (-1.70) *	-1.37 (-1.20) ***	-2.77 (-1.41) **	-0.318 (-0.31)
SE	0.58	0.75	0.71	0.58	0.40	0.53	0.53
n	44	58	64	45	52	44	61

a. All variables preceded by L are in natural logs and symbols MUR, ASST, ROB, BUR, LAR and AUTO represent murcer, assault, robbery, burglary, grand larceny and auto theft. All Figures are rounded to the nearest hundred. The t-statistics are reported in parenthesis under the coefficients, SE represents standard error of the regression and n represents the sample size.

b. Significant at 5 per cent (*), Significant at 10 per cent (**), Significant at 15 per cent (***), Significant at 20 per cent (****).

TABLE 10.2
Two Stage Least Squares Estimates of Crime Equations for Low Severity Cities

	LMUR	LASST	LRAPE	LROB	LBUR	LLAR	LAUTO
Constant	2.31 (0.52)	-29.49 (1.08) ***	-12.70 (-1.30) **	8.69 (0.67)	9.33 (1.65)	6.41 (1.61) **	2.49 (0.37)
LINC	-0.028 (-0.052)	2.93 (1.03) ***	1.13 (1.0) ****	-0.841 (-0.57)	-0.309 (-0.46)	-0.10 (-0.21)	0.272 (0.35)
LNW	0.584 (6.12) *	1.0 (4.29) *	0.469 (2.78) *	0.909 (3.65) *	-0.159 (-1.19) ***	-0.107 (1.28) ***	0.212 (1.65) **
LU	-0.014 (-0.06)	0.59 (0.81)	0.120 (0.27)	-0.305 (-0.39)	-0.695 (2.16) *	0.284 (1.28) ***	0.289 (0.86) ****
LGINI	0.95 (1.69) *	1.64 (0.62)	0.240 (0.14)	0.727 (0.50)	1.20 (1.27) ***	0.234 (0.32)	1.38 (1.13) ***
LP	0.004 (0.008)	1.51 (0.91) ****	0.098 (0.23)	-1.96 (-2.27) *	0.527 (1.83) *	0.60 (3.79) *	-0.50 (-2.81) *
LS	-0.247 (-1.07) ***	3.95 (1.19) ***	1.19 (2.09) *	-0.815 (-0.85) ****	0.717 (1.37) **	1.40 (3.25) *	-0.381 (-0.76)
SE	0.54	1.14	0.85	0.96	0.48	0.42	0.54
n	68	54	48	67	60	68	51

Note: see notes a. and b. in Table 10.1.

ing is already in the books in one form or another, while States like Michigan, Ohio, etc., are gearing up to pass such a law. Such a law is intended to take away some discretion in sentencing from the judges and hence, in general, it tends to increase the severity of punishment. Our findings suggest that, even if one may question the propriety as well as the effectiveness of such a law and therefore of severity, it does tend to increase the effectiveness of certainty on crimes. However, it is not suggested here that the implementation of such a law as well as its effect on the prison system is costless. We have only presented the deterrent aspects of such a law in this paper. These findings are preliminary and should be used with caution. More conclusive evidence would require better and more comprehensive data on certainty and severity of punishment for cities.

FOOTNOTES

1. In General we expect 'U' 0 hence our result will follow. However, if preferences are such that U_{cc} 0 and U_{nn} 0 we get just the opposite result, i.e., $^2t_i/ s_i$ 0.

2. The data for crimes in 1960 are obtained from **Uniform Crime Reports**[13] of the F.B.I. ; the length of prison sentence for each crime (to calculate the severity measure) and for prison admissions (to construct the certainty index) are obtained from **National Prisoner Statistics** 1960[12]; general revenue from **City Government Finances,** 1960-61[11]; and for the rest of the variables from the 1960 **U.S. Census of Population**[10].

3. This measure of centainty suffers from certain drawbacks. It does not represent the proportion of offenders convicted or imprisoned nor does it consider multiple offenses and penalties other than imprisonment. For details see Bailey and Smith[2]. In cases where more admissions than reports of such offenses occurred we assigned a value of 0.99 to the certainty index. Fortunately there were not many such cases in 1960.

4. The 1980 U.S. census data on socio-economic variables for cities of the U.S.A. are not yet available.

5. It must be noted that the sign of severity coefficient could be positive in the case of a risk preferer.

REFERENCES

1. Bailey, William C., David Martin J., and Louis N. Gary, "Crime and Deterrence: A Correlation Analysis," **Journal of Research in Crime and Delinquency** 11 (July 1974), 124-143.
2. Bailey, William C., and Ronald W. Smith, "Punishment: Its Severity and Certainty, "**Journal of Criminal Law, Criminology, and Police Science** 63 (Dec. 1972), 530-539.
3. Becker, Gary, "Crime and Punishment: An Economic Approach," **Journal of Political Economy** 76 (Mar/Apr 1968), 169-217.
4. Bentham, Jeremy, "Principles of Penal Law," in J. Browning (ed.), **The Works of Jeremy Bentham 1748-1832** (N.Y.: Russell & Russell, 1962).
5. Ehrlich, Isaac, "Participation in Illegitimate Activities: A Theoretical and Empirical Investigation, **Journal of Political Economy** 81 (May/June 1973), 521-565.
6. Gibbs, Jack P., "Crime, Punishment and Deterrence," **Social Science Quarterly** 48 (March 1968), 515-530.
7. Gray, Louis N., and David Martin J., "Punishment and Deterrence: Another Analysis of Gibb's Data," **Social Science Quarterly** 49 (September 1969), 289-295.
8. Mathur, Vijay K., "Economics of Crime: An Investigation of the Deterrent Hypothesis for Urban Areas," **The Review of Economics and Statistics** 60 (August 1978), 459-466.
9. Tittle, Charles R., "Crime Rates and Legal Sanctions," **Social Problems** 16 (Spring 1969), 409-423.
10. U.S. Department of Commerce, Bureau of Census, **Census of Population 1960, Characteristics of Population** (Washington, D.C: Government Printing Office.)
11. U.S. Department of Commerce, **City Government Finances,** 1960-61 (Washington, D.C.: Government Printing Office).
12. U.S. Deprtment of Justice, Bureau of Prisons, **Characteristics of State Prisoners, 1960 National Prisoner Statistics** (Washington, D.C.: Government Printing Office).
13. U.S. Department of Justice, Federal Bureau of Investigation, **Uniform Crime Reports,** 1960 (Washington, D.C.: Government Printing Office).

SECTION FOUR
POLLUTION AND HEALTH IN CITIES

ELEVEN

S.Q.A. Rizvi

Changing Direction and Intensity of Air Pollution of an Urban Centre

A case study of Gorakhpur City

The study of urban growth and functional morphology of an urban centre aims at bringing out a sound plan and a prosperous urban life for which every nation is making efforts. The ultimate goal of such a study of a city and its surrounding region is not merely a plan determining the layout of the ground arrangement of roads and streets and designs of buildings but also to aim at ameliorating public health and sanitation.

Sanitation does not mean physical and visual cleanliness only. It envisages control of environmental pollution also. Clean air, clean water and even unpolluted soil must be provided to every citizen. It is, therefore, imperative to make a rational approach to and a proper understanding of the existing environmental conditions which tell upon the human health and activity and thereafter to probe possibilities and to suggest measures for their betterment.

The environmental conditions of a city, such as Gorakhpur, which immediately arrest the attention of geographers and town planners are recurring floods, water-logging, drainage and swerage, water-supply, electricity and sanitation. Last but not the least is the study of the problem of environmental pollution, a gift of modern scientific and mechanical developments. The pollutants may be solid, liquid or gaseous. While solid pollutants are confined to a definite spot, the liquid pollutants follow the hydrology of the town. But the gases depend on the sources and the weather conditions for movement.

At Gorakhpur, the Thermal Power Plant, the Chimneys of Loco Workshop, the Fertilizers Factory, the Airways and Roadways and other transport centres and various workshops emit thousands of tons of gases including carbon-mono-oxide, sulphur dioxide, hydrocarbons and other chemicals as liquid or solid pollutants which sometimes exceed the tolerance level of the environment and increase the pollution burden rsulting in discomfort, headache and even death also.

AN ANALYTICAL STUDY

Gorakhpur, by far the largest city of the plain north of the river Ghaghra in the Sub-Himalayan region of eastern U.P. is located in the Saryupar plain in between 26° 42' N and 26° 47' N latitudes and 83° 20' E and 83° 25' E longitudes. It is situated on the left Bank of the river Rapti near its confluence with the tributary—the Rohini. It is the only city of the Saryupar plain with the population of 2,30,701 (1971).

The characterstics of weather around Gorakhpur are dampness, moderate heat and rare as well as intermittant west-winds, both in hot and cold seasons. Of the total frequency of wind about 28% is calm. The west-winds set in November and become dry and strong in March. Towards the close of April, these dry west-winds are prevailed over by the eastern and north-eastern winds moving vigorously from April to October. The days and nights are coolest during the month of December and January while the warmest are those of May extending sometimes, to September.

The air is mostly calm from April to June. The eastern as well as the north-eastern wind sets in the month of April with a speed of 3 to 6 km. per hour and starts disappearing in October yielding place to western winds, 2-5 km per hour in speed, due to intensity of the air. The month of July experiences the most varied types of winds coming from all directions except South and south-west. The frequency of winds at Gorakhpur in a year is as follows:

Direction	N	NNE	NE	ENE	E	ESE	SE	SSE	S	SSW
Frequency	23	7	63	23	90	4	2	2	1	1

Direction	SW	WSW	W	WNW	NW	NNW
Frequency	2	5	85	10	44	3

The temperature at Gorakhpur varies between 5°C and 45° C. The hot wind that is called 'Loo' is not as common in

Gorakhpur as in various places of western U.P. In some years it is experienced only for a few days. During the days the temperature is high, the content of moisture is also high. As a consequence thereof, a high relative humidity is recorded from June to October when it is generally more than 80%. The highest humidity is experienced in the month of August. For 25 times out of 60 in August 1962, it was recorded above 90%.

Frequency and direction of wind as well as the temperature and relative humidity influence the environmental condition. Constinuously high temperature, dampness and relative humidity result in outbreak of a number of diseases. During winters the bracing cold is accompanied with increasing density of air also. Sometimes, dense fog obscures the morning and at evening the city and the outskirts are hidden under its own pall of smoke.

The direction and intensity of air pollution changes from time to time depending on temperature, density and humidity of the air. As revealed by the analysis given above the temperature is sometimes recorded upto 45°C during summer which results in decrease of the density of the air.

Due to low density the speed of the wind increases to 3 to 6 km/hour. These conclusions are just in accordance with the Gas Law derived from Boyle's Law and Charles Law. According to 'Gas Law', PV = RT, temperature is directly proportional to volume. If the temperature increases, the volume also increases. But the volume itself is inversely proportional to the density of a Gas. If the volume increases, the density will consequently decrease.

At Gorakhpur, with the increase in temperature and advent of NE winds whose frequency is 63, the density of air decreases in April and May. The unenervating polluted air, therefore, rises up to minimise its influence. After the month of June, the relative humidity rises from 80% to 95% in the month of August increasing dampness. With the decrease in temperature, the density of the air increases after September. During the month of October, the NE winds are replaced by the western and north-western winds changing the direction of the pollution. Thus, high percentage of relative humidity followed by increasing density of air as a consequence of lowering temperature to the extent of 5°C during the month of December and January reduces the speed of the wind also from 5 km per hour to 2 km per hour. The polluted air, therefore, does not rise up quickly or move away speedily. The gaseous particles of carbon dioxide, unburnt hydrocarbons, sulphur-dioxide and carbon monoxide remain suspended in the air for long till they are either inhaled by the inhabitants or they make respiration difficult and sometimes, create unnoticed suffocation. The direction and intensity of such an air mass changes after the month of March with the change in direction of wind and rise in temperature.

As already mentioned, the air pollution takes the direction of the prevailing wind. If more closely examined, almost all the sources of air pollution are located in the north-eastern northern and north-western part of the city of Gorakhpur. The two most important sources are the Thermal Power Plant of 15000 Kw. started in 1957 just north of Mohaddipur Colony and the Fertilizers Factory producing 80,000 tons of nitrogenous contents annually since 1963. The industry alone covers more than 10% of the municipal land. The 'Wind-Rose' for Gorakhpur city reveals that the frequency of wind for Gorakhpur is 90 from East, 63 from North east, 85 from west and 44 from the North West. Besides, the eastern and north eastern winds are very frequent from May to September whereas the Western and the north-western winds are frequent from Ocrtober to March. Following the direction of the prevailing wind, therefore, air pollution will tell upon the health of the residents of the Railway colony, durana Gorakhpur, Jata Nagar and Humayunpur as well as the inhabitants of the Hydel Colony, Mohaddipur Colony, Cantonment and the Civil Lines to the maximum since they fall in the direction of both the eastern as well as the western winds.

Prior to the installation of the Power House and Fertilizers Factory, the northern part of the city was the least polluted due to extensive open space-parks and gardens as well as the fringing forest and groves of trees.

OCCASIONAL POLLUTION

It was mostly dampness and heat pollution which made weather oppressive. Dilapidated and worn metalled and deplorable dusty unmetalled roads added to the pollution of air generously. They created a dusty scene after passing of every vehicle resulting in pollution of the breathing air. In addition to the above, as remarked by Warner H. Terjung, "The city is an emitter of artificial heat pollution and water vapour". The city is an emitter of artificial heat pollution and water vapour". The core of the city of Gorakhpur, particularly, Urdu Bazar and Sahibganj with high density of population and tall buildings show low terrestrial radiation while the periphery experiences a comparatively lower temperature. Consequently, the core of the city becomes polluted and unhealthy.

CONCLUSION

A map of the area with lines drawn parallel to the direction of the prevalent winds from the different sources of pollution as well as a wind rose help in demarcation of the polluted area of;

(i) Pollution under warm-moist and fast E winds during summers.

(ii) Pollution under cool, dense and slow W winds during winters.

(iii) Pollution under both.

The area under first category is the urban region of low intensity of pollution and makes frequent changes with pollutants rising upwards. The area under second category is the urban region of high intensity of pollution. Changes are not frequent. The pollutants are effective due to high density and low velocity of the wind. The third category is the area of the maximum pollution as it falls in the way of both the rising as well as settling down pollutants.

In order to reduce the influence of pollution the following measures are suggested besides legislation etc.

(i) Building of residential houses or colonies should be discouraged near the sources of pollution.

(ii) Installation of industrial plants should be prohibited in N & NE.

(iii) Plantation of trees and green spots should be encouraged as far as possible.

(iv) Both the sides of the roads should be shaded with trees.

(v) Plantation of trees and afforestation should also be encouraged around the sources of pollution particularly the industrial area and in the direction of the prevalent winds which make frequent changes.

TWELVE

John C. Chicken

Community Organizations' Influence on Local and Regional Decision Making

INTRODUCTION

This paper describes some of the findings from a study I made of the various factors that have influenced the formation of nuclear power hazard control policy in Britain[1].* In the context of this workshop interest in this study stems from the fact that many of the groups and the techniques they have used to influence the formation of nuclear power hazard control policy are similar to those associated with other forms of public policy. In this study I consider only the civilian use of nuclear power and avoid the military implications.

The period covered by my study is from 1948 to the late 1970's. In this period there was a complete metamorphosis of the way nuclear hazard control policy was developed. At the beginning of the period policy decisions were made mainly on the advice resulting from fairly confidential deliberations by specialists working in the nuclear field. By the end of the period discussion of policy decisions was open and often very protracted, as typified by the Windscale Inquiry into the application by British Nuclear Fuels Limited for planning permission to build a re-processing plant for nuclear fuel.[2] The Inquiry lasted 100 days and it is claimed cost about ?2 million.

BACKGROUND TO NUCLEAR POWER IN BRITAIN

Throughout the world the use of nuclear power has grown considerably. At least 80% of all the world's electricity is generated by nuclear power. In some countries the percentage has reached 20% and in Britain it is about 14%.

----

* Paper presented at the European Meeting on Applied Urban Research, 1981.

As nuclear power grew in Britain so did the external factors that had conditioned the environment the policy making machine had to work in. During the early years there was growth of concern about the environment, then there was growth of terrorism from the mid-1960's onwards and from the mid-1970's onwards there was the growth of the movement for more open government. During this period the opposition movement had an increasingly significant influence on policy.

THE NATURE OF OPPOSITION

The way in which opposition to nuclear power has grown has varied from country to country. The origins of this anti-nuclear movement can perhaps be seen as developing as part of the environmentalist movement, which in some ways was a response to the public concern generated by Rachel Carson's book in 1962 "The Silent Spring",[3] which dealt with the environmental problems related to the use of DDT. This concern about the impact of technology was fuelled by Ralph Nader's book in 1965 "Unsafe at any Speed"[4] and of course by his second book "The Menace of Atomic Energy"[5] which he wrote in 1977 with Abbotts. Nader's second book was very specifically against nuclear power, part of it was a manual on how to organise citizen opposition at national and local level. These opposition techniques can be applied to any policy making situation.

Looking at the kind of national variations there have been in the way that opposition to nuclear power has grown, it can be seen that in Germany there have been more extreme forms of anti-nuclear demonstrations than in Britain. The demonstrations against the German Brokdorf reactor are examples of this extreme form of anti-nuclear demonstration. In the November 1976 Brokdorf demonstration, which was one of the more violent demonstrations, 25,000 people demonstrated against the reactor. About 3,000 of these people attempted to break into the reactor site at several points. They were armed with long bars, ladders, goggles, some had gas masks, others had Molotov Cocktails, and some had anchors with ropes that could be used for tearing down the barbed wire fences and power cables. In their attack this army of 3,000 people three stones, roof shingles torn from nearby sheds, and road surfacing material torn from the road. To defend the power station several hundred policemen were brought in armed with water cannon, tear gas, and rubber sticks. In addition to the policemen the site was protected by a ditch, barbed wire, and a strong wire mesh fence. The demonstrators failed to break into the site and retired after three hours. The cost of the attack was 79 policemen and 50 demonstrators injured, and an estimated

$250,000 worth of damage to the site. This estimate of damage excludes the cost of damage to police cars, one of which was burned out by a Molotov Cocktail.

The demonstration was organised by a local group called the Citizens Initiative Environmental Protection Organisation of the Lower-Elbe area. Appeals from church leaders before the demonstration asking them to refrain from violence had clearly failed.

Similar martial type anti-nuclear demonstrations have been held in Switzerland, France and Spain. But it is important to remember there have also been demonstrations and marches in favour of nuclear power. In America one result of the opposition to nuclear power has been to increase the time taken to obtain a licence for a nuclear plant from 265 days in 1966 to 607 days in 1970, mainly due to the additional questions that have to be answered.

In Britain the nuclear approval procedure has also been lengthened, and a new feature of the British approach has been the adoption of an extended public inquiry, such as the Windscale Inquiry, which allows all opposition groups to voice their views. Also through the established procedure questions about nuclear power were raised by groups working through Members of Parliament and given full answers. Some indication of the way the procedure to obtain a licence for a nuclear plant in Germany has had to adapt to increased opposition is reflected in the fact that the range of the number of objections raised against particular nuclear power stations increased from 4 to 100 in 1967 to 600 - 100,000 in 1974. These examples demonstrate how increasing public participation and consultation slows down the policy making process.

THE WINDSCALE INQUIRY

Opposition to nuclear power in Britain came to a head when BNFL proposed to build an additional nuclear fuel reprocessing plant at their Windscale Establishment in Cumbria.

The Government chose to have a Public Inquiry into this proposal at which not only the ordinary planning aspects could be ventilated, but also all the safety issues and environmental issues that seemed to be causing some public concern. The Inquiry started on 14 June 1977 and lasted for 100 days[2]. It was conducted by an eminent Judge, Justice Parker, who was supported by two eminent assessors, Sir Edward Pochin and Professor Sir Frederick Warner. Evidence was taken from 196 witnesses and 1,500 documents were submitted. Considering the volume of evidence presented the report on the Inquiry was prepared with remarkable speed and was presented to the Secretary of State for the Environment on 26 January 1978.

The main participants in the Windscale Inquiry are shown in Fig. 12.1. It is easy to recognise the association that the pro-groups have with the nuclear industry. The anti-groups can easily be divided into groups formed simply to oppose the Windscale development and more permanent groups that had wider interests.

PRO-GROUPS

BRITISH NUCLEAR FUELS LTD
SOUTH OF SCOTLAND ELECTRICITY BOARD
CENTRAL ELECTRICITY GENERATING BOARD
CUMBRIA COUNTY COUNCIL
COPELAND BOROUGH COUNCIL
ELECTRICAL, ELECTRONIC, TELECOMMUNICATIONS AND PLUMBING UNION
UNITED KINGDOM ATOMIC ENERGY AUTHORITY
NATIONAL RADIOLOGICAL PROTECTION BOARD
NUCLEAR INSTALLATIONS INSPECTORATE
DEPARTMENT OF ENERGY
DEPARTMENT OF THE ENVIRONMENT

ANTI-GROUPS

FRIENDS OF THE EARTH, LONDON LTD
FRIENDS OF THE EARTH, WEST CUMBRIA†
NATIONAL CENTRE FOR ALTERNATIVE TECHNOLOGY
SOCIALIST ENVIRONMENT AND RESOURCES ASSOCIATION
NETWORK FOR NUCLEAR CONCERN*†
TOWN AND COUNTRY PLANNING ASSOCIATION
POLITICAL ECOLOGY RESEARCH GROUP
THE WINDSCALE APPEAL*†
ISLE OF MAN GOVERNMENT BOARD†
NATIONAL PEACE COUNCIL
WINDSCALE INQUIRY EQUAL RIGHTS COMMITTEE*†
FRIENDS OF THE LAKE DISTRICT†
COUNCIL FOR THE PROTECTION OF RURAL ENGLAND
LAKE DISTRICT SPECIAL PLANNING BOARD†

*GROUPS FORMED TO OPPOSE THE WINDSCALE PROPOSAL
†GROUPS WITH LOCAL INTERESTS

Fig 12.1 **MAIN PARTICIPANTS IN THE WINDSCALE INQUIRY**

Of the national groups the Friends of the Earth organisation, founded in Britain in 1974, was one that had a very significant influence on the proceedings. The Friends of the Earth organisation is relatively small with a regular income of only about 150,000, about one-third of which represents the annual 5 subscription of the 9,000 supporters. About 170 local community Friends of the Earth groups have been formed, so they are following a well established political technique of spreading their influences by having widespread cells of activists.

Two other local groups that are of particular interest are the Network for Nuclear Concern and the Windscale Appeal. These groups were formed after the announcement was made that there would be a public inquiry, and this is typical of the way groups are formed to contest any urban development. Each of the groups is a consortium of mainly smaller groups. The Network for Nuclear Concern represents Half Life Lancaster, Friends of the Earth West Cumbria, Half Life Furness, Half Life West Cumbria, Friends of the Earth South Lakeland, Friends of the Earth Lancaster University and Ambleside Nuclear Concern. The Windscale Appeal represented Concern Against Nuclear Technology Organisation, The Conservation Society, Cornwall Nuclear Alarm, The Ecologist Magazine, The Ecology Party, Greenpeace (London), Irish Conservation Society, Society for Environmental Improvement, Wexford Nuclear Safety Association.

The Inquiry examined a very wide range of topics that were currently associated with discussions about the acceptability of nuclear power. These topics included proliferation of nuclear weapons, terrorism and civil liberties, the need for reprocessing, risks from routine discharges, risks associated with accidents, size of plant, public hostility, conventional planning issues and the efficacy of such inquiries.

The proceedings of the Inquiry were given extensive coverage by the news media and a general impression was given that all the issues were examined quite impartially. To answer questions about the risk of eating locally caught fish that may be contaminated, the contamination of potato crops in the Isle of Man, and the contamination of drinking water drawn from the Lake District, tests were performed during the Inquiry. The results of these tests were judged to show that the risks involved were acceptable.

The conclusion that the Inquiry reached was that the proposed extension of the nuclear fuel reprocessing plant at

Windscale was acceptable. This view was accepted by the Government and the plant is now being built.

THE SITUATION AFTER THE INQUIRY

Many of the opposition groups disagreed with the outcome of the Inquiry. Partly to answer criticism of the Inquiry procedure and partly to try to find a way of improving the system, the Social Science Research Council funded a study by Professor Pearce of Aberdeen University into the efficacy of a Windscale type of inquiry as a way of satisfying the democratic requirements that the public should be able to participate in the examination of the acceptability of major high technology projects.[6] The changes that Professor Pearce proposed were evolutionary rather than revolutionary. They suggested a certain amount of satisfaction with the existing system in the following way:

"In the United Kingdom the combination of plant inspection, democratic national bodies, express Parliamentary investigation and advisory units represents a politically powerful means for making sensible and responsible decisions. If, however, their decisions are predictable regardless of the content of the arguments put to them then the system will have legitimised other tactics wittingly or unwittingly".

With the stress that they place on public participation it is easy to understand their view that the adoption of a Freedom of Information Act is a prerequisite for the improvement of the planning process. The view they take is that only when the public have free access to all the relevant information will they be able to participate in the planning process in an informed way. To further support the private objectors it was proposed that they should be helped from public funds, so that their status would be the same as proposals from the public sector. They recognise the problem of controlling such things and suggest the funds should be controlled by a national commission. The important point about this for other policy making situations is its aim to ensure that those likely to be affected by the policy have access to the relevant information and funds to present their case.

Among the other suggestions that were made for satisfying the democratic requirements were Bishop Montefiore's for judging the acceptability of important projects by a public referendum[1]. My own view is that there is considerable merit in developing the Public Inquiry procedure further. The advantages and disadvantages of the Public Inquiry System are as follows:-

Advantages of the Public Inquiry

(1) The Public Inquiry exposes the public to the strengths and weaknesses of the case for and against a particular project.
(2) It provides a way of de-fusing a conflict situation.
(3) A favourable Public Inquiry into a project makes it easier for the authorities to obtain the necessary resources (men and money) for the project to continue.
(4) It allows an element of public participation in the policy making process.
(5) The simple existence of a Public Inquiry tends to emphasize the problems associated with the projects examined.

The Disadvantages

(1) An inquiry slows down the decision making process.
(2) The cost of preparing the case for an Inquiry and the cost of representation at the Inquiry add to the total cost of the project. Tax payers bear a large proportion of the cost.
(3) It is not an intrinsic characteristic of Public Inquiries that only technically correct information about the proposal is presented (it is my impression that at the Windscale Inquiry Justice Parker and his two assessors had to spend a lot of time checking and correcting the views put forward by those in opposition to the Windscale proposal).
(4) The wrong impression about the proposal can be given by the media concentrating on the emotional issues raised without checking their technical validity.
(5) A Public Inquiry does not allow a detailed examination of the alternatives to the proposal being examined.
(6) It is not always easy to find an impartial Chairman able to evaluate the technical arguments.
(7) It may be that the organisations putting forward the proposal to be examined by a public inquiry are at a disadvantage as they do not operate at the same level of public relations activity as those opposed to the argument.
(8) The opposition may not be representative of the whole community. An important factor that determines the effectiveness of a policy making process is the accuracy with which the policy makers perceive the public beliefs and views about the policy being made.

A joint study by the International Atomic Energy Agency

and the International Institute for Applied Systems Analysis of policy makers' perception of public beliefs showed that the policy makers they examined had a reliable picture of the general public's attitude towards nuclear power. The IAEA/IIASA study examined particularly the opinions of senior Austrian civil servants concerned with energy matters, and their understanding of the public acceptability of the Zwentendorf reactor. The conclusion reached in the study was that four major independent dimensions had been found to underlie public views towards the use of nuclear energy; psychological risks; economic/technical benefit; socio-economic risks; environmental/physical risks. In terms of these four dimensions policy makers were able to satisfactorily reproduce the general attitudes of public groups in favour of or against the use of nuclear energy. Part of the study also evaluated differences in attitudes between five countries with different cultural backgrounds. These studies showed that there was a close correlation in the views about the risk aspect of nuclear power in all five countries. The importance of the IAEA/IIASA study is that it showed a sound understanding of public opinion can be obtained by opinion sampling techniques and this is an important technique that the policy maker should use to help him assess the requirements of the public.

CONCLUSIONS

The study showed that in recent years relatively small groups have had a significant influence on nuclear hazard control policy. The action of anti-nuclear interest groups led to the Public Inquiry into British Nuclear Fuels Ltd proposals to expand their Windscale plant. There are also indications that to demonstrate that all local and regional interest groups have a proper forum they can use for presenting their views a refined version of the Public Inquiry procedure supplemented by opinion sampling procedures could be a satisfactory solution.

Many of the problems identified in dealing with interest groups in the nuclear energy field are analogous to the problems associated with introducing policies in other fields, such as urban development. This study has tempted me to postulate a model of the policy making process that helps to give a structured approach to the identification of the factors that influence policy making in any area. The steps in the construction of this model are first to identify the factors that make up the environment of the policy making process in general. The second step is to identify the specific and unique environment for the policy making process being considered. Fig. 12.2 shows the specific composition of the environment for the nuclear hazard control policy making subset. A similar subset can be constructed for any policy making system. Fig. 12.3 indicates how variables interact in the nuclear policy making systems. The third step is to recognise that no environment stays constant with time and in any analytical situation you have to argue from the environment as it is made up at the present time to the way it will be made up in the future. This variation with time may have to take account of changes in government policy that may take place, new legislation thåt will be introduced, changes in leading figures and other major projects coming to fruition. Something of the feel for the way the environment may change with time is showin in Fig. 12.4.

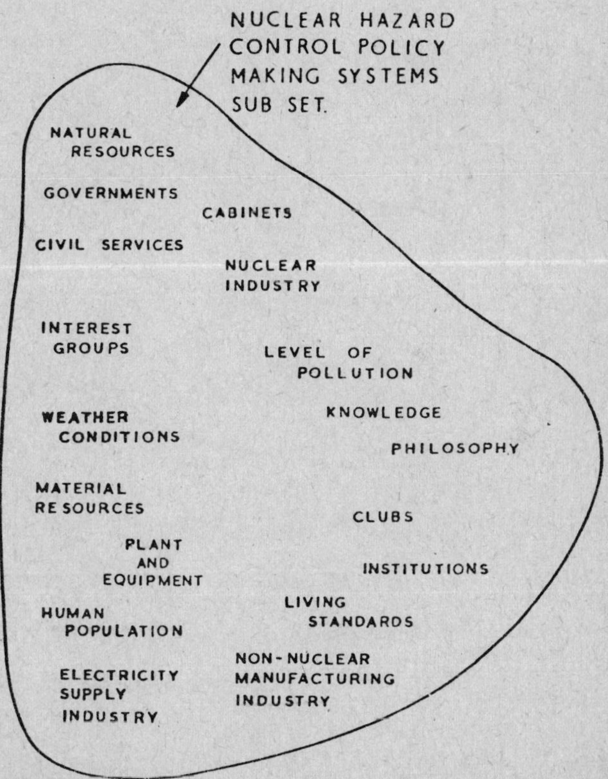

FIG. 12.2

ELEMENTS THAT MAKE UP THE ENVIRONMENT IN THE NUCLEAR HAZARD CONTROL POLICY MAKING SUB SET.

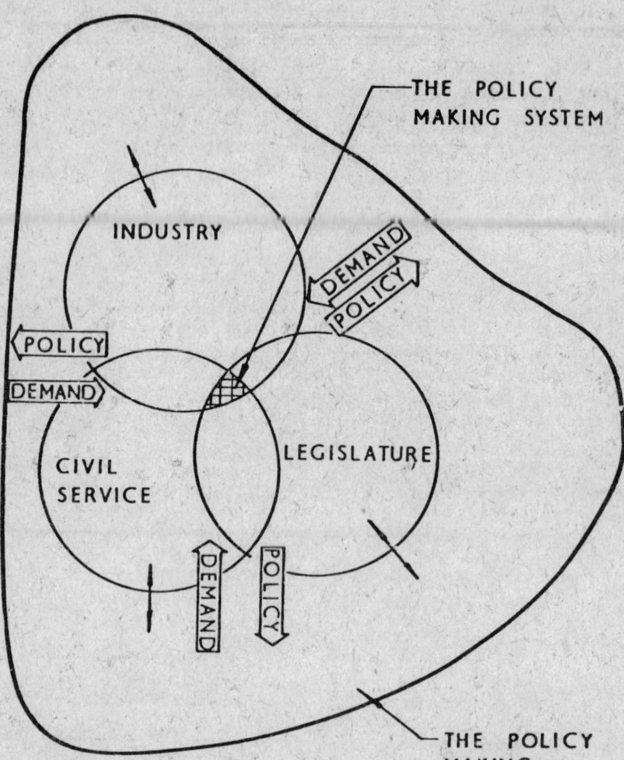

NOTES

1. DIFFUSION OF KNOWLEDGE AND IDEAS SHOWN ⟷
2. THE GROUPING OF INTERACTING VARIABLES SHOWN APPLIES EQUALLY TO NATIONAL OR INTERNATIONAL POLICY MAKING

FIG.12.3 INTERACTING VARIABLES ASSOCIATED WITH POLICY MAKING

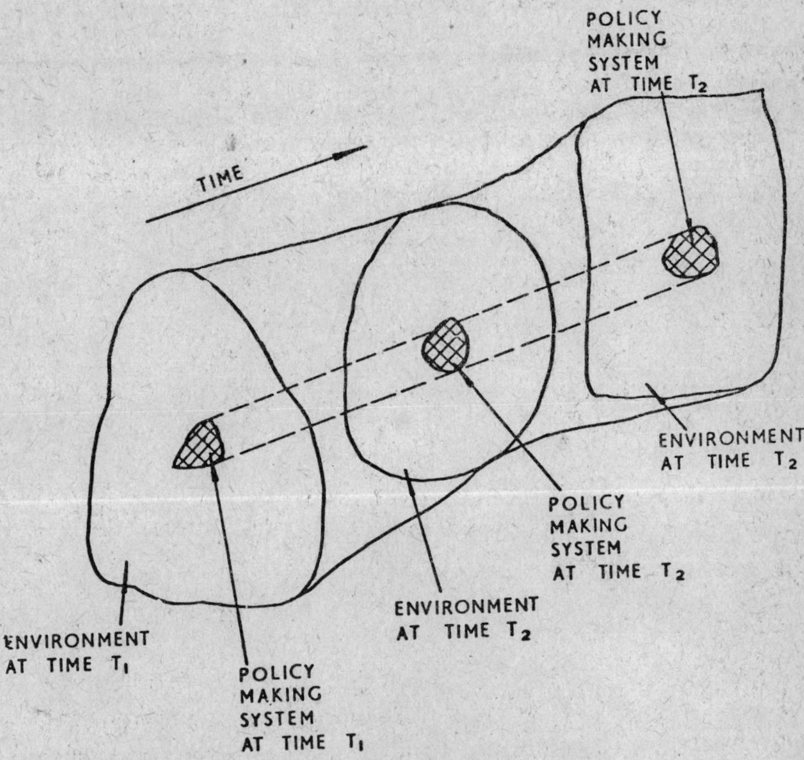

FIG.12.4 VARIATION OF ENVIRONMENT AND POLICY MAKING SYSTEM WITH TIME

REFERENCES

1. Chicken, J C. (1981). Nuclear Power Hazard Control Policy. Pergamon Press, Oxford.
2. The Windscale Inquiry. (1978). Her Majesty's Stationery Office, London.
3. Carson, R. (1962). The Silent Spring. Riverside Press, Cambridge.
4. Nader, R. (1977). Unsafe at any Speed. Grossman Publishers, New York.
5. Nader, R. and Abbotts, J. (1977). The Menace of Atomic Energy. W W Morton & Co Inc, New York.
6. Pearce, D, Edwards L, Beuret, G. (1979). Decision Making for Energy Futures. The Macmillan Press Ltd, London.

THIRTEEN

Terrel L. Rhodes and Kathleen K. Loewy

Policy Issues
Emergency Response Planning for Nuclear Power Plants

INTRODUCTION

Nuclear generation of power is a fact of life in many countries and will be in more by the end of the century. The initial promise has been modified by more realistic assessment of relative costs and hazards posed by accidents and waste products. The worst case, according to a recent article in **Scientific American** (1980), will be the explosion of a nuclear weapon on or near a nuclear power plant. Such an occurrence would create a lethal zone of 500 square miles. An area of 180 square miles would continue to expose any occupant to a dose of 2 rem per year for more than a century. Such an event could devastate a substantial part of Europe. Of more immediate concern is the possibility of an accident resulting in release of radioactive water or emissions in the air. The frequency of incidents at nuclear power plants caused by design and construction faults and human error suggests the real likelihood of such a release.

Some figures of U. S. Licensee Event Reports support this concern. There were 20,000 of these reports by the end of 1979. In 1980 it was expected that there would be 3,400 or an average of 10-15 per day. Even these figures may be low since "the decision as to whether or not an event should be reported is made by the individual licensee, applying NRC written guidelines" (Fetter and Tsipis, 1981). They are limited to safety-related systems and subject to interpretation. Designs, nomenclature and license conditions vary from plant to plant. Interpretation of the reporting threshold varies from utility to utility. Some use very narrow definitions to limit the paperwork or to not look bad. Others overreport to be conservative. There is a clear factor of self-interest involved in information given both to the government and the public. In the U. S., as long as this is a private sector business run for profit, such problems will continue to occur.

There are a number of public policy issues concerned with nuclear power generation. The first, of course is the decision whether or not to include it in national energy planning. Modern industrial nations have already made this choice. Other policies concern location of facilities, safety of persons and property, and waste disposal. The proximity of nuclear plants to urban areas raises the issue of whether nuclear plants should be sited so close to such large concentrations of people. Isn't the potential for disaster heightened in a radiological emergency? Western Europe, however, does not have the luxury of locating plants away from urbanized areas. There are existing plants already on the periphery of cities; such plants are not likely to be relocated. Therefore, what follows is a comparison of the emergency response plans (ERP) of four industrialized nations as they relate to procedures and policies for protecting the general citizenry who live in the vicinity of a nuclear power plant. Issues regarding the siting of plants and the technical operations of plants will not be addressed in this paper. Ideally, a comparison of all nations with nuclear power generation capabilities would be desirable but the limited information available to the authors at the time of preparation focused attention primarily on four nations: The United Kingdom (UK), France (FR), the Federal Republic of Germany (FRG), and the United States (US). When appropriate and possible, reference is made to the emergency response plans of other nations.

The focus of this report is on emergency response plans designed to moderate or forestall the hazard to the population most likely to be adversely affected. An emergency response plan is an official document which outlines the responsibilities of actors and the actions to be taken in the event of an accident or potential accident at a nuclear power electrical generating station. The plans usually encompass a range of accidents from minor fires to massive release of radioactivity into the environment. In each case the purpose of an emergency response plan is to provide immediate response alternatives to the threat of injury and suffering to persons, and destruction and damage to public and private property as a result of natural and man-made destructive forces. Such a plan should also deal with measures necessary to return the area to a normal state as quickly as possible or isolate contaminated areas as well as protecting the population from unsafe food and water. "In the event of an accident, the decision-making authorities must try to apply protective measures aimed at reducing radiological exposures to the public to a value as low as reasonably achieveable" (IAEA, 1981, p. 9).

A major focus will be on issues of responsibility, both intergovernmental and interorganizational. Interovernmental relations (i.e., what level of government has responsibility for making which decisions pertaining to which components of an ERP?) and interorganizational relations (i.e., which governmental and which non-governmental organizations have responsibility for implementing which components of an ERP?) represent the context within which we examine the ERPs of these four nations. Such plans generally require a great deal of coordinated effort by many organizations and levels of government and shifts in authority from one to another depending upon the definition of the emergency situation.

To facilitate the comparison of the plans, we have divided the analysis into three stages: (1) Procedures and responsibilities for warning the populace of an emergency or the potential for an emergency; (2) Procedures and responsibilities for evacuating the populace from the affected area; and (3) Procedures and responsibilities for restoring the affected area and the return of the populace to that area. In addition to questions of responsibilities and procedures, a further consideration is the extent of involvement of the general citizenry and local governments in the decision-making and development of ERPs.

INFORMING AND WARNING THE PUBLIC

All four nations have a system of emergency action levels (EALs) which defines the types of emergency that may occur and the measures that should be taken in response to the EALs (See Table 13.1). Each nation sets out rather detailed levels of emergency, which distinguish between more conventional accidents or incidents contained within the plant perimeter, e.g.,a fire or leak, and more extraordinary accidents or incidents of a radiological nature which threaten the environment and people surrounding the plant. Each nation also specifies a steadily expanding and complex set of measures to be taken in response to the EALs (although the UK and FRG report the least detailed set of measures). Clearly, there is a recognition of the variety of potential incidents at nuclear plants and the need to have appropriate response measures (See Table 13.2).

In the event of an emergency, especially an emergency of a radiological nature, it is necessary to have clearly assigned

TABLE 13.1
Emergency Action Levels and Warning Systems

LEVELS FRG	FR	UK	US
(A) Early Disaster Alert -operational failure -effect on environment nil or slight	(A) Conventional Alpha Alert -within facility perimeter -without victims -nonradiological	(A) Site Incidents - Standby -contained within site security fence -Situation exists or imminent	(A) Unusual Event -potential degradation of safety of plant
(B) Special Water Alert -operational failure or accident -dangerous release of radiation to water, but not air	(B) Conventional Bravo Alert -same as Alpha, but with victims	(B) Site Incident - Alert -contained within site fence -incident is verified	(B) Alert -actual or potential substantial degradation of safety of plant
(C) Disaster Alert -operational failure or accident -dangerous release of radiation to air occurred or imminent	(C) Inside Alpha Alert -radiological character -without consequences for environment of power plant -without victims	(C) Emergency - Standby -hazardous condition likely to harm public -incident exists or imminent	(C) Site Area Emergency -actual or likely major failure of plant functions needed for protection of the public
	(D) Inside Bravo Alert -same as Alpha, but with victims	(D) Emergency - Alert -hazardous condition likely to harm public -incident verified	(D) General Emergency -actual or imminent substantial core degradation or melting with potential for loss of containment integrity
	(E) Outside Alert -radiological character -threat outside plant perimeter		

Table 13.1 continued.....

EMERGENCY MEASURES FRG	FR	UK	US
Class 1: -alarms raised upon receipts of alert from licensee -prepare for futher alert	First Level Alert (A,B above) -contact Prefecture government -fire fighting department -emergency medical -civil air resources -report to Directorate of Civil Safety	All events -verbally notify key plant personnel -sirens and public address system notification of remaining plant personnel -telephone regional and other governmental personnel to activate fan-out network	Notify Nuclear Regulatory Commission (NRC) -may activate Emergency Operations Facility (EOF) (established by licensee apart from site capable of monitoring all pertinent radiological, meteorological and plant system data) -Federal Emergency Management Agency (FEMA, has liaison at EOF
Class 2: -urgent prevention of acute dangers	Second Level Alert (C,D above) -all of above, plus Prefecture alert: -radiological detection team -Disaster Control Center -Central Service for Protection Against Ionized Radiation -Atomic Energy commission Control Team		Notify NRC -may activate EOF -FEMA at EOF -NRC liaison for on-site actions, FEMA liaison for state actions -state requests Federal assistance -state sets its Emergency Command post. FEMA official there - notifies all state agencies -Communications links established -Notify local government - County Civil Defense Office - they notify all affected units - fire, police, medical, shelter
Class 3: -eliminate dangers that still exist	Third Level Alert (E abcve) -all of above, plus -appropriate measures -no designation of agencies		Notify NRC Must activate EOF -all above
			Notify NRC -must activate EOF -all above

TABLE 13.2
Responsibility for Emergency Actions

LICENSEE

FRG	FR	UK	US
-primary responsibility in alarm phase -operator notify/alarm governmental authorities and offices, especially disaster control authority -contact licensee's expert liaison to coordinate until radiological protection specialist arrives from disaster control authority -designate and equip command post outside plant for licensee's disaster squad management team in case evacuate plant -measure radiation levels in environment of plant and inner zone (2km) -develop and maintain own "alert plan" (required under licensing plan)	-operator notify authority and report changes -satisfy within plant -prepare/maintain emergency plan for plant -designate linkage person with outside assistance	-specific individuals who can declare alert from plant superintendent down to shift change engineer on duty -notify other utilities & government officials -most senior person present Emergency Controller (EC) -overall command of emergency operation -safety of on-site personnel -operation of plant -safety of public -assess risk to public -take counter measures -Emergency Control Center (EC, duty health physicist, reactor physicist, administrative officer, telephonist) -fire teams (each shift) -emergency survey team -first-aid team -rescue team -damage control team -cancel alert	-Shift supervisor/Emergency coordinator/Station Manager alerts local (calls local government designated 24 hour number), state (State Warning Paid, federal agencies, licensee management -monitors and evaluates situation -requests state aid -recommends evacuation to state after confirming with local governments -primary responsibility within the site boundaries

Table 13.2 continued....

GOVERNMENT FRG	FR	UK	US
-overall federal plan (Atomgesetz) -primary responsibility to state -primary agencies = public safety (radiological emergency part of overall disaster plan) -federal agencies brought in only upon request (Army, National Weather Service, River Police) -specific Disaster Control plans classified -maintain alert diagrams for alert phases (who does what, when) -designate reallying points for marking disaster personnel -the DCM (disaster control management raises the alert) (see Table 13.1) -measurement of radiation levels off-site (middle and outer zones - 10 km & 24 km)	-local and regional governments should call on national governmental agencies, e.g. police fire-fighting Special Aggressive Forces - for detection and decontamination Public Health Dept. Atomic Energy Comm. Central Service for Protection Against Ionizing Radiation (SCPRI) in Ministry of Health Directorate of Civil Safety in Ministry of Interior technical department advisors Mobile cells for radiological control (CMIR) - rapid development decontamination squads Electricite de France - detection, lab, locate radiological sources & medical assistance	LOCAL: UPON NOTICE -county police channel communic. for other county agencies issue potassium iodate tablets carry out evacuation when directed by EC -fire help if an alert -ambulance service - assist plant rescue and first-aid team -welfare - temporary housing -other plants - personnel and equipment NATIONAL -Health & Safety Branch of UKAEA staff expedite radiological survey, remedial measures and lab serv. -Meteorological Office - weather information -Ministry of Agriculture, Fisheries and Food - control distribution of milk & farm products -Depart. of Environment - advise locals on water undertakings	FEDERAL GOVERNMENT -NRC coordinating all technical (primarily radiological) response of Fed. Govt. -FEMA coordinating all non-technical (primarily logistical) -DOE coordinating off-site radiological & monitoring activities of Fed. Govt. -upon request by Governor STATE GOVERNMENT -assume overall management of off-site response when team is in place (approx. 6 hrs.) -principally responsible for emergency operations in the area of the ingestion exposure pathway (80 km) -specific assignments by State Emergency Response team leader LOCAL GOVERNMENT -local government bears the primary responsibility for emergency response within its jurisdiction -county is first source of governmental assistance for municipal governments. Direction and control by local gov. officials for 1st 6.hrs. after notifi. -Civil preparedness fire, med., ambulance & rescue -Quasi government & private? notif. or warning of person in affec. areas evacuation as necessary

responsibilities for warning specific individuals and organizations so that they may initiate their assigned activities. The assignment of primary responsibility in the event of a radiological emergency varies widely among the nations studied, but all rely heavily on the local levels of government. The FRG relies heavily on the states which have general disaster control plans, including sections on radiological emergencies. Federal agencies are brought in upon request from local agencies. The disaster control plan (Rahmenemphehlungen fur den Katastrophen schutz in der Umgebung Kerntechnischen Anlagen) for the vicinity of nuclear installations only presents a framework; the specifics are classified. It would appear, though, that the German plan is well detailed and extensive. There are clear descriptions of what actions should be taken under the three alerts and the three classifications within the alerts (although classes 2 and 3 relate primarily to the latter two alerts). The states have also worked to standardize and unify their emergency response plans nationwide. The major weaknesses in the German plans appear to be the seemingly high opportunity for confusion or at least lack of coordination among the disparate governmental agencies that are to respond in an emergency and the lack of widespread and frequent testing of the emergency plans themselves, which might provide valuable information on the question of coordination among responsible agencies.

The overall objective of emergency response plans is to provide dose savings (and in some cases immediate life saving) for a spectrum of accidents that should produce off-site doses in excess of Protective Action Guides (PACs). (U.S. NRC/FEMA, 1980), p. 5. The U.S. also relies heavily on local levels of government in an emergency, especially the county and state.

Planning is related to two exposure pathways: (1) a **plume exposure pathway** - whole body exposure to gamma radiation and deposited material and inhalation exposure; and (2) **and ingestion exposure pathway** - ingestion of contaminated water or foods. **Emergency Planning Zones** (EPZs) are described ascon centric circles centered at the nuclear power plant site but would have the actual shape modified by characteristics of a particular site. The plume exposure EPZ would be about 16 km in radius. The ingestion exposure EPZ would be about 80 km in radius.

The initial response to an off-site emergency is assigned to the county in which the plant is located and other counties within the plume exposure EPZ. Each county must have an approved plan which must be in conformity with the state site specific ERP. IF the emergency is not terminated quickly or if it escalates the operator may request the State to send in its

Emergency Response Team which will take over coordination and control responsibilities for the county(ies). Federal aid is primarily in research and training and as a backup in an extreme case.

In all cases the government is dependent upon the site shift supervisor for information and evaluation of the level of emergency, present or potential. State and federal officials on site may work with the shift supervisor in these determinations. The termination of the alert is also initiated by the licensee.

The French place the primary burden of response on the perfecture, but the actual response to the emergency and the provision of services comes primarily from national governmental agencies. France was divided into zones with each zone having a team of 15-30 people who could assemble in hours in response to an accident. A strong sense of the preeminence of national agencies and services is conveyed through the planning documents that are available. As with Germany, the specifics of emergency response are classified. No indication is given as to which agency has responsibility for specific activities, or who would provide coordination to activities and responses. The available documents are only plans in support of the ORSECRAD, the primary emergency response plan of the French government, which is classified.

The UK approaches the issue of emergency response in a manner similar to the U.S. The British vest primary responsibility in the plant operator, or more specifically, the Emergency Controller, who is the most senior plant personnel present. The Controller, with the assistance of additional designated plant personnel, declares the alert, assesses risks, indicates appropriate counter measures for plant personnel and the public and candels the alert when he deems it safe to do so. Local government, the county as in the U. S., is the primary governmental level of response to an emergency, but acts in a support capacity to the plant personnel. The national government's involvement also is primarily an enormous burden on emergency officials on the scene.

The four emergency response plans present basic assignments of responsibility between the organizational actors involved in a radiological emergency; however, only the U. S. documents suggest that on-going, extensive tests of the emergency response plans actually occur. From what we know of the myriad difficulties that arise in interorganizational relations, it would seem to be an essential part of any effective national emergency response plan that frequent and extensive operational testing of the plans be required of the licensees as well as local and national governmental agencies and individuals.

The final concern in the primary warning system is the notification of the public (See Table 12.3). Warning procedures concentrate on notification of governmental actors, not the general public. The details and procedures for notifying the general public are also sketchy, although most rely on a combination of television, radio and press announcements, mobile and stationary public address systems and sirens. Only Germany (and the U. S. in some areas) appear to systematically distribute much information to the public concerning procedures to follow in emergency. The lack of prior educational efforts for the general public would suggest the possibility of greater confusion and panic by the populace in an emergency than if efforts were increased to adequately inform people in advance. Part of the low priority assigned to public education and information may be traced to the pre-Three Mile Island feeling that there was little danger of a radiological emergency at a nuclear power facility. Greater attention has been given to educating and informing the public since that time.

EVACUATION PROCEDURES

Most of the plans also do not give much attention to evacuating the populace in the event of an emergency. Again, most licensees and governmental officials take a position that there is little likelihood of an accident that would effect anyone outside the perimeter of the plant. Only in the US is evacuation considered a high priority response to a radiological emergency. Germany advises its citizens to remain indoors and to seal their homes until the plume passes the area, but in the event that evacuation is determined by the Disaster Control Management team to be necessary a detailed plan and announcement are available. The prepared text briefly describes the danger, gives tips on securing property, preparing luggage, private and public transportation, and temporary accommodations outside the affected area. The evacuation plan calls for estimates of the number of people involved, available transportation (private and public), travel routes, emergency vehicle routes, accommodations for people, medical care, food supply, populations with special needs (handicapped, prisons, hospitals), and decontamination. That this elaborate plan is a back-up plan is remarkable since many nations appear to have much less developed plans as their primary response. The one weakness again appears to be the lack of assigned responsibility for evacuation management and coordination.

TABLE 13.3
Informing the General Public

FRG	FR	UK	US
-Disaster control Management set-up Information Bureau to update citizens -prepare text Stay inside house, and close it up Decontaminate self it have been out (wash clothes, self -traffic out - decontaminated at collection point -other traffic dealt with according to own disaster plan -distribution of iodine tablets -provision of educational materials prior to an emergency	-Prefecture notifies public in event of Conventional and Inside Alerts, no mention of who in event of Outside Alert -reference to response of information and Public Relations Service of the ORSEC plan (classified) -no details	-establish Information Center -Regional Public Relations Officer - sole contact brief press upon instructions from Emergency Controller	-operator local and state emergency officials (list supplied) -licensee gives reports & eval. to state/local officials -State officials are responsible for keeping the populace adequately informed (prepare news releases, hold press conferences) -NRC responsible for reporting federal technical response -FEMA responsible for reporting non-technical support activities. Both report to White House and Congress -if licensee, local, state, and federal officials deem it necessary, public will be informed (licensee recommends evacuation to the State) -Alert primarily depends upon sirens and institutional warning systems -Emergency Broadcast System - signal to turn to specified frequency for information -Aircraft - flares and leaflets House by House Warning by fire departments

The British plan calls for evacuation if "two or more off-site measurements indicate a beta/gamma air count greater than 2×10^6 dpm/m^3 action" (NUREG/CR-1979, 1980, p. 71). If evacuation is necessary a plan exists in the Essential Services Emergency Plan, which details police and welfare services, but its breadth does not approach that of the German plan.

The French evacuation guidelines vaguely refer to concentrations of "radioactive substances in a specified area" with evacuation "justified in a very restricted number of hypotheses" (NUREG/CR 1979, p.88) with no specific mention of who, when, how, where or if.

The US plans call for evacuation of all persons in a sector of the 16 im EPZ exposed to the radioactive plume. The site specific plan has detailed maps and analysis of the population. Shelters are established in public buildings outside the affected zones which are staffed by local government personnel and emergency services including such organizations as the Red Cross. Persons leaving the EPZ are checked for radiation exposure and decontamination of persons and vehicles carried out before they are permitted to leave the zone. The plan does not call for long-term operation of shelters. Reentry is permitted upon recommendation of the licensee to the State.

Plans for evacuation of the 80 km ingestion EPZ are not as detailed and are not tested by actual drills.

Evacuation is not viewed as a primary or even a desirable option in the European countries for a variety of reasons ranging from the existence of more substantial residential structures than is the case in the US to the greater difficulty in Europe presented by the density of population surrounding many nuclear facilities. However, the German plan in particular is a more detailed and comprehensive plan of action in many respects than the US plans, which do contain evacuation of the general public as a primary response.

RESTORATION OF AFFECTED AREAS AND THEIR POPULATION

A final aspect of safety planning in response to a radiological emergency presumably would include a plan for restoring the affected area and for returning the population to their homes, businesses, etc.

The FRG plan seeks only of decontamination which relates to individuals and property within or departing the affected area. Restoration of the area is not discussed. Neither the British nor the French plans mention restoration.

The US plans are similar to those of the FRG. The licensee may recommendthe return of residents to the area. The State government, assisted by federal agencies, would monitor affected areas. A control of milk from cattle fed contaminated feed is mentioned - there is mention of a table top exercise to test the ingestion parhway exposure (80 km radius) but no discussion of its effectiveness. (Plant McGuire Site Specific Radiological Emergency Preparedness Exercise, p. 7).

Perhaps the issue of restoration of the affected area is not a major concern because all of the nations examined still do not consider a radiological disaster that would involve radioactive release into the environment a very likely possibility. Three Mile Island has prompted a reexamination and revision of national, local and site specific plans, but the sense of the documents and governmental officials seems to remain one of confidence in the ability of well-trained plant personnel to handle any mechanical difficulty that might arise. The emphasis is still on mechanical, equipment-based accidents, not on people-related problems, although changes in operational procedures have been made in the wake of TMI.

An additional factor which has affected the issue of restoration, is the question of who will bear the financial cost and/or actually provide the restoration services? Most national plans leave the question unanswered and occasionally unasked. Only in Switzerland does there appear to be a clear concern that the operator bear the costs of informing the public and providing emergency procedures as a result of events at their facilities. The US places most of the financial burden on local and state governmental institutions with limited promise of federal assistance. The operator's liabilities are extremely limited through federal assistance insurance and statutes. This is clearly an issue that governmental decision makers would prefer to avoid if at all possible.

SUMMARY AND CONCLUSIONS

One of the main benefits of efforts to compare national policies is that we increase our opportunities to learn from each other and to build on our strengths. The preceding comparison has elucidated the general emergency response plans of four major industrial nations as they relate to off-site measures to protect the general population residing near nuclear electric power facilities. From the information that is available, there is a heavy emphasis, rightfully so, on measures to control and contain accidents within the nuclear facility itself. Plans for the protection of the surrounding population, however, are largely too vague and inadequate to demonstrate much promise of effectively protecting local citizenry.

Even where more extensive plans exist (FRG, US) there is little emphasis placed on continual testing and updating of the procedures and assignments of responsibility. Although sheltering is a reasonable response if sturdy structures are available, evacuation of the populace, if initiated in the early phase of an accident, would greatly reduce contamination. Given the importance the International Atomic Energy Agency (IAEA) has placed on the protection of the general public in the event of a radiation accident, e.g., "Evacuation is the protective measure that can be implemented if suitable conditions exist. . . the ideal time to implement evacuation is prior to the plume arrival." (IAEA, 1981, p. 19), the need for frequent drills and exercises to test the plans should be apparent. Contrary to the IAEA recommendations, it also would seem advisable to periodically involve the general public in emergency response exercises, including at least limited evacuation drills. Experience in an actual US emergency response drill (McGuire Nuclear Power Plant, December 4-5, 1980) reinforces the need for testing ERP's. The two major failings of this exercise were in communications and in coordination between the licensee and the many government jurisdictions and agenceis involved. A particular problem arose with the transfer of powers from county to state emergency response teams.

An additional serious problem, one also mentioned in reports of European drills, was the lack of radiological monitoring equipment and personnel properly trained to use it. This would create grave difficulties in decisions about appropriate actions during the emergency and decisions about reentry. In the US the separation between health related units and emergency control units at all levels of government makes coordination still more difficult.

The US Nuclear Regulatory Commission now requires yearly drills for license renewal. If these drills are enlarged to include evacuation much could be learned which would facilitate the improvement of plans. However, the population in general is resistant to the idea of evacuation; businesses, schools and other institutions are against the disruption such exercises would cause. Most drills are held on weekends for this reason. The constant message that serious accidents are extremely unlikely contributes to this "head in the sand" attitude.

In heavily populated areas, the potential danger of large scale human contamination and injury is increased, and therefore efforts that could prevent harm to the populace must have a very high priority. Though siting has not been our focus in this report, the IAEA states that "if a proposed site for a nuclear facility presents particular difficulties to be overcome in developing and implementing an emergency response plan, this could be sufficient reason for not selecting the site" (IAEA, 1981, p. 2). One of the difficulties mentioned is population density. Most European nations, unlike the US and Canada, do not have the option of locating nuclear facilities in sparsely populated areas, yet even in North America nuclear plants are placed in close proximity to densely urbanized areas. Localities are not usually involved in the decisions to locate nuclear plants near them; their involvement only comes later when efforts are made to prepare an emergency response plan that requires the participation of local agencies and personnel. Emergency response planning must be done as a part of determining site selection.

A final lesson to be learned from this examination is the need for clearly delineated central control of emergency responses. Most plans do specify functional responsibilities, but they do not provide for comprehensive, coordinated control of response activities. The Canadian plan does provide a model that might be applied elsewhere through the creation of an interagency Control Group within the Ministry of Health, which has responsibility for on-site and off-site activities, as well as for ensuring the coordination of all operating procedures and actions under the plan and at local and municipal levels. Again, a lack of critical testing makes it difficult to judge the effecitveness of the body in action. The design does offer a greater likelihood of reduced conflict, duplication and confusion in highly stressful situations.

It is unlikely that industrialized or industrializing nations will totally abandon nuclear power generation as one alternative to their energy needs, although France's new government has moved to halt that nation's program. Even if development of a nation's nuclear power plants was halted and existing plants were closed down, the threat to the public safety continues in the form of nuclear waste and fuels, and the lack of any viable plan to decommission nuclear plants.

A further complication arises from the location of a nuclear plant by one nation on the border of another, thus creating a burden on the resources of the second nation and its people. European nations have been very aware of this issue and have drawn-up agreements between and among national governments to address the problem.

The overall policy implications remain. Nuclear power facilities exist and new ones are expected over the coming years. Even though the on-the-job safety record for nuclear facilities is good, potential disaster persists as a real threat for large numbers of people living in the vicinity of a plant. Emergency response plans are essential, but they **must** be tested, including involvement of the affected populations. As this study has indicated: (1) detailed, comprehensive plans appear to be lacking or at least are not readily available to those organizations and citizens who may be told to implement or follow the plan in an emergency; (2) education and involvement of the general population is virtually non-existant; (3) specification of responsibility for unified **coordination** of the emergency response is often absent; (4) plans for evacuating the populace are usually weak and perhaps too late; (5) plans for restoring the affected area are not available in any detail; and (6) the plans that do exist have not actually been tested in extensive field exercise (with the exception of the US).

Those who prepare emergency response plans are torn between the technical aspects of the various components of a plan and a desire not to alarm the general populace. The threat of widespread harm, however, which far surpasses the threat from other energy generation technologies, requires that the governments of nations fully inform their citizenry of the potential dangers and consequences of an accident, and that they take the most extensive steps possible to protect their citizens in the event of a radiological emergency. Protecting a few people in a rural area is quite different from protecting a highly urbanized and industrialized population. Those outside the present planning process should perhaps be more directly involved in the development of emergency response plans. At a very minimum, those who are involved in ER planning must be required to test their plans thoroughly and to inform and involve the public in these major decisions that so drastically affect their lives. "The dangers of nuclear power to present and future generations are too great to leave decision to the so-called experts. There is a growing effort by citizens to remove nuclear power decisions from an estranged bureaucracy and technological elite and place these decisions in the hands of the citizenry." (Nader, 1977, p. 68).

REFERENCES

Fetter, Steven A., and Tsipis, Kosta. (1981). "Castastrophic

Releases of Radioactivity," **Scientific American**, Volume 244 No. 4, pp. 41-47.

International Atomic Energy Agency. (1981). **Planning for Off-Site Response to Radiation Accidents in Nuclear Facilities: Recommendations**, Safety Series No. 55.

Nader, Ralph, and Abbotts, John. (1977). **The Menace of Atomic Energy**. W.W. Norton and Company, Inc., New York.

Nuclear Safety. (1981). Volumes 22-23.

Plant McGuire Site Specific Radiological Emergency Preparedness Exercise Observations and Recommendations of the Federal Observer Team. (1980).

Schuller, C.R., et al. (1980). **Emergency Preparedness for Nuclear Electric Generating Facilities in Foreign Countries: A Brief Survey of Practices**. (NUREG/CR-1979) U.S. Nuclear Regulatory Commission, Washington, D.C.

FOURTEEN

C. Thangavel, P. Jayapal, K.M. Kulkarni

Spatial Patterns of some Infectious Diseases
A Case Study of Ahmedabad City

INTRODUCTION

Urbanization and Industrialization have their own impact on the urban mosaic, both positive and negative. On the one hand, they bring various advantages to the Society in the form of agglomeration economies, and on the other hand, they have far reaching negative effects such as overcrowding reflected in high density of population, high density of housing and high internal living density. The phenomenon of high density of population may perhaps give rise to several social problems like social disorders, social tensions, social ill-health and social injustice and among these the problem of social ill-health deserves special attention. Many of the social diseases of the urban area have been attributed to high density of population or overcrowding (Allan Booth 1976). The communicable diseases spread quickly in the neighbouring areas of high density of population in the huddled houses.

In large urban centres, the higher proportion of residents live in the areas of traumatic environmental conditions such as densely populated core areas, slums and shanty-towns. The inhabitants will have poor knowledge of the health care and facilities and so will be more susceptible to the communicable diseases. This needs careful health planning in terms of eradication programmes. However, such programmes require background material such as the pattern of occurrance of various diseases, their frequency and intensity, the quality of physical and social environment, including the important ones like density of houses,

---

* Submitted to the international symposium on Incidence of Infectious and Chronic Diseases: Geographical Perspectives, Held at Madras during December 1-4, 1981.

quality of houses (condition), number of persons per room, density of population and micro variation in the quality of air, water and intensity of temperature.

Data base and methodology

Data regarding the monthly incidence of Jaundice, Measles, Diptheria, Gastroenteritis and Chicken-pox were collected for different wards from the Municipal Corporation of Ahmedabad, for the year 1980 (Refer Table 14.1). The study takes into account a few physical and social variables* such as density of population, density of houses, number of persons per room, percentage of residential tenements having out ratable value less than Rs. 300 to total residential tenements and percentage of ward population below the age group 14** to understand the spatial association with the occurrance of diseases. Data pertaining to the physical and social variables were collected from the census handbook (1971) and minucipal corporation of Ahmedabad.

Data were used in mapping both to identify the spatial patterns and associations. Quantities were used as class intervals for drawing the choropleth maps. The 'independentness' of the variables were also tested by using the multiple regression.

Study Area

Our study area is confined to Ahmedabad city which is the seventh largest city in India. It is one of the most densely populated cities in the world, with an approximate population of over 2.2 million (1981). The city came under British rule in the year 1817 and subsequently experienced the advent of Industrialization, particularly in the ancient textile sector. This led to a dramatic period of economic reconstruction. By 1900 A.D. Ahmedabad became a leading textile manufacturing centre in the country which attracted population from far and wide. Population attained a sizeable magnitude due to the accelerated migration. Physically it is divided into two parts by the Sabarmati river, with the old city and its outgrowth on the eastern side and the nearby developed areas on the western side.

---

* These are the few chosen variables which form the limitation of the paper.

** Wardwise population below the age 14 is computed from the total population of the city in that age group with the assumption that it has uniform proportion in all wards.

TABLE 14.1

Incidence of Infectious Diseases, Ahmedabad 1980 (Per 10000 Pop.)

	Ward Name	Disease					Total Population
		Jaundice	Gastro-enteritis	Diptheria	Measles	Chicken Pox	
1.	Khadia	4.6	1.1	1.8	0.03	0.5	78588
2.	Kalupur	3.4	1.5	0.7	0.0	0.3	91174
3.	Jamalpur	6.7	2.1	1.2	0.6	0.0	80150
4.	Shahpur	4.6	1.2	0.6	0.0	0.6	102785
5.	Dariapur	1.6	0.9	0.2	0.1	0.0	80459
6.	Raikad	3.3	0.2	1.0	0.0	0.4	47571
7.	Saraspur	97.7	0.0	7.4	0.4	0.0	22921
8.	Rakhial	9.2	0.2	2.1	0.0	0.3	186622
9.	Gomthipur	16.6	5.2	1.6	0.0	0.0	74003
10.	Asarwa	3.7	0.1	0.6	0.0	0.2	179387
11.	Ellisbridge	4.5	0.6	0.8	0.1	0.4	223954
12.	Sabarmathi	5.1	2.2	1.1	0.0	0.4	44951
13.	Maninagar	7.3	0.8	0.5	0.1	0.2	182123
14.	Mattupura	1.0	0.0	0.8	0.0	0.5	132662
15.	Behrampura	1.7	5.4	0.7	1.7	1.0	59186
16.	Danilimda	2.4	24.2	1.0	3.4	2.4	20621

Source: Municipal Corporation of Ahmedabad.

Conceptual Framework

In the field of medical geography, as in other branches of Geography, isolating specific and single casual factor is probably a dangerous thing (Emvys Jones and John Eyles, 1976). Jacques May (1950) points out that 'Disease is a multiple phenomenon which occurs only if various factors coincide in place and time'. The reasons for the occurrance of a disease could be physical, biological and social. The present analysis takes into consideration some of the physical and social factors.

The occurrence of many diseases is closely related to their environmental conditions. The organisms will succeed in jeopardising the health of a person only when both the external environment (geographical and socio-cultural) in which it originates and the internal environment (the human body) in which it grows offer favourable conditions for multiplication (Misra R.P. 1970). Some of the diseases are waterborne. They occur and spread because of the use of contaminated water. The high density of population, high density of dwelling units and more number of persons per room, either singly or together can offer susceptible environment. The chances of easy contamination and quick spread of diseases are possible mainly because of illiterate members of the society, lack of general awareness and crowded living. There is greater chance for the occurrence and spread of diseases in conditions of high population density and lower quality of housing (which could be explained by the amount of rent paid (G.E.A. Daver) or the net ratable value of the housing (Sundaravel, 1981). Considering the inadequate urban facilities such as housing, protected water supply, sewage disposal etc., in the urban areas it should not be surprising to find greater incidence of various diseases.

Patterns of Diseases

Jaundice

Jaundice is caused by virus infection mainly through contaminated water and unhygenic food. Though there could be several other factors, which account for its occurrence, the selected five variables (Table 14.2) - population density, dwelling density, persons per room, low housing condition and population below age 14 together explain 81% of the (Table 14.3) variation in the occurrence of jaundice. Though all these variables together explain 81%, the density of dwelling units explains greater association. Density of population shows a significant negative relation with the incidence of jaundice. This clearly reveals that the incidence of jaundice is related to the density of dwelling units which influence the amount and quality of water. The other variables show insignificant relation.

The map showing the spatial pattern of the incidence of Jaudice (Figure 14.1) conforms to the above findings. The greater incidence of disease has been observed in the wards of Saraspur, Maninagar, Rakhial and Gomthipur where the density of dwelling units is also relatively high, while the least occurrence of disease is observed in Danilimda, Behrampura, Dariapur and Mattupura where there is low density of dwelling units. The incidence of jaundice was observed to be uniform throughout the year in fairly large areas except some wards such as Danilimda, Mattupura, and Behrampura. These wards show the peak of occurrance during the months of April, May and September (Appendix 14.1).

Gastroenteritis

Gastroenteritis is a viral disease which results from the use of contaminated water. The variables explain 72% of the variance (Table 14.3) in the occurrence of the disease. The variable representing the number of persons per room shows significant positive relation. The crowded dwelling units increases the incidence of disease mainly due to the possible contamination of water. Eventhough population density shows insignificant positive relation, the other variables show significant positive relation, the other variables show significant negative relation. This indicates that either the density of dwelling units or the housing condition and or children population in the age group 0-14 are related to the incidence of gastroenteritis. The spatial pattern of the incidence of gastroenteritis (Figure 14.2) also shows an association with the areas having greater number of persons per room. The areas of high incidence of gastroenteritis are Behrampura, Danilimda, Gomthipur and Sabarmathi which also show high density per room. The relatively low incidence of the disease is associated with the lower number of persons per room. The monthwise analysis of the incidence of gastroenteritis shows a bias for the monsoon season. The incidence of disease is maximum from July to October (Table 14.4 and appendix 14.2).

Diphtheria

Many diseases are directly related to the intake of unhygrenic food. Diphtheria causes mainly because of the consumption of infected food. The variables under study explain 81% of the variation in the incidence of diphtheria (Table 14.3). Among the variables the density of dwelling units show significant posi-

TABLE 14.2
Physical and Social Variables

Ward Name	Population* density (km^2)	No.of Dwelling** units (km^2)	No. of persons per room**	Net ratable Values Rs. 300	Percentage* of popution below age 14
1. Khadia	105274	19020	2.51	52.85	4.89
2. Kalupur	107612	17362	2.88	60.03	5.68
3. Jamalpur	89595	14101	3.05	64.99	5.00
4. Shahpur	86679	14593	3.14	63.57	6.39
5. Dariapur	141023	22838	3.46	35.90	5.00
6. Raikad	48052	8213	2.41	67.31	2.96
7. Saraspur	143256	28600	3.86	55.32	1.42
8. Rakhial	27690	5123	3.41	76.72	11.55
9. Gomthipur	43495	9092	3.45	84.36**	4.60
10. Asarwa	18746	3676	2.93	77.83	11.16
11. Ellisbridge	6321	1149	3.38	30.72	13.94
12. Sabarmathi	8990	1780	2.40	49.51	2.79
13. Maninagar	16617	3154	3.25	51.91	11.34
14. Mattupura	22677	4290	2.92	71.26	8.26
15. Behrampura	19239	3447	3.84	81.04	3.68
16. Danilimda	3919	702	3.70	50.70	1.28

Source: * Compiled from census handbook 1971
** Municipal corporation of Ahmedabad.
*** Data is only for Railwaypura, but Gomthipur ward includes Mattupura's Gomthipur.

TABLE 14.3
Multiple Linear Regression Analysis

Dependent variable	a Population Density (X_1)	Dwelling Density (X_2)	Persons per room (X_3)	Low Housing conditions (X_4)	Percentage of pop. below Age 14	R^2(%) (X_5)	
Jaundice	-2.2776	-0.000165 -4.2324*	0.00108 4.7438*	1.0601 1.4685	-0.01739 -0.7511	-0.03148 -0.3497	81.63
Gastro-enteritis	0.05564	-0.000015 1.2710	-0.000132 -1.6590	0.6424 2.8678	-0.01119 -1.5575	-0.10750 -3.8475	72.43
Diptheria	-0.004647	-0.000012 -4.5373	0.00083 4.9981*	0.0441 0.8364	-0.00098 -0.5833	-0.00360 -0.5480	81.00

* Significant at 0.01 level
** Significant at 0.05 level

TABLE 14.4
Monthly incidence of Diseases* 1980

	January	February	March	April	May	June	July	August	September	October	November	December
Jaundice	7.5	7.5	8.3	9.1	11.3	8.5	7.5	8.8	9.5	10.6	5.0	5.7
Diptheria	2.9	-	5.2	1.7	4.1	4.1	8.8	22.9	20.0	7.6	7.0	11.7
Gastro-enteritis	1.3	0.1	6.3	8.1	6.3	4.0	12.0	48.0	1.3	3.0	6.3	2.0
Measles	-	-	-	10.7	-	3.5	3.5	-	-	-	39.0	42.8
Chicken pox	12.9	24.0	30.6	24.0	3.2	3.2	-	-	-	1.6	-	1.6

* Figures represent percentage to the total cases

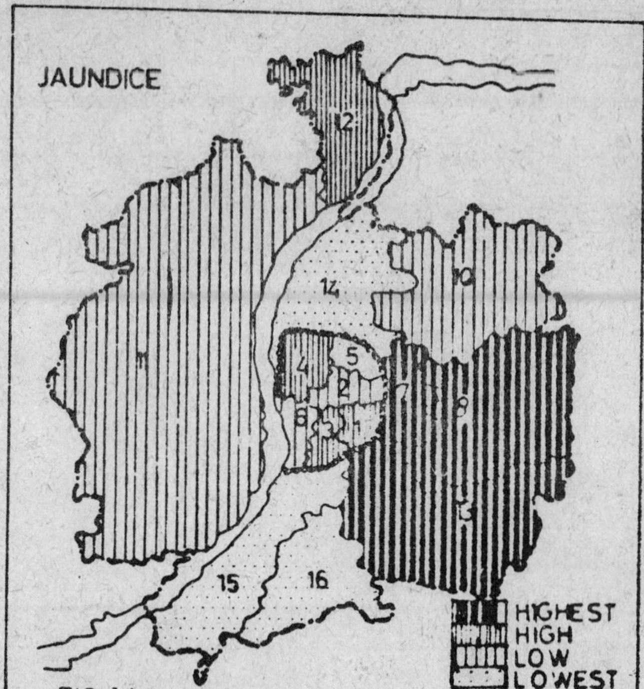

FIG: 14.1

SPATIAL INCIDENCE OF SOME INFECTIOUS DISEASES AHMEDABAD

1 KHADIA
2 KALUPUR
3 JAMALPUR
4 SHAHPUR
5 DARIAPUR
6 RAIKHAD
7 SARASPUR
8 RAKHIAL
9 GOMITIPUR
10 ASARVA
11 ELLISBRIDGE
12 SABARMATI
13 MANINAGAR
14 MADHUPURA
15 BEHRAMPURA
16 DANILIMBDA

tive relation whereas the density of population shows negative association. The density of dwelling units affect the quality of micro-urban environment. The residents' habits of throwing garbage, washing vessels and clothes etc., affect the cleanliness of the environment and insects. The other variables under study are found to be insignificantly related.

The figure shows (Figure 14.3) that the Khadia, Sarapur, Gomthipur and Rakhial wards have higher incidence of diphtheria. They are also the wards with relatively high density of dwelling units. Other wards like Danilimda, Behrampura, Maninagar, Ellisbridge etc., show low incidence of diphtheria with low density of dwelling units. The incidence of diphtheria is more common during the monsoon season beginning from June and prevails till October (Appendix 14.3)

Measles

Measles is a highly infectious virus disease with an incubation period of about 10 to 14 days depending on the symptoms. There are several studies which indicate that the children are relatively more prone to this disease. The visual comparison of the figure (Figure 14.4) showing the spatial pattern of the incidence of measles and the percentage of population below the age group 14 (Table 14.2) (Percentage indicates to the total city's population in that age group) shows negative association with each other. Saraspur, Danilimda, Behrampura and Jamalpur wards show the lowest proportion of children in the age group below 14 whereas the incidence of measles is highest in those wards. The areas of Asarwa and Rakhial show relatively higher proportion of children but the incidence of measles is low. However, it is necessary to relate the incidence of measles with the actual proportion of children in the respective areas. The detailed study of the age of the patients in the case of measles and the differences in micro-temperature conditions serves our purpose of knowing its proneness. The incidence of measles is maximum during the peak Summer months (April-May) (Appendix 14.4)

Chicken-pox

The spatial pattern of its occurrence over the city shows fairly good association with the industrial areas and the polluted areas (Figure 14.5). The areas having low incidence of this disease are mainly the major residential areas. This clearly reveals that the urban micro climate in terms of quality and content of air exert some influence. The monthwise analysis of its occurrence also clearly shows that it occurs mainly during

~~fullpageblank~~

Fig.

and

Fig.

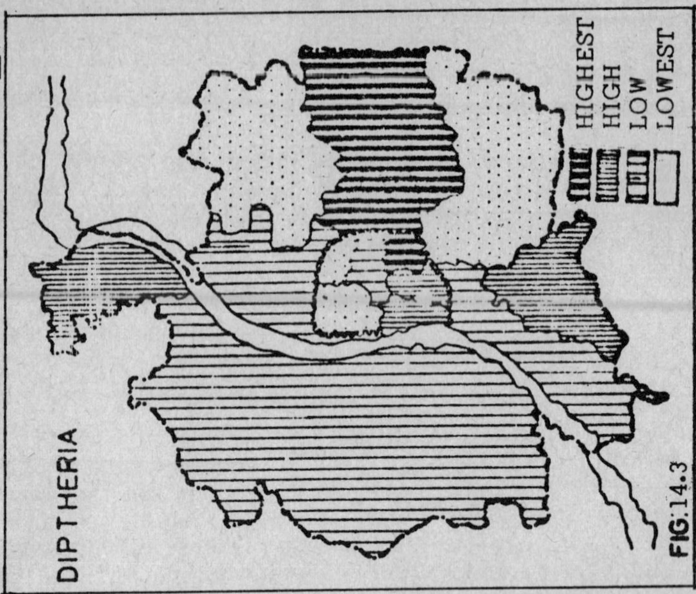

FIG.14.3

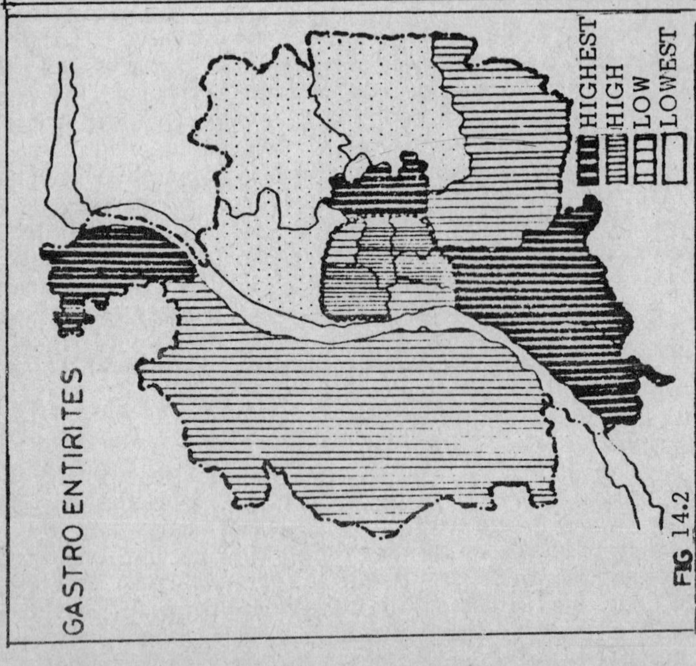

FIG 14.2

the summer season. The high temperature condition together with industrial smoke, waste and pollutants cause the greater incidence of chicken-pox, which is fairly well reflected in the figure 14.5 and Appendix 14.5.

CONCLUSIONS

The preceding discussion with its limitations of data and analytical tools brings our certain salient aspects with regard to the patterns of some infectious diseases in micro-urban environment of Ahmedabad city. However, such studies are worth carrying out elsewhere in similar urban situations for understanding the significant conformities and departures in the spatial patterns of infectious diseases. The salient observations of the study are as follows:

1. It is significant to note the spatial association of the occurrence of measles and chicken-pox in Jamalpur and Behrampur areas which are characterised by low lying terrain, poor housing conditions, habitation of muslims, industrial workers, hawkers and peddlers. The incidence of measles and chicken-pox is higher in these areas perhaps due to their outdoor activities and perspiring in the hot sun. Either they peddle around the city in hot sun for earning their bread or are engaged in household activities such as printing of the fabrics, beedi making and tailoring which take place almost outside their tiny single room house.

2. Jamalpur, Rakhial and Saranpur areas show higher incidence of jaundice and diphtheria. The areas are characterised by the high density of population, intensive commercial and industrial (textile mills and associated activities) activities with greater possibility of water and food contamination.

3. The study also observes, through the multiple linear regression analysis, the occurrence of gastroenteritis in the areas of high density of population and the occurrence of jaundice and diphtheria in the areas of high density of dwelling units. This observation needs further supplementary studies.

4. It is interesting to make observations regarding the fluctuations in the incidence of infectious diseases. It helps the planners to make effective programmes incorporating both the curative and preventive measures. The incidence of Jaundice is almost throughout the year. Gastroenteritis and diphtheria diseases mainly occur during the monsoon season, between June and October months. The incidence of chicken-pox is greater during the summer months when the hot days prevail whereas the

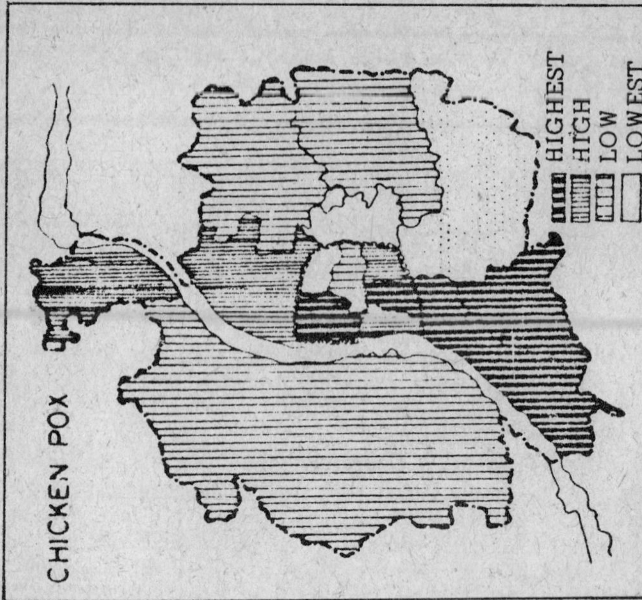

FIG: 14.5

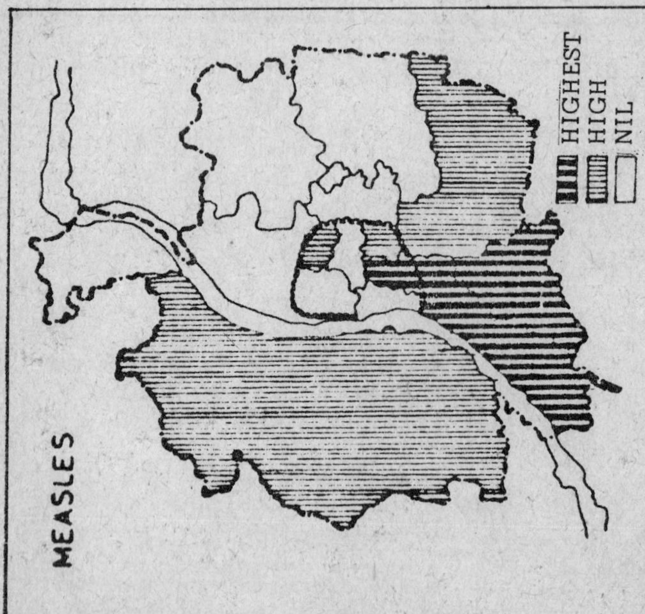

FIG. 14.4

April when the air is hot and dry as well as during the monsoon when the atmosphere is hot and humid.

5. The study, by and large, brings out the impact of physical and social densities on the spread of some infectious diseases.

REFERENCES

Booth Allan (1976): **Urban Crowding and its consequences, Pvaeger Publishers, New York.**

Herbert, D.T. and Smith, D.M. (ed) (1979): **Social Problems and the city: Geographical Perspectives.**

Jones, E. and Eyles, J. (1977): **An Introduction to Social Geography,** Oxford Press.

Lear Month A.T.A. (1978): **Patterns of disease and hunger:** A Study in Medical Geography.

Mcglashan, N.D. (ed) (1972): **Medical Geography:** Meshuan Co. Ltd., London.

Misra, R.P. (1970): **Medical Geography of India,** National Book Trust, Delhi.

Pyle, G. (1973): Measles as an urban health problem. The case of Akron, **Economic Geography,** Vol. 49.

Pyle, G. (1976): Foundations to Medical Geography, **Economic Geography** Vol. 52.

Sundara Vol, E. (1981): **Factorial Ecology** of **Ahmedabad,** Unpublished dissertation, School of Planning, Ahmedabad.

Wilcocks and Manson, Behr (1972): **Manson's Tropical diseases** Macmillan Pub.

APPENDIX 14.1
Monthly Incidence of Jaundice* 1980

	January	February	March	April	May	June	July	August	September	October	November	December
Khadia	2.77	8.30	5.30	2.77	16.60	11.10	2.77	13.80	5.50	11.10	-	22.8
Kalupur	12.90	16.10	3.20	12.90	3.20	3.20	9.60	3.20	6.40	22.50	3.20	3.20
Jamalpur	5.40	-	5.40	5.40	20.00	9.00	14.50	12.70	11.00	12.70	3.60	-
Shahpur	4.16	4.16	10.40	6.25	12.50	2.00	4.10	6.25	12.50	16.60	12.50	8.30
Dariapur	7.60	15.30	7.60	23.00	7.00	15.30	7.60	-	-	7.60	-	7.60
Raikhad	6.20	-	6.20	-	31.20	-	6.20	-	-	18.70	12.50	25.00
Saraspur	7.58	7.14	8.90	5.80	10.71	12.90	8.40	7.10	9.30	10.71	5.35	5.85
Rakhial	10.46	7.55	6.90	6.90	11.00	11.00	7.50	8.70	10.46	8.10	4.60	6.30
Gomthipur	4.80	7.30	13.80	6.50	7.30	4.80	1.60	7.30	12.10	19.50	7.30	7.30
Asarwa	5.90	8.90	1.40	17.90	10.40	5.90	1.40	8.90	7.40	4.40	7.40	4.40
Ellisbridge	6.90	7.90	5.90	12.80	14.80	2.90	11.88	12.80	4.90	11.80	4.90	2.00
Sabarmathi	4.30	8.60	4.30	-	4.30	4.30	8.60	13.00	8.60	13.00	17.00	13.00
Maninagar	8.90	9.70	14.10	16.40	7.40	9.70	9.70	10.00	8.90	2.20	0.007	1.40
Mattupura	7.60	7.60	-	7.60	7.60	-	15.00	-	46.00	7.60	-	-
Berampura	-	-	-	10.00	30.00	30.00	10.00	10.00	10.00	-	-	-
Danilimda	20.00	-	-	40.00	40.00	-	-	-	-	-	-	-

* Figures represent percentage to the total year.

APPENDIX 14.2

Monthly Incidence of Gastro-Entiries* 1980

	January	February	March	April	May	June	July	August	September	October	November	December
Khadia	-	-	-	22.0	11.0	-	11.0	44.0	-	-	11.0	-
Kalupur	7.1	-	7.0	7.0	7.0	-	-	20.0	14.0	-	7.1	14.0
Jamalpur	5.8	5.8	17.6	23.0	5.8	5.8	17.6	7.6	-	-	-	-
Shahpur	-	-	-	-	-	-	7.6	84.6	-	-	-	7.6
Dariapur	-	-	-	-	-	48.0	-	57.0	-	-	-	-
Raikhad	-	-	-	-	-	-	100.0	-	-	-	-	-
Saraspur	-	-	-	-	-	-	-	-	-	-	-	-
Rakhial	-	-	-	-	-	-	33.0	-	-	33.0	33.0	-
Gomthipur	-	-	-	-	10.2	-	10.2	77.0	-	-	2.5	-
Asarwa	-	-	-	-	-	-	-	-	100.0	-	-	-
Ellisbridge	7.6	-	15.3	7.6	7.6	-	15.3	46.0	-	-	-	-
Sabarmathi	-	-	10.0	-	-	30.0	30.0	-	-	20.0	10.0	-
Maninagar	-	7.10	7.10	-	7.1	-	7.1	42.0	28.0	-	-	-
Mattupura	-	-	-	-	-	-	-	-	-	-	-	-
Berampura	-	-	12.5	28.1	9.3	3.1	21.0	18.0	-	3.1	3.1	-
Danilimda	-	-	4.0	2.0	4.0	2.0	2.0	44.0	-	8.1	16.8	-

* Figures represent percentage to the total year.

APPENDIX 14.3
Monthly Incidence of Diphtheria*

Ward Name	January	February	March	April	May	June	July	August	September	October	November	December
Khadia	-	-	-	-	7.0	7.0	21.4	21.4	14.0	-	7.4	21.4
Kalupur	16.6	33.0	-	-	-	-	-	16.6	16.6	-	-	16.6
Samalpur	-	-	20.0	-	20.0	-	10.0	20.0	10.0	10.0	10.0	-
Shahpur	16.0	-	-	-	16.0	-	16.0	16.0	16.0	16.0	-	-
Dariapur	50.0	-	-	-	-	-	-	-	-	-	-	50.0
Raikad	-	20.0	-	-	30.0	-	-	-	-	-	20.0	40.0
Saraspur	-	-	-	-	-	-	11.7	41.0	23.0	6.0	6.0	11.0
Rakhial	2.5	25	7.5	2.0	5.0	2.0	5.0	27.0	20.0	5.0	10.0	10.0
Gomthipur	-	-	-	-	-	16.0	7.0	16.0	16.0	-	25.0	16.0
Asarwa	-	11.0	11.0	-	-	-	-	22.0	22.0	11.0	-	22.0
Ellisbridge	5.0	5.0	-	-	-	11.0	5.0	27.0	16.0	22.0	-	11.0
Sabarmathi	-	-	-	-	-	-	20.0	20.0	40.0	20.0	-	-
Maninagar	11.0	-	-	-	-	-	-	22.0	22.0	22.0	-	22.0
Mattupura	-	9.0	-	-	-	9.0	18.0	9.0	36.0	-	9.0	-
Behrampura	-	-	2.5	-	-	-	-	50.0	-	-	25.0	-
Denilimda	-	-		-	-	-	50.0	-	50.0	-	-	-

* Figures represent percentage to the total year

APPENDIX 14.4

Monthly Incidence of Measles* 1980

Ward Name	January	February	March	April	May	June	July	August	September	October	November	December
Khadia	-	-	-	50	-	-	-	-	-	-	50	-
Kalupur	-	-	-	-	-	-	-	-	-	-	-	-
Jamalpur	-	-	-	-	-	-	20	-	-	-	80	-
Shahpur	-	-	-	-	-	-	-	-	-	-	-	-
Dariapur	-	-	-	100	-	-	-	-	-	-	-	-
Raikhad	-	-	-	-	-	-	-	-	-	-	-	-
Saraspur	-	-	-	-	-	-	-	-	-	-	100	-
Rakhial	-	-	-	-	-	-	-	-	-	-	-	-
Gomthipur	-	-	-	-	-	-	-		-	-	-	-
Asarwa	-	-	-	-	-	-	-	-	-	-	-	-
Ellisbridge	-	-	-	100	-	-	-	-	-	-	-	-
Sabarmathi	-	-	-	-	-	-	-	-	-	-	-	-
Maninagar	-	-	-	-	-	-	-	-	-	-	100	-
Mattupura	-		-	-	-	-	-	-	-	-	-	-
Behrampura	-	-	-	-	-	-	-	-	-	-	30	70
Danilimda	-	-	-	-	-	14	-	-	-	-	14	71

* Figures represent percentage of the total year.

APPENDIX 14.5

Monthly Incidence of Chicken-pox* 1980

Ward Name	January	February	March	April	May	June	July	August	September	October	November	December
Khadia	-	25	50	25	-	-	-	-	-	-	-	-
Kalupur	-	64	-	33	-	-	-	-	-	-	-	-
Jamalpur	-	28	16	28	-	28	-	-	-	-	-	-
Shahpur	33	50	-	16	-	-	-	-	-	-	-	-
Dariapur	-	-	-	-	-	-	-	-	-	-	-	-
Raikad	-	-	-	100	-	-	-	-	-	-	-	-
Saraspur	-	-	-	-	-		-	-	-	-	-	-
Rakhial	16	-	33	50	-	-	-	-	-	-	-	-
Gomthipur	-	-	-	-	-	-	-	-	-	-	-	-
Asarwa	50	25	25	-	-	-	-	-	-	-	-	-
Ellisbridge	11	11	66	11	-	-	-	-	-	-	-	-
Sabarmathi	-	100	-	-	-	-	-	-	-	-	-	-
Maninagar	-	-	-	33	-	-	-	-	-	33	-	33
Mattupura	16	50	16	16	-	-	-	-	-	-	-	-
Behrampura	33	-	56	-	-	-	-	-	-	-	-	-
Danilimda	-	20	40	40	-	-		-	-	-	-	-

* Figures represent percentage to the year.

FIFTEEN

A. H. Harris

Economics and Epidemiology
A Critical Review of the state of the Art

THE ISSUES

The use of aggregate data on populations to infer the health effects of a reduction in air pollution has been the subject of contention for some time. Many scientists would distrust outright the results of statistical "natural experiments" on populations exposed to varying levels of environmental quality. They would prefer to rely on at best clinical tests or at least detailed individual case histories of exposure and health state. As Lave and Seskin (1979) observe:

> "... some scientists will not accept epidemiological evidence as proof of causation no matter how elaborate it is."

Most researchers would agree that before finally accepting any such evidence as causal we sould be careful that any statistical association between air pollution and health is supported by a consistent theoretical model specifying the disease mechanism. However, since experimental work on humans is deemed unethical, experimental work on animals is not always suitable, and detailed study of cohorts time consuming and expensive, if the policy maker requires some basis for decisions in the near future the use of epidemiological evidence may be the only answer. This crucially depends on the confidence which can be placed on the results of a statistical association between air pollution and human health. The advantages of low cost and quick results may well be outweighed by the accuracy of other methodologies such as the study of 'controlled' populations.

Perhaps the pillars on which such confidence should rest are the specification and form of the estimated relationship between air pollution and health. Analysis of the relationship at the aggregate level requires not only that all confounding influences be removed from the statistical relationship but also that the relationship be properly specified. It is these two issues which have occupied the attention of the best work in this area. The problems are severe. Not only is it difficult to draw up a list of variables which might be assumed to affect mortality and morbidity and which are correlated with air pollution, but once this is decided upon it is all too often the case that there exist only very imperfect measures of these variables. The specification of the estimated relationship is also problematic. While laboratory experiments would suggest a non-linear dose response curve of an 'S' shape, it is often difficult to estimate a significant relationship of this form. Instead linear or log linear estimates are used as an approximation with the assumption that there exists no threshold level of pollution below which health effects are negligible. If, as has been suggested, individuals do not passively react to levels of air quality, then the dose-response function estimated by these techniques must take account of such behaviour. A simple model which attempts to estimate an aggregate physiological relationship may not achieve this if the effects of ambient air quality on health are mitigated by defensive or avertive action on the part of the sufferers. In this way the economic cost of air pollution may depend on the economic actions of those affected.

More generally the use of aggregate data may lead to misleading results if errors of aggregation are severe enough to bias the estimates and to give spurious significance to otherwise unrelated variables. The use of the "representative person" in city level data for example cannot only reduce the variance of the sample and increase the explanatory power of the statistical technique but also disguise relationships witin the melting pot of the city.

In this paper an assessment is made of an attempt by Crocker **et al.**, (1979) to estimate a set of complex models specifying the aggregate relationship between health and air pollution. This is contrasted with the earlier work of Lave and Seskin (1977) in order to determine the usefulness of this approach.

TWO RECENT STUDIES

Lave and Seskin (1977)

Since 1970, Lave and Seskin have pioneered the use of cross-section aggregative studies of mortality rates and their statistical association with air pollution. Their work has consistently suggested an association between both particulates and sulphates and mortality[1]. These results have been used by themselves and others to assess the economic benefits of air pollution control. Table 15.1 presents an example of their work. Using 1960 and 1969 data on mortality rates in US Standard Metropolitan Statistical Areas (SMSAs) they regressed mortality on a number of socioeconomic variables characteristic of each population.

Criticism of the work of Lave and Seskin has centred around three issues:

(1) The original data contained serious measurement errors which have biased the results.
(2) The multiple regression techniques used were inadequate for the purpose of estimating a complex relationship.
(3) The list of variables used in the regression was incomplete and several apparently significant influences on mortality were ignored.

Although the most glaring of measurement errors (measure of sulphate) were eliminated in later work there remained the problem common to all studies of this type—the accuracy and relevance of the pollution concentration measures. Not only are the techniques used to measure the various pollutants far from perfect but they usually pertain to the central business district of the SMSA. This data will not be representative of a whole SMSA (the relevant area for other data) and indeed the measurment error is likely to be correlated with city size. There is also the question of which of the pollution variables to inclued in any regression. Lave and Seskin acknowledge the strength of multicollinearity between the pollution variables and tend to use minimum sulphate and minimum particulate variables with dubious justification.

Another source of measurement error which could bias the results is the use of current period pollution variables. Chronic illness arises out of long term exposure and there is no evidence to suggest that the long term history of air pollution is the same for each SMSA. It is likely that cities in certain regions have had considerably worse histories of air pollution exposure. When dummy variables were used by Lave and Seskin to allow for these considerations, however, the coefficients on the pollution variables became non-significant and negative. For this reason, Lave and Seskin ignored this possibility of error in future estimates without any detailed investigation of the problem.

TABLE 15.1
Alternative Specifications of Total Mortality Rates, 1969 from Lave and Seskin (1977)

	Unadjusted					
	Basic regression	Log-log	Quadratic	Dummy variable	Linear spline	Outliers deleted
	7.4-1	7.4-2	7.4-3	7.4-4	7.4-5	7.4-6
R^2	.805	.827	.811	.807	.814	.820
Constant	330.647	124.635	255.197	390.043	192.370	227.954
Air pollution variables Min S	.774 (2.11)	.023 (1.73)	.542 (.37)		.176 (.05)	.567 (1.54)
$(\text{Min S})^2$			-.013 (-.08)			
Mean P	.818 (3.39)	.088 (3.34)	2.757 (2.51)		2.916 (1.46)	.655 (2.37)
$(\text{Mean P})^2$			-.931 (-1.78)			
Mean S x Mean P			.040 (.30)			
Sum AP elasticities	11.63	11.08	22.34	7.47	27.30	8.87

TABLE 15.1 (Cont.)

	Unadjusted					
	Basic regression	Log-log	Quadratic	Dummy variable	Linear spline	Outliers deleted
Socioeconomic variables						
P/M^2	.131	.020	.127	.142	.127	.043
	(2.54)	(1.97)	(2.43)	(2.62)	(2.37)	(.29)
65	6.568	.694	6.532	6.426	6.526	7.812
	(18.09)	(18.87)	(17.94)	(16.94)	(17.52)	(19.61)
NW	.204	.021	.200	.186	.220	.502
	(2.27)	(1.92)	(2.20)	(2.04)	(2.31)	(4.62)
Poor	.557	.092	.612	.658	.596	.191
	(2.29)	(3.62)	(2.50)	(2.70)	(2.39)	(.70)
Sum SE elasticities	74.99	82.66	75.08	74.39	75.13	86.69
Log Pop	-.365	.021	-.403	-.393	-.373	-.328
	(-1.94)	(-2.20)	(-2.10)	(-1.98)	(-1.93)	(-1.58)

TABLE 15.1 (Cont.)

	Basic regression	Log-log	Age-sex-race-adjusted Quadratic	Dummy variable	Linear spline	Outliers deleted
	7.4-7	7.4-8	7.4-9	7.4-10	7.4-11	7.4-12
R^2	.348	.373	.365	.322	.380	.357
Constant	918.657	259.306	872.868	968.808	823.706	860.393
Air pollution variables						
Min S	.784	.021	.428		.304	.617
	(2.48)	(1.89)	(.34)		(.09)	(1.78)
$(\text{Min S})^2$			-.024			
			(-.18)			
Mean P	.723	.082	2.128		2.210	.651
	(3.48)	(3.72)	(2.24)		(1.29)	(2.51)
$(\text{Mean P})^2$			-.732			
			(-1.61)			
Mean S x Mean P			.061			
			(.53)			
Sum AP elasticities	10.04	10.25	16.97	5.65	20.64	8.42

TABLE 15.1 (Cont.)

	Basic regression	Log-log	Age-sex-race-adjusted Quadratic	Dummy variable	Linear spline	Outliers deleted
	7.4-7	7.4-8	7.4-9	7.4-10	7.4-11	7.4-12
Socioeconomic variables						
P/M^2	.092	.016	.089	.102	.092	.003
	(2.07)	(1.89)	(1.98)	(2.12)	(2.01)	(.02)
65	.315	.041	.285	.214	.286	.971
	(1.00)	(1.36)	(.91)	(.64)	(.89)	(2.59)
NW	.109	.011	.104	.086	.109	.315
	(1.40)	(1.18)	(1.31)	(1.06)	(1.33)	(3.08)
Poor	.640	.078	.679	.709	.676	.341
	(3.06)	(3.71)	(3.21)	(3.29)	(3.14)	(1.33)
Sum SE elasticities	11.14	14.68	11.11	10.59	11.20	16.26
Log Pop	-.283	.017	-.318	-.288	-.296	-.243
	(-1.74)	(-2.15)	(1.92)	(1.64)	(-1.78)	(-1.25)

Based on data for 112 SMSAs except 7.4-6, 7.4-12 103 SMSAs.
t statistics in parenthesis.

Even if all the specified variables are measured accurately there still exists the problem of specifying the parameters of the mortality model. Explanatory variables such as age, sex, life-style, and personal habits are likely to be important. The exclusion of important explanatory variables which vary with the level of pollution will have the effect of biasing the results. The inclusion of variables collinear with the level of air quality will confound the interpretation and significance of the pollution coefficient. One problem here is the high degree of collinearity between the air pollution measures themselves due in part to the similarity of sources and measurement techniques. A second is the availability of reliable data on such a **priori** important factors as diet and smoking.

Lave and Seskin concentrate on two types of pollutant, sulphate (SO_4) and particulates (TSP), and always in combination. To this extent they cannot distinguish the effects of either pollutant or others which have been omitted and are correlated with these two. The best that this analysis can hope to provide is an assessment of the general effects of air pollution on human health.

The form of the equation estimated is also of considerable importance. The US Clean Air Act Amendment (1970) talks of a threshold level below which there is no damage to health. Lave and Seskin investigated whether such a threshold existed and consequently whether a simple linear model was unsuitable. They suggest that no alternative functional form fits the data better than a simple linear form and see no reason to reject a linear relationship. The fact is that the acceptance of a non-linear relationship and/or of a threshold could have profound effects on the estimated benefits from pollution control and that Lave and Seskin do not satisfactorily demonstrate the non-existence of threshold effects[2].

It should be clear that there is much room for interpreting the results of aggregate studies of health status. Indeed the Lave and Seskin studies have not even unambiguously sown there is a consistent significant statistical relationship between aggregate mortality and air pollutants. Of the estimates made of the relationship between mortality rates and sulphate/particulate emissions by no means all were significant. When disaggregated into age, sex, race, age and cause of death categories this lack of significance became more apparent. In spite of the apparent association between air pollution and cancer deaths there was no significant association with respiratory causes, a result which is extremly surprising.

In fact the more variables that were added to the estimated relationship the less significant were the pollution coefficients. When occupation and home heating were added, the sulphate coefficient lost significance. The exclusion of smoking as a variable is undoubtedly a major stumbling block in accepting the magnitude of the coefficients on SO_4 and particulates. If individuals are seen as more than passive acceptors of their state of health then the level of smoking will be related to the ambient pollution level and the exclusion of per capita smoking levels will bias the pollution coefficient in an upward direction.

Crocker, Schultze, Ben-David, Kneese (1979)

This study consists of a number of component parts. First estimates of the relationship between aggregate mortality data in sixty US cities and a number of supposed influences on the variation in that data. Second an examination of data from the University of Michigan Survey Research Centre on time and budget allocations of 5,000 heads of household for the years 1968 to 1976. The latter date provide an opportunity to study the morbidity effects of air pollution and any resulting impact on labour productivity. Crocker **et al.**, presents two models which permit estimation and evaluation of these effects.

Sixty-City Study

The authors are very aware of the difficulties involved in obtaining reliable and consistent estimates of a relationship between air pollution and human health. Aggregate epidemiological studies have generally been criticised for failing to produce such reliable estimates. The authors place a great deal of emphasis on the novelty of their approaches in this study. The claims which they make of increased accuracy are based on the innovations which they introduce. In the analysis of mortality data perhaps the major innovation is the recognition that individuals do not treat their state of health as given. They can affect their health state by economic and non-economic actions. Individuals may affect their health state not only by cigarette smoking, excercise, diet and workload but also by recourse to preventive and ameliorative medicine. In the study of morbidity the use of disaggregated survey data and a large data set allows the authors to develop and use a theoretical model of the demand for health in estimating the productivity effects or air pollution.

The authors claim two major advantages which this study has over previous work in this area. First they have made use of a larger number of variables in explaining the response of mortality to air pollution changes. A major innovation here is the account taken of smoking and diet on health. Earlier work on dose-response functions has been criticised for its failure to standardise for smoking and dietary variables. Second, the authors have attempted to account for influences on mortality rates which are not independent of the level of mortality itself. As the authors claim, the aim of the study is to include influences on health which are not exogenous to the individual but are affected by direct decisions. The authors stress that the individual may make a conscious decision (in response to increasing ill health) to take ameliorative action. If the individual chooses to consume more medical care, for example, this will have a direct effect on the level of health. The increase in air pollution is expected to lead to a direct negative effect on health, but the observed change in the health is likely to be less since the individual will have increased expenditure on medical care. Although the authors single out this example as of prime importance, the general principle is clear. If a change in air pollution causes indirect effects on income, consumption habits, diet etc., this will affect the state of health of the individual in this indirect manner. An estimated relationship which attempts to explain the effects of a change in air pollution on health states ought to take account of any significant indirect effects of individuals reactions to that change. Although previous studies have implicitly regarded these effects as insignificant the authors feel that the consumption of medical care is likely to have significant effects on the state of health as a result of a pollution induced change in health. Of course this is but one possibility. For example the individual may respond to a pollution-induced change in bronchitis by smoking less, working less in a polluted city or by moving out of the area.

A single equation model may not give unbiased estimates if health states and any of the independent variables are jointly determined. For example one cannot explain changes in mortality by patterns of lifestyle if a change in the state of health will lead the individual to alter his or her lifestyle. A single equation system will give biased estimates of the dose-response relationship if any of the alleged explanatory variables are jointly determined with the dependent variable. Depending on the specification of the 'dose-response' relationship the estimated effect of a change in pollution on human health may be under or overestimated. In order to avoid the possibility of such bias all jointly determined variables would have to be explained within a more complex system of equations. For example, the relationship between the level of smoking and the health state, income etc., would have to be specified. Even the use of median age as an explanatory variable may not be desirable if the median of the population varies with some other of the explanatory variables in addtion to the mortality rate.

The advantages to be gained from a more complex model must be balanced against the disadvantages. The reduction in bias may be quite small in relation to the errors introduced by the use of ill measured and inappropriate variables to proxy for the simultaneous nature of the relationships.

For example, the authors focus exclusively on the relationship between medical care and mortality. They argue that medical care is not an exogenous variable but is determined to some extent by the state of health of the individual. People who live in cities with higher levels of mortality will suffer higher levels of illness per capita and will therefore seek out greater levels of medical care. There is undoubtedly some truth in this argument. The difficulty, however, is in choosing a variable which measures the demand for medical care. Crocker **et al.**, choose doctors per capita as the appropriate variable. A demand for health improvement does not necessarily increase the demand for doctors let alone lead to an increase in their numbers. There is a danger here of introducing bias by the use of an inappropriate variable in an attempt to reduce bias in a simultaneous equation system.

The authors used a two stage least squares procedure to estimate a relationship of the form

Mortality Rates = f (Diet, Medical Care, Socioeconomic Factors, Smoking Environmental Factors, Age) 2.1

Medical Care = g (Socioeconomic Factors, Mortality Rate, Age) 2.2

The data used were:

(1) 1970 city wide mortality rates;
(2) dietary patterns 1955 and 1965;
(3) medical doctors per capita for 1970 or near year;
(4) socioeconomic factors for 1970;
(5) smoking patterns for 1956 and 1968;
(6) air quality for each city for 1970 or near year; and
(7) median age of population in 1969.

There are at least three problems at this stage: (i) the choice of variables to be included, (ii) the measurement problem, and (iii) the aggregation problem. A well-known problem in this type of study is that many of the factors which **a priori** are hypothesised to influence mortality rates are highly collinear. The inclusion of all of these variables would lead to multicollinearity and make interpretation of the coefficients a serious problem. This problem is usually serious in respect of the pollution variables. The choice is often whether to include all of the supposed relevant pollutants and thereby risk increasing the standard errors on the coefficients or to include only one as a proxy for all the others and by doing so confound the interpretation of that variable.

Crocker **et al.**, chose to focus on SO_2 and TSP, and nitrogen dioxide (NO_2), and based on the collinearity of SO_2 and SO_4, SO_2 was used as a proxy for both. Multicollinearity may have been less of a problem in this study since many of the simple correlations were surprisingly low in comparison for example with the work of Lave and Seskin; e.g. for SO_4 and TSP the R^2 = 0.37 whereas in Lave and Seskin for 1960 data R^2 = 0.586. Of course the relatively low simple partial correlations between variables is not a strong test for the absence of multicollinearity. The authors chose a rule of thumb to assess the importance of multicollinearity.

> "Typically multicollinearity problems can be avoided if the simple correlations between explanatory variables are less than 0.4 to 0.6". (p.44)

Using this rule the authors find serious multicollinearity problems associated with the dietary variables and some of the air pollution variables. This rule, although useful, cannot be regarded as totally accurate and one would want to look more carefully at the relative magnitude of the coefficient of determination and the multiple correlation coefficient before coming to any conclusion concerning the absence of serious multicollinearity. To the extent that multicollinearity presents a problem, it becomes difficult to interpret the coefficients of any of the variables and particularly difficult to attribute the significance and extent of the influence of any one on the dependent variable, mortality.

The study uses a subset of the available number of possible independent variables but the procedures for narrowing these down are not clear. The selection was largely based on **a priori** knowledge rather than statistical tests. This is preferable in many cases, but the authors frequently make choices for reasons which remain obscure. One example of this was the use of estimated doctors per capita in the second stage of the estimation precedure in spite of very poor statistical results in the estimation of the reduced form equation relating doctors per capita to socioeconomic factors, mortality rate and age. In fact, none of the independent variables was significant in the reduced form equation casting doubt on the usefulness of the synthetic variable estimated doctors per capita. If the variable is judged a **priori** to be so important as to justify its retention, more care should be used in specifying the equations.

In this respect a problem of interpretation arises from the use of the variable doctors per capita. As discussed above the authors assume that there is a fixed supply of doctors at a fixed price. In this way they interpret the variable doctors per capita as the quantity of medical care demanded. If, however, the number of doctors at any location was not in perfectly elastic supply and thus allowed the price to vary it would become difficult to interpret the reduced form equation. In fact it may represent a combination of demand and supply effects. An area with low levels of pollution may have more doctors per capita not only because of a high demand for socioeconomic reasons but also because doctors choose to locate in areas of low pollution. Similarly, the price of medical care may vary between areas reflecting the variable supply of doctors. If in order to identify the health effects of a change in pollution it is necessary to specify the response of medical services consumption to a change in illness it seems necessary to fully specify the relationship between doctors per capita and the relevant variables. It may be argued that the authors fail to do so. They choose to interpret an equation of the form 2.2 as a demand equation when it may be interpreted as a mixture of demand and supply considerations. The effects of such a possible misinterpretation could be to bias the results in an upward direction and/or change the sign on one or more of the explanatory variables.

One final problem of data selection in this study is the use of lagged variables. Both the intra urban and inter urban mobility of the population coupled with changing levels of pollution over time make single year observations of pollutants unsatisfactory. Air pollution is likely to have long term cumulative effects on human health and a single measure of pollution in one year is an imperfect measure of lifetime exposure. One must therefore not only take some account of mobility but also variations in air pollution levels through time.

A more basic problem wich plagues work in this area is that of measurement error. This generally applies to measurement of ambient pollution concentrations where measurement techniques are not always as accurate as might be hoped and where it is difficult to make a choice between aspects of the air quality distribution. For example the Crocker study generally used the arithematic mean of daily pollution concentrations, but in cases where insufficient data was not available the 50 per centile of the data available was used. This would generally underestimate the true value of arithmetic mean. Another problem is that the method of measurement for some pollutants is known to be either unreliable or at least incapable of reliably measuring levels of SO_2 lower than 13 ug/m^3, a level above many of the sixty cities under consideration.

A potential advantage of this study was the inclusion of a **priori** relevant variables which have been missing in earlier work. Both diet and smoking are likely to have significant effects on mortality rates. Their inclusion in a system of equations explaining overall mortality could be expected to improve the performance of the estimation. However, the available data on each of these are unreliable and unavailable at the required level of disaggreagation. The authors had therefore to construct a synthetic variable based on fifteen year old dietary data for four regions, income and urbanization data for each city within the regions. The smoking variable was constructed from data on state-wide tax receipts. It is difficult to assess the extent of measurement error and this errors in variables problem should be seen as a limitation on the results. This is the case since both the synthetic dietary variables on the smoking variable could be interpreted in a number of way, including a proxy for income and lifestyle.

Empirical Results

The method of two stage least squares gives unbiased and consistent estimates in large samples. The procedure in a two equation system is generally to obtain estimates of a reduced form equation by using ordinary least squares to estimate an endogenous variable as a function of all the exogenous variables. Using the estimated value of this endogenous variable as a replacement for the original variable the structural equation may be estimated using ordinary least squares. In this case one would expect the authors to estimate medical care as a function lf all exogenous variables including air pollutants. The resulting estimated data set could be used instead of actual doctors per capita on the right hand side of the equation specifying mortality rates as a function of social and environmental variables. In fact the estimated reduced form equation includes only some of the exogenous variables (Tables 15.2, 15.3, 15.4, the regression estimates from Crocker **et al**).

TABLE 15.2

Reduced Form Equation from Crocker et al (1979)

Dependent Variable MDOC

Independent Variable	Coefficient	T Statistic
-NONW	50.447	1.1020
-MAGE	1.3513	0.50439
-IN69	0.61649D-02	0.86708
-EDUC	1.9399	1.3418
-DENS	161.53	-0.26107
-COLD	-0.12806	-0.53850
-CI68	0.45771	1.4919
-XPRO	0.22302D-01	1.4136
-XCAR	0.22804D-02	0.72804
-6SFT	0.24002D-01	1.9402
CONSTANT	-1691.3	-2.7124

R-SQUARE = 0.3877 SSR = 0.1062D+06 DF = 49

Variable List for Tables 15.2 - 15.4

MO70	deaths per 100 pop 1970
MDOC	MD's/100,000 pop 1970
NONW	fraction non white pop
MAGE	median age of pop 1969
IN69	median income of pop 1969
EDUC	% 25 with H.S. diploma 1969
DENS	% 1.5 person per room 1969
COLD	days temp 0°C 1972
C168	packs per year per capita 1968
XPRO	gr protein/capita/yr 1965
XCAR	gr carbohd/cap/yr 1965
6SFT	gr animal fat/cap/yr 1965
NO69	NO_2 ppm 1969
SO70	SO_2 g/m^3 1970
PA70	particulates g/m^3 1970

TABLE 15.3
Total Mortality Crocker et al. (1979)

Dependent Variable	Independent Variables	Coefficient	T-Statistic
MO70			
	-DOCH	-0.53031D-01	-4.7501
	-NONW	5.6092	5.0448
	-MAGE	0.66172	12.360
	-DENS	31.910	2.4494
	-COLD	0.14370D-01	3.1093
	-CI68	0.21896D-01	3.0758
	-XPRO	0.19325D-02	3.7525
	-XCAR	-0.82907D-04	-1.5347
	-6SFT	0.36251D-03	1.5938
	CONSTANT	-78.675	-3.7169
R-SQUARE = 0.8195		SSR = 49.74	DF = 50
MO70			
	-DOCH	-0.52797D-01	-4.3493
	-NONW	5.6276	4.5620
	-MAGE	0.65893	11.540
	-DENS	31.772	2.3469
	-COLD	0.14436D-01	2.9089
	-CI68	0.21968D-01	2.8120
	-XPRO	0.19196D-02	3.5522
	-XCAR	-0.79431D-04	-1.3612
	-6SFT	0.39783D-03	1.4508
	-NO69	1.6457	0.35799
	-SO70	-0.31302D-02	-0.34850
	-PA70	0.10744D-02	0.20059
	CONSTANT	-79.296	-3.5155
R-SQUARE = 0.8205		SSR = 49.48	DF = 47

(Variables as for Table 15.2)

The results of such a procedure will be that the estimated coefficients may no longer be unbiased or consistent. The authors do however report on p.67 that they did fully implement a two stage least squares procedure. In this case air pollution variables are included in the reduced form equation for doctors per capita. If successful this should give unbiased results if the specification is correct. They find however that when air pollutants are included in the estimated reduced form equation there appears to be a negative association between doctors per capita and air pollution. When estimates are made for particular disease categories (as opposed to total mortality) the coefficients on the pollution variable in the estimated dose response function become negative. The real issue here is not, however, whether to include or exclude air pollution variables from the reduced form equation but the failure to properly specify the model. The omission of equations to account for other endogenous variables (such as the supply of doctors) is likely to have severe effects on the accuracy of the results.

TABLE 15.4

Pneumonia and Influenza Crocker et al. (1979)

Dependent Variable	Independent Variables	Coefficient	T-Statistic
PN70			
	-DOCH	-0.12925D-02	-1.2098
	-NONW	0.18381	1.7274
	-MAGE	0.19920D-01	3.8880
	-DENS	2.9692	2.3816
	-COLD	0.13030D-02	2.9460
	-CI68	0.61524D-03	0.90310
	-XPRO	0.70654D-04	1.4336
	-XCAR	-0.11329D-05	-0.21914
	-6SFT	0.3801CD-05	0.17462
	CONSTANT	-3.0478	-1.5046
R-SQUARE = 0.4108	SSR =	0.4556	DF = 50
PN70			
	-DOCH	-0.38115D-03	0.37068
	-NONW	0.13820	1.3226
	-MAGE	0.16194D-01	3.3484
	-DENS	2.6677	2.3264
	-COLD	0.10428D-02	2.4807
	-CI68	0.61816D-03	0.93415
	-XPRO	0.46048D-04	1.0060
	-XCAR	-0.10027D-05	-0.20286
	-6SFT	-0.49261D-05	-0.21208
	-NO69	0.55215	1.4180
	-SO70	-0.47719D-03	-0.62722
	-PA70	0.14272D-02	3.1456
	CONSTANT	-2.1183	-1.1075
R-SQUARE =0.5409	SSR =	0.3550	DF = 47

(Variables as for Table 15.2 except PN70 deaths per 1000 pop from pneumonia and influenza 1970).

The results themselves suggest only a very limited relationship between various air pollutants and human health measured by general or disease specific mortality rates.[4] Unlike Lave and Seskin (1977) who found significant associations between a variety of pollutants and specific diseases the authors find only two significant relationships using this model: (1) between particulate concentrations and pneumonia and influenza, and (2) between SO_2 and early infant disease. As the authors point out these diseases are short term, causing death only in the very young and very old. This framework seems incapable of capturing the long term effects (if any) of air pollution on health in the average person. Not only that but one cannot endow these two groups with the characteristics of the population as a whole. Excessive aggregation will not capture either the propensity of these two groups to illness, their ability and willingness to seek medical care or their attitude to risk.

Given an accurately estimated dose-response relationship the population at risk and a value of life it may be possible to estimate the total benefits from a reduction in air pollution. The authors use the estimated linear dose response relationships for SO_2 and particulates to do this. Since the estimated dose response relationships are linear it is reasonable only to discuss small changes around the mean of the sample values of the variables. The linear form is presumably an approximation to non-linear form and as such can only give accurate estimates of small changes around the mean values. The authors present figures for the value of the health benefits associated with a sixty per cent reduction in SO_2 and particulate concentrations. This is far from satisfactory representing, as it does a very crude approximation to the true value. Moreover, this requires a value to be put on human life, an exercise which is not only dubious in itself but which can also give rise to quite dramatic variations in the estimated values depending on how the value of life is calculated.[5]

Conclusions on the Sixty City Study

The basic methodology of this study although practised and accepted by many is not without its critics. The authors themselves clearly outline the statistical problems associated with aggregate epidemiology. Among the more serious of these are specification and aggregation biases. The gains which the authors make over previous studies by using a two equation model may seem substantial, but there is little reason to expect simultaneity to end where the authors might hope. They have made **a priori** judgement as to the usefulness of continuing to search for other endogenous variables and by doing so have rejected alternative interpretation of the data. In addition no a **priori** evidence for the linear shape of the dose response function has been presented. Not only might the function be non linear and non continuous but it may also differ systematically between individuals. The latter factor is obscured by the use of highly aggregative data. These factors combined with the use of a number of inappropriate and ill measured variables may lead to misleading results. The results may not represent a good estimate of either the dose response relationship or the value of changes in human health consequent upon a change in air quality. The strength of these sources of inaccuracy is a matter of judgement. The authors choose to assume that they do not negate their attempts to define at least 'order of magnitude' results but without more detailed consideration this seems difficult to justify.

Michigan Survey Experiment

The objectives of this study are to quantify the economic losses associated with morbidity caused by the level of air quality. The basis consists of a nine year set of data for several thousand heads of household on health status, time and budget allocations.

There are four basic aims in this study: (1) using reported data on number of days absent from work as a proxy for acute illness, linear regression techniques were used to estimate a relationship between illness and mean annual air pollution; (2) using reported data on the length of disability of the head of household as a proxy for chronic illness, similar techniques were used to estimate a relationship with air quality; (3) using a fairly sophisticated recursive model of the interaction between the aforementioned morbidity variables and the determinants of labour market behaviour Crocker **et al.** attempt to estimate the labour supply response to chronic and acute illness; in doing so they hope to estimate some of the labour productivity losses associated with air pollution; (4) using a model of the demand for health, the authors estimate an expression alleged to quantify consumers' willingness to pay to avoid chronic and acute illness.

The estimation of the relationships followed the familiar pattern. The proxies for illness were regressed on a number of socioeconomic variables, environmental variables and personal characteristics.

The authors themselves no more than tentatively conclude that the variables used including air pollution "probably play a significant role in acute illness". This is not an unreasonable conclusion; however, it says nothing about the absolute or even relative contribution of each variable to ill health. Again as the authors point out, none of the estimated dose-response functions explain more than 31% of the variation in acute illness and of the credit for this must go to the constant term which explains more of the variation than all of the other variables put together. Even among the health variables the largest contribution seems to come most often from the two chronic illness variables.

Three-quarters of the estimated chronic illness dose-response expressions display significant contributions from air pollution variables. However, as in the case of acute illnesses it is impossible to attribute the strength of contribution to any particular pollutant due to a high degree of collinearity between the air pollution variables.

The other major problem with the chronic illness dose-response expression is the nature of the chronic illness variable itself. As discussed by the authors since the variable used is not continuous or monotonic, one must assume that the intervals of time measured by the discrete values of this variable are identical if any sense is to be made of the coefficients on the explanatory variables. Even if this is done one must still remember that since all the equations are of a linear form it is only reasonable to discuss small changes of all variables around their respective means. Thus the implication that air pollution is on on average associated with an increase of from 1 1/2 to 3 1/2 days in the duration of chronic illness must be treated with great caution. First, one must grant the assumption that people who have been disabled for at least eight years have not been disabled for more than ten years. Second, this implication is only an average which may encompass extreme variation.

None of the biological or social endowments were consistently significant or even displayed the expected signs (with the exception of age) in the chronic illness or the acute illness expressions (with the exception of black or non-black and childhood backgroud). This may not be due to the fact that these variables do not play an important part in the production of good health, but that the investigations have failed to capture their effects.

The lifestyle variables were often statistically significant in the acute illness expression, but are never significant in the chronic illness expressions. As for the suggestion that they consistently have the expected signs, in many cases it is difficult to guess just what the expected sign should be. The variable representing fundamental religious affiliations is but one extreme example.

With the exception of the variable measuring the degree of disability, none of the explanatory variables explains substantial proportions of the variation in the measure of the duration of chronic illness. The air pollution variables as a whole never explain more than 2% of the variation.

The limitations on these estimates are very similar to those on the sixty-city mortality estimates. With the possible exceptions of aggregation bias and heteroscedasticity the econometric problems are identical. Even the absence of any aggregation bias in the results is open to doubt. The use of linear estimates to approximate a dose response function for the representative individual in the sample may disguise extreme variations within the sample. In particular one would expect the effects of air pollution on illness to vary substantially with age. The use of a single value for the coefficient on air pollution therefore must be regarded as a weighted average of the effects of air pollution on groups of individuals. The greater the difference between the groups and the greater the number of groups the less accurate is this averaging process.

Many of the other problems with this study have been discussed above. Perhaps some of the more crucial issues are:

(1) The results of this exercise may be biased to some unknown extent and in unknown directions by the simple specification of the model. In particular once again insufficient attention has been paid to the effects of cumulative exposure on health. The use of a single equation system seems to be at variance with the analysis of the sixty city study and the succeeding sections of the study. The assumption in this part of the study is that the individual accepts as given the current state of health and makes no effort to improve or maintain that state through either medical care, diet or habits. All questions of simultaneous determination of variables are absent from this section of the study.

(2) Once again many of the variables used in this study can only be described as crude approximations to the desired variables. This is particularly true of the morbidity variables themselves, medical care and dietary variables. Errors in variables will of course lead to biased results and a certain ambiguity in the interpretation of those results.

(3) In addition there are certain characteristics of the Michigan Survey which may lead to biased results. In particular the response of individuals to questions on why they have been absent from work seems hard to credit. It would appear that these individuals never absent themselves from work unless they are ill. The exculsion of those who died between interviews from the sample for that period will have biased the results in a downward direction.

Of course just how serious these sources of inaccuracy are is open to judgement. The authors clearly believe that these problems do not seriously damage the approximation to the dose-response relationships they have obtained, but this can only be regarded as a statement of faith and not of hard evidence.

The Effects of Air Pollution on Labour Productivity

In this part of the study the authors attempt to estimate the labour productivity effects of changes in the level of air pollution concentrations. The model is an extension of the morbidity relationships postulated in the previous section.

The authors assume that the individual has no influence on his/her state of health in the current period. Investment in health is a long term decision unaffected by short term influences such as price changes. The authors go on to describe the determination of earnings partly by market conditions in the labour market and partly by the individual's ability to perform work. The ability to work and earn is determined by such factors as education and health state. In this way a change in the health state is seen to affect not only the hours available for work but also the wage which the individual can obtain in the market. Since the wage rate is also a determinant of the number of hours worked the influence of health on total earnings will be complex. In the case of acute illness the only effect on labour supplied will be the direct effect on the number of hours worked. In the case of chronic illness on the other hand prolonged illness will affect productivity and the wage rate obtained per hour of employment. Since the wage rate affects the quantity of labour supplied chronic illness may lead to a further reduction in the hours worked over and above the days lost directly through absence from work due to illness. (Of course it may lead to an increase if a reduction in the wage rate required increased hours of work to pay for the maintenance of the health state.)

The authors attempt to capture both the direct and indirect effects of a change in health status (consequent upon a change in air quality) using a system of four equations. The general form of this system is reproduced below.

Chronic Illness = f (Biological and Social Endowments, Lifestyle, Medical Care History, Environment) 2.3

Acute Illness = g (Chronic Illness, Biological and Social Endowments, Lifestyle, Medical Care, Environment) 2.4

Marginal Hourly Wage Rate = h (Chronic and Acute Illness, Cost of Living, Experience, Biological and Social Endowments) 2.5

Hours Worked = k (Wage Rate, Chronic and Acute Illness, Transfer Income, Wealth) 2.6

The general form of this four equation recursive system is not inconsistent with the Grossman (1972) model of health as a capital good. That is to say the individual treats the health state as an exogenous variable in the current period. It is of course different from the earlier model used in the sixty-city study where individuals were seen as determining their health state by consuming medical care in the current period. In addition it seems likely that individuals will have some influence over their state of health both by varying diet and lifestyle as well as by the choice of a number of hours of work which ensures an optimal level of health. If this is the case then illness is no longer an exogenous variable in this system and the authors' treatment of it as such produces the possibility of simultaneous equation bias. If air pollution increases acute or chronic illness and these in turn reduce the number of hours worked the individual may further reduce hours worked in order to permit a faster recovery. Alternatively they may increase the number of hours worked in order to earn sufficient income to obtain a reasonable diet or pay for medical care. The direction and magnitude of this source of bias is therefore unclear. The point is that conditions and hours of work are likely to be major factors in the determination of the health state.

Results of the Recursive Morbidity Estimate

An example of the estimated system is reproduced in Table 14.5. The estimations of equations 2.3 and 2.4 should produce identical results to those obtained earlier. The conclusion that

"calculated at the arithmetic means, the elasticity of LDSA (chronic illness) with respect to NOXM (nitrogen dioxide ambient geometric mean) is 0.47 and for TSPM (suspended particulates geometric mean) is 0.95". (p. 134)

does not seem to agree with the earlier estimates (pp.114-145) where the range of elasticities is 0.2 to 0.5. The difference is due to the use of a 830 day weighted arithmetic mean of intervals in the chronic illness index. In the earler example a figure of 770 days was taken to be the length of the interval. Obviously the assumptions made concerning this variable are significant for the results, yet no clear case is made for choosing any particular length of interval. A change from using 770 days to 830 days for example means that the range of values for the number of days of illness induced by a unit change in ambient pollution concentration changes from 1.5 - 3.8 days to 1.6 - 4.1.

TABLE 15.5

Empirical Results for a 1971 Sample Recursive Labour Supply Crocker et al* (1979)

1. LDSA = -1.018 + 0.06 (NCIG) - 0.17 (DSAB)* + 0.05 (RELG) -0.40 (CITY)*
(0.04) (0.07) (0.68) (0.19)
-0.05 (FEDU) + 0.06 (EDUC) + 0.15 (FOOD) + 0.005 (AGEH)*
(0.04) (0.05) (0.19) (0.006)
+0.001 (COLD) + 0.001 (ULTV) - 0.002 (SULM) + 0.005 (NOXM)*
(0.002) (0.002) (0.003) (0.002)
+0.008 (TSPM)*
(0.004)
$R^2 = 0.21$; F (13, 305) = 5.76; S.E.= 1.56

2. ACUT = 35.397 + 0.25 (NCIG) - 0.38 (DSAB) - 4.98 (LDSA) - 47.39 (EXER)
(6.20) (9.40) (7.59) (35.76)
+5.14 (EDUC) - 0.36 (AGEH) + 0.06 (COLD) - 0.01 (ULTV)
(4.85) (0.87) (0.27) (0.02)
-0.38 (SULM) + 0.06 (NOXM) + 0.49 (TSPM)
(0.44) (0.31) (0.52)
$R^2 = 0.15$; F (11,307) = 0.43; S.E. = 215.15

3. WAGE = -5.619 + 0.08 (BDALO) + 0.02 (ACUT) - 156.70 (SEXH)*
(0.06) (0.10) (44.41)
+33.46 (LOCC)* - 3.00 (DSAB) - 41.73 (LDSA)* + 20.31 (EDUC)*
(10.81) (14.35) (15.72) (10.20)
+50.80 (RACE)
(32.08)
$R^2 = 0.20$; F (8, 310) = 9.72; S.E.=367.66

4. WORK = 2011.671 - 0.12 (BDALO) - 0.01 (ACUT) - 0.05 (ICTR)*
(0.15) (0.23) (0.01)
+123.40 (SVGS)* - 10.55 (DSAB) - 212.00 (LDSA)* + 0.50 (WAGE)*
(26.35) (34.26) (36.52) (0.13)
$R^2 = 0.35$; F (7, 311) = 23.68; S.E.= 865.51

Standard errors in parenthesis.
* Significant at the 0.05 level of the one tailed t-test.

Variable List Table 15.5

LDSA	Length of Disability 2 yrs = 1; 2-4 yrs = 2; 5-7 yrs = 3; 8 yrs = 4.
ACUT	Weighted Workdays ill
WAGE	Marginal hourly earnings rate in cents (head of household)
WORK	Annual hours working (head of household)
NCIG	Daily cigarettes per adult family member
DSAB	Degree of disability
RELG	Fundamental religious preference (fundamentalist = 1; others = 0)
CITY	Grew up in city = 1; otherwise = 0
FEDU	Father's education
EDUC	Education
FOOD	Food expenditures relative to needs
AGEH	Age of family head
COLD	Number of days below 0°C in 1972
ULTV	Ultraviolet radiation
SULM	Sulphur dioxide annual 24 hour geometric mean
NOXM	Nitrogen dioxide annual 24 hour geometric mean
TSPM	Total suspended particulates annual 24 hour geometric mean
EXER	Energetic participant = 1; others = 0
SEXH	Sex of family head
LOCC	Length of present employment
DDALO	Regional cost of living 1970
ICTR	Non-work family income
SVGS	Savings greater than twice monthly income = 1; less = 0

While the authors admit a number of the above objections and summarise the crude assumptions necessary for their interpretation they insist that they have at least estimated the order of magnitude of the labour productivity effects of air pollution. There seems little basis on which to make this claim. The simple addition of estimated hours lost due to extreme changes in particulate concentrations to estimated hours lost due to extreme changes in nitrogen dioxide concentrations is perhaps the most gross procedure. To use this estimate multiplied by a measure of marginal productivity (marginal wage) as an estimate of the value of lost productivity seems not only crude but possibly misleading. The overall effect of assuming linearity in all relations in the study (not just the equations themselves but also the effects of various pollutants and the conversion of an index into a continuous variable) would seem to negate any confidence in even estimates of the correct order of magnitude. To claim that the results conform to intuitive possibilities is to place too much weight on intuition.

One cannot but notice also that there is no agreement in results between the four samples used. Indeed the significance of acute and chronic illness in the effects on labour supply vary from sample to sample. This could easily be due to severe mis-specification.

In conclusion then the authors seem to be over-optimistic in claiming anything more than suggestive results. The gross nature of the assumptions and the underlying over-simplicity of the model make claims of obtaining 'order of magnitude estimates' over-ambitious. The authors are at pains to stress that the results can only be regarded as suggestive at levels of pollution and characteristics of the sample individuals in the immediate neighbourhood of their averages. Such estimates may contain wide variations within the sample and severely limit the applicability of the results to a nationwide setting.

The Demand for Illness

The authors clearly see the need to include the effects of work hours on health in any estimate of the effects of air pollution on productivity. In addition they accept the notion that individuals place a value directly on good health. Differences in the value of good health between individuals will obviously influence their reaction to a change in the level of health. The authors develop and estimate a model of the demand for health. The model in essence is very simple. The individual is seen as seeking to maintain an optimal level of health given the cost of maintaining any level and value which the individual attaches to it. The individual's choice of the optimal number of days ill will be affected by the opportunity cost of time spent ill and the ability of the individual to maintain any given health state. The number of days ill chosen may thus be expressed as a function of those variables which influence the price of time (wages), the shadow price of health (general endowment variables), and a budget constraint. The authors estimate expressions designed to express the optimum number of days ill as a function of the sacrifices the individual is willing to make in order to avoid illness time given certain pre-determined attributes. The form of the expression to estimate the demand for acute illness is:

Acute Illness = f (wage rate, non-earned income, environmental variables, cost of living, endowment variables) 2.7

The major difference between this equation and one of the form earlier described is that income variables are now included on the right hand side. The explanation for this follows from the implications of the theoretical model. The optimal amount of illness time given the predetermined levels of air pollution etc. will be influenced by the price of time. In the case of chronic illess since the wage is partly determined by the degree of illness a simultaneous equation procedure is used after specifying a relationship between the wage rate and chronic illness.

The authors estimate relationships of the form of 2.7 and interpret them as demand functions for the avoidance of acute or chronic illness. As an approximation to the pecuniary amount the individual would have to receive to avoid an increase in acute or chronic illness the authors calculate

$$\frac{\text{change in illness time}}{\text{change in pollution from mean}} \cdot \text{wage rate}$$

The estimated relationships are in fact similar to the illness expressions in the recursive system above. In addition the monetary valuation of the health effects is identical to the procedure employed to calculate the pecuniary equivalent of the recursive effect of air pollution upon labour. One would therefore expect the use of what might be interpreted as a reduced form equation for a more complete model of labour supply where the number of hours worked, and consequently illness, are functions of the wage rate, and therefore determinants of labour supply. This is not how the authors choose to interpret the equation. They place intepretations on the expressions (and the variables) in line with their model of human behaviour which sees the health state as a choice variable. While an **a priori** model is essential for the interpretation of an empirical relationship the model does not preclude other interpretations of the results. In this case it would be perfectly reasonable to explain the results of the estimated equations in a manner more in line with their previous section. That is to say as an additional argument in a more complex model. The assignment of an interpretation for example to "days lost through illness" as "the demand for avoiding increased hours of acute illness" should not obscure the fact that the variable is invariant to the interpretation placed upon it. The expressions could be seen just as easily as an improperly specified dose-response relationship or at least as part of a wider system of equations. It requires some degree of abstraction to interpret variables measuring the number of days lost through illness or the number of years chronically ill as the chosen number of days or years ill. This perhaps is a useful approach, yet the authors in accepting the Grossman model of health reject all other views on the production of health and seem unable to place any interpretation on their equations but those which conform to such a model. The

Grossman approach is but one suggested approach to the economics of health. It is an insightful approach but not the only one. Not everyone is prepared to accept the view that individuals can or do treat their health as an investment good. Indeed when onc examines the significant variables in the equations estimated they bear a close resembelance to more simple dose response relationships. For example sample 2 in their table 5.12 has an estimated relationship for the significant variables of the form

Weighted work days ill = f (Diet, Risk Medical Insurance, Transfer Income, Particulate Concentration) 2.8

The absence of a significant coefficient on the wage rate must cast some doubt on the authors' interpretation since the wage rate has no estimated significant influence on the optimal length of illness. It is difficult to be confident of the results of willingness to pay to avoid acute illness in the light of this absence in any of the estimated expressions.

In addtion the expressions only manage to explain less than 10% of the variation in the number of workdays ill, suggesting that at least some important variables are missing.

The estimated expressions for chronic illness use two stage least squares since the wage rate is assumed to be endogenous dependent as it is on the length of time of chronic illness. In this case the wage variable is significant in all samples quoted; however, only one pollutant (particulates) in one sample has a statistically significant influence on the index of years disabled. Even if we allow ourselves to generalise from one sample, however, the estimated increase in the number of days of chronic illness chosen as a result of one more unit of particulates can only be assessed as an average for a representative person chosen at the time in their life when earning the average wage. Not only is this an average for the sample of individuals at an average value of time but it also assumes a constant marginal valuation of pollution damage.

When one considers that variables such as climate or urban environment have not been included in either the acute or chronic health relationships, the problem of mis-specification must undermine the confidence which we place in these results. In addition the health effects of work, the induced choice of leisure in place of work and the role of medical care are not properly modelled. The confusion of biases resulting from these problems may be severe limitations on the accuracy of the estimates.

Measurement errors are also particularly apparent in this study. Not only do we see the usual measurement problem for air pollutants but also the unsatisfactory use of bounded discrete variables to represent continuous values. These are both potentially serious sources of bias associated with important variables such as medical care and length of diability.

Conclusion on Crocker et al.

The study represents one of the most sophisticated epidemiological studies carried out by economists. It is a major step forward in the literature in that it recognises the complexity of the issues involved and uses a formal model to interpret the results. The results however ,cannot be said to be convincing. The sophistication of the theory cannot be said to be matched by the data or the applied econometric work. Even the underlying theory is not without its faults and it may even be said to obscure other perhaps more simple explanations of the success and failure of estimated relationships. Impressive though the techniques, the theory and the data are, they cannot be said to produce anything approaching conslusive results even to the extent of offering estimates of the correct order of magnitude.

GENERAL CONCLUSIONS

In general our consideration of two of the most detailed studies of the aggregate relationship between air pollution and human health suggests that we have insufficient evidence to come to any conclusion on the significance of the relationship. The Lave and Seskin (1977) and Crocker (1979) studies are amongst the most detailed and influential work in this area.[6] Most of the criticisms of their work which have been outlined are applicable to the other studies. This pessimistic conclusion is unfortunate given the concern by polcymakers to obtain accurate estimates of the health damage of air pollution. It would seem to be highly dangerous, however, to place sufficient confidence in so called aggregate "dose response functions" to warrant producing damage estimates. Undoubtedly reworking of data, addition of variables, new functional forms and exploitation of new data sets could improve the estimates. Although there is no guarantee of this it would seem better to be cautious at this stage rather than waste resources on a policy which might have little or no effect on the target. If decisions must be made soon then they must be made on other criteria than the results of these experiments.

NOTES

1. The emission of sulphur dioxide into the atmosphere leads to the creation of sulphur particles (sulphates). Ambient concentrations of sulphate particulates tend to be correlated with sulphur dioxide concentrations although the correlation is not always high for urban areas since sulphates have a number of other origins and are more widely dispersed.
2. The breakpoints chosen are somewhat arbitrary and the inconsistencies which arise when the threshold analysis is used could have alternative explanations such as model misspecification.
3. As Lipfert (1978) points out the 24 hour pararosaniline-sulfamic acid bubbler method used to collect NASN data on SO_2 has a reliable lower detectable limit of 13 g/m^3.
4. The use of disease specific mortality rates may not be more satisfactory than using total mortality rates. This is because each disease has its own separate characteristics in terms of severity, duration and age pattern. This will exacerbate the failure to adequately account for other lags in the system and the mobility of the population.
5. Since the subjective value of life may differ according to age this factor may be important in the overall estimates of value of life lost through air pollution.
6. There are a large number of other studies which use similar data and techniques but often produce conflicting results. Examples include Mendelson and Orcutt (1979) and Lipfert (1978)

REFERENCES

Crocker, Thomas D., William Schulze, Shaul Ben-David and Allen V. Kneese (1979) - "Methods Development for Assessing Air Pollution Control Benefits - Volume I Experiments in the Economics of Air Pollution Epidemiology." EPA-600/5-79-001a, February 1979, US Environmental Protection Agency, Washington DC.

Lave, L.B. and Seskin E.P. (1977) - **Air Pollution and Human Health.** Johns Hopkins University Press for Resources for the Future.

Lipfert, F.W. (1978) -"The Association of Human Mortality with Air Pollution: Statistical Analysis by Region, by Age and by Cause of Death". Ph.D. dissertation, Union Graduate School, Yellow Springs, OH.

Mendelson, Robert and Guy Orcutt (1979) - "An Empirical Analysis of Air Pollution Dose Response Curves", **Journal of Environmental Economics and Management**, 6, 85-106.

SECTION FIVE
THE SOCIAL CONSEQUENCES OF POPULATION

SIXTEEN

K. M. Dykes

The Women's Movement Relation to Social Movements in the United States

THE CONTEMPORARY WOMEN'S MOVEMENT AND IT'S HISTORICAL TRADITION

A movement for women's rights has surfaced every time drastic change has shaken the established social order. The women's suffrage movement in the United States grew out of the drive to abolish slavery. The contemporary women's movement was begun largely, but not completely, by women who had been involved in the civil rights movement, in the anti-war. movement, in student movements, and in left politics (Morgan, 1970).

The new feminism began to arise in the early 1960's coming to wide public attention in the last two years of that decade. In 1959, Elanor Flexnor's, **A Century of Struggle, A History of American Feminism** was published and well received, as a reminder of feminist activity; it likely acted as a spur to the new developing feminism. Also, in 1959, Mabel Newcomer's, **A Century of Higher Education,** showed that women's involvement in academic life had declined over the past decade. In 1963, **The Feminine Mystique,** concerning women's discontent by Betty Friedan was widely read.

The year for organizational beginnings for the new feminism was 1966, resulting in the formulation of the National Organization for Women (NOW), with Betty Friedan as the first president. NOW's membership was mostly composed of middle and upper-class women and men (it is among the few groups in the women's movement that allow male members). The majority of it's members are professional middle aged, white women. This organization which has members in every state has been called the National Association for the Advancement of Colored People (NAACP), of the women's movement because it fights within the system, lobbying, concentrating on job discrimination etc. The charter of NOW reads in part, "to bring women into full participation in the mainstream of American society excersizing all the privileges and responsibilities thereof in truly equal partnership with men." NOW was nearly solely responsible for the Equal Employment Opportunities Commission ruling that segregated male-female help-wanted ads in newspapers were discriminatory and illegal. They worked hard to change abortion laws and to call attention to education discrimination. NOW is essentially a reform organization.

At the same time that NOW was being organized, feminist activity was flourishing among younger, more radical women. In 1967 the "Women's Manifesto" was adopted by a national conference of the Students for a Democratic Society (SDS). In this statement the women compared their status with that of peoples of the third world, in that women held a colonial status in relation to men. They claimed that women must fight for their own individuality, and that such a fight would strengthen the revolutionary movement. Women called upon the SDS to work for communal child care centres staffed by women and men, for the right to choose when to have children, and the requirement that every person in a household assume equal participation in the maintenance of a home.

In July of 1971 the National Women's Political Caucus (NWPC) was formed to "awaken, organize, and assert the vast political power represented by women." This group has had the direct affect or running an increased number of women for elected office.

The women's movement is a radical movement, whether radicality is viewed as starting with new premises or as giving new direction to old orders. The term "women's liberation" is said to have been coined by the women's groups that began to meet separately from new left political bodies in 1966. The women's liberation movement of young radical political, educated women had a distinct identity as one part of the contemporary feminist movement. Feminism is typically defined as a position advocating women's rights, while women's liberation implies advocacy of the full freedom of women.

Repeatedly in discussions of the new feminism the analogy was made between the experience of black people and of women, between racism and sexism, and between the women's movement and the black movement.

The contemporary women's movement shares many of the concerns and motivations of the nineteenth century women's movement. They understood economic oppression, political and educational deprivation, but did not understand sexual oppression in the concept of patriarchy. Though it was Elizabeth Cady Stanton, nineteenth century feminist, who coined the phrase, "a woman has a right to her own body and her own self". What nineteenth century women meant by this was voluntary motherhood, the right of women to control her sexual behaviour and abstainance in marriage as the answer. Twentieth century women view sexuality as an essential ingredient in women's subordination.

The nineteenth century women's movement developed apart from the most downtrodden women. Emphasis on the ballot eventually influenced nineteenth century women's tactics, the feminist movement leadership became racist, nativist, and indifferent to the needs of working women (Lerner, 1979).

Nineteenth century women struggled to gain equality as citizens in society, along with women's right to her own body, the right to self determinism, martial reform and birth control.

The moderate wing of the American suffrage movement became The League of Women Voters. As a deliberately nonpartisan group The League could not make use of the ballot for direct purposes of women's self interest as other interest groups traditionally have done. Since public feeling, together with party practices (and women's growing reticence in the face of both), combined to prevent candidacy or election to office for women the vote grew more and more meaningless as reaction set in. Prejudice against the employment of women mounted during the depression and was repeated again after World War II. In the fifties anti-feminism culminated in a fairly solid feeling against women's participation in public life. The groundswell of the women's movement was utterly spent by the fifties, feminism nad become a derogatory term.

The chief weakness of the nineteenth century movement's concentration on suffrage, the factor which helped it to fade, disappear, and lose ground when the vote was gained lay in its failure to challenge patriarchal ideology at a sufficiently deep and radical level to break the conditioning processes of status, temperament and role. A reform movement, is not likely to propose the sweeping changes in society necessary to bring about the completion of a necessary sexual revolution—changes in social attitudes and social-structure in personality and institutions. (Millett, 1969).

Sociologist Elsie Boulding has noted that perhaps the quiet

nineteen-fifties were not so timid in that women as full time homemakers were breeding a set of revolutionaries who powered the anti-war movement, the civil rights and black movements and finally in the sixties the women's liberation movement (Boulding, 1977).

THE FEMINIST TRADITION IN ARCHITECTURE, PLANNING AND SOCIAL WORK

Urban Planning Professor Dolores Hayden has written about the first feminists in the United States to identify the economic exploitation of women's domestic labour by men as the most basic cause of women's inequality. She terms them material feminists because they dared to define a "grand domestic revolution" in women's material conditions. During the nineteenth century they demanded remuneration for women's unpaid household labour. They proposed a complete transformation of the spatial design and material culture of American homes, neighbourhoods and cities. While other feminists campaigned for political or social change with philosophical or moral arguments, the material feminists concentrated on economic and spatial issues as the basis of material life.

The loss of the material feminist tradition has led scholars to misunderstand feminist ideology as a whole (Hayden, 1981). The arching theme of the late nineteenth and early twentieth century feminist movement was to overcome the split between domestic life and public life created by industrial capitalism, as it affected women. Every feminist campaign, Hayden notes, for women's autonomy must be seen in this light.

In the 1960's when Betty Friedan searched for a way to describe the housewife's "problems that have no name" and settled on the "feminine mystique," Charlotte Perkins Gilman's, **Women and Economics, The Economic Factor Between Men and Women as a Factor in Social Evolution,** (1910) had been out of print for decades. Feminists avidly read Gilman's work again, in the late 1960's but the books reappeared without any rediscovery of the historical context of the material feminist thought or political practice that inspired them.

The Utopian and pragmatic sources of material feminism, its broad popular appeal, and the practical experiments it provoked are not well known. Since the 1930's, very few scholars or activists have ever suspected that there might be such an intellectual, political and architectual tradition in the United States.

In her book Hayden traces the realtionship of the cooperative housekeeping movement to the growth in major cities of apartment hotels—those buildings in which residents lived in small, kitchenless suits and dined in communal facilities. These buildings in their time were thought to constitute a grave threat to family life. The materialist feminist movement was closely tied to the communitarian socialist movement—in both cases, the single-family house was seen as a barrier to an ideal community.

The material feminist movement lost ground in the 1920's, largely owing to the rapid rise of the middle class and to the technological developments that made housework, in Hayden's words, "not work but consumption." The suburbanized American culture seemed, at least for a few generations, to make the cause of feminism less urgent.

Charlotte Perkins Gilman, nineteenth century radical feminist theorist, (1860-1935), synthesized the thinking of suffragists, home economists and utopian novelists to produce a comprehensive vision of what the domestic environment might become. Gilman's goal was to change women's role. She has been judged the most original feminist the United States has ever produced, on the basis of her economic, social, and architectual arguments for collective domestic life, she has been described by scholars as representing "the full elaboration of the feminist impulse; and as putting forward radical proposals based on socialist premises" (Hayden, 1981). Gilman stated that women were holding back human evolution because of their confinement to household work and motherhood. Her original contribution was the promption of the development of socialized domestic work and new domestic environments which would be seen as promoting the evolution of socialism, rather than following it. Daring to speak of domestic revolution, Gilman and other material feminists developed new definitions of economic life and settlement design that many socialists in the United States and Europe also accepted.

Hayden notes that the debates the material feminists raised are continuing today. Recently many of the same questions about women's domestic roles and the larger economy are once again being asked, but the importance of the design of housing and the organization of neighbourhoods for these issues has been largely forgotten. Most families still inhabit single-family housing designed around the ideal of woman as full-time homemaker. As women's participation in the paid labour force continues to rise, women and men see the conflicts that outdated forms of housing and inadequate community services create for them and their families. It is difficult to imagine alternatives. It requires spatial imagination to understand that urban regions designed for inequality cannot be changed by new roles in the lives of individuals. The material feminist tradtions can stimulate that imagination, a spatial imagination, by providing feminists visions of different ways to live our lives.

In 1931 the Nobel Prize for Peace was awarded to Jane Addams for recognition of her struggle for international peace. She is one of the most widely known and respected of American women of the twentieth century. She and Ellen Gates Starr founded Hull House, a settlement house in a deçayed section of Chicago largely populated by immigrants. In 1899 Chicago had a million citizens; of these nearly three-quarters had been born outside of the United States. Hull House existed to help these diverse elements melt into the American mainstream. A day care centre was set up, a health clinic, a boarding house for working girls. The Hull House group, dedicated reformers, took up the fight for the rights of people it was trying to help. Garbage collection and municipal corruption became targets as did child labour and sweat shop conditions. The city establishment which had welcomed the settlement workers were later to grow uneasy due to their unswerving loyalty to the population they were determined to assist. The city leaders, being American born and feeling that the foreign born were dangerous, turned against Hull House, its interests, and Jane Addams due to her willingness to deal with anarchists and Hull House efforts to organize labourers.

The reforms undertaken by Hull House illustrate some of the broad trends in social work and illuminate the ties between the residents of settlement houses, who developed many community outreach programs, and home economists, who were involved in research, teaching, and demonstration work in nutrition, child rearing, housing, and sanitation. Jane Addam's enormous contribution in creating a supporting female network and new structures for living, Gerda Lerner wrote, has often been ignored by historians, who have concentrated on her role as a progressive reformer, or as representative of a group of frustrated college trained women with no outlet for their abilities (Lerner, 1975).

Hull House Maps and Papers, by Julia Lathrop (1895) has been recognized as a major pioneer work in urban sociology, reflecting the residents efforts to analyze their own problems and act upon them. Because of their understanding of urban life and politics, Hull House residents did influence social legislation as well as the emerging field of urban sociology (Hayden, 1981). Through the 1890's they lobbied effectively for industrial health and safety, the limitation of child labour, and the legal recognition of trade unions.

Jane Addams wrote that the educational activities of a settlement, as well as its philanthropic, civic, and social undertakings, are but differing manifestations of the attempt to socialize democracy, as is the very existence of a settlement itself. They called upon sociologists, psychiatrists, sought the services of artists, economists, gymnasts, case-workers, dramatists, trained nurses, and the anthropologists.

During its first two decades, Hull House with other American settlements, issued various studies and fact-finding analysis of the city areas with which they were most familiar. The settlement movement antedated by three years the first sociological departments in the universities and by ten years the establishment of the first foundations. Jane Addams viewed the settlements as pioneers in the field of urban research, saying these early efforts in research made for cordial cooperation between social workers and university men. The School of Civics and Philanthropy founded by the Chicago Commons and Hull House was, after twenty years, taken over by the University of Chicago and developed into a graduate school of Social Service Administration. This early relationship between the settlements and the universities had direct and immediate influence on American thinking about industrial questions, and on the course of social practice (Addams, 1935).

By the mid 1890's, twenty women were residents of Hull House, and over forty activities drew two-thousand people per week to the House. Many of the social workers reformers, and scholars (Charlotte Perkins Gilman among them) who came to vist stayed to live and work in the settlement. By 1911 their were over four-thousand settlement houses in the United States. Jane Addams was president of the national association they formed. In her book, **Democracy and Social Ethics** (1902) and **Twenty Years at Hull House** (1910), she explained her reform philosophy, in her administrative positions she strived to implement it. She was chairperson of the Women's Peace Party, a president of the International Congress for Women at The Hague, and the first president of the Women's International League for Peace and Freedom.

Women gathering away from home to discuss their common concerns and to help each other grow represents an act heavy with the potential for social change. This phenomenon was a popular method with the consciousness-raising groups of the early 1970's. What is not so well known is that such gatherings were precedented one-hundred years earlier in the formation of the first women's clubs of America. In both eras women were motivated to come together by their discontent with isolation in the home. The energy of the club movement and the need which it met resulted in a membership of two-hundred-thousand women in 1902. Having bettered the lives of women members as well as implementing social reforms, the movement became the breeding ground for the political activity which achieved women's suffrage (Rock, 1981).

Reform topics discussed by club members such as "Living Conditions in the Poorer Parts of the City", "Homes as They Are-Homes as They Should Be" contrasted with, "Women as Sincere Friends" express the tension between the idea of the clubs for women's individual improvement and the desire to act in the public sphere. It is important to note that at the same time, black women were forming their own clubs, which focused on educational and welfare issues in their communities. In 1896 the National Association of Coloured Women was established.

Researcher Cynthia Rock concludes that in the post suffrage era these women's clubs, like the feminist movement retreated from the fight for women's progress and took on a social role and its place in community reform. The radical aspect of early club ideals reappeared in the second wave of feminism in the late 1960's and 1970's when women once again founded new institutions for themselves.

REFERENCES

Addams, Jane (1935). **Twenty Years at Hull House.** The Macmillan Co. p. 306.

Barnard College (1981, April 11). **The Scholar and Feminist Conference.** Blanche W. Cooke and unidentified speaker.

Boulding, Elsie (1976). **The Underside of History, A View of Women Through Time.** Westview Press, Boulder, Co. p. 9

Daniels, Arlene, Kaplan (1978). "Studying Women's Worlds" in **Society** magazine. Transaction, Inc. p. 45.

Davis, Angela (1981). Quoted by Cheryl Shultze at **Scholar and Feminist Conference** ibid.

Flexnor, Elanor (1959) in **Sexual Politics** by Kate Millett. Avon. p.115

Hayden, Dolores (1981). **The Grand Domestic Revolution: A History of Feminist Designs for American Homes, Neighbourhoods and Cities.** The MIT Press. Cambridge Mass. & London England. pp. 1,5,26-28, 164, 306. And (1981). "The Feminist Paradise Palace". in Heresies. **Heresies** periodical # 11, New York. p. 56.

Lerner, Gerda (1970). **The Majority Finds It's Past, The Placing of Women in History.** pp. 33-36, 67. and (1975). "Placing Women in History Definitions and Challenges," in Feminist Studies, 3 Fall. p. 6.

Millett, Kate (1969). **Sexual Politics.** Avon Books, New York. p. 119.

Morgan, Robin (1970). **Sisterhood is Powerfull, An Anthology of Writings From the Women's Liberation Movement.** Random House, New York p. xx.

Rock Cynthia (1981). "Building the Women's Club Movement in Nineteenth Century America," in **Heresies,** ibid. p.88

SEVENTEEN

Ira M. Sheskin and Howard G. Eisenstadt

The Impact of Planned Dade Country Rapid Transit Upon the Accessibility of the Elderly*

While the decreasing physical and mental abilities of many elderly suggests the need for various paratransit programs, it is clear that, perhaps due in part to the selective nature of elderly migration to Dade County,[1] large groups of Dade's elderly employ both the private automobile and the public transit system[2]. The purpose of this paper is to examine the effects of an expanding public transit system upon the accessibility of the elderly to various destinations, including health centres, social service centres, and the central business district[3]. First, brief descriptions of Dade's elderly and planned rapid transit system are provided. Then, the methodology used to analyze accessibility changes is presented. Finally, selected results are shown. These results show that: (1) the elderly enjoy a somewhat greater level of accessibility than the general population; and, (2) will experience decreased walk access times and total travel times, but will have an increased need to make transfers in 1985.

THE ELDERLY IN DADE COUNTY

The elderly in the United States comprised about 11.0 percent of the population in 1978. Florida, with its 1.6 million elderly residents, has the greatest proportion of elderly in the nation with 17.7 per cent of its population in the over 65 cohort. Dade County has one of the largest concentrations due in part to the large in-migration of elderly from other states who seek the tropical climate and a somewhat lower cost of living than is found in northern metropolitan areas[4]. The elderly

----

* Paper presented at the 8th National Conference on Transportation for the Elderly and Handicapped, Sarasota, Florida, October, 1981.

population of Dade County has been increasing in both absolute and relative terms. In 1970, approximately 172,700 (13.6 per cent) of Dade County's residents were 65 or over; the comparable figures for 1979 were 247,870 (16.3 percent), a 44 percent increase. Approximately one-third of the elderly persons in Dade County are considered to be of lower income. Dade County has large numbers of Jewish, Black, and Spanish elderly. South Maimi Beach has been characterized as an urban geriatric ghetto; other elderly neighbourhoods are in suburban areas.

In 1974 the Dade County Office of Human Resources[5] identified four "significant problems" faced by most elderly: (1) reduced and/or static incomes coupled with inflation; (2) increased demand for health care; (3) deficits of decent housing; and (4) alienation and frustration.

Although mobility problems were not identified as "significant," they obviously underlie other difficulties. Income problems affect automobile ownership and the ability to afford public transit. Income-related mobility problems may restrict a person's access to lower-priced shopping opportunities. Health care problems are often related to difficulty in accessing health care services. Mobility restrictions caused by either monetry considerations or physical deterioration often require elderly people to live in less desirable areas. Alienation and frustration may well result when a formerly mobile individual becomes spatially restricted.

Transportation needs of the elderly had become an acknowledged issue by 1978 when the four-volume "Elderly and Handicapped Transportation Needs Study" was issued by the Dade County Office of Transportation Administration (OTA)[6]. Since then, senior citizens, via the "Concerned Seniors of Dade," and handicapped persons, via the "Commission for the Advancement of the Physically Handicapped," have been lobbying for improved transportation services for their constituents who represent over 25 per cent of all public transit users. Also, a number of Dade County social workers have indicated their feelings that mobility is a serious problem for the elderly. Thus, the problem of elderly accessibility is well-recognized in Dade County.

PLANNED CHANGES IN THE DADE COUNTY TRANSIT SYSTEM

Metropolitan Dade County Florida currently is constructing an integrated multimodal public transit system to consist of a 21-mile elevated rail rapid transit line, a 4.2-mile downtown people mover (DPM), and a bus system that will expand from the current 550 to 1000 buses. The rail line will run from the Dadeland Shopping Centre in the South, past the University of Miami, Coconut Grove, and the high-rise, high-income condominium area of Brickell Avenue to the outskirts of the central business district (CBD). From the Miami CBD, the rail line will proceed north to the Dade County Government Centre/University of Miami-Jackson Memorial Hospital Complex, though the depressed Liberty City area, and then west past the Hialeah Race Track. These two legs will serve a predominantly middle-class, white (mostly nonhispanic) population to the south, the black population of Liberty City and Coconut Grove, and the Hispanic residents of Hialeah, as well as the upper-income residents of the Brickell area, but will not pass through the elderly areas of the county. This route was selected as a result both of an alternatives analysis in which various proposed alignments were examined and the political reality of the need to pass two county-wide referenda on the issue of whether or not to build a public transit system. The route will include twenty stations and will cost a minimum of 867 million dollars which will come from federal (77 per cent), state (10 per cent), and local (13 per cent) funds. About 200,000 passengers are expected to use the rail line daily when it opens in 1984.

The rail line will connect to the 92 million dollar Miami Downtown People Mover (DPM) on the outskirts of the CBD, where 73,700 persons currently are employed. More than two-thirds of the route will be within existing right-of-way on an elevated guideway, thus minimizing disruption. The goals are to eliminate the need for buses to enter the CBD and to reduce the number of automobiles driven into the CBD daily.

Areas of high elderly concentration will be connected to the rail system via the bus system which will be realigned into a modified grid network. Many routes will act in a "feeder" capacity to the rail system, feeding into the rail rapid transit and DPM stations. One fare will be paid and in most cases "free body transfer," in which riders get off the bus and onto the train without waiting on a line to buy tickets or hand in transfers, will be in effect.

This fully integrated system is designed to help satisfy nine policy statements or goals as defined by the Dade County Transit Development Program[3] and adopted by the Dade County Board of County Commissioners. One stated "goal" of the new transit system is to "provide adequate transit service to elderly and handicapped citizens... by increasing travel opportunities at times of day relevant to these residents." This paper examines the extent to which this goal is likely to be attained. A brief synopsis of the techniques used to analyze accessibility changes is provided in the next section. Following that, the likely impacts of the new public transit system upon the accessibility of the elderly are presented.

METHODOLOGY FOR ACCESSIBILITY ANALYSIS

The methodology developed consisted of comparing the accessibility of the elderly on the "existing (1975)" and "proposed (1985)" Dade County public transit system described above[7,8]. For this analysis, three measures of accessibility were defined:

(1) **Walk time,** including walking to, from, and between transit vehicles (at an assumed speed of three miles per hour);
(2) **Total travel time,** including walk time (as defined above), waiting time, and in-vehicle time; and,
(3) **Number of transfers** between transit vehicles.

Accessibility was examined to each of four different types of destinations: social service agencies, health care centres, activity centres (shopping centres), and the Miami CBD. Because travel characteristics vary between the peak (7-9 AM and 4-6 PM) and off-peak periods and because the goal stated above calls for "increasing travel opportunities at times of day relevant to these residents," separate analyses were conducted for the peak and off-peak periods.

The following procedure was employed to calculate the three accessibility measures for each of the four destinations for the peak and off-peak periods. The necessary demographic data for 1975 and 1985 for each of Dade County's 723 Traffic Analysis Zones (TAZ's) were made available by the Dade County Planning Department as were the locations of relevant destinations (hospitals, shopping centres, etc.). The centroids of each TAZ were used as origin points and, where appropriate, as destinations. That is, for example, if a TAZ contained a hospital, its centroid became a possible destination as a health care center. A shortest path algorithm was then run over the graph of the Dade County transit networks for 1975 and 1985 to find the shortest paths from each origin centroid to each designated destination centroid.

For each of the three accessibility measures, Accessibility Standards were established. For walk time, the three standards used were "under 5 minutes," "5-10 minutes," and "over 10 minutes" The categories for total travel time were "under 10 minutes," "10-20 minutes," "20-30," "30-45," "45-60," and "over

60 minutes". Five categories were established for the use of transfers: "0 transfers," "1," "2," "3," and "4 transfers." Combining the demographic data with the calculated travel times it was possible to determine the percentage of the elderly population in each accessibility category during each time period (peak, off-peak). The data were grouped by relevant destination types producing Accesibility Classes such as the percentage of elderly people requiring "under 5 minutes" of walk time during a trip to a health centre during the off-peak period.

Two analysis techniques are employed in evaluating the changes in accessibility from the existing 1975 to the proposed 1985 transit systems. First, for each Accessibility Class, for each possible destination type, for the peak and off-peak periods, an Accessibility Histogram was produced showing the percentage of the population within each Accessibility Standard for the 1975 and 1985 transit system.

The second analysis technique employed was the Index of Dissimilarity (1)[9] which was used to compare the percentage distributions for 1975 and 1985 on each histogram. The index varies between zero and 100. Zero indicates that the two percentage distributions are exactly the same. Thus, in the context of this study, an 1 of zero indicates that no change in accessibility occurred between 1975 and 1985. An I of 100 indicates total dissimilarity, or the maximum change in accessibility. An I of ten, for example, is interpreted as a ten percent improvement (or decline) in accessibility.

RESULTS

The impact of the proposed Dade County rapid transit system on the accessibility of the elderly is shown in Table 17.1 (via indices of dissimilarity) for trips for social services, health and activity (shopping) centres, and the CBD and in Figure 17.1 (with histograms) for social service, health centre, and CBD trips. Table 17.1 also shows indices for the entire population to permit comparison. This section highlights some of the more important results.

Table 17.1 indicates that the greatest improvement in walk time for the elderly will occur in the off-peak period, particularly for social service trips, for which about 23 percent of the population will experience shorter walk times. (See also Figure 17.1.). Overall, however, little improvement is seen in walk times. For 1975, the modal class is 5-10 minutes (except for health centre trips, where it is 0-5 minutes). Thus, it would be difficult for any transit system to lower walk times

TABLE 17.1
Indices of Dissimilarity

		1975-1985 Comparision of Transit Accessibility				Elderly - Total Population Comparison	
		Total Population		Elderly			
Trip Type		Off-Peak	Peak	Off-Peak	Peak	1975	1985
Social Services	Walk Time	2.0	17.0	.9	22.8	9.5	8.4
	Total Time	15.3	14.7	13.0	11.5	8.6	10.8
	# Transfers	12.6	12.7	11.3	10.5	2.4	1.5
Health Centre	Walk Time	4.1	8.3	9.3	11.8	10.3	8.1
	Total Time	15.7	15.6	20.2	13.4	18.8	17.0
	# Transfers	19.6	16.4	20.3	17.4	4.8	5.0
Activity Centre	Walk Time	5.0	3.8	3.0	3.9	10.1	8.1
	Total Time	24.0	25.1	21.6	22.9	10.7	7.6
	# Transfers	16.6	17.7	9.8	13.2	2.7	5.5
CBD	Walk Time	9.8	8.5	9.3	10.3	8.5	6.1
	Total Time	23.6	28.2	12.9	20.0	17.0	8.8
	# Transfers	39.5	50.1	41.8	48.8	5.0	5.5
Average for All Trip Types	Walk Time	4.4	8.5	5.6	12.2	NA	NA
	Total Time	19.2	20.2	16.9	17.0		
	# Transfers	20.8	22.3	20.8	22.5		

Sources: (3).

significantly.

Compared to the entire population the elderly were walking shorter distances in 1975 and will be walking shorter distances in 1985. The size of this disparity will remain about the same over time. (Table 17.1) shows the I between elderly and total population to be 9.5 in 1975 and 8.4 in 1985. Figure 1-B (1 = 11.8) shows some increases and some decreases in elderly walk time for health centres. Figure 1-A (1 = 10.3) shows decreases in walk time for elderly CBD-oriented trips.

Total travel time for the elderly also will be reduced for 1985, particularly for trips to health centres during the peak period, trips to activity centres, and trips to the CBD in the off-peak. Overall, however, only about 17 percent of elderly will experience decreased travel time. Two reasons may be cited. First, the area of highest elderly density, (Miami Beach) is already well-served by transit. Second, the elderly, on the average, live closer to the CBD than the general population and thus already experience short travel time to most destination types.

Table 17.1 also shows that elderly travel times were shorter than those for the general population in 1975 although this advantage will decrease, particularly for CBD trips. Figures I-A,-D, and-G show the details of the types of changes to be expected. Figure I-D, for example, shows that for CBD trips, many elderly experiencing travel times over 60 minutes will have their trips shortened to below 60 minutes.

Unlike for walk time and total travel time, the indiices of dissimilarity in Table I indicate increases in the need to transfer in 1985 due to the multi-modal nature of the proposed system as described above. As would be expected from a CBD-oriented rail and DPM, the greatest increases in the need to transfer is for CBD-oriented trips. Obviously, the new system will create some difficulties for those with mobility problems who have problems getting on and off vehicles. A trip that can be accomplished currently by use of a single bus will in many cases, require a bus to the rail to the DPM.

Table 17.1 also shows that there will be little change in the slightly lower need for the elderly to transfer. Figure I-G shows that for the CBD about forty percent of elderly who currently can travel downtown without the need to transfer, will need one or more transfers in 1985.

FIGURE 17.1

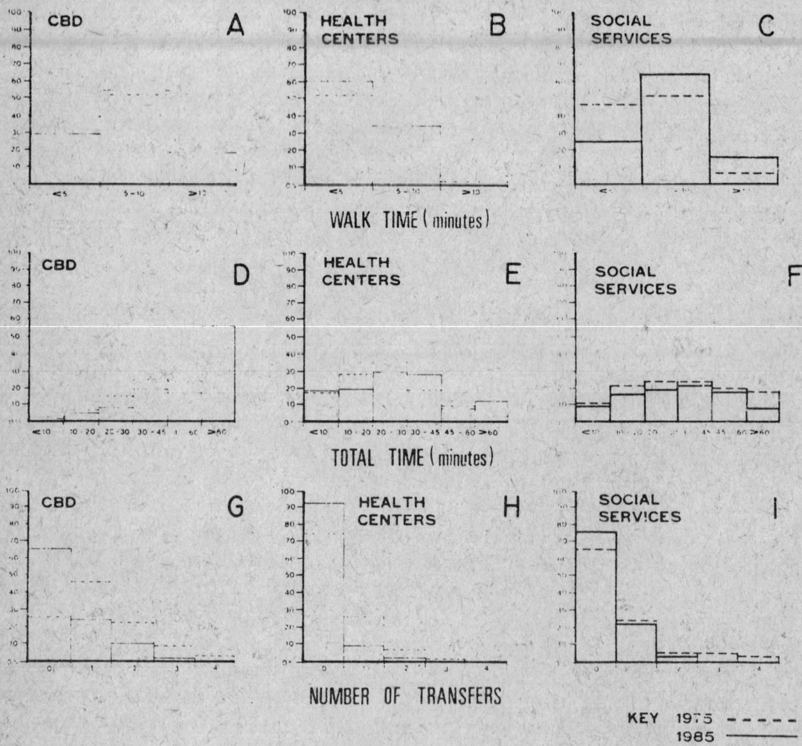
CBD
A
HEALTH CENTERS
B
SOCIAL SERVICES
C
WALK TIME (minutes)
CBD
D
HEALTH CENTERS
E
SOCIAL SERVICES
F
TOTAL TIME (minutes)
CBD
G
HEALTH CENTERS
H
SOCIAL SERVICES
I
NUMBER OF TRANSFERS
KEY 1975
1985

CONCLUSION

The results of the methodology presented above indicate that Dade County's elderly population will experience increased transit service characteristics upon implementation of proposed transit system improvements. Specifically, we found that: (1) the elderly will experience decreases in walk time and travel time, but will suffer from a significant increase in the need to transfer; and (2) the elderly enjoy somewhat better accessibility than the general population given both the current transit system and the planned system.

REFERENCES

1. R. Schultz and Camarco, T. Jr., "Migration to and from Southeast Florida, 1965-70," **Southeastern Geographer,** 17 (1977); 33-48.
2. I. M. Sheskin and H. A. Friedman, "Aging and Mobility in Dade County, Florida," **The Florida Geographer,** April 1981, pp. 17-24.
3. This paper is based upon an analysis performed by the authors for Dade County, and may be found in Appendix B of: Office of Transportation Administration, **Transit Development Program,** Dade County, Florida, 1980.
4. J. Kraft and C. C. Osterbind, (Eds.) **Older People in Florida '80 - '81,** Gainesville, Florida: The University presses of Florida, 1981.
5. Dade County, Office of Human Resources, **Profile of the Elderly,** Dade County, Florida, 1974.
6. Dade County, Office of Transportation Administration, Division of Planning and Programming, Elderly and Handicapped Transportation Needs Study, 1978, 4 vols.
7. The analysis of elderly accessibility on an urban areawide basis has been increasing. See, for example: S. Golant, **The Residential Location and Spatial Behavior of the Elderly: A Canadian Example,** The University of Chicago, Department of Geography Research Paper no. 143, 1972; S. Golant, **Location and Environment of Elderly Population** (Washington, D.C.: V. H. Winston & Sons, 1979); G. Rowles, **Prisoners of Space? Exploring the Geographical Experience of Older People** (Boulder, Colorado: Westview Press, 1978); R. Wiseman, Spatial Aspects of Aging, Association of American Geographers Resource Paper no. 78-4 (Washington, D.C., 1978); and the July, 1980 issue of **The Pennsylvania Geographer.** The most complete work on elderly travel is: M. Wachs, **Transportation for the Elderly** (Berkeley, California: University of California Press, 1979).
8. A discussion of accessibility in terms of such issues as costs

and vehicle characteristics may be found in: U. S. Department of Transportation, **Transportation for the Elderly and Handicapped,** Programs and Problems **2,** October, 1980, pp. 1-33.

9. D. M. Smith, **Patterns in Human Geography,** New York: Crane, Russak & Company, Inc., 1975.

EIGHTEEN

A.T. Salau

Population Movements within the Nigerian Urban System

INTRODUCTION

Population movement within an urban system takes place on two levels. On a microlevel, people move within a city in the process of carrying out their daily routines (travelling to work, shopping, visiting friends or relatives, etc.). On a macrolevel, urban residents also travel to locations outside their communities, in particular to other cities for recreational, business or visitation purposes. All these movements can be further categorized as (1) circulation and (2) migration.

Circulation embraces movements which are usually repetitive in nature and where there are no intention of changing residence either permanently or for a long period of time. Migration, on the other hand, are those movements involving long-term or permanent change of residence.

These movements are manifestations of part of the processes taking place within an urban system. As Burgess (1925) aptly puts it: 'movement may be thought of as the pulse of the community. Like the pulse of the human body it is a process which reflects and is indicative of all changes which are taking place in the community'.

Information on the degree and nature of population movements within the Nigerian urban system can only be gleaned from some few case studies in the absence of national census migration data. The available studies are few in number but some are sufficiently detailed enough in enhancing our knowledge and answering many inter-related questions pose by population movements.

The study is divided into two sections. The first section concentrates on the population movements between Nigerian cities (inter-urban migration) while the second part focuses on circulation within Nigerian cities (intra-urban movements).

Inter-urban Movements (Migration)

This section is concerned with the urban population movements in Nigeria. This type of movement has long been a neglected aspect of population movements in Nigeria. Most studies have concentrated on and emphasized the rural-urban population movements. The reason for this is not far-fetched. The rural-urban migration has been the most noticeable and one which in fact has effected the most radical change in the spatial distribution of people in Nigeria as in all countries at one time or the other. Several studies have indicated the massive nature of these movements. According to Milone and Green (1973), p.6), 644,000 people migrated into Lagos within a single decade (1953-1963) and the World Bank (1972) had also calculated that migrants accounted for 75 per cent of the total population growth in Lagos between 1952 and 1963. However, it is now agreed that as the process of urbanization gains momentum in a country, natural increase within the city becomes an increasingly dominant contributor to urban growth because of the sheer size of the urban population relative to the rual population (Davis, 1972). Most of the largest cities in Nigeria have undoubtedly reached the stage where most of their growth can now be attributed to natural increase rather than migration from the rural areas. Migration from other urban areas is perhsps more important now than that from the rural areas. For example, in a study of migration to Calabar, Ilorin and Warri, (Ekanem and Adepoju (1977), it was found that the most common form of migration to these cities was urban to urban. As can be seen on Table 18.1, the largest proportion of moves was in the urban-urban category regardless of the order of move for Warri and Calabar. In the case of Ilorin, the only deviation from this pattern is the third move which is mostly rural to urban. This result is consistent with the earlier findings of Adepoju (1975-76) in Ife and Oshogbo where about two-thirds of the migrants were from other urban areas rather than from rural areas. The genral conclusion then is that stepwise migration has become prevalent whereby instead of movement from villages directly to, for example, Lagos, a potential migrant moves first to a small town, then after a short time there, he may move to a bigger town (a medium size city which may invariably be one of the state captials). From there, he may finally move to the nation's capital or one of the nation's metropolitatn centres. One can justifiably presume that most movements are now terminated at the state capitals. This is due to the fact that these cities are not too far and the migrants are in familiar environments with most of the urban residents probably belonging to their ethnic groups. With increasing opportunities (jobs and other services) available in these cities, they serve as countermagnets to cities like Lagos, Kano, Kaduna, Ibadan and Enugu.

On the determinants of migration, most studies have buttressed the well known fact that the major factor is economic in nature. Indeed, in view of the existing high level of unemployment in most of the major cities in the country, it is still rational and profitable for people to migrate there. In a study by Fapohunda, Adegbola and Sada (1972), the attraction of Lagos for the unemployed residents was found to be mainly three in number: economic opportunity, amenity and family relationships. As can be seen from Table 18.2, the dominant reasons for migrating to Lagos were economic in nature. Employment related reason account for over half of all reasons given with 43.83 per cent of the respondents having come to Lagos mainly to look for work. The second most important reason for migrating to Lagos is the desire of the respondents to partake of the better social amenities available there, especially the opportunities for higher education. This is in line with many studies which have found that there is a positive correlation between educational attainment and migration. There are many ways in which education affects migration. It is often found that the higher the level of education the higher the propensity to migrate. This fact may not be surprising in that Nigerian educational curriculum prepare students for the kinds of jobs which are invariably only avilable in the big cities. Also, the fact is that in order to acquire higher education (especially technical and post secondary education), most students are obliged to go to cities where they are often concentrated. In Nigeria, majority of the universities, for example, are located in the major cities (Table 18.3) and thus students come from the rural areas and other cities to attend them.

Ekanem and Adepoju (1977) also found that the income expectation of all migrants were very high before they left their areas of origin. About 80 per cent of all migrants to Warri, Calabar and Ilorin were optimistic of getting more income (Table 18.4). Also, more than half of these migrants were employed before they left their areas of origin. Therefore, it can be concluded that not all migrants are necessarily jobless and thus being 'pushed' out. As has been found elsewhere, people migrating from one city to the other in Nigeria, are generally young. In Oshogbo and Ife, the average age is less

TABLE 18.1

Direction of moves by migrant heads of households in Warri (1974), Calabar & Ilorin (1975)

Order of Move	calabar				Percent* Ilorin				Warri			
	R—R	R—U	U—U	U—R	R—R	R—U	U—U	U—R	R—R	R—U	U—U	U—R
FIRST	6.6	13.4	68.6	1.1	11.6	24.6	32.6	0.9	48.2	3.6	43.8	1.6
SECOND	4.3	5.3	71.7	5.0	5.8	10.4	42.8	4.3	10.2	3.6	73.1	6.4
THIRD	2.3	7.6	68.0	8.3	4.2	47.8	26.4	3.7	9.3	2.7	70.5	5.3
FOURTH	3.2	8.2	53.3	5.5	1.6	8.2	14.9	6.9	8.6	4.3	67.6	2.4

*Excluding No response

—direction, U = urban; R = rural

Source: Ekanem and Adepoju (1977 p.62)

than that of non-migrants. Two-fifths of the migrants in Ife were between the ages of 20 and 29 compared to one-quarter of the non-migrants. The migrants are also predominantly males. In both Oshogbo and Ife, migrants were found to be generally better educated than non-migrants and most migrant house-hold heads were married but about forty percent were single (Adepoju, 1975-76, p.5).

TABLE 18.2
Reasons for coming to Lagos by unemployed Respondents

Reasons	Absolute Frequency	Relative Frequency(%)
1. **Economic**	803	54.26
(a) to look for work	649	43.85
(b) to learn a trade	141	9.53
(c) bad village/house life	13	0.88
2. **Amenities**	224	15.14
(a) to school	206	13.92
(b) city attraction	18	1.22
3. **Family Relationship**	84	5.68
(a) to meet/join parents	50	3.38
(b) parental advice	34	2.30
4. **Other Reasons**	99	6.69
5. **Have Always Lived in Lagos**	270	18.24
TOTAL	1480	100.0

Source: Fapohunda, Adegbola & Sada (1972)

The creation of new states in 1967 and 1976 has contributed greatly to the modification of migration pattern in the past few years. Some new state capitals have emerged as major destination points for migrants who might have otherwise gone directly to Lagos or cities like Kaduna, Kano, Enugu or Ibadan. With new manufacturing activities being established in the cities designated as state capitals and with the budgeoning employment opportunities in the state civil services, which did not exist before state creation, this modification is inevitable.

TABLE 18.3
Location of Universities in Nigeria (1981)

Settlement Size	Absolute Frequency	Relative Frequency(%)
Small cities (20,000-50,000 population)	0	0
Medium cities (50,000-250,000 population)	10	58.82
Large cities (above 250,000 population)	7	41.18
Total	17	100.0

TABLE 18.4
Income Expectation and Employment Status of Migrants to Warri (1974) Calabar and Ilorin (1975)

Variables	PERCENTAGE Warri	Calabar	Ilorin
1. Pre-Migration Income Expectation			
More	77.4	87.3	85.9
Less/same	11.1	8.1	0.7
No response	11.5	4.5	13.4
2. Pre-Migration Employment Status			
Employed	53.2	51.7	56.8
Unemployed	38.8	45.8	30.3
No response	8.0	2.5	12.8
Number	1204	1100	819
Total (%)	100.0	100.0	100.0

Source: Ekanem and Adepoju, op. cit., p. 56

The study of Warri, Calabar and Ilorin shows that the attraction of these cities is a recent phenomenon. As can be seen on Table 18.5, only about one tenth or less of the migrants in these cities arrived before the country became independent in 1960. Between that period and the begining of the political crisis in 1966, about one-fifth of them arrived although the proportion is much higher in Warri being only one-tenth. Following the creation of states in 1967 and until the end of the civil war in 1970, between 12-16% arrived in Calabar and Ilorin but the proportion was higher for Warri (33%). Most of the migrants arrived since the end of the civil war. These movements could thus be associated with the political developments taken place in the country. Calabar and Ilorin were made state capitals in 1967 and the movements to these cities increased dramatically after that period.

The high volume of inter-urban migration can be expected to continue, if not increase, as time goes on. This is so, when one realizes that the urbanization level for the nation is still reckoned to be only 30%. Thus, the increase in the level of urbanizarion will undoubtedly be accompanied by increasing mobility of people from cities to cities. Studies have also shown that some of the 'costs' of migration are not borne directly by the migrants. Majority of them are always able to get temporary accomodation with friends and relatives (usually free of charge or at nominal rate) already in those cities. For example, more than half of all migrants to Calabar and Ilorin in 1975 resided with friends or relatives (Ekanem and Adepoju, 1977, p.67).

As has been noted, the major factor responsible for migration is economic in nature. Specifically, it is the need to get a job or better employment opportunity. One would have expected the migration stream to be reduced when information of high level of unemployment in these cities gets back to the areas of origin. However, this is not the case because a substantial number of these migrants still do manage to get jobs, the type of jobs is another matter. For example, in Calabar, Ilorin and Warri, over sixty percent of all migrant heads of household spent less than a year before securing one kind of job or the other (Table 18.6). Perhaps more important is that majority of the migrants has a favourable opinion about their new abodes.

INTRA-URBAN MOBILITY

Circulation within the city is a very important aspect of urban processes and growth. These intra-urban movements involve both the day-to-day movements of people from their places of residence to work and service as well as to recreational and social trips. The ease with which urban residents interact or move from one part of the city to another is a critical indicator of the efficiency of the urban system.

TABLE 18.5

Reported time of arrival by origin of migrant heads of households Warri (1974), Calabar and Ilorin (1975)

Time of Arrival	PERCENT Calabar Urban	Calabar Rural	Calabar Total	Ilorin Urban	Ilorin Rural	Ilorin Total	Warri Urban	Warri Rural	Warri Total
Before 1960	14.9	7.9	11.8	11.8	3.6	7.2	4.7	6.9	5.0
1960-1966	1.6	1.1	1.4	-	4.3	2.2	12.4	2.5	10.7
1967-1970	14.4	19.0	16.3	9.9	16.6	12.3	37.8	33.6	37.7
After 1970	61.8	62.4	62.0	49.4	43.0	46.1	40.8	46.3	42.0
No Resp.	7.3	9.6	8.5	28.9	33.0	32.3	4.3	4.7	7.6
Number	550	550	1100	1368	451	819	557	647	1204
Total (%)	100.0	100.0	100.0	100.0	100.0	100.0	100.0	100.0	100.0

Source: Ekanem and Adepoju (1977, p.65)

TABLE 18.6
Duration of unemployment on arrival in Calabar, Ilorin (1975) and Warri (1974)

Period	Per cent Calabar	Ilorin	Warri
Under 6 months	63.8	64.7	69.2
6-12 months	8.1	7.0	11.3
12 + months	11.1	2.0	19.5
No response	17.0	26.3	-
Number	1100	819	1204
Total (%)	100.0	100.0	100.0

Source: Ekanem and Adepoju (1977, p. 67)

As has been indicated earlier, urban trips are made for a number of reasons but most studies have shown that the major one is the trip to and from places of employment from a place of residence (journeys-to-work). In a study of Lagos (Olayemi, 1977), it was found that the Journey-to-work and school trips dominate the intra-urban movements. These two categories of trips accounted for 44.8% and 34.5% respectively of the total daily trips in Lagos. Thus, almost four-fifths of the total trips within the city on an average weekday are made up of work and school trips. Next importance were business trips which accounted for about 9% of the total (Table 18.7).

TABLE 18.7
Characteristics of intra-urban Movements in Lagos, (1974)

Purpose of Movements	Absolute Frequence	Relative Frequence
Work	4344	44.83
School	3338	34.45
Business	864	8.92
Shop	622	6.42
Job seeking & Apprenticeship	401	4.14
Social and others	121	1.24
Total	9690	100.0

Source : Olayemi (1977, p.21)

Ragarding the means of transportation used by urban

residents, most trips in Nigerian cities are being made on foot, minibuses, buses, taxis, motor-cycles, bicycles and private automobiles. In Lagos, 79.5% of journeys-to-work and 50.4% of shcool trips depend on bus transport (buses and minibuses) while 8.5% of journeys-to-work and 19.6% of school trips were made on foot (Fig. 18.1).

An indicator of the effectiveness of urban planning is the length or distance people have to travel in the pursuance of their daily activities. The result of an effective planning is the minimization of the distance. In Lagos, only 14.2% of residents travel less than two miles daily from their residence to work while the figure for school trips was 22.1%. More than 50% of these trips were between two to five miles (Olayemi, 1977, p. 25). In contrast, in a study of Jos, Ayeni (1979, p. 101) found that for the journey-to-work, quite a high proportion of people (38.5%) travel less than 1 kilometre and as for the journey-to-services, the figure was 26.08%. Perhaps more important is that overall, 59.88% and 62.44% of all respondents travel less than two kilometres daily to work and services respectively in Jos. This is a reflection of the degree of the ease of movement in the two cities and the complexity of the urban structures.

Many hypotheses have been postulated concerning the relationship between trip frequency and socio-economic characteristics of urban residents in the cities of the more developed countries. The only study known to this author which have tried to uncover these relationships in Migerian cities is that of Ayeni (1979) on Jos. Ayeni divided the Jos households into three income groups (low, middle and upper) and found that there was a difference in trip frequencies between the low and upper income on the one hand and the middle and low income on the other. Above an income of 600 naira, differences in trip frequency of households virtually become insignificant (Table 18.8). With the use of analysis of variance (where the F value of 9.28 was highly significant at the .001 level), he thus concluded that the higher income groups generate more trips than the low income groups. The implication of this finding becomes very obvious in that as the standard of living of urban residents improves, there is a propensity for them to make more trips (as the distance factor, particularly its cost seems less significant) in order to partake to the fullest all the amenities and services available in the city. Secondly, most of the private automobiles in the city are invariably owned by people of middle and upper income groups. Perhaps more important, while the low income group would be making few trips daily (for example, the petty traders and others belonging to the informal sector usually travel to and from the markets or their stalls twice a

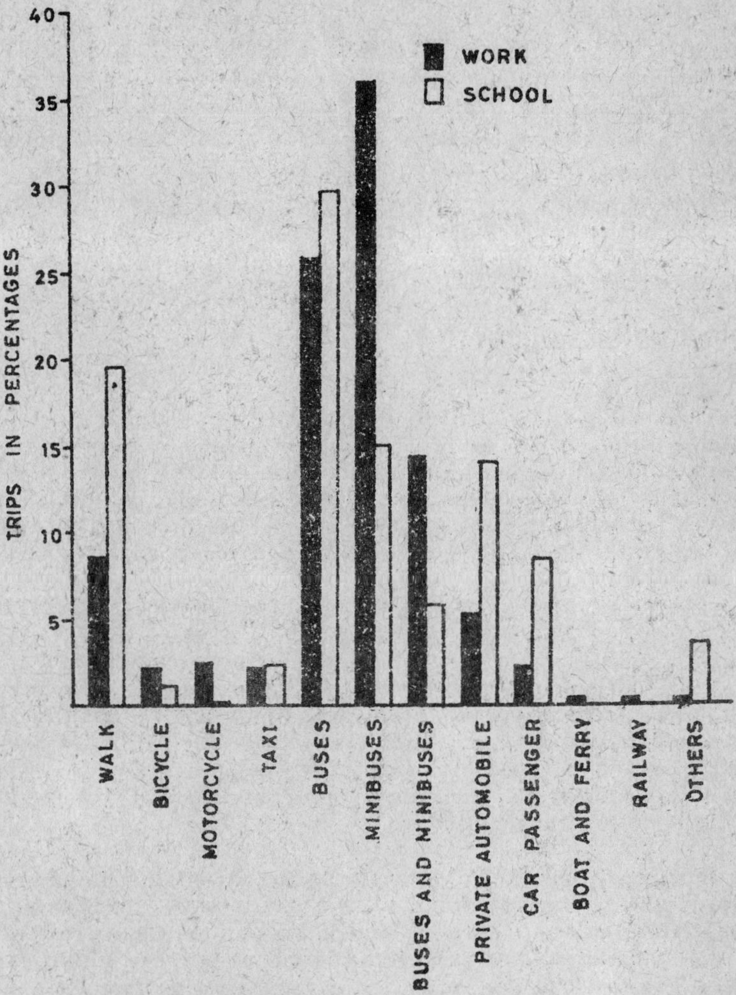

FIG18.1 COMMUTERS MODE OF TRAVEL IN LAGOS
Source: Olayemi (1977 P. 23)

TABLE 18.8
Household trip frequency by wage classes in Jos, 1972

Income Group	No of Observation	Mean Friquency trip	Standard Duration
Low Income (N600 p.a.)	114	16.59	8.96
Middel Income (N600-1600 p.a.)	114	22.96	15.35
Upper Income (Above N1600 p.a.)	56	23.50	12.62

Source: Ayeni, op. cit., p.94

day) the people in the civil service, manufacturing and industries often make many trips daily. Since the low income groups relies on walking or public transportation while those of the middle and upper income groups generally prefer to use private automobiles, an improvement in the standard of living will invariably necessitate more investment on roads and parking spaces within the urban areas.

CONCLUSION

The continuing improvement in the standard of living of Nigerians cannot but lead to an increasing rate of mobility both between and within the cities. Thus, the implication of this is that there is a need for effective spatial planning without which our cities and highways would be plagued by mounting problems of traffic congestion.

Thus study has shown that population movements between and within cities occur mainly in the efforts by the people to satisfy their needs. There is a need to pay particular attention to the allocation and efficient arrangement of activities in space. The lopsided concentration of activities in few cities will ensure that most movements within the national urban system will be in their direction. As for the intra-urban mobility, the volume and distance travelled is determined by how far the necessary facilities are separated from the places of residence. A more rational and efficient arrangement of these activities will go a long way towards minimizing the costs of intra-urban movements and enhance the effective functioning of the city.

REFERENCES

Adepoju, A. (1975-76) 'Urban Migration Differentials and selectivity: The Example of Western Nigeria' **African Urban Notes,** Vol. 11, Number 1, pp.1-24.

Ayeni, B. (1979) **Concepts and Techniques in Urban Analysis,** London, Croom Helm.

Burgess, E.W. (1925) 'The Growth of the City' in R.E. Park et al. (eds.) **The City,** Chicago, Univ. of Chicago Press.

Davis, K. (1972) **World Urbanization, 1950-70,** Population Monograph Series 9, University of California, Berkeley.

Ekanem, I and Adepoju A. (1977) **Migration into selected medium-sized towns of Nigeria,** Research Monograph, Dept. of Demography and Social Statistics, University of Ife.

Fapohunda, O., Adegbola, K. and Sada, P. (1972) **Population, Employment and Living Conditions in Lagos,** Human Resources Unit Research Project, Univ. of Lagos.

Milone, V. and Green L. (1973) **Urbanization in Nigeria: A Planning commentary,** New York, Ford Foundation.

Olayemi, O.A. (1977) 'Intracity person travel in Metropolitan Lagos' **Geoforum,** Vol.8.

NINETEEN

Hans Blumenfeld

Where Did All the Metropolitan Cities Go?

THE CONCEPTUAL FRAMEWORK OF THE PROBLEM

For several centuries a trend toward concentration of activity and population in relatively few urban centres has been observed. This trend has been generally accelerating and spreading from the "developed" to the "developing" countries. For at least a century this centripetal trend has been supplemented by a centrifugal trend from urban centres to their "umland". The resulting new form of human settlement has been recognized as a "Metropolitan Area" by the Census of the U.S.A., and under the same or another name, by many other countries. The Metropolitan Area is essentially defined as a commuter watershed, constituting a common labour and housing market. It has long been recognized that such a concentration leads to a substantial increase of activities and population well beyond its boundaries, up to a travel distance of about two hours from its centre.

These activities are of two kinds, productive, primarily manufacturing, which draw on the services of the centre; and recreational services to the population of the central area. John Friedmann, while expressly recognizing only the second function, has proposed the term "Urban Field" for this large unit. I have called it a "Metropolitan Region," consisting of a "Fringe" surrounding a "Core," constituted by a Metropolitan Area. The boundary between core and fringe is blurred and becoming more so, as work places move increasingly from the centre toward the periphery of Metropolitan areas.

In no country have these "Metropolitan Regions" been defined officially, nor their characteristics investigated systematically. While "growth pole" and "satellite town" theories and policies are widely accepted, few comparisons have been made between the growth rates of towns within or without Metropolitan orbits. A small study of the 17 towns in Ontario which passed the 20,000 population mark between 1941 and 1969 showed that the growth rates of 10 towns located within metropolitan orbits averaged more than twice those of seven located outside such orbit[1].

Metropolitan Regions are potentially very large: if two hours travel time is identified with 150 km, one such area could cover almost 70,000 km^2, over twice the size of Belgium! Indeed, in the most urbanized parts of the world, such as West Central Europe, the Northeast of the U.S.A., and most of Japan, there is hardly an area left outside such regions. If their inhabitants are defined as "metropolitanites," there is for them no place to go (or to come from), except abroad. The question formulated by the title loses its meaning. The United Kingdom has established "Metro Economic Labour Areas". Although these by definition are less extensive than "Urban Fields", they accounted in 1971 for all but 4.3% of the population and 4.0% of the employment of the British Isles.

In most parts of the world, however, including most of North America, extended areas are definitely "non-metropolitan", and have been defined as such by U.S. Census. A difficulty arises because the census definition of a Metropolitan Area includes numerous areas which are much smaller than those denoted in common parlance as "metropolis", generally thought of as units of at least half a million or a million population. On the other hand, an investigation limited to these large units encounters the difficulty that their number in most countries is so small that the potential weight of random deviations makes statistical analysis somewhat hazardous.

Renewed discussion of the problem has been touched off by the fact that the U.S. Census showed an actual decrease of the population of some of the largest Metropolitan Areas in the country since 1970. Prior to that time a reversal of growth had been observed in only two cases: Vienna and Berlin (both East and West), after they had lost their role as imperial capitals; both, in addition, are located in countries with decreasing populations. Other cities which have lost their role of national capital—Istanbul, Leningrad, Calcutta, Rio de Janeiro—continue to grow.

An added impetus was given to the discussion when U.S. census figures on internal migration showed a sizeable reversal of the long established flow from Non-Metropolitan to

Metropolitan Counties. While from 1965 to 1970 the sum of all Metropolitan Counties gained 352 thousand persons from the Non-Metropolitan Counties, from 1970 to 1975 they lost 1,594 thousand to them. The trend continued with a loss of 396 thousand from 1975 to 1976.

This surprising phenomenon gave rise to various explanations, not necessarily mutually exclusive. A few observers saw it merely as a repetition of the return of unemployed to their home communities, which had been observed during the depression. This may be a contributing factor, but probably a minor one. Most scholars interpret it as a continuation of the historical centrifugal trend beyond the metropolitan boundaries established by the Census; others see a "clean break", a return to life in the countryside and the small town.

There can be no question that metropolitan life extends increasingly beyond the official boundaries. Residential "sprawl" has been amply documented. Perhaps even more significant is the fact that a rapidly growing percentage of the work places of the metropolitan population is located beyond these boundaries. Table 19.1 presents the relevant data for the five largest metropolitan areas of the Northereastern United States, all of which have lost population since 1970. It is evident that this loss is inconclusive, and that much larger areas must be analyzed before jumping to the conclusion—which may or may not be valid—that the diseconomies of city size now outweigh its long established economies. Even less founded is the hypothesis of a "return to the land". Farm population continues to decrease; in the U.S.A. four out of five "rural" dwellers are now classified as "non-farm".

TABLE 19.1

Percentage distribution by location of place of work of workers resident in five S.M.A.'s, U.S.A., 1960 & 1970

	Central city		Other S.M.A.		Outside S.M.A.	
S.M.A.	1960	1970	1960	1970	1960	1970
New York	79.2	71.0	18.7	24.4	2.1	4.6
Chicago	68.1	51.9	30.3	46.0	1.6	2.1
Philadelphia	55.6	45.8	41.0	48.5	3.4	5.7
Detroit	55.9	37.5	42.3	60.0	1.8	2.5
Boston	42.8	36.0	53.6	59.0	3.6	5.0
Unweighted average	60.3	48.5	37.2	47.6	2.5	4.0

Source: Alex Anas and Leon N. Moses, Transportation and Land use in the Mature Metropolis; in: Charles L. Levin, The Mature Metropolis, Lexington Books, 1978, p. 158, Table 8-1.

In opposition to those who believe that the "overspill" resulting from the historical centrifugal trend provides a complete explanation, a number of observers have emphasized the growth of counties located well beyond metropolitan overspill. These have been defined by two different measures: first, counties not adjacent to metropolitan areas, and second, counties with less than 3% of the labour force commuting to Metropolitan Areas. The former accounted for only 12.5%, and the latter for 13.1% of the population of the United States in 1974.

An interesting new twist was given to the discussion by the studies of Daniel R. Vining, Jr.[2] Vining is interested in the most spectacular form of centripetal movement, the trend toward concentration in one (more rarely two or more) primate cities. In order to encompass any conceivable overspill, he overbounds their area. This in fact shifts the investigation from a comparison between non-metropolitan and metropolitan regions, and between various size classes of the latter, to the relation between core and periphery, or the regional distribution of a nation's population. This is an even more complex problem, related to the former one in ways which may be contradictory as well as concurrent. Another peculiarity of Vining's approach is his emphasis on net internal migration as the most significant factor of population change. I have had the benefit of a wide exchange of views with Mr. Vining which, in fact, provided the stimulus for this paper.

PROBLEMS OF THE DATA BASE

All the relevant data for study of population change are derived from official statistics. While their authors never fail to point out the margin of error of these data, their precise numerical form makes it easy to forget that they cannot be more reliable than the individual answers which they summarize. If deviations of answers from facts are entirely random, they are irrelevant because of the "law of large numbers". Estimates of biased deviations are always speculative, but may be still worth considering.

The primary data in dealing with population change are periodic census counts, based generally on oral or written replies of the head or other member of the household. Overcounting of persons with two residences is probably eliminated with modern methods of data processing; a seasonal bias dependent on the date of the count may exist, but is probably not significant. However, undercounting may be serious. It may be assumed that persons distrustful of public authority will try, often successfully, to avoid being enumerated. This certainly applies to illegal immigrants, but may include other groups hostile to "the Establishment". It is probable that these are concentrated in metropolitan areas, and incrasing in number. A significant and growing undercount of metropolitan populations is a distinct possibility.

Population changes are the combined results of demography (births minus deaths) and of net migration. Probably the substitution of place of occurrence for place of residence which has long bedeviled vital statistics has now been practically eliminated in developed countries. Net migration is given as the difference between the change derived from vital statistics and that found by successive census counts, and is as reliable as these. Gross migration, however, is elusive. No data, nationally or locally, are available for out-migration. National data on in-migration are notoriously deficient because of substantial illegal immigration.

For movements between different areas of a given country the main sources are answers to census questions concerning a person's place of residence at a previous (usually 5 years) point in time. By processing these data, movements between areas can be defined, including movements from (but not to) places abroad.

On this basis a distinction has been made between "Internal Migration" and "Foreign Immigration", Vining and most other authors treat them as clearly distinct and independent variables. This is questionable. First, some of the persons who lived abroad at the defined previous point in time, are not "immigrants", but returning from temporary residence abroad. Second, illegal immigrants, and quite likely some legal ones also, will substitute a place within the country—almost certainly a major city—for their actual previous location abroad. Third, when does an "immigrant" become an "internal migrant"? According to the questionnaire classification, the moment he arrives in the country. In Canada almost all immigrants "land" in one of the three largest metropolitan areas, Montreal, Toronto, or Vancouver. Most of them stay there for shorter or longer periods of acculturation, until they find jobs and permanent residence all over the country, approximating the general population distribution. A case in point is Toronto; from 1971 to 1976 there was a "net internal migration" loss of about 20,000 but immigration of 200,000. In the preceding five-year period immigration had been even higher. Certainly far more than 20,000 of these moved to other places in Canada between 1971 and 1976. Should they be counted as "internal migrants"?

Another point raising doubts about the reliability of figures on net internal migration derived as residuals from gross internal migration is the fact that the former usually represent a small fraction of the latter. In the City of Munich, Germany, e.g., a gross migration (both directions) of 217,000 resulted in a net migration of -546. It is evident that an error of less than 1% in the data for either gross direction could have reversed the sign of net migration.

Finally, the large size and irregular shape of the territorial units of measurement—counties in the U.S.A.—is a potential source of error; e.g., a county with less than 3% commuting may well contain municipalities, from which 10% of the labour force commute to a metropolis.

For all these regions the following findings must be regarded as highly tentative.

OBSERVED CHANGES IN THE U.S.A.

The changes in population between 1940 and 1977 of Metropolitan and Non-Metropolitan Counties are summarized in Table 19.2. In their interpretation it should be kept in mind that counties may shift from non-metropolitan status, while the opposite shift has not occurred. Somewhat surprisingly, the data do not indicate any decrease in the annual growth rates of metropolitan populations up to 1975; only the last two years show a definite slowing down, but not yet a reversal of growth.

TABLE 19.2
Metropolitan and Non-Metropolitan Population, U.S.A., 1940 to 1977

Year	Per cent of total	Metropolitan 1000	Metropolitan av. annual change (%)	Non-Metropolitan 1000	Non-Metropolitan av. annual change (%)
1940	52.8	69,535	-	62,135	-
1950	56.0	84,854	2.2	62,135	0.0
1960	62.9	112,886	2.8	66,438	0.7
1970	68.6	139,419	2.2	63,793	-0.4
1975	72.7	155,021	2.2	58,153	-1.8
1976	73.0	156,754	1.1	58,114	-0.1
1977	73.0	157,968	0.8	58,570	0.8

Note: Average annual growth is calculated as equal fraction of period.
Source: U.S.A., S.M.S.A. Population (Statistical Abstract 1979, No. 14).

A reversal can, however, be observed in the annual grcwth rate of non-metropolitan areas from -1.8% from 1970-1975 to 0.8 from 1976-1977. It may be noted that this rate is only nominally higher than that observed 1950-1960 (0.7%). More significant is the fact that in 1976-1977 the growth rate of non-metropolitan equalled that of metropolitan areas. Also, a definite slowing down of the growth rate already during the 1970-1975 period occurred in the largest SMSA's, those with populations over 1.5 million, together with a nominal slowing down in the smaller SMSA's and a tripling of the growth rate of the non-metropolitan counties (Table 19.3 and 19.4).

TABLE 19.3
Percentage Distribution of Population of SMSA's, U.S.A. 1970 & 1977

Size group (1000)	1970 1000	1970 per cent	1977 1000	1977 per cent	per cent change 1970 to 1977
Over 3,000	39.3	26.3	38.8	24.6	-1.1
1,000 -3,000	45.8	30.6	49.3	31.2	7.5
500-1,000	23.8	15.9	25.3	16.0	8.4
250- 500	22.9	15.3	25.0	15.9	9.1
100- 250	15.8	10.6	17.4	11.0	10.2
under 100	2.0	1.3	2.1	1.3	5.9
All groups	149.6	100.0	158.0	100.0	5.6

Source: U.S.A., SMSA population (Statistical Abstract 1979, No. 15).

TABLE 19.4
Population of the U.S.A., by three size groups of settlement units, 1960, 1970 and 1975

Unit	1960	1970	1975	per cent change 1960-70	per cent change 1970-75	per cent change 1960-75
SMSA						
over 1.5 m	69,262	81,472	82,899	17.6	1.7	19.7
under 1.5m	58,676	68,355	73,198	16.5	7.1	19.7
non-SMSA	51,373	53,478	56,954	4.3	6.6	10.9
U.S.A.	179,311	203,305	213,051	100.0	100.0	100.0

Source: U.S. Census, estimates of the population of counties and metropolitan areas, July 1, 1974 and 1975.

It can be hypothesized that it is precisely the largest SMSA's which have overflown their boundaries and that this overflow accounts for the increase of the non-metropolitan population. Some support of this hypothesis can be derived by a breakdown of the data by four major regions of the U.S.A. (Table 19.5). These show that only in the North-East, where SMSA's account for almost 60% of the population, has the share of the non-metropolitan population shown any increase between 1970 and 1975, from 14.2% to 14.3%. In the other three regions their share continued to drop; in the South, with only 22% in large metropolitan areas, the drop was precipitous, from 38.8% to 33.4%.

TABLE 19.5
Population of SMSA's with population over 1.5 million and of non-SMSA counties as percentages of four regions, U.S.A., 1960, 1970, 1975

Region	SMSA's over 1.5 million			Non-SMSA		
	1960	1970	1975	1960	1970	1975
Northeast	58.9	59.0	58.0	14.7	14.2	14.3
North-Central	38.8	40.0	39.4	33.3	31.3	30.8
South	18.4	22.0	22.1	41.2	38.8	33.4
West	45.2	46.7	44.2	23.9	21.2	20.0

Source: U.S. Census Estimates of the population of counties and metropolitan areas, July 1, 1974 and 1975.

A valuable contribution to the analysis of the problem has been made by Peter A. Morrison and his associates,[3] by breaking down the non-metropolitan counties into those "adjacent" and "non-adjacent" to SMSA's. They have also divided the 2,469 non-metropolitan counties of the U.S.A. into 321 "urban", 865 "less urbanized", and 1,283 "rural" (Tables 19.6, 19.7 and 19.8).

TABLE 19.6
Non-Metropolitan Counties in 26 States of the U.S.A. which showed growth from 1970 to 1974; Annual Net Migration 1960-1970 and 1970-1974, for three groups of counties

Groups of Counties	1960-1970	1970-1974	Change from (1960-1970)-(1970-1974)
Urbanized	-.23	.52	.75
Less urbanized	-.77	.83	1.60
Rural	-1.00	1.30	2.31

Source: McCarthy, Kevin F. and Morrison, Peter A., The Changing Demographic and Economic Structure of Non-Metropolitan Areas and in the United States. Rand Corp., Santa Monica, January 1979, p. 34-37.

A comparison between Tables 19.4 and 19.6 indicates the fragility of the data. A lowering of the threshold of "large" from 1.5 to 1.0 million population and a one-year reduction of the period, from 1970-1975 to 1970-1974 results in the disappearance of the relative decrease of the "large SMSA" population. In Table 19.6 growth rate is positively correlated with population size of SMSA's. However, the large SMSA's are the only one of the nine groups in which the 1970-1974 growth rate has dropped below that of the preceding decade. Growth has accelerated far more in the adjacent than in the non-adjacent counties, and in the rural than in the urban ones. The significant net result is an equalization of growth rates among the nine groups, the range being reduced by about 70%. By contrast, within SMSA's the difference between core and fringe areas has increased by almost 65%. The importance of the over-flow as a source of the apparent reversal of metropolitan growth is strongly confirmed by data presented in the study by McCarthy and Morrison, which show an opposite reversal in the counties adjacent to SMSA's. The study divided the U.S. into 26 regions. While from 1960 to 1970 more than three quarters of these (23) showed a migration loss, including five with a total population loss, from 1970 to 1975, all but three showed migration gains.[4]

Of the three regions in which non-adjacent counties showed a net migration gain already in the 1960's, two "N-E Metro Belt" and Florida,[5] have a metropolitan structure which makes overflow beyond adjacent counties highly probable. In the N-E Metro Belt the migration gain in the non-adjacent counties accelerated to an annual rate of 1.7%.[6]

All data so far presented indicate continued strength of the centrifugal trend within metropolitan orbits, both with in SMSA's and in the adjacent counties, defined as the "Fringe" in Table 19.7. The table compares the actual changes from 1970 to 1974 with those which would have occurred if population distribution between the three groups of counties had remained stable. Of the 0.75% loss by metropolitan counties of share of the national population, 0.62% were absorbed by "fringe" and only 0.13% by non-adjacent counties. in the 1970-1974 period 82.6% of the metropolitan loss appears to be due to "over-spill" and only 17.4% to "reversal". This is a very tentative conclusion; post-1974 data may show a different picture.

SOME CANADIAN DATA

The Canadian Census identifies, in addition to 23 Metropolitan Areas, with populations over 100,000 also 88 smaller

"Urban Areas". From 1971 to 1976 the median growth of the former was 6.80%, of the latter only 0.25%. Twelve of the 23 Metropolitan Areas, but only 27 of the 88 smaller urban areas, increased by more than 6.79%; only two of the larger areas lost population (only 0.4% in both cases), but 23 of the smaller ones showed decreases, in nine cases exceeding 5.0% (Table 19.8)

TABLE 19.7
Net shift of population from SMSA's to "fringe" and "other" counties, U.S.A., 1970 to 1974

County	Population (million)		Change, 1970-1974		Shift from national average	
	1970	1974	million	%	% of 1970	million
SMSA	149.8	154.9	5.1	3.5	-0.5	-0.75
Fringe	26.8	28.5	1.7	6.3	2.3	0.62
Other	26.7	27.9	1.2	4.5	.5	0.13
USA	203.3	211.3	8.0	4.0	0.0	0.00

Source: Peter A. Morrison, The Current Demographic Context..., in: L.S. Bourne/J.W. Simmons, Systems of Cities, Oxford University Press, 1978, p. 477.

Within the universe of 23 Metropolitan Areas growth rates were not consistently correlated with size, either positively or negatively, but were clearly determined by specific local factors. The very small (2.2%) growth of the largest (in 1971) area, Montreal, is clearly due to adverse shifts in economic geography and an unfavourable industrial profile. The two other areas with populations over one million, Toronto and Vancouver, each grew by 7.7%, above the median rate. The highest growth rate occurred, not surprisingly, in the oil-boom area of Calgary. It was closely followed by Kitchener (14.0%) and Oshawa (12.3%), industrial towns within the metropolitan orbit of Toronto, at distances of 60 and 30 miles, rspectively, from its centre. The other nine areas with growth rates above or at the median are all capitals, federal or provincial, reflecting the fact that during this period government was one of Canada's leading growth industries.

A comparison of the 1951-1976 growth of Canadian towns, urban areas, and metropolitan areas by five size groups shows a consistent positive correlation between growth rate and size, from 25.2% for those between 5,000 and 10,000, to 46.6% for those over 500,000. It appears that in Canada the centripetal trend to larger agglomerations has not been reversed, though it is certainly slowing down.

TABLE 19.8
Average annual net migration, per cent, 1960-1970 and 1970-1974, U.S.A., by type of County

Type of County	Annual per cent change 1960-1970	1970-1974
Metropolitan		
over 1 million	1.46	1.03
250,000-999,999	.47	.96
50,000-249,999	.17	.72
Adjacent to Metropolitan		
urbanized	.13	.66
less urbanized	-.56	.73
rural	-.82	1.18
Non-adjacent to Metropolitan		
urbanized	-.45	.16
less urbanized	-1.02	.40
rural	-1.37	.64
Range	2.83	.87
Within Metropolitan Counties		
Core	.30	-.46
Fringe	1.89	2.15
Range	1.59	2.61

Source: McCarthy, Kevin F. and Morrison, Peter A., The Changing Demographic and Economic Structure of Non-Metropolitan Areas and in the United States. Rand Corp., Santa Monica, January 1979, p. 23, Table 1.

The opposite, smaller-scale, centrifugal trend within-metropolitan orbits is certainly continuing vigorously. From 1971 to 1976 the three inner municipalities of the Municipality of Metropolitan Toronto lost 8.6% of their population, the three outer ones gained 10.4%, while the surrounding municipalities within the Toronto SMSA increased by 36.2%. There is little doubt that a sizeable overspill over the SMSA boundaries has occurred in this and other Canadian metropolitan areas. This overspill may account for most or all of the increase in the national share of the "rural" population from 24.0% in 1971 to 24.5% in 1976.

THE ROLE OF MIGRATION

While overspill clearly accounts for most of the relative,

and in some cases absolute population loss of Metropolitan Areas which has been observed so far, reversl toward a shift to non-metropolitan forms of settlement certainly is the more surprising and interesting phenomenon. As differences in birth and death rates between metropolitan and non-metropolitan areas have almost disappeared in developed countries, the shift is due to changes in net migration—which, as noted previously, is a generally small residual of much larger volumes of two-way gross migration. It is worth noting that the net movement of 396,00 persons from metropolitan to non-metropolitan areas of the U.S.A. represents only 5.7% of the gross two-way movement between these two types of areas.

Caution in the use of Census data on internal migration is also advisable because of incomplete reporting. Out of a population of 183.5 million persons over 5 years of age enumerated in the United States in 1975, 19.0 million lived in non-metropolitan areas at both periods. A group more than half that numerous, 10.4 million, are listed as "no report on mobility", in addition to 3.6 million "moved from abroad".[7]

It is well known that migration is highly selective. In the period 1970-1975 no less than 72% of those aged 25-29 and 60% of those aged 30-34, but only 20% of those over 65 changed residence.[8] A comparison of the population by age group anticipated in Metropolitan Toronto by moving forward the age cohorts of 1971 to 1976 with the age groups enumerated in 1976 indicated a strong net migration gain of the same young adult groups, and a net loss of all others.

While the influx of young adults testifies to the continuing attraction of the metropolis as a labour market, the movement in the opposite direction, from metropolitan to non-metropolitan counties, is strongly concentrated among persons relying on sources of income other than labour. Of every 100 males aged 16 years or over that had made this move between 1970 and 1975, no less than 35 were not in the Labour Force[9]. It may well be that the growth of genuinely non-metropolitan areas is due mainly, maybe exclusively, to an increase in the number of persons permanently or temporarily not working. Both the first ("retirement") and the second ("recreation") group induce of course also a growth in the number of persons working to service them.

This hypothesis receives some support from the aforementioned study by McCarthy and Morrison. If I understand the study correctly, it identified 753 non-metropolitan counties which showed positive net migration gains from 1970 to 1974, by "concentration" of one or more functions; in 98 cases there was more than one concentration, resulting in a universe of 671 cases in 26 selected states of the U.S.A. Out of these more than a third (244) were identified as "retirement", followed by 135 for "recreation"; government accounted for 125, energy for 124, and manufacturing only for 43 cases. If my understanding of the study is correct, it did not identify concentration in counties with population loss; their number may will be higher in the case of manufacturing, and possibly also in the cases of energy and government.

The changes in the rate of change 1970-1974 versus 1960-1970 were least pronounced for "urban", more pronounced for "less urbanized" and strongest for "rural" counties, both for net population (0.33, 1.16, 1.85) and for net migration (0.75, 1.60, 2.31)[10]. The most significant changes, those of net migration in rural counties, are summarized in Table 19.10. By far the greatest change, 3.46 annual net migration, was found in recreation counties, which also were the only category which had experienced a net migration gain in the 1960's. They are followed by "retirement" with 2.54 and lower values for the three other, work-based categories.

INTERACTION BETWEEN METROPOLITAN-NON-METROPOLITAN AND NATIONAL CORE-PERIPHERY POPULATION SHIFTS

As already noted, this important area has been opened up by Vining. His studies attempt to deal with both at once by applying the general concept of "concentration". By an ingenious application of the "Hoover Index of Concentration" to areas of different sizes in the United States he shows, first, that the results vary strongly with size of area and, second, that for the first time in the history of the United States the Index showed increased deconcentration for all size units. He concludes that the secular trend toward concentration has been reversed since 1970.

He then proceeded to an investigation of the same problem in 20 other countries and summarizes his conclusions as follows: "...suggests a law of spatial development whereby deconcentration becomes possible only in the mature phase of a country's industrialization." It is true, as Vining states, that in the "developed" countries the trend to concentration in major urban areas is "exhausted", while in "developing" ones it is still continuing apace.

As noted earlier, Vining's studies provide information

TABLE 19.9

Population change of urban areas with population over and under 100,000, respectively, grouped by rate of change, Canada, 1971-1976

Population of area, 1976	Percent change 1971-1976: Decrease No.	Decrease %	0.0-4.0 No.	0.0-4.0 %	4.01-7.0 No.	4.01-7.0 %	Over 7.0 No.	Over 7.0 %	Total No.	Total %
over 100,000	2	8.7	3	13.0	7	30.5	11	47.8	23	100.0
under 100,000	23	26.2	23	26.2	15	17.0	27	30.6	88	100.0
					Median percentage change					
over 100,000					6.80					
under 100,000					.25					

Source: Census of Canada, 1976, Population, Metropolitan Areas, Urban Area.

TABLE 19.10
Annual Net Migration Rate, Rural Counties Only by Predominant Function

Function	1960-1970	1970-1974	Change from (1960-1970)-(1970-1974)
Recreation	.54	4.00	3.46
Retirement	-.24	2.30	2.54
Energy	-1.48	.48	1.96
Government	-.23	1.55	1.78
Manufacturing	-.87	.88	1.75
All	-1.00	1.30	2.31

Source: McCarthy, Kevin F. and Morrison, Peter A., The Changing Demographic and Economic Structure of Non-Metropolitan Areas and in the United States. Rand Corp., Santa Monica, January 1979, p.37, Table 5.

primarily on population shifts between core and peripheral regions of nations rather than on those between metropolitan and non-metropolitan regions (however defined). However, shifts between national regions cannot be understood in terms only of the two "classical" trends: national-scale centripetal towards major agglomerations, and smaller-scale centrifugal towards the expanding periphery of thse agglomerations. At least five other general trends can be identified:

1. Older-to-newer regions.
2. Unpleasant-to-pleasant climate and scenery.
3. Declining-to-growth industries.
4. Depression-to-boom (the business cycle).
5. Catastrophe-affected to safe.

The meaning of "old" and "new" is different for long-settled countries and for those of relatively recent white settlement, such as the U.S.A., the U.S.S.R., Canada, or Australia. For these "old" areas are, by definition, the core areas. In long-settled countries the "old" regions are those first industrialized, usually comprising both the region of the capital and of location of the "old" industries, coal-steel and/or textiles.

The interactions of shifts between geographic regions of a country and shifts between metropolitan and non-metropolitan regions are multiple and complex.

In developing countries, a substantial part of the population, frequently the majority, are employed in agriculture. Only in the core region is a substantial part of the population urban. As urbanization proceeds, even if it proceeds at the same or faster pace in peripheral regions, the share of the core region is bound to increase. It is therefore erroneous to conclude from this that the metropolitan share or urban population must have increased. A separate investigation of this share is required. In the case of the Soviet Union and other East European countries such an investigation shows an actual decrease of this share absorbed by the largest cities,[11] contrary to Vining's conclusions.

If and when development in one or more peripheral regions proceeds faster than it does in the rest of the country, generally—though with significant variations—the growth rate of both rural and urban (not necessarily metropolitan) population will be above the national average. Frequently one or more urban nodes in such a growing region will transcend the metropolitan threshold, and further growth of such a region may indicate strength, rather than weakness of metropolitan concentration.

Vining's studies, which take into account only the inverse, less ambiguous effect of growth rate of a metropolis being reflected in the growth rate of their region, are therefore inconculsive as to the problem which has been brought to the fore by recent developments in the United States population shifts between metropolitan and non-metropolitan forms of settlement. However, their significance as pioneering efforts in the field of international comparisons warrants further discussion of at least some of his cases.

Vining's "classical" first two cases are those of Japan and Sweden. In both countries he compares the population growth rates of the three largest metropolitan areas, first defined more narrowly, roughly corresponding to the U.S. concept of "Metropolitan Areas" and, second, defined much more broadly, corresponding to my concent of "Metropolitan Regions". However, by regrouping his data (Tables 19.11 and 19.12), I arrive at different conclusions.

In Japan the share of the three "Metropolitan Areas" continued at the same annual rate of 0.3% from 1970 to 1975 as during the preceding 50 years. In the "metropolitan fringe":, here "the rest of Tokaido", the modest annual decrease of -0.1%, observed 1920 to 1970, has stopped after 1970. I interpret this to mean that the centripetal "country-to-metropolis" movement is now being balanced by the centrifugal "overflow' from the three "Metropolitan Areas". The decrease in the share of the "rest of the country" has accelerated from an annual rate of -0.2% during the half-century prior to 1970 to -0.3% after that date.

TABLE 19.11

Percentage distribution of population of Japan by three major metropolitan regions, rest of central (Tokaido) region, and rest of Japan, 1920, 1970 and 1975

Region	Per cent of pop'n 1920	1970	1975	Annual per cent change 1920-1970	1970-1975
Tokyo, Nagoya, Osaka	29.6	44.6	46.1	0.3	0.3
Rest of Tokaido	19.5	14.5	14.5	-0.1	0.0
Rest of Japan	50.9	40.9	39.4	-0.2	-0.3
Japan	100.0	100.0	100.0	0.0	0.0

Source: Daniel R. Vining, Jr., and Thomas Kontuly. Population dispersal from major metropolitan regions: an international comparison. RSRI Discussion paper series, No. 100, Septemeber 1977, p. 7, Table 1.1.

TABLE 19.12

Percentage distribution of population of Sweden, by three major metropolitan areas, their umlands, and rest of Sweden, 1900, 1960 and 1975

Region	Per cent of pop'n 1900	1960	1975	Annual per cent change 1900-1960	1960-1975
Stockholm, Goteborg, Malmo	23.8	33.7	35.9	0.167	0.147
Their umlands	37.8	32.5	33.3	-0.090	0.053
Centres with umlands	61.6	66.2	69.2	0.770	0.200
Rest of Sweden	38.4	33.8	30.8	-0.770	-0.200
Sweden	100.0	100.0	100.0	0.0	0.0

Source: Daniel R. Vining, Jr., and Thomas Kontuly. Population dispersal from major metropolitan regions: an international comparison. RSRI Discussion paper series, No. 100, September 1977, p. 7, Table 2.1.

In Sweden the centrifugal movement has been stronger, resulting in a slowing of the annual share increase of the three metropolitan areas from 0.167 during the period 1900-1960 to 0.147 from 1960 to 1975. Correspondingly the annual change in the share of the fringe, or "umland", has reversed from -0.090 to 0.053. In the rest of Sweden it has slowed down from -0.770

to -0.200. As the second period presented for Sweden includes also the 1960's, these data do not preclude a reversal after 1970. However, this appears highly unlikely in the light of data for net total (internal plus external) migration to the three metropolitan areas, also given by Vining, which I have summarized as follows:[12]

1973	-9,940
1974	2,337
1975	6,542
1976	11,314
1977	16,392
1978	10,502

Vining is of course correct in showing that internal net migration alone has been negative for the three metropolitan areas in recent years. However, for reasons presented earlier, I consider this to be less relevant than total population change.

Of the other countries investigated by Vining, I will deal only with the two Germanies. Vining notes that the strong population shift towards the provinces ("Laender") located in the watershed of the Rhine, which was characteristic of Germany since the middle of the 19th century, has stopped in the post-war Federal Republic. He defines this very large area, which comprises fve of the ten provinces, as the "core" and interprets the change as a "long-term secular decline in net immigration from peripheral regions". I believe that a more adequate explanation of recent changes is provided by the shift from North to South (Table 19.13).

TABLE 19.13

Percentage of population in northern, middle and southern provinces of German Federal Republic, 1960 and 1975

	Percentage of population	
Region	1960	1975
North	51.1	49.3
Middle	17.3	17.3
South	31.8	33.5
F.R.G.	100.2	100.1

North: Nordrehin-Westfalen, Niedersachsen, Schleswig-Holstein, Hamburg, Bremen. Middle: Hessen, Rheinland-Pfalz, Saar. South: Bayern, Baden-Wurttemberg.

Source: Daniel R. Vining, Jr., and Thomas Kontuly. Population dispersal from major metropolitan regions: an international comparison. RSRI Discussion paper series, No. 100, September 1977, p. 7, Table 9.1.

Certainly it cannot be interpreted as a shift from metropolitan to non-metropolitan areas, because five of ten areas identified by German geographers as agglomerations ("Ballungen") are located in the South and have considerably increased their national share in recent years. In the North the growth of three of its four metropolitan areas has been slower because of their industrial profile: in the Ruhr-Rhine region coal-steel, and in Hamburg and Bremen overseas trade, which has largely shifted to Rotterdam and to the Baltic ports of East Germany and Poland.

In East Germany, Vining recognizes the decreasing share of its industrial heartland, formed by its four southeastern provinces, but assigns it to the group of countries in which "net migration into the core regions remains high and positive". This conclusion is based on the assumption that the growth of the two eastern provinces (Frankfurt and Cottbus) contiguous to East Berlin is due to overflow from the capital. This assumption is in error. There is no overflow from East Berlin, as was confirmed orally by East German planners in 1980. The growth of these two provinces is due entirely to the growth of five new (or enlarged) towns on the Oder river, which from 1969 to 1976 increased their population by 53,100, or 21.8%, while the balance of the provinces, including the umland of Berlin, lost 36,900 or 2.8%. The share of the population of Berlin itself, which had dropped from its prewar level of 9.5% to 6.3% in the 1960's, has increased to 6.6.% in 1976, as a result of a reversal of government policy. This reversal applies however only to the captial, apparently for reasons of prestige. The general shift from larger to smaller towns, continues: from 1967 to 1975 the five cities with populations over 200,000 (in 1969) increased only by 0.7%, while the sixteen with populations between 50,000 and 200,000 increased by 7.9%. The conclusion of my earlier study appears still to be valid: the countries with centrally planned economies have achieved some 'deconcentration', with population shifts both from core to periphery and from larger to smaller urban units.

Perhaps the most interesting result that can be derived from Vining's data on the share of national population concentrated in the core area is its almost miraculous stability (Table 19.14). In conjunction with the previously noted stability of the shares of the national population living within and outside "Metropolitan Regions" achieved in the United States in the 1970's, this points to the tentative conclusion that population distribution, in these terms, in the most developed market (including "mixed") economy countries has reached maturity. It is significant that this term is being used not only by Vining, but also by another astute observer of the phenomena under study, Charles L. Leven[13].

TABLE 19.14
Range of change of share of national population concentrated in core areas, five European nations, various recent periods

Country	Region	Length of Period years	Range per cent
Sweden	Stockholm, Goteborg, Malmo	4	0.1
Italy	Piedmonte, Lombardia, Ligure Toscana, Lazio	5	0.1
Norway	Ostlandet	5	0.3
Germany	Nordrhein-Westfalen	14	0.4
France	Paris Region	14	0.3

Source: Daniel R. Vining, Jr., and Thomas Kontuly. Population dispersal from major metropolitan regions: an international comparison. International Regional Science Review, Vol. 3, No. 1, 1978, pp. 56, 57, 58, 62. Same authors and title, RSRI Discussion Paper Series, No. 100, 1977, p. 45.

THREE POSSIBLE INTERPRETATIONS OF RECENT STABILITY

It should be noted that the observed stability is, in fact, compatible with the three previously mentioned different interpretations of net migration from metropolitan to non-metropolitan counties in the United States.

It is compatible with the hypothesis of a temporary interruption of the trend to metropolitan concentration by the economic stragnation of the 1970's, presumed to be part of a business cycle.

It is compatible with the hypothesis of "reversal". In this case it would represent the movement at which the pendulum is at rest between swings toward concentration and deconcentration, respectively.

Finally, it is obviously compatible with the hypothesis of achievement of "stability" or a "stable state".

Only the analysis of future events will enable us to determine which hypothesis is the true one.

THE SIGNIFICANCE OF THE CONCEPT OF "METROPOLITAN REGION"

In must be emphasized that the stability of the share of the Metropolitan Regions does not apply to their cores, the Metropolitan Areas. It is maintained because their loss in terms of share of national population is compensated by the gain of the "Fringe" of the Metropolitan Region.

For the United States this conclusion is strongly supported by data from Morrison's studies. Morrison has broken down the non-metropolitan counties by percentage of the labour force commuting to S.M.S.A.'s into four groups: over 20%, 10%-19%, 3%-9%, and less than 3%. Their annual rates of growth 1970-1974 averaged 2.0, 1.4, 1.3, and 0.6 per cent respectively, compared to 0.8% for the S.M.S.A.'s.

I tentatively identify the counties with less than 3% commuters which accounted for only 13.1% of the U.S. population, as genuinely non-metropolitan, and those with higher percentages of commuters accounting for 13.5%, as the Fringe. My rationale—not tested, but plausible—for rating counties with a commuting share of the labour force as low as 3% as part of a Metropolitan Region is as follows:

By definition, the Fringe is the area beyond normal commuting range, which attracts both residents seeking recreational services and establishments seeking business services within the range of easy accessibility of the metropolis. Commuting requires about 240 round trips annually. Both recreational sevices, e.g., summer cottages, and establishments needing intermittent metropolitan services, e.g., factories, may need no more than 24 round trips annually, an average of two per month to induce them to choose a location within the metropolitan orbit rather than beyond it. It can therefore be hypothesized that their number is likely to be ten times that of the commuters who make the same trip ten times as frequently, or 30% for 3% commuting. Together with the population serving them, they will account for the majority of the population of such a county.

As Charles L. Leven notes: "It is not so much that metropolitan life is being forsaken for a return to a small town or rural existence, but rather that metropolis is actually moving to the countryside."[14] It is, however, equally valid to note that these moves do reflect a preference for a location other than a metropolis.

The debate whether these moves should be interpreted as a

continuation of the centrifugal trend toward metropolitan expansion or a reversal of the centripetal trend of metropolitan concentration is really a quarrel about semantics. They are both. We are dealing with a dialectical process which can be adequately explained only by the concept of "reversal (Umschlagen) into its opposite", so dear to Hegel and Marx. The continuing urban, or metropolitan expansion into the countryside reaches the point where it becomes "ruralization" of urban population and activities. ("Rus" includes many small and some not so small towns.) The age-old distinction between city and country is beginning to lose its meaning.

TENTATIVE CAUSAL EXPLANATIONS

In the social sciences incontrovertible identification of cause-effect regulations is never possible. In trying to explain the recent population movements away from metropolitan areas, the small size of the universe, and the small number of years during which this phenomenon has been observed, make such attempts particularly speculative.

There is fairly unanimous consent that the reason for metropolitan concentration is primarily the economic one of greater productivity of labour, due to agglomeration economies which are refleted as "external economies of scale" for the individual enterprise. The preference of enterprises for metropolitan location sets in motion the well-known cycle—vicious or virtuous—of enterprises attracting workers and supplementary enterprises, and the presence of these two factors attracting more enterprises. The concentration of people and of purchasing power also greatly enlarges the choice of services and contacts of all kinds. In addition to its primary attraction as a place for "making a living" the metropolis also has attractions as a place for living.

It has been argued that the observed "reversal" is due to the "dis-economies of scale" having outgrown the "economies of scale". This is questionable. The strictly economic "diseconomies" affecting enterprises are time losses in short-distance transportation due to street congestion and higher local taxes due to higher cost of services. There is no evidence to show that either of these has increased more in metropolitan areas than in smaller agglomerations; or even has increased at all, though it may frequently be perceived as having done so.

It is more likely that the "external economies of scale" have decreased, though the changes are not all one-way. Access to the most effective forms of long-distance transportation for both persons (frequent and direct air and rail service) and goods (big and specialized ships, unit trains, pipelines) is increasingly concentrated in the largest metropolitan areas. However, improvements in transportation and, in particular, in communication have made many business services as accessible to small communities as to the metropolis. This is particularly true for those located in the "fringe", which continue to have substantial advantages over more distant ones in access to services requiring personal presence as well as to highly specialized goods.

However, it is likely that the recent acceleration of the movement away from the metropolis and, in particular from its core, to more dispersed forms of settlement, both within and beyond the fringe, is due primarily to a basic shift in attitude, encouraged by prosperity, from seeking a place "to make a living" to choosing a place for "living". This is reflected in the greatly increased emphasis on "environment" and on the "quality of life". Most of the goods and services previously found only in the metropolis, are now to be found almost everywhere in developed countries; those that are not in particular personal contact, are becoming more accessible by greater ease of travel. The relative advantages of the metropolis as a place for living have been greatly reduced.

On the other hand, its relative disadvantages are weighted far more heavily and perceived as growing inexorably. They are numerous: congestion, pollution of air and water, noise, anomie, and, in particular in the United States, insecurity of person and property and unsatisfactory schools. The rural and small-town environment is attractive not only, as it has always been, because it offers access to the world of nature, more space and privacy, but also as providing stronger community ties.

The growing importance of environmental amenity is confirmed not only by the previously mentioned dominant role of retirement and recreation in the growth of non-metropolitan counties, and the correlation of their rates of growth with "rurality", but also by the fact that out of the 14 areas which showed the highest growth among the S.M.S.A.'s of the U.S.A since 1970, nine are located in Florida.

It is also important to keep in mind that any net gains of non-metropolitan areas are residuals of a much larger and highly selective two-way movement. Despite the rejection of the "consumer society" by a significant minority, the majority of young adults still is attracted by the economic opportunities of the Metropolis. As Charles L. Leven notes, on the basis of migrations observed in the U.S.A. from 1970 to 1975 the chances of a person moving from a non-metropolitan county to a metropolitan county were 1.7 times greater than the reverse.[15]

WHAT MAY THE FUTURE HOLD?

In very general terms, probably "more of the same".

The contrast in the rate of metropolitan growth between "developing" and "developed" countries is bound to increase simply because the former have a much higher rate of growth and a huge and growing "surplus" of agricultural population. By contrast, the population of the developed nations is approaching stability or even beginning to decrease, and the total non-metropolitan population is small in relation to the majority already concentrated in metropolitan regions. There is little left "to come from", except foreign countries.

In the developing countries metropolitan concentration is reinforced because the infrastructure and services making a place attractive both for economic activity and as a living environment are to be found only in primate cities. This increases their advantage in productivity, because the small number of educated and qualified people strongly resist living in "backward" areas.

I am also hypothesizing that these same factors generally will limit metropolitan expansion to areas much smaller than the metropolitan regions of developed countries. An exception is China which has implemented a policy of locating industry in "new towns" at considerable distances from the centre. This has however, led to time- and energy-consuming commuting from the central cities, the volume of which, in places like Peking and Shanghai, far exceeds that of inbound commuting. It remains to be seen if, with the present emphasis on the "four modernizations", this policy will be fully maintained.

In the Soviet Union, after exhaustive discussions, the policy of limiting the growth of big cities has been somewhat relaxed. Soviet policy now favours small and medium-sized cities within "agglomerations", or, in my terms, metropolitan regions. East German planners consider their present population distribution as generally satisfactory. Moderate preference is, as before, given to development of the less industrialized northern and eastern provinces, and of some provinical captials, to which more recently Berlin has been added. In addition, there is a strong effort to contain the spatial expansion of all settlements, large and small, in the interest of preservation of agricultural land.

In the developed market economy countries the main shifts to be expected are, first, those between regions. These wil be determined in part by the predominance of new industries, but primarily by the increasing importance given to climatic and scenic amenities. Second, and even more important, will be the rate, location, and form of the outward shift within the metropolitan regions.

In the "old" and relatively small countries of Europe and Japan, and also in the equally densely populated and highly urbanized northeastern part of the United States these are the only questions. In the large "new" countries, including the U.S.A. as a whole, most of the areas, though only a relatively small part of the population, are certainly non-metropolitan and the question of their development is highly relevant.

Growth in these areas, and to a considerable extent also in the "fringe", is likely to be increasingly selective in terms of environmental amenities. This means that the majority of municipalities in non-metropolitan regions, and many in the fringe, are more likely to lose than to gain populatiuon. Planning theory so far has always been dealing with growth; we are ill-prepared to deal with conditions of decreasing population. Such decrease will increasingly occur not only in scattered small communities, but in a rapidly extending area of all core cities. Here the task is to provide a higher quality of urban environment for a smaller quantity of people.

The toughest problem however, will be posed by increasing scatteration of "urban" activities and population. The danger is twofold. First, exclusive reliance on and greatly increased use of motor vehicles for all movements, of goods as well as of persons. Second, loss of agricultural prodction, both by direct occupancy of land and by disruption of farming by other uses.

The obvious remedy is channeling of development into relatively compact clusters. Continuing and increasing conflicts are predictable between such attempts and the apparently insatiable desire for more space, supported by a strongly rooted belief in the right of the individual to freely own and use land.

Many observers believe that the increasing price of oil will force a reversal of this trend. I consider this unlikely for two reasons. First, the wellhead price of oil is now well above the cost of producing an equivalent amount of coal in the United States; it is therefore more likely to decrease than to increase, in real terms, in the future. Second, the traditional American cars are so fantstically inefficient that fuel consumption can easily be reduced by two-thirds by a switch to smaller lighter cars. This argument has been countered by the statement that "smaller, lighter cars...do not lend themselves to one-way work trips of thirty and more miles because they are uncomfortable."[16] To this writer, who has travelled all over Canada from coast to coast in a V W Beatle, this statement is not convincing. Nor is the same author's expectation that multinucleation will induce people to work in the nearest nucleus confirmed by experience.

DESIRABLE FUTURE RESEARCH

As noted earlier, the data published by the U.S. Census on metropolitan and non-metropolitan counties do not provide an adequate basis to evaluate changes in metropolitan concentration for two reasons. First, the definition of "metropolitan" is much broader than that normally and meaningfully associated with the term "metropolis", and, second, the country may contain areas with radically different characteristics.

I suggest a special study of the Metropolitan areas in the United States with a population over 1 million and of their surrounding regions up to a distance of 150 km from the metropolitan centre. In Canada, because of the paucity of areas of this population size, half a million is a more suitable lower limit. A supplementary study of U.S. areas with populations between 500,000 and 1,000,000 would, of course, also be welcomed.

All smaller metropolitan areas, whether outside of or within metropolitan regions, would have to be treated as non-metropolitan in dealing with all movements, commuting as well as migration. This should, of course, not preclude additional studies dealing with them. In many cases neighbouring metropolitan regions will overlap. The boundary between two such neighbours can easily be determined by the preponderance of commuting to one or the other. Within the metropolitan regions I recommend collection of data by Census Tracts or, where these are not available, by municipalities, and their grouping by concentric circle around the metropolitan centre, as well as by location in the fringe and its S.M.S.A., respectively. With the aid of available computers, this is not excessively laborious.

As for the population shifts and migrations affecting the distribution of the national population by major regions, only a detailed investigation of all relevant factors can provide valid answers. I completely agree with the statement made by Daniel

R. Vining Jr. in a letter to me of 10 October 1978 "that a satisfactory theory of the phenomenon of deconcentration will be more complx, richer, and more interesting than monocausal explanations".

FOOTNOTES

1. Hans Blumenfeld, **Metropolis—and Beyond.** John Wiley & Sons, New York, 1980, p. 132.
2. D.R. Vining, Jr., A. Strauss. A Demonstration That the Current Deconcentration of Population in the United States is a Clean Break with the Past. **Environment and Planning** A, 1977, Vol. 9, pp. 751-758; also: Daniel R. Vining, Jr., Robert L. Pallone, Chung Hsin Yang. Population Dispersal from Core Regions: A Description and Tentative Explanation of the Patterns in 20 Countries. Working Description and Tentative Explanation of the Patterns in 20 countries. Working Paper No. 26, University of Pennsylvania, February 1980.
3. McCarthy, Kevin F. and Morrison, Peter A. The Changing Demographic and Economic Structure of non-Metropolitan Areas in the United States. Rand Corporation, Santa Monica, January 1979. Also: Peter A. Morrison, The Current Demographic Context...in: L.S. Bourne/J.W. Simmons, Systems of Cities, Oxford University Press, 1978, pp. 473-479.
4. Op. cit., p. 14.
5. Op. cit., p. 17, fig. 4.
6. Op. cit., p. 16.
7. U.S. Bureau of the Census, Series P-20, No. 285, October 1975. Mobility of the Population of the United States, March 1970-March 1975, Table 19.1
8. Ibid, Figure 19.1.
9. Ibid, Table 19.10.
10. Op. cit., p. 37, Table 19.5.
11. Hans Blumenfeld, **Metropolis—and Beyond,** John Wiley & Sons, New York, 1980, pp. 181-187.
12. Daniel R. Vining, Jr., Robert L. Pallone, Chung Hsin Yang, Population Dispersal from Core Regions. **Working papers in Regional Science and Transportation,** University of Pennsylvania, No. 26, p. 12, Table 2.
13. Charles L. Leven. The Mature Metropolis. Lexington Books, O.C. North & Co., Lexington, Mass. 1978.
14. Op. cit., p. 7.
15. Op. cit., pp. 29-30.
16. Alex Anas and Leon N. Moses. Transportation and Land Use in the Mature Metropolis; in Charles L. Leven, op. cit., p.164.

INDEX